CLEAVAGES, PARTIES, AND VOTERS

CLEAVAGES, PARTIES, AND VOTERS

Studies from Bulgaria, the Czech Republic, Hungary, Poland, and Romania

Edited by
Kay Lawson, Andrea Römmele,
and Georgi Karasimeonov

Westport, Connecticut
London

Library of Congress Cataloging-in-Publication Data

Cleavages, parties, and voters : studies from Bulgaria, the Czech Republic, Hungary, Poland, and Romania / edited by Kay Lawson, Andrea Römmele, and Georgi Karasimeonov.
    p. cm.
Includes bibliographical references (p.) and index.
ISBN 0–275–95589–3 (alk. paper)
1. Political parties—Europe, Eastern. 2. Political parties—Europe, Central. 3. Elections—Europe, Eastern. 4. Elections—Europe, Central. I. Lawson, Kay. II. Römmele, Andrea, 1967– III. Karasimeonov, Georgi.
    JN96.A979 C54 1999
    324.24′009171′709049—dc21   98–31078

British Library Cataloguing in Publication Data is available.

Copyright © 1999 by Kay Lawson, Andrea Römmele, and Georgi Karasimeonov

All rights reserved. No portion of this book may be reproduced by any process or technique without the express written consent of the publisher.

Library of Congress Catalog Card Number: 98–31078
ISBN: 0-275-95589-3

First published in 1999

Praeger Publishers, 88 Post Road West, Westport, CT 06881
An imprint of Greenwood Publishing Group, Inc.

Printed in the United States of America

The paper used in this book complies with the Permanent Paper Standard issued by the National Information Standards Organization (Z39.48–1984).

10 9 8 7 6 5 4 3 2 1

Tables

1.1	The Four Thresholds according to Lipset and Rokkan: A Summary	5
1.2	Cleavages, Critical Junctures, Issues, and Party Families: A Summary	8
4.1	Rokkan's Model of Development Linkages	48
6.1	Ethnic Composition of Polish Society in 1931	81
6.2	The Second Republic of Poland. Elections and Political Fragmentation of the Seym (Polish Parliament)	83
6.3	Social Structure of Poland in 1930s (estimation)	84
6.4	The Republic of Poland and People's Republic of Poland. Elections and Political Composition of the Seym (Polish Parliament)	87
7.1	Results of the Romanian Elections Held on December 20, 1937	97
9.1	Results of 1990, 1992, and 1996 Parliamentary Elections: for the Composition of Czech Government, Federal Government, and Federal Assembly after Election (over 5 percent of votes)	125
10.1	Assessment of the Importance of Hungarian Political Objectives (on a continuum from 1 to 5)	148
12.1	Economically Active Population in Romania (percent in various branches)	170
12.2	Stratification of Romanian Households according to Living Standard (in percent)	171
12.3	Relative Strength of the Main Romanian Party Camps (in percent)	174
13.1	Bulgarian Parliamentary Elections of 1990, 1991, 1994 (percent of vote)	188
13.2	Bulgarian Parliamentary Elections of 1994 (Results in Seats)	188
13.3	Composition of the Bulgarian Electorate	190
13.4	Structure of the Electorates of the Two Main Bulgarian Political Parties (coalitions)	194

13.5	Bulgarian Citizens' Attitudes toward the State	196
13.6	Bulgarian Citizens' Attitudes toward Democracy	199
13.7	Bulgarian Citizens' Attitudes toward Elections	199
13.8	Results of Parliamentary Elections (April 1997)	201
14.1	Election Results in 1990 (the Czech National Assembly [Mandate])	204
14.2	Election Results in 1992 (the Czech National Assembly [Mandate])	205
14.3	Election Results in 1996 (first chamber of Czech Parliament–Chamber of Deputies)	207
14.4	Election Results in 1996 (round 2 for Czech Senate)	207
14.5	Voters' Decisions from the Perspective of Their Social Class	209
15.1	Election Results in 1990 and 1994 (in percent) (Hungary)	217
15.2	Opinions of Party Supporters Regarding Social and Ideological Tensions in Hungary in 1993 (percentage saying high level of tension)	218
15.3a–g	Attitudes of Party Supporters	219
15.4	Ideological and Attitudinal Responses of Party Supporters (differences between the HSP and the others–logistic regression)	222
15.5	Factor Analysis by 18 Scales	224
15.6	Voter Types on the Basis of Factor Characters (Hungary)	225
15.7	Economic Winners and Losers according to HSWP Membership (Hungary)	226
15.8	Placement of Factors on the Market–Democracy Coordinate System (Hungary)	227
15.9	Parliamentary Parties on the Left–Right Scale according to MPs (Hungary)	228
15.10	MP Opinions on Social Tensions by Party (mean–one way, analysis variance)	229
15.11a	Support for European Integration as a Left-wing Value according to MPs (Hungary)	230
15.11b	Support for European Integration as a Right-wing Value according to MPs (Hungary)	230
16.1	Results of the 1991 and 1993 Elections to the Polish Seym	243
16.2	Results of the 1991 and 1993 Elections to the Polish Senate	245
17.1	Returns of the General Election of May 20, 1990, in Romania and Party Preferences One Year Later	263
17.2	Returns of the General Elections of September 27, 1992, and November 3, 1996, in Romania. Chamber of Deputies and Senate (in percent)	264
17.3	Party Choice in Urban and Rural Areas in the 1992 and 1996 Elections (in percent) (Romania)	267
17.4	Socioeconomic Status and Party Preference in 1992 and 1996 General Elections (Romania)	269

Acknowledgments

The principal debt of any edited volume is always to the contributors, and this book is no exception. We thank them all: those who waited so patiently while others found the time to finish, those who responded so readily to requests for revisions, and those who accepted so graciously what may have sometimes seemed a pretty heavy editorial hand. It was a pleasure to work with all of them.

In addition, three agencies provided invaluable aid in the preparation of this volume. The Paul Lazarsfeld Gesellschaft für Sozialforschung, under the leadership of Ernst Gehmacher, and the Bank of Austria, guided by Vice President Heinz Kienzl, provided the funding and logistical support for our first meeting in Vienna, while the Lazarsfeld Gesellschaft arranged and paid for our second meeting. Special thanks to Elizabeth Stoïc for her help with the former and to Birgit Weiss for hers with the latter. ZEUS (Zentrum für Europäische Umfrageanalysn und Studien) at the Mannheim Centre for European Social Research provided very generous assistance, allowing for constant communication among the editors and between editors and contributors, as well as for the hard and loyal work of Sven Kersten, who kept us electronically viable, prepared all the tables and graphs, and otherwise came to the rescue time and again. We also want to thank Andreas Reich, Peter Wagner, and Stephan Soltys for checking the spelling and accent marks throughout. James Dunton and James Sabin of Praeger showed steady and deeply appreciated faith in the concept and in our ability to do the job. And finally, the editors thank one another: we helped and nagged one another, worried together, rectified each other's work, and stayed good friends.

Kay Lawson
Andrea Römmele
Georgi Karasimeonov

Preface

Ernst Gehmacher

This collection of essays summarizes and explains one of the most fascinating developments of contemporary history: the peaceful revolution of the central European nations from a long period of authoritarian regimes to Western democracy. This process is still in full movement, so there is no escape from disturbing questions: Is this transition already achieved? Or is this a long-term evolution oscillating between ups and downs? Could the new political culture fail and collapse to a less flexible and humanitarian polity?

A simple answer cannot be given. But this book offers rich material and keen observations by some of the most knowledgeable political analysts in these countries. From such a treasure of information and analyses some fundamental regularities can be extracted. A preface may serve best in its function as signpost and leader to the book by waking the reader to these natural laws of emerging democracy in the process of modernization.

Modernization is the more recent part of the historical process of civilization—and is still going on rapidly.

Modernization means innovation: Open, mobile societies and the introduction of democracy accelerate and increase its dynamics. Change is introduced by mostly "new" elites.

A sequence of characteristic cleavages typifies the modernization process, from religious and national wars to social class and economic conflicts.

The evolutionary dynamics of innovation create new winners and losers; thereby, existing political cleavages are aggravated and new ones are created. In developed economies and democratic welfare states, winners and losers are partialized into "interest groups," "minority groups," "subcultures," and "deviant-majority cleavages." At the same time, globalization, high mobility, and communication power make for new cultural cleavages. The outcome is a high volatility of voters and parties. The compartmentalization of societies increases the demand for social and political coherence.

Innovation and coherence are contrasting and conflicting phenomena. After periods of rapid modernization and growth, cleavages rise to a point of "hard regulation" by conflict, breakdown, and retreat—eventually to fundamentalism, dictatorship, or anarchy. After a turnaround or a takeover by more successful polities, a new push of modernization follows. The length and depth of such political "waves" are difficult to forecast. Shorter and less violent fluctuations are desirable, and may be attained by democratic buffering and heightened self-reflection.

This book will make a valuable contribution to such a process of democratic pacification, especially if widely read and discussed in the countries treated within it.

Part I

Introduction

1

Cleavage Structures and Party Systems in East and Central Europe

———————————— *Andrea Römmele*

The newly developing democracies of East and Central Europe have given social scientists a unique opportunity to study the process of cleavage formation, party response, and voter alignment. In these nations, new relationships are still developing between social groups and parties, and between parties and their voters. New party images are being created and transmitted. Citizens are learning—or relearning—to use the process of electoral choice in the pursuit of representative democracy.

To take advantage of this opportunity, the contributors to this volume have found it useful to take the concept of cleavage as the point of departure. But *cleavage* is a difficult concept, one on which agreement is limited and debate is enthusiastic. It is therefore important to begin by examining this concept and, in particular, its development over the past thirty years and the ways it is applied to the study of elections and parties. Such an examination is the purpose of this chapter.

There is a large body of research that tests and explores the cleavage concept. The seminal work, it is widely agreed, is the edited volume by Seymour Martin Lipset and Stein Rokkan, *Party Systems and Voter Alignments,* and in particular their own contribution to that volume, "Cleavage Structures, Party Systems, and Voter Alignments: An Introduction" (Lipset and Rokkan, 1967). In that chapter the authors focus on the genesis of the system of cleavages then prevalent in the democracies in Western Europe, note the conditions necessary for the development of a stable system of cleavage and oppositions, and analyze the response of citizens to the resultant party systems. They also launch one of the most fruitful theoretical discussions in the social sciences in the second half of the twentieth century.

This volume continues that discussion. The framework developed by Lipset and Rokkan provides a strong starting point for our effort to apply the concept of cleavages to the emerging party systems of East and Central Europe. Yet it can be only a starting point. Before moving forward we must examine the development of the concept since the original study, and we must make at least a rudimentary attempt to set out the key differences (and similarities) between the conditions present in the Western European nations analyzed by Lipset and Rokkan, and those present today in East and Central Europe. These are the tasks of this chapter.

We begin by exploring the literature regarding two key points: the meaning of cleavage, and the usefulness of the freezing hypothesis. Our brief review cannot do justice to the details of the various authors' elaborations, but it does show the range of meaning given to the term and the passion with which the chapter's most provocative assertion has been met. A third section turns to the special situation that East and Central Europe are facing after the breakdown of Communism, and seeks to compare that situation to Western Europe thirty years ago. What are the key situational differences? What are the similarities? What questions must most urgently be posed when examining these new democracies through the lens of cleavage theory?

THE MEANING OF CLEAVAGE

The substantial literature on cleavages offers no single coherent definition of what cleavages actually are. There is no agreement on what the necessary and sufficient conditions are nor what a useful typology of cleavages would look like.

To begin with, however, it is clear that the concept of cleavage contains two kinds of components: structural and substantive. There are three different structural components: the *divisional* (an existing differentiation among a social group); the *conflictual* (the consciousness about the differentiation); and the *organizational* (organization in defense of the group's identity and goals) (adapted from Bartolini and Mair, 1990). Substantively, there are *social* and *political* cleavages. The concept can be used when analyzing the impact of social stratification on institutions and behavior or the impact of political institutions on social structure and change (Allardt, 1964). *Social* cleavages are commonly defined in terms of social attitudes and behaviors, and are seen as reflecting traditional divisions of social stratification. *Political* cleavages are usually defined in terms of political attitudes and behaviors.

Social cleavages. When Lipset and Rokkan sought to identify the critical lines of cleavage that have historically structured the party systems of Western democracies, they identified four major social divisions and carefully traced their origin and development. The Reformation and Counter-Reformation and the various national revolutions were the *critical junctures* for the development of the divisions between *Center and Periphery* and between *State and Church*. Most of the conflicts taken up by parties representing ethnically, linguistically, or religiously distinct populations of the peripheries of the newly emerging nation-states of Europe could be traced back to these critical points in Western history. Similarly, Lipset and Rokkan pointed out that the industrial revolution gave rise to two further forms of social divisiveness: *rural versus urban* and *worker versus owner.*

Lipset and Rokkan identify four "thresholds" that must be crossed by any political organization on the path to incorporation in a nation's party system (see Table 1.1). However, on closer examination, we find that these "thresholds" are actually barriers that the system may or may not keep in place against the formation of a cleavage (thresholds 1 and 2) and its entry into the political system as a new organization (thresholds 3 and 4).

Other authors have also stressed the social dimension. Michael Gallagher, Michael Laver, and Peter Mair offer this definition: "First, a cleavage involves a social division that separates people who can be distinguished from one another in terms of key social characteristics such as occupation, status, religion or ethnicity . . . Second, the groups involved in the division must be conscious of their collective identity—as workers or employers, for example—and be willing to act on this basis . . . Third, a cleavage must be expressed in organizational terms. This is typically achieved as a result of the activities of a trade union, a church, a political party, or some other organization that gives formal institutional expression to the interests of those on one side of the division" (Gallagher et al., 1992: 91 ff; see also Bartolini and Mair, 1990, and Mair, 1997).

For the authors cited above, a cleavage is not merely a division within society that might or might not lead to a conflict; it is a conflict within society *that is organized.* As Adam Przeworski and John Sprague note, cleavages cannot be

Table 1.1
The Four Thresholds according to Lipset and Rokkan: A Summary

Threshold of Legitimization	Is there a right of petition, criticism, and opposition? Can the differences among groups be openly expressed and articulated?
Threshold of Incorporation	Are all members of a social group allowed to participate?
Threshold of Representation	Must the new movement join larger and older movements to ensure access to representative organs, or can it gain representation on its own?
Threshold of Majority Power	Are there built-in checks and counterforces against numerical majority rule in the system, or will a victory at the polls give a party or an alliance power to bring about major structural changes in the national system?

Source: Lipset and Rokkan, p. 27.

reduced simply to outgrowths of social stratification; rather, "social distinctions become lived as cleavages because they become organized as such" (Przeworski and Sprague, 1977).

However, not all definitions stressing the social dimension include the organizational aspect. In their often-cited work, *The Analysis of Political Cleavages,* Douglas Rae and Michael Taylor offer the following: "Cleavages are the criteria which divide the members of a community or subcommunity into groups, and the relevant cleavages are those which divide groups with important political differences at specific times and places" (Rae and Taylor, 1970: 1). They further suggest that there are three principal types of cleavage: (1) ascriptive, or "trait," cleavages, such as race or caste; (2) attitudinal, or "opinion," cleavages, such as ideology or preference; and (3) behavioral, or "act," cleavages, manifested by such activities as voting or joining organizations. In regard to the structural dimension, Rae and Taylor see neither conflict nor organization as a necessary condition for the existence of a cleavage.

Jan-Eric Lane and Svante Ersson agree with Rae and Taylor that conflict and organization are not essential elements in their definition of cleavage. However, they lay considerably greater stress on the possibility of conflict: "A cleavage is a division on the basis of some criteria among individuals, groups or organizations among whom conflict may arise. The concept of cleavage is thus not identical with the concept of conflict; cleavages may lead to conflict, but a cleavage need not always be attended by conflict. A division of individuals, groups or organizations constitutes a cleavage if there is some probability of a conflict" (Lane and Ersson, 1994: 53). In contrast to Rae and Taylor, this definition sees the *possibility* of a conflict as a necessary condition for the emergence of a cleavage. But—as in Rae and Taylor—the organizational aspect of a cleavage is not systematically taken up and not regarded as a necessary condition for the existence of a cleavage.

The Rae and Taylor typology has been criticized by Bartolini and Mair, among others, who see this use of the term "cleavage" as making it a catch-all concept capable of embracing almost every conceivable type of political division (Bartolini and Mair, 1990: 215). Whereas Rae and Taylor regard the three types of cleavages listed as mutually exclusive classes of different cleavages, Bartolini and Mair see these three types simply as different aspects of cleavage. They suggest that "the term 'cleavage' should be restricted to the indication of a dividing line in a polity which refers to and combines all three aspects and . . . alternative terms should be adopted when referring to objective social distinctions or to ideological, political and organizational divisions per se" (Bartolini and Mair, 1990: 216; see also Pappi, 1979).

Political cleavages. For other authors, political attitudes and behaviors are the key factors in determining when cleavages exist. These scholars are more likely to stress relatively stable patterns of political polarization, in which certain groups support certain policies or parties, while other groups support opposing policies or parties. The groups in question may or may not be *social* groups; what counts is that there are divisions that are given *political* form.

Empirical analysis has shown that class is one of the most powerful bases of political cleavage (see Rose and Urwin, 1970, and Rose, 1974). However, social change that has taken place during the recent past has brought about cleavages that are no longer based on class, nor even on social groups, but rather on values or ideologies. The translation of social divisions into political oppositions has weakened (Schmitt, 1987). Ronald Inglehart argues that the cleavage structures underlying politics in Western nations have changed profoundly since World War II as individuals have moved from material to postmaterial values (Inglehart, 1977, 1981, 1990). Postmaterialists give priority to such goals as a sense of community and the nonmaterial qualities of life, although they live in societies that have traditionally emphasized economic gains above all. The rise of postmaterialist issues (such as the environment, male/female equality, unilateral disarmament, opposition to nuclear power, abortion, and gay rights)[1] has, it is claimed by Inglehart and his followers, reduced the saliency of political polarization on the basis of class. The new political divisions originate not in social inequalities but in ideological and value-based differences. Such cleavages may assume organizational form as new political parties, but are even more likely to take the form of *social movements* (Merkl, 1988: 582). Whereas social cleavages become visible in (mass) organizations and political parties, political cleavages do not have this organizational transmission. They are loosely organized in single (issue) movements.

Although some definitions (for example, Lane and Ersson, Gallagher et al.) clearly privilege the social and others (for example, Inglehart) the political, the distinction is often blurred. The line between definitions of cleavage that stress social elements but require an organizational component and those that emphasize political components but see traditional social divisions as the point of departure is not an easy one to draw. Like many of those we have reviewed, our own definition falls somewhere in the middle. Our focus is on the parties that have emerged in these new systems and thus we might reasonably be expected to stress political elements. On the other hand, we and our contributors search for the source of cleavages in old and new social divisions, trying to discover which seem likely to endure and which are actually being given political representation by the parties. For our purposes, then, the definition we find most useful is mixed: Cleavages are long-term structural conflicts that give rise to opposing positions that competing political organizations represent. We do not presume that all social divisions produce cleavages, nor that all cleavages are social, nor that those that do exist are represented by parties rather than by other forms of organization. We do not take for granted that parties that say they are representing important existing divisions in society are in fact doing so. Our definition forces us to consider both social and political elements; it allows us to see the ways they interact—and the ways they sometimes do not.

THE FREEZING HYPOTHESIS

As of 1966, the party systems of Western Europe appeared to Lipset and Rokkan to be "frozen." "Party systems of the 1960s reflect, with but few significant exceptions," said Lipset and Rokkan, "the cleavage structures of the 1920s" (1967: 50). The evolution of mass parties and the high degree of electoral mobility left little room, they claimed, for the development of new parties (51). The differences among political parties could be traced directly back to the social divisions dominant at the time of their founding. These structured conflicts formed a general pattern across Western Europe and brought about mass organizations for electoral action. Parties were "alliances in conflicts over policies and value commitments within the larger body politic" (5). (See Table 1.2.)

The freezing hypothesis offers a theoretical as well as historical explanation for the stability of European electoral behavior in the 1950s and 1960s. This was the period in which the potentially vulnerable new West German party system stabilized and the policies of the British Labour Party became almost indistinguishable from those of the centralist Conservative government. It was during this era that the long-term control of the center-right Christian Democrats was established in the polarized party system of Italy, and the French adopted the quasi-presidential constitutional system that served to eliminate much of the efferves-

Table 1.2
Cleavages, Critical Junctures, Issues, and Party Families: A Summary

Cleavage	*Critical Juncture*	*Issues*	*Party Families*
Center–Periphery	Reformation–Counter-Reformation (16th–17th centuries)	National vs. supranational religion; national language vs. Latin	Ethnically and linguistically based parties
State–Church	National Revolution, 1789 and later	Secular vs. religious control of mass education	Religious parties
Rural–Urban	Industrial Revolution, 19th century	Tariff levels for agricultural products; control vs. freedom for industrial enterprise	Agrarian parties; conservative and liberal parties
Owner–Worker	The Russian Revolution, 1917–1991	Integration into national polity vs. commitment to international revolutionary movement	Socialist and Communist parties

Source: Lipset and Rokkan, p. 47.

cence of their previous party systems. And in Scandinavia, Social Democratic hegemony continued unchanged (Gallagher et al., 1992: 99).

Inasmuch as the evidence was suggestive and the hypothesis was provocative, it is not surprising that the idea of "freezing" prompted a large body of party system and electoral research over the next thirty years. The first study to offer a broad empirical test appeared in 1970 and its authors, Richard Rose and Derek Urwin, offered Lipset and Rokkan significant support: "Whatever index of change is used," they concluded, "the picture is the same: the electoral strength of most parties in Western nations since the war has changed very little from election to election, from decade to decade, or within the lifespan of a generation . . . the first priority of social scientists concerned with the development of parties and party systems since 1945 is to explain the absence of change in a far from static period of political history" (Rose and Urwin, 1970: 295).

However, much of the scholarship based on the freezing hypothesis over the next thirty years moved in the opposite direction. If, in fact, the parties had been frozen, the new studies suggested the glacier was in retreat, and a great thaw had begun. One of the earliest thorough and comprehensive analyses of electoral volatility in Western Europe was conducted by Mogens Pedersen (1979, 1983), whose own work was stimulated by Denmark's "earthquake election" of 1973. Pedersen found significant "unfreezing" of European party systems, and subsequent works concurred (Dalton et al., 1984; Shamir, 1984; Wolinetz, 1979, 1988). Maria Maguire (1983) replicated the Rose/Urwin study and found that there had been a strong shift among parties since 1960 and that the older and more powerful parties in particular had suffered major losses. Klaus von Beyme (1982) identified a tendency toward greater fragmentation of Western European party systems: The number of parties gaining more than 2 percent of the vote had grown significantly in numerous nations (see also Harmel and Robertson, 1985).

Ronald Inglehart's work on value orientation and value change (see previous text) persuaded him that the postmaterialists had succeeded in raising a new set of issues, creating a political dimension that cut across the conventional left-right axis. The powerful new political organizations (environmentalist, peace, women's movements, and so forth) they had formed had, he argued, challenged and changed the established party systems (Inglehart, 1990, 1981, 1977).

Oddbjørn Knutsen carried even further the postmaterialist argument against freezing. The new issues, he said, cut across established cleavage lines based on social alignments and thereby weakened not only the parties that served them but the very bonds themselves. For members of the middle class who were drawn to the political program of the environmentalists, for example, class solidarity naturally became less important. According to Knutsen, the postmaterialists also threatened to erode the ruling parties' oligarchic control of political representation, stressing as they did the need for more opportunities to participate in political decisions and the further democratization of society and politics. Furthermore, the new issues were attracting the attention of social groups that had hitherto been weakly integrated in traditional social alignments: the young, the new middle class, the better educated, and the nonreligious (Knutsen, 1989).

More recently, Bartolini and Mair have taken the argument back in time, analyzing variance in class-cleavage volatility over the past century. The resultant picture is mixed, but lends more support to the notion of freezing than some earlier studies: "The one element to emerge with greatest clarity from our analysis is that this century of mass politics in Western Europe can be seen as a century of electoral stabilization," they conclude (Bartolini and Mair, 1990: 287). But they do not suggest that nothing has changed. Voters have indeed changed parties, acknowledge Bartolini and Mair; however, those who were on the left have tended to move to other parties also on the left, while those on the right have shifted to other right-wing parties. In the broadest sense, then, the party systems have remained frozen, say Bartolini and Mair, even though voters may have moved about. They are correct to remind us of the difference. The unit of analysis in regard to a cleavage is neither a voter nor a party; it is all the parties representing one side or the other of an existing social division. Decline in voter support for a particular party does not necessarily mean the overall decline of a cleavage.

Nevertheless, it is clear that the link between parties and groups in the party systems of Western Europe has not remained as static as the term "frozen" would imply. The established parties within these systems have proved ever more ready to enlarge their programmatic offers to reach out to voters not formerly considered likely to give them support, and new parties, representing new issues, have emerged. Furthermore, this process was almost certainly well under way even as Lipset and Rokkan were formulating their hypothesis. In a work published the same year as *Party Systems and Voter Alignments,* Otto Kirchheimer argued that the weakening of the old links between parties and social groups had begun to produce a new kind of party, the catch-all party, a party that deliberately sought to take advantage of the wider electorate that could be attracted by moderating and bridging the cleavages of the past (Kirchheimer, 1966; see also Epstein, 1967). In 1984, Russell Dalton demonstrated that the postwar determination of German Christian Democrats to bridge historic religious differences between Catholics and Protestants, and the 1959 Bad Godesberg decision of German Social Democrats to move to the center together brought about a significant lessening of social and partisan conflict in that nation, permitting individuals who had been only marginally tied to traditional social networks or who were strongly influenced by new political concerns to form new partisan ties (Dalton, 1984). Later studies have linked such changes in party programs to organizational changes within the parties, and to new forms of campaign strategy (Lawson, 1994; Katz and Mair, 1995; Ware, 1996).

Furthermore, as many old parties jettison what they now judge to be superfluous ideological and programmatic baggage, new organizations continue to be formed around postmaterialist and other newly salient issues. Such organizations are seldom originally formed as parties. Indeed, the antagonism against parties and other traditional forms of political organization has often been strong. Participation should be direct and leaders should be instructed by followers. Politics should be performed through movements, not through parties. Nevertheless, Green parties have emerged and taken their place in several European parliaments (Poguntke, 1993; Müller-Rommel, 1993) and a women's party, the Women's Alliance, had been founded in Iceland, where it took 5.5 percent of the national vote in the Allting election in 1983, and 10 percent in 1987 (Styrkársdóttir, 1986; Knutsen, 1989).

Thus it appears that in recent years the party systems of Western Europe have thawed considerably, far beyond that which can be ascribed merely to the shifts of voters among parties on the same side of an ideological spectrum, or to the replacement of one party by another of very similar stripe. The freezing hypothesis requires modification now; the circumstances governing the formation of party systems may determine their general contours for many years, but only so long as the parties concerned find no better way to attract voters than to continue to appeal to the same kind of supporters who gave them their initial success.

THE PROSPECTS FOR FORMING PARTIES IN RESPONSE TO CLEAVAGES: CONTRASTING CONDITIONS IN WESTERN AND EASTERN/CENTRAL EUROPE

In addition to considering how the concept of cleavages fits contemporary parties in general, we need to consider its usefulness for the specific cases at hand. The contributors of the fifteen case study chapters make this assessment in detail, and Kay Lawson offers some summarizing observations in the second part of this Introduction. Here, drawing on the observations of other scholars, we conclude by reminding our readers of four key differences governing the formation of these new governments and these new parties, four conditions not to be found in Western Europe in the 1920s:

Pace and complexity of the transition. As Claus Offe has pointed out, post-communist Europe is in fact undergoing a "triple transition," a process involving not just democratization, but also marketization and wholesale economic transformation as well as state-building itself. What Western Europe "mastered over a centuries-long sequence (from the nation state to capitalism, and then to democracy)," post-communist nations must endeavor to accomplish simultaneously, and within the shortest possible time (Offe, 1992: 14).

Differences in the electorate. Although Western party systems are probably no longer frozen and Western electoral alliances have been shown to be more and more unstable (Franklin, Mackie and Valen et. al., 1992), there remains a strong bias toward continuity and persistence within the established party systems of the West (Bartolini and Mair, 1990; Mair, 1997). In East and Central Europe, on the other hand, the electorate is far more open and available, far more volatile and uncertain. Old cleavages may or may not reappear but even when they do they must find ways to assert themselves in vastly changed conditions. The early years of these systems and of their newly democratized electorates are inevitably marked by instability; prediction has proved dangerous election after election.[2]

Differences in party type. As they formed, Western European parties were able to mobilize collective political identities and draw upon organizational networks that were already in place as they established semi-permanent liaisons with those on one side or the other of important cleavages. Electorates were consequently "effectively segmented . . . into relatively stable and closed partisan blocs" (Mair, 1997: 183). The circumstances of the fall of communism, entailing as they did the extensive repudiation of preexistent identities and networks, have given the new parties of East and Central Europe no such advantages. The new parties are more likely to be charismatic and clientelistic than programmatic. Charismatic parties, which are little more than an unstructured mass of people rallying around a leader, avoid high costs of organization and political consensus-building; clientelistic parties, particularly patronage organizations, are better organized and are obliged to provide a constant flow of resources to their followers (Kitschelt, 1995: 449). Neither charismatic nor clientelistic parties are able to develop the kind of societal and political anchors (for example, the collective identities and organizational networks posited by Mair) that permit them to establish close programmatic coordination among party supporters and leaders. (They may in fact have no interest in doing so.) The absence of such coordination makes it less likely that the parties will recognize and respond to the divisions of opinion—cleavages—actually present in their societies.

Role of the media. The media was heavily censored and controlled under communist rule in the nations of Eastern and Central Europe, serving as an instrument of the ruling elite to popularize state policies and the ruling ideology. Post-communist policies of liberalization and privatization have produced rapid change (Splichal, 1994: 29) and contemporary political actors have proved quick to adapt to the new freedom. The politics of marketing have taken hold, complete with spiralling costs of campaigns, an emphasis on candidates who make a strong personal appeal, and the quest for "catchy" issues. The mediatized commercialization of politics, a process that has been so strong a factor in weakening old ties between parties and voters in the West, appears to be in place from the outset in the East. To the extent that campaigns are used to manipulate, rather than respond to, opinion, the bond between social divisions and political parties seems likely to be weak.

The conditions in place in East and Central Europe now thus suggest it is unlikely the process of party formation will provide strong parallels to the Western past. But we do not need to rely upon suggestion. To find the answers we seek, we can turn to the close study ten indigenous scholars of five Eastern and Central European nations have made of their countries' political development before, during, and after the fall of communist rule.

NOTES

1. Not all these issues fit into Ingelhart's postmaterialist category. For example, the questions of economic rights and physical security raised by women's movements fall *per definitionem* under the category of materialist.

2. Two large projects are presently underway. Studies in Hans-Dieter Klingemann and Charles Lewis Taylor's series on *Founding Elections in Eastern Europe* (Berlin: Sigma Edition) examine the early elections and government formation in the political transformations that are taking place in the new democracies of Central and Eastern Europe. Scholars from each of the new democracies analyze their early democratic elections and document the pre- or postelection surveys that they have undertaken. A separate volume of description and pre-analysis is published for each country. Chapters include topics such as an overview of the recent transition process, a history of the development of political parties, an examination of the effects of the electoral system on the election outcome, an analysis of the voting behavior of the population, a study of the candidates that stood for election, and an investigation of the process of government formation after the election. Also included are the legislative act that regulates the formation and operation of political parties, and the act that defines and establishes the electoral system. Since 1991, Richard Rose has annually conducted the New Democracies Barometer (NDB)—a nationwide sample survey—across Central and Eastern Europe. In each of ten countries—the Czech Republic, Slovakia, Hungary, Poland, Romania, Bulgaria, Slovenia, Croatia, Belarus, and Ukraine—about a thousand respondents are interviewed face-to-face about economic, political, and social attitudes and behavior. Because the same questions are repeated in each NDB country, cross-national comparisons can be made. Because key questions are repeated from year to year, trends can be analyzed within each country and across a wide variety of post-communist societies.

REFERENCES

Alford, Robert R. 1963. *Party and Society: The Anglo-American Democracies*. Chicago: McNally.

Allardt, Erik. 1964. *Cleavages, Ideologies and Party Systems*. Helsinki: The Academic Bookstore.

Andersen, J. G. and T. Bjorklund. 1990. "Structural Changes and New Cleavages: the Progress Parties in Denmark and Norway." *Acta Sociologica* 33: 195–218.

Baker, Kendall, Russel Dalton and Kai Hildebrandt. 1981. *Germany Transformed. Political Culture and the New Politics*. Cambridge: Harvard University Press.

Bartolini, Stefano and Peter Mair. 1990. *Identity, Competition, and Electoral Availability*. Cambridge: Cambridge University Press.

Ben-Rafael, E., H. Shteyer and E. Lewin. 1989. "Israel as a Multi-Cleavage Setting." *Plural Societies* 19: 21–40.

Berglund, Sten and Jan A. Dellenbrant, eds. 1991. *The New Democracies in Eastern Europe: Party Systems and Political Cleavage*. Aldershot: E. Elgar.

Brown, Robert. 1995. "Party Cleavages and Welfare Effort in the American States." *American Political Science Review* 89: 23–33.

Dalton, Russell J. 1996. "Political Cleavages, Issues, and Electoral Change." In Lawrence LeDuc, Richard G. Niemi, and Pippa Norris (eds.), *Comparing Democracies. Elections and Voting in Global Perspective*, 319–342. Thousand Oaks/London/New Delhi: Sage Publications.

Dalton, Russell J., Scott C. Flanagan and Paul A. Beck. 1984. *Electoral Change in Advanced Industrial Democracies*. Princeton: Princeton University Press.

Eckstein, Harry. 1966. *Division and Cohesion in Democracy. A Study in Norway*. Princeton: Princeton University Press.

Epstein, Leon. 1967. *Political Parties in Western Democracies*. London: Pall Mall.

———. 1980. *Political Parties in Western Democracies*. New Brunswick: Transaction Books.

Franklin, Mark N., Thomas T. Mackie, Henry Valen et al. 1992. *Electoral Change: Responses to Social and Attitudinal Structures in Western Countries*. Cambridge: Cambridge University Press.

Gallagher, Michael Laver and Peter Mair. 1992. *Representative Government in Western Europe*. New York: McGraw Hill.

Grove, John D. 1977. "A Cross-National Examination of Cross-Cutting and Reinforcing Cultural Cleavages." *International Journal of Comparative Sociology* 18: 217–27.

Hallenberger, Gerd and Michael Krzeminski. 1994. *Osteuropa. Medienlandschaft im Umbruch*. Berlin: Vistas.

Harmel, Robert and John D. Robertson. 1985. "Formation and Success of New Parties: A Cross-National Analysis." *International Political Science Review* 6 (4): 501–23.

Harmel, Robert and Lars Svasand. 1997. "The Influence of New Parties on Old Parties' Platforms: The Cases of the Progress Parties and Conservative Parties of Denmark and Norway." *Party Politics* 3: 315–40.

Hoel, Marit and Oddbjørn Knutsen. 1989. "Social Class, Gender, and Sector Employment as Political Cleavages in Scandinavia." *Acta Sociologica* 32: 181–201.

Howell, Susan and James Vanderleeuw. 1990. "A Social Cleavage Model of Ideological Identification." *Southeastern Political Review* 18: 1–15.

Inglehart, Ronald. 1977. *The Silent Revolution: Changing Values and Political Styles among Western Politics*. Princeton: Princeton University Press.

———. 1981. "Postmaterialism in an Environment of Insecurity." *American Political Science Review* 75: 880–900.

———. 1990. *Culture Shift in Advanced Industrial Society*. Princeton: Princeton University Press.

Jahn, Detlef. 1993. "The Rise and Decline of New Politics and the Greens in Sweden and Germany: Resource Dependence and New Social Cleavages." *European Journal of Political Research* 24: 177–94.

Johnston, Richard and William Irvine. 1985. "The Reproduction of the Religious Cleavage in Canadian Elections." *Canadian Journal of Political Science* 18: 99–114.

Katz, Richard and Peter Mair. 1995. "Changing Models of Party Organization and Democracy: The Emergence of the Cartel Party." *Party Politics* 1: 5–28.

Kirchheimer, Otto. 1966. "The Transformation of the Western Party System," in Joseph La Palombara and Myron Weiner, *Political Parties and Political Development*. Princeton: Princeton University Press.

Kitschelt, Herbert. 1995. "Formation of Party Cleavages in Post-communist Democracies: Theoretical Propositions." *Party Politics* 1: 447–72.

Knutsen, Oddbjørn. 1989. "Cleavage Dimensions in Ten West European Countries: A Comparative Empirical Analysis." *Comparative Political Studies* 21: 495–534.
———. 1990. "The Materialist/Post-Materialist Value Dimension as a Party Cleavage in the Nordic Countries." *West European Politics* 13: 258–74.
Körösenyi, András. 1993. "Stable or Fragile Democracy? Political Cleavages and Party Systems in Hungary." *Government and Opposition* 28: 87–104.
Lane, Jan-Eric and Svante O. Ersson. 1994. *Politics and Society in Western Europe*, 3rd ed. London/Thousand Oaks/New Delhi: Sage.
Laponce, Jean A. und R. Uhler. 1974. "Measuring Electoral Cleavages in a Multiparty System: The Canadian Case." *Comparative Political Studies* 7: 3–25.
Lawson, Kay, ed. 1994. *How Political Parties Work: Perspectives from Within*. Westport: Praeger.
Lijphart, Arend. 1971. *Class Voting and Religious Voting in the European Democracies: A Preliminary Report*. Glasgow: University of Strathclyde.
Lijphart, Arend. 1981. "Political Parties: Ideologies and Programs." In David Butler et al. (ed.), *Democracy at the Polls. A Comparative Study of Competitive National Elections*. Washington: American Enterprise Institute.
———. 1982. "The Relative Salience of Socio-Economic and Religious Issue-Dimensions." *European Journal of Political Research* 10: 201–11.
Lipset, Seymour M. 1959. *Political Man*. New York: Doubleday.
Lipset, Seymour M. and Stein Rokkan. 1967. "Cleavage Structures, Party Systems, and Voter Alignments: An Introduction." In Lipset, Seymour M. and Stein Rokkan, *Party Systems and Voter Alignments: Cross-National Perspectives*, 1–64. New York: The Free Press.
MacHale, Vincent and Dennis Paranzino. 1975. "Development Change and Electoral Cleavage in France. Government and Opposition in the 5th Republic." *Canadian Journal of Political Science* 8: 431–53.
Maguire, Maria. 1983. "Is There Still Persistence? Electoral Change in Western Europe, 1948–1979." In Hans Daalder and Peter Mair (eds.), *Western European Party Systems. Continuity and Change*, 67–94. London: Sage.
Mair, Peter. 1997. *Party System Change: Approaches and Interpretations*. Oxford: Oxford University Press.
Menahem, Gila. 1992. "Social Cleavage and Political Devisions in Community." *International Journal of Contemporary Sociology* 29: 97–113.
———. "Social Cleavage, Political Division and Local Political Leadership Recruitment." *Journal of Theoretical Politics* 5: 375–95.
Merkl, Peter H. 1988. "The Challengers of the Party Systems." In Kay Lawson and Peter H. Merkl (eds.), *When Parties Fail: Emerging Alternative Organizations*, 561–588. Princeton: Princeton University Press.
Michels, Robert. 1966. *Political Parties. A Sociological Study of the Oligarchical Tendencies of Modern Democracies*. New York: Free Press.
Müller-Rommel, Ferdinand. 1993. *Grüne Parteien in Westeuropa: Entwicklungsphasen und Erfolgsbedingungen*. Opladen: Westdeutscher Verlag.
Offe, Claus. 1992. "Capitalism by Democratic Design? Democratic Theory Facing the Triple Transition in East-Central Europe." In György Lengyl, Claus Offe, and Jochen Tholen (eds.), *Economic Institutions, Actors and Attitudes: East Central Europe in Transition*, 11-22. Budapest: University of Economic Sciences.

Offerlé, Michel. 1987. *Les Partis Politiques*. Paris: Presses Universitaires de France.
Ostrogorski, Moisei. 1970. *Democracy and the Organization of Political Parties*. New York: Haskell.
Panebianco, Angelo. 1988. *Political Parties: Organization and Power*. Cambridge: Cambridge University Press.
Pappi, Franz U. und P. Mnich. 1992. "Social Structure and Party Choice in the Federal Republic of Germany since the 1960s." In Mark Franklin and Thomas T. Mackie et al., *Electoral Change*. Cambridge: Cambridge University Press.
Pappi, Franz U. und M. Terwey. 1982. "The German Electorate: Old Cleavages and New Political Conflicts." In Herbert Döring and G. Smith (eds.), *Party Government and Political Culture in Germany*, 174–96. London und Basingstoke.
Pappi, Franz U. 1979. "Konstanz und Wandel der Hauptspannungslinien in der Bundesrepublik." In Joachim Matthes (ed.), *Sozialer Wandel in Westeuropa*. Verhandlungen des 19. Soziologentages Berlin, Frankfurt: Campus. 465–79.
Pedersen, Mogens N. 1979. "The Dynamics of European Party Systems: Changing Patterns of Electoral Volatility." *European Journal of Political Research* 7(1): 1–26.
Pedersen, Mogens N. 1983. "Patterns of Electoral Volatility in European Party Systems: Explorations in Explanation." In Hans Daalder and Peter Mair, *Western European Party Systems: Continuity and Change*. London: Sage.
Pizzorno, Allesandro. 1981. "Interests and Parties in Pluralism." In Suzanne Berger (ed.), *Organizing Interests in Western Europe: Pluralism, Corporatism, and the Transformation of Politics*. Cambridge: Cambridge University Press.
Poguntke, Thomas. 1993. *Alternative Politics: The German Green Party*. Edinburgh: Edinburgh University Press.
Powell, Bingham. 1976. "Political Cleavage Structure, Cross-Pressure Processes, and Partisanship: An Empirical Test of the Theory." *American Journal of Political Science* 20: 1–23.
Przeworski, Adam and John Sprague. 1977. *A History of Western European Socialism*. Paper presented to the Annual Meeting of the American Political Science Association, Washington, D.C.
Rae, Douglas W. and Michael Taylor. 1970. *The Analysis of Political Cleavages*. New Haven/London: University Press.
Rae, Nicol. 1992. "Class and Culture: American Political Cleavages in the 20th Century." In *Western Political Quarterly* 45: 629–50.
Ragin, Charles. 1977. "Class, Status, and 'Reactive Ethnic Cleavages': The Social Bases of Political Regionalism." *American Sociological Review* 42: 438–50.
Rokkan, Stein. 1980. "Eine Familie von Modellen für die vergleichende Geschichte Europas." In *Zeitschrift für Soziologie* 9: 118–28.
Rose, Richard and Derek W. Urwin, 1970. "Persistence and Change in Western Party Systems Since 1945." *Political Studies* 18: 287–319.
Rose, Richard, ed. 1974. *Electoral Behaviour: A Comparative Handbook*. New York: Free Press.
Sartori, Giovanni. 1976. *Parties and Party Systems. A Framework for Analysis*. Cambridge: Cambridge University Press.
Scase, Richard. 1977. *Industrial Society: Class, Cleavage and Control*. New York: St. Martin's Press.
Schmitt, Hermann. 1987. *Neue Politik in alten Parteien*. Opladen: Westdeutscher Verlag.

Schneider, William. 1974. "Issues, Voting, and Cleavages: A Methodology and Some Tests." *American Behavioral Scientist* 18: 111–46.

Scholten, Ilja. 1987. *Political Stability and Neo-Corporatism: Corporatist Integration and Societal Cleavages in Western Europe*. London: Sage Publications.

Seiler, Daniel. 1977. "Cleavages, Regions, and Political Science: Application of a Schema of Analysis to Switzerland and Belgium." *Canadian Journal of Political Science* 10: 447–72.

Shamir, Michael. 1984. "Are Western Party Systems 'Frozen'? A Comparative Dynamic Analysis." *Comparative Politicial Studies* 12: 35–79.

Smith, Gordon. 1976. "Social Movements and Party Systems in Western Europe." In Martina Kolinsky and William Patterson (eds.), *Social and Political Movements in Western Europe*. New York: St. Martin's Press.

Sparks, Colin and Anna Readon. 1995. "Re-regulating Television after Communism: A Comparative Analysis of Poland, Hungary, and the Czech Republic." In Farrel Cocrcoran and Pachal Perston (eds.), *Democracy and Communication in the New Europe. Change and Continuity in East and West*, 31–50. Cresskill: Hampton,

Splichal, Slavko. 1994. *Media Beyond Socialism. Theory and Practice in East-Central Europe*. Boulder: Westview.

Styrkársdóttir, Audur. 1986. "From Social Movement to Political Party: The New Women's Movement in Iceland." In Drude Dahlerup (ed.), *The New Women's Movement*. London: Sage Publications.

Stinchcombe, Arthur. 1975. "Social Structure and Politics." In Fred Greenstein and N.W. Polsby (eds.), *Macropolitical Theory, Handbook of Political Science*, vol. 3, 557–622. Reading: Addison Wesley.

Svallfors, Stefan. 1995. "The End of Class Politics? Structural Cleavages and Attitudes to Swedish Welfare Policies." *Acta Sociologica* 38: 53–74.

Taylor-Gooby, Peter. 1986. "Consumption Cleavages and Welfare Politics." *Political Studies* 34: 592–606.

von Beyme, Klaus. 1982. *Parteien in westlichen Demokratien*. München: Piper Verlag.

Voye, Liliane and Jean Remy. 1986. "Persistence of Traditional Cleavages and Differences in Priorities." *Tijdschrift voor Sociologie* 7: 165–87.

Ware, Alan. 1996. *Political Parties and Party Systems*. Oxford: Oxford University Press.

Wolinetz, Steven B. 1979. "The Transformation of Western European Party Systems Revisited." *West European Politics* 2: 4–28.

Wolinetz, Steven B., ed. 1988. *Parties and Party Systems in Liberal Democracies*. London and New York: Routledge.

Wright, James und Daniel Holub. 1979. "Social Cleavage and Party Affiliation Revisited: A Comparison of West Germany and the United States." *Sociology and Social Research* 63: 671–97.

Zuckermann, Alan. 1975. "Political Cleavages: A Conceptual and Theoretical Analysis." *British Journal of Political Science* 5: 231–48.

———. 1982. "New Approaches to Political Cleavages." *Comparative Political Studies* 15: 131–44.

2

Cleavages, Parties, and Voters

Kay Lawson

INTRODUCTION

As Andrea Römmele has noted, and as the contributing authors will show in detail, the study of cleavages and parties in East and Central Europe provides an unusual opportunity to study the process of cleavage formation, party response, and voter alignment. The fifteen chapters to follow tell us a great deal about how that process began and continues in this part of the world. But they do more than that. They also offer us the chance for new insights into the interrelationships among cleavages, parties, and voter preferences. They suggest, above all, the crucial importance of separating these three elements.

This chapter is divided in two sections. The first offers a brief overview of the book and an explanation of how it was written. The second, based on a fairly extensive review of the contributors' work, seeks answers to the following questions: Do true cleavages presently exist in these nations? Are they revivals of old cleavages? Whether old or new, or a combination, are the parties capitalizing on them, presenting themselves as representative of those on one side of such a cleavage? What does the public make of all this—how have the voters been responding to the choices offered them? This second section concludes with a consideration of a larger question: What do these studies suggest, in general, regarding the nature of the interrelationships among cleavages, parties, and voter preferences?

OVERVIEW, WITH COMMENTS ON METHOD

The fifteen chapters that follow my own are organized not country by country, but topic by topic, with all five nations covered by separate chapters under each topic. Part II examines the cleavages and parties existent prior to 1989; Part III considers cleavages and parties after 1989; and Part IV looks at how the voters have responded to the parties in recent elections. This organization has two advantages. It facilitates focus on the commonalities in these nations' political pasts and presents and it makes clear the importance of distinguishing among our three topics: Although all three are treated in all three Parts, the discussion of *cleavages* becomes dominant in Part II, *parties* hold center stage in Part III, and *voters* are the stars of Part IV.

The authors of the individual substantive chapters are all citizens and residents of their nations. Petre Datculescu, writing about Romania, is the only author to cover all three topics for a nation. Georgi Karasimeonov covers both the pre- and post-1989 eras for Bulgaria, while Vladimir Shopov analyses the response of the voters in the recent past. Similarly, György G. Márkus analyses parties and cleavages in both eras of Hungarian history, but leaves it to János Simon to provide the breakdown of the vote in that nation. Lubomír Brokl takes up the challenge of the Czech past, shares the coverage of post-revolutionary cleavage and party development with Josef Blahož and Zdenka Mansfeldová, and coauthors the final Czech chapter with Mansfeldová. The Polish chapters are written by Hieronim Kubiak, Jerzy J. Wiatr, and Jacek Raciborski.

All the authors are established political scientists affiliated with prestigious academic or survey research institutions in their countries; their backgrounds and accomplishments are more fully detailed in the List of Contributors. Here, however, I wish to further emphasize that they are indigenous scholars and what this means for the book.

Arjun Appadurai has posed a mighty challenge to those who would conduct research across national and cultural borders:

If we are serious about building a genuinely international and democratic community of researchers—especially on matters that involve cross-cultural variation and intersocietal comparison—then we have two choices. One is to take the elements that constitute the hidden armature of our research ethic as given and unquestionable, and proceed to look around for those who wish to join us. This is what may be called *weak* internationalization. The other is to imagine and invite a conversation about research in which . . . the very elements of this ethic could be subjects of debate, and to which scholars from other societies and traditions of inquiry could bring their own ideas about what counts as new knowledge and about what communities of judgment and accountability they might judge to be central in the pursuit of such knowledge. This latter option—which might be called *strong* internationalization—might be more laborious, even contentious. But it is the surer way to create communities and conventions of research in which membership does not require unquestioned prior adherence to a quite specific research ethic. (Appadurai, 1997)

This book moves only a small step in the direction Appadurai recommends, but it is perhaps an important one. We cannot claim to have opened the whole Western research ethic to question. We did, however, take the important step of inviting only indigenous authors to comment on the new parties forming in their own lands; and we did make an effort to hear what it was our contributors wanted to say on this subject. These two steps made an enormous difference. Our original suggestion to this team was that they continue the work on the internal life of political parties already begun by the Workgroup on Political Parties and Elections.[1] However, the parties were too new for most of our authors to believe it made sense to focus on the internal organization of any of them. They believed there were far more important matters at hand, and they were determined to write about them. Most of them believed it was essential to provide a thorough understanding of the past before they could talk about the present. They also wanted to address the question of how that past influenced present politics. There was disagreement about whether or not the parties were picking up old cleavages, whether there were new cleavages, and whether the parties were actually representing any cleavages—the word cleavages would not go away.

Appadurai says working to achieve strong internationalization can be "laborious, even contentious" and he is right. But by the end of our second meeting we had hammered out an outline that satisfied everyone sufficiently for all to proceed. We agreed to have three chapters on every nation: One on the past relationship between cleavages and parties, one on present relationships, and a final one on voter response.

There followed a very long period of editing, much of which was devoted to bringing the substance of the three chapters for each nation into greater conformity with the overall scheme, while trying at the same time to respect the authors' own approaches and conclusions. Although the contributors to this book all work comfortably within the empirical norms of Western party scholarship, some of them (e.g., Blahož, Brokl, Kubiak, Márkus) brought an unusual wealth of historical knowledge and philosophical understanding to bear as well, while others (co-editor Karasimeonov and fellow contributors Datculescu, Mansfeldová, Raciborski, Shopov, Simon, and Wiatr), while obviously fully knowledgeable about the past, laid greater stress on contemporary scholarship and methods.

In addition to this diversity, which the editors have sought to protect and encourage within the general scheme of the book, these authors also *shared* many characteristics, characteristics that we believe have also immensely enriched this enterprise and that we could never have hoped to find in scholars less intimately familiar with these nations' politics. Many were themselves active in their countries' revolutions and are presently active in politics (one, Jerzy J. Wiatr, completed his chapter while serving as Minister of Education; another author actually had to withdraw because earlier work had attracted the ire of her prime minister; she was too busy defending academic freedom—her own—to stay with us). Furthermore, as dedicated scholars *and* citizens, they shared the capacity to blend strong patriotism and pride in their nations' revolutions with a determination to discuss difficult and painful conditions, past and present, with absolute honesty. The overall result is a rich combination of data, insight, and interpretation, strongly rooted in the particular national context, deeply informed by experience and by feeling.

Certainly we all share the hope of Ernst Gehmacher (see Preface) that these studies will be well read within the countries concerned. But we also believe they will offer readers outside East and Central Europe an unusually varied and textured approach not only to the recent political histories of these countries, but to the science and art of party scholarship as well.

CLEAVAGES, PARTIES, AND VOTERS IN EAST AND CENTRAL EUROPE

Turning to the second purpose of this chapter, I seek now to determine whether or not it makes sense to say that true cleavages exist in these nations, that the parties recognize and capitalize on such cleavages, and that the voters recognize themselves and their own deep divisions in the political offer and respond accordingly. I must stress at the outset that although I begin this section by summarizing, country by country, what the authors have to say that seems to me to bear most pertinently upon these questions, it is certainly possible that others, including perhaps some of the authors themselves, would make this summary differently, and would arrive at different conclusions. In particular, I use one of the more rigorous definitions of cleavage (see Römmele, Chapter 1, for the many choices possible). For my purposes, *cleavages are long-term structural conflicts that give rise to opposing political positions, which may or may not be represented by parties.* I leave it to our readers to decide which definition they prefer, and—having read the chapters that follow—how sound this summary and interpretation may be.

Bulgaria

Georgi Karasimeonov reminds us that Bulgaria's first parties did not appear until the establishment of a constitutional monarchy in 1879. The Conservatives and the Liberals represented a division between elites: those who sought to keep the propertied elite in power and those who sought to apply the philosophies of the French Revolution and of British Liberals to Bulgaria. Although the period 1889–1894 was marked by near dictatorship, party formation continued during and afterwards. However, the early years of Bulgarian independence (up until World War I) were marked by partisan fragmentation and intrigue, when no stable ruling majority could be established, and the king maintained strong personal control. There were no significant differences in the party platforms and, according to Karasimeonov, no significant cleavages were represented in the political arena prior to 1918.

At the conclusion of World War I the party representing the peasant masses against the urban elite gained new vigor; however, urban domination, in cooperation with dictatorial monarchical rule, was firmly established by 1934. Although the rural/urban cleavage did not reappear after the war, given Communist elimination of the market economy, of private property, and of all intermediary organizations, a new division between the ruling nomenklatura and those favoring the establishment of a civil society did appear and spread into the ranks of the party itself, taking the form of pro-Western modernizers versus pro-Soviet traditionalists.

Given the weakness of any earlier Bulgarian attempts to establish a structurally responsive democratic party system, there has been little temptation since 1989 to return to partisan politics based on center–periphery, urban–rural, church–state, or even worker–employer divisions. Karasimeonov makes a valiant effort to discover possible new cleavages emerging. One may be sociopolitical: the state versus "islands of civil society" (the media, the universities, some nongovernmental organizations, some private entrepreneurs). A second may be national versus ethnic, although the only evidence is the Movement for Rights and Freedoms representing the Turks, 10 percent of the Bulgarian population. Religious and cultural cleavages are also hard to find, although Karasimeonov believes a widespread concern for the absence of cultural values has been responsible for the creation of many religious groups and sects and some strengthening of Islamic fundamentalism. Bulgarians do have different opinions regarding international policy and orientation, and can be divided into those who are pro-Europe and those who are panslavic and nationalist, but for Karasimeonov this is an issue for discussion, not a powerful cleavage.

To the extent that there is any echo at all of ancient battles, it appears to be heard within, not between, the two leading parties. The anti-communist coalition is divided between those who would like to return to the past ("restaurationists") and modernizers, between those who favor radical decommunization and those who hope for more moderate evolutionary change, and even, says Karasimeonov, between those motivated by values and those who care only for the conquest of power. The ex-Communists have also been divided between those who are pro-reform (some radically so, others more moderately) and those who are conservative old guard marxist hardliners.

But for Karasimeonov none of this represents real cleavages or even serious divergences of opinion, but simply a struggle to find the ideological basis for taking over what is still a powerful bureaucracy unrestrained by either a strong private business sector or a well developed civil society.

When the ex-Communist forces took power in 1994—with a strong majority, and good turnout—they appeared to represent one side of a newly defined socioeconomic cleavage, ready to serve an electorate that had its focus firmly fixed on its material needs. In fact, they focused on enriching themselves by hidden privatizations of property formerly belonging to the state.

Vladimir Shopov shows that although the voters for the two forces are different, they are not sharply so. It is rare that the total in any demographic category ready to declare it would vote for one of the two parties exceeds 60 percent; more often the two parties share about 40 percent of a given category. Shopov's data tend to confirm as well Karasimeonov's views that the central emerging division is between those who are winning and those who are losing (regardless of one's class identity), that the latter category is by far the most numerous, and that the parties are more remarkable as agencies of ambition (if not outright corruption and venality) than as honest representatives of divergent popular interests.

Karasimeonov and Shopov agree there is a cleavage. It is rich versus poor, and the parties are not addressing it when in power. The concerns of the large majority of the population find little echo in programs of the parties among which they must choose.

The Czech Republic

The bitter struggles between Catholics and Protestants and between German colonists and indigenous peoples in the "Czech lands" during the seventeenth and eighteenth centuries produced an array of divisions to which Lubomír Brokl has no difficulty applying the classic concept: Cleavages existed between serf and feudal lord, between periphery and center, between Protestantism and Catholicism, and between the speakers of the Czech and German languages. There were, however, no organized political manifestations of these divisions, which surfaced instead in peasant rebellion and in religious, moral, and literary dissidence.

It was not until the middle of the nineteenth century that political parties and other political movements began to form, and not until a constitutional monarchy was established in 1861 that the Czech bourgeoisie and intelligentsia who aligned themselves with the underprivileged possessed the necessary arena for waging their struggle in electoral politics. Even then, although the new parties addressed some aspects of the earlier cleavages, the continued domination by foreign powers meant that such divisions were subordinated to the quest to assert Czech identity and gain greater autonomy.

After World War I Czechs and Slovaks were reunited in the independent Czechoslovak Republic, and a true democracy, albeit one that was to endure for only twenty years (1918–1938), was established. Czech politicians could now campaign more openly on the issues that divided them from each other (particularly rural versus urban and church versus state) or from their Slovak compatriots. However, during the succeeding period of totalitarian rule, lasting more than forty years, all organized manifestations of political divisiveness were suppressed. Furthermore, policies during the Communist era, which removed most of the German population and many Hungarian inhabitants, favored rural development (to the extent that rural incomes were sometimes higher than those in town), destroyed the economic power of the church and spread atheistic propaganda, all served to weaken the old divisions. Despite the important signs of dissent they note during the Communist era, Josef Blahož, Lubomír Brokl and

Zdenka Mansfeldová seem to agree that the old cleavages effectively disappeared during the era of totalitarian rule.

The reintroduction of democratic politics in 1989 led in Czechoslovakia, as elsewhere, to an explosion of new parties, associations, and trade unions. Some of the new parties were revivals of earlier parties, some were highly ephemeral. When the political dust finally settled, noticeably unrepresented was the political center. In fact, the Czech authors argue, the two strongest parties have themselves both always taken centrist positions on policy when in power.

There are many questions that divide Czech public opinion, and some which divide those in politics without being of much concern to the general public. Although every party supports privatization and there is no significant current of public opinion opposed, the methods to be followed, the role to be played by the state, the right of former communists to take part, and the role to be permitted foreign companies are all matters of debate. Other issues include the relationship between civic society and the political system, the maintenance or reduction of social expenditures, the environment, human rights (which ones? for whom?), the extent of decentralization desirable, the "German question," and the role of the Czech Republic in the institutions of Europe and NATO.

The Czech parties address most of these issues, and do so in ways that distinguish one from the next, although often only marginally. There is little party interest in the ecology and only extremist parties have attempted to make anything of the German question or have strongly opposed Czech membership in Europe and NATO. The parties make much of the matter of decentralization; the general public does not find the question particularly salient.

But these issues do not in themselves create divisions that meet the more rigorous definition of cleavage. Only one such cleavage may be beginning to emerge; according to these authors the socioeconomic division, which they define as economic populism versus market liberalism, is a true cleavage. Considerably more tentatively, they add cosmopolitan versus nationalist (incorporating questions of how to protect Czech security, readiness or reluctance to accept foreign influence and foreign capital, and attitudes toward the German population, ethnic minorities, and asylum policy). They specifically reject the categories of rural versus urban, church versus state, and owners versus workers; although they acknowledge the divisions between worker and owner have not disappeared, they believe new systems of consultation and cooperation will work and point out that no party represents the interests only of workers and employees. (Economic populism versus market liberalism is not about workers versus employees; it is about what kind of socioeconomic system to develop.)

In summary, despite an earlier period of strong democratic government, the two periods of totalitarian rule have served to eliminate several of the older cleavages in the Czech Republic, apparently for good, and post-1989 politics show little sign either of their renascence or of the substitution of new cleavages with unambiguous partisan representation.

Hungary

For György Márkus, Hungary is "a distinctive medieval state" that became a "historical–geopolitical buffer zone." Its boundaries have been continuously redrawn, and Hungarians' sense of national identity precedes the nation state.

Márkus identifies one key cleavage as dominating the precommunist past: traditionalists versus westernizers. The traditionalists were those who stressed Hungarian nationhood above all, favored strong authority, a strong church, and the community, and maintained particularist rather than universalist values. They never ceased to dream of bringing all Hungarians together again. Westernizers, on the other hand, were keen for catch-up modernization, favored individualism, multicultural diversity, a secular state, and human rights, and privileged universalist over particularist values. They were ready to address the problems of Hungarians living elsewhere by insisting on their rights and liberties rather than trying to redraw existing boundaries.

For Márkus this division carries forward into the communist era. The "populist" writers, historians, and social scientists who worried about various threats to Hungarian identity, but were never strongly anti-regime, were, he says, the traditionalists. The followers of George Lukacs, the Jewish minority, the human rights activists, the reformists in the ruling party, and in general all those who offered some form of "moral resistance" to the regime were modernists.

Furthermore, Márkus claims, even today the strongest parties in Hungary carry forward this historic cleavage. The Hungarian Democratic Forum (the MDF), including the Christian Democrats and the Smallholders parties, represents the traditionalist side, albeit somewhat more Christian and more middle class, and less populist, than such movements in the past. In power after the 1990 election, the MDF and especially Prime Minister Antall (1993–1994) stressed the importance of creating a "single spiritual community," restoring religious education, giving the church back its schools, guaranteeing that the media were "genuinely" Hungarian and Christian, and taking what action it could on behalf of Hungarian minorities abroad. Yet at the same time this was a government moving steadily toward a capitalist social market economy, the rule of law, and the integration of Hungary into Europe and NATO.

When the Socialist "modernizers" came to power in 1994 they focused heavily on technocratic solutions, and went so far as to devise a "stabilization" program designed to stimulate exports, reduce public spending on social and health services, limit consumption, impose wage restraints, and reduce employment in public education, public health, and scientific research. For Márkus, this is the old modernist current, caught up in a strange new world, a world in which their most powerful allies—and their most dangerous competitors for power—are the forces of the new global economy, including the IMF.

Strange rifts developed among the out of power traditionalists as they sought to distinguish themselves from the Socialist austerity program. Now it was they who spoke on behalf of welfare state, even Keynesian, policies, going so far as to claim that not to measure the social effects of government policies was "antinational." Not surprisingly, the party broke apart over this line, giving Hungary an opposition divided between more moderate, more European, and *more* professional forces and what we might call the more traditional (and populist) traditionalists.

Márkus believes these later developments are signs the parties are struggling to move past the old cleavage. His name for the new cleavage is commodification versus decommodification. But what he tells us suggests not so much a new cleavage as an effort to bring the old one forward into a strange new world. The traditionalists are updating the essence of traditionalism—resistance to change—and defending the old, which now means the welfare state. The modernists are discovering that socialism is not modern, and it is socialism itself that is being jettisoned, despite the victory of those who call themselves by that label.

As for the general public, they appear to be confused and displeased. When they name their priorities, they are staunchly pragmatic and little interested in such matters as whether or not to strengthen national feeling, purge ex-Communists or increase the role of religion. Very few have a sense of identification with a party and only a handful have joined a party. Abstention is 40 percent or higher, and when asked "Where are the greatest tensions in society?" they do not respond in the terms the parties have offered them. However, János Simon does find evidence of distinct differences among the supporters of the different parties. He identifies six voter types: Nonvoters, Great Winners, Powerless, Technocrats, Authoritarian, and Indifferent, and his findings suggest that the divisions among Hungarians may be more numerous and more structured than Márkus believes and that even if the parties do not campaign or govern in terms of those divisions as unambiguously as their supporters might desire (Simon does not consider what the parties are actually saying and doing), those supporters are nonetheless developing reasonably strong links to "their" parties.

In sum, although the two major political forces in Hungary may both be seeking ways to update an old cleavage that no longer makes sense to most Hungarians (and perhaps never did) and in the process disassociating themselves from some of the values they have each professed to hold most dear, Hungarian voters appear able to choose among the parties in ways consistent with their own (divided) opinions. Simon is content to call such divisions cleavages. In fact only the religious issue would seem to meet the requirement of being a "long term structural conflict," and some of the issues (attitudes toward the communist past in particular) seem inevitably transient. However, his findings regarding the importance of the division between winners versus losers fits well with Márkus' insistence that here in fact is the most important cleavage presently forming in Hungary.

Poland

Hieronim E. Kubiak points out that parties began to form in Poland nearly a quarter of a century before Poland's own democratic government was installed, because Poles often had the right to elect representatives to other nations' legislatures during that time. During this period, the key question was whether to put all political energies into gaining independence, or to focus on other issues (such as workers or farmers' rights, or the need to develop a national identity). Religious and ethnic diversity was very great, and often translated into partisan fragmentation and mutual hostility.

When independence brought a new constitution and a proportional representation electoral system in 1918, thirty-two parties were formed. The democratic experiment was not an overwhelming success, and the parties do not seem to have formed in response to structured divisions embedded in the popular will. There was little if any supraparty consensus about the nature of the state or of the public good, and little resistance to the coup d'etat which overthrew the government in 1926.

Poland was divided between the Soviet Union and Germany during World War II. By war's end, ethnic cleavages had largely disappeared, not because different peoples had learned to live together peacefully but rather because they no longer lived together at all. In addition to the decimation of Polish Jewry by the Holocaust, the nation lost 47 percent of its territory, lands that had been populated mostly by national and religious minorities, ethnic Germans returned to Poland, and ethnic Poles returned to Poland (from the USSR). Poland had become homogeneous, 95 percent Polish and Catholic.

Poland came fully under Communist rule in 1945 and, here as elsewhere, Soviet rule meant radical measures to suppress old divisions, and the elimination of all channels of dissent (the church being a partial exception). In addition, there was great economic change during the communist era: the land-owning nobility lost its land and the bourgeoisie came under heavy control from the state (rich and poor still existed, but it *was* a more equal society). There were, however, important divisions of opinion during this era, such as on the question of support for the nation versus support for the USSR, as well as on broader issues of church versus party, and society versus the state. In all such issues, the basic division was between those who sought to maintain some sense of traditional nationhood and those whose support for the Communist regime was unconditional; Wiatr sums it up as "us" versus "them," but not real class politics, not a genuine cleavage.

In any case the parties (and there continued to be more than one) could play no effective role during this period vis à vis such divisions. The existent parties were steadily forced to consolidate, and there was no well established legal opposition. There was no open competition for elite selection, no need for politicians to seek social acceptance, no development of pluralist skills and practices, and the police and military were entirely politicized.

Did new divisions emerge after 1989? Wiatr finds that post-Communist Poles almost unanimously decline to respond to arguments regarding authoritarianism versus democracy or Westernization versus nationalism (they are all pro-democracy, they all favor some measure of Westernization). They organize themselves instead around three divisions, which Wiatr believes are the new cleavages:

1. Socioeconomic: haves versus have nots. The radical economic reforms introduced since 1989 have led to greater income differences than existed before. The "haves" are younger, better educated, and live in regions of high economic activity (and thus employment). The have-nots are their opposites, plus most farmers.
2. Secular versus religious state: The Church remained strong throughout the Communist era and after 1989 became the most powerful social institution, partly because still able to offer religious instruction in the schools. But this cleavage is stronger in opinion than in party positions. Only two parties are forthrightly secular, none is forthrightly for a religious state.
3. Historical responsibility for the communist era. This question produced two grounds for divisiveness after 1989: Should ex-communist-bureaucrats be excluded from positions of leadership? Was everything about the communist era utterly bad and to be condemned? Public opinion is sharply divided on the first, but most people find the latter question of little interest.

These three divisions are not cross-cutting for the parties, but neither are they fully dichotomous. Wiatr identifies parties of the Left (for the have nots, secularism, opposed to decommunization); of the Liberal Right (for the haves, moderately pro-Church and moderately pro-decommunization); and of the Conservative Right (middle of the road as to haves and have nots, strongly pro-Church and pro-decommunization).

What do the voters make of all this? In the first place, Jacek Raciborski says, turnout was very low in the first elections, the number of parties immense (for example, 111 in 1991), and voter loyalty to party almost nonexistent. The 1993 vote was largely a protest vote against a right wing government seen as failing to keep its promises—70 percent saw the economic situation as poor, and most did not approve of the religious state, of strong decommunization, nor of the conflict revealed within the ruling elite. Subsequent shifts further left, then partially back to the right, have apparently done little to stabilize Poland's highly fluid politics. No party other than the Polish Peasant Party can count with certainty on any demographic group and whatever "alignments" appear in a single election tend to be both partial and transient. In sum, the findings of the Polish authors suggest that although new divisions are apparent, and some appear to be assuming the status of genuine cleavages, they are not strongly served by the parties, and the parties, in turn, are not strongly supported by the public.

Romania

Romania is a small country that has been repeatedly occupied or threatened by other states. Its economy in the nineteenth and earlier twentieth century was largely owned and controlled by foreign interests, and most Romanians have made what living they could from the land. Ethnically, Romanians have long been relatively homogenous; early cleavages did not pit ethnic group versus ethnic group but rather foreign versus indigenous elites, and, domestically, the ruling class versus the excluded classes (the peasants and workers were, says Petre Datculescu, "mere spectators" in the game of politics).

Thus it is no surprise that the earliest party began as a movement against foreign domination, and that when it divided into two factions, one side represented large landowners and the other smaller landlords interested in moderate agrarian reform. Although many new competing parties were formed when the former disappeared at the end of World War I, the other dominated party politics from 1866 to 1933. Its efforts to build up the nation's financial and industrial infrastructure benefited few beyond foreign investors and a narrow indigenous elite.

Throughout the inter-war period right and extreme-right parties grew steadily stronger, and by 1937, the date of the last free elections prior to World War II, the stage was set for the establishment of fascist dictatorship which endured until 1944.

Any improvements in the lot of the Romanian masses after Communist takeover in 1944 were soon erased after Nicolae Ceaușescu came to power in 1965. Ceaușescu's efforts to achieve economic growth by boosting industrial development despite the nation's inadequate resources and the state of the world market were a predictable failure, and the repression of individual rights became ever more severe. By the 1980s living standards, never high, were decreasing dramatically and ideological repression, including censorship of all political, artistic, social and scientific information from the West, was growing ever worse.

Datculescu sees such conditions as producing two important cleavages in the final years of the Communist regime: that between the political elite and the working class, and that between the political elite and the technocrats. Both workers and technocrats had been favored under early Communist rule, and both were disillusioned when the effects of steady economic deterioration reached their own privileged positions. However, the political elite was not entirely unsympathetic: Datculescu says that most of the nomenklatura (about ten thousand at most) were themselves suffering from the drastic economic decline and were "not at all persuaded of Ceaușescu's infallibility."

Following a brief period of economic improvement immediately after the revolution, low-level social and economic homogeneity continued after 1989. Privatization was largely rural, and meant little more than the restoration of traditional peasant households living in poverty. The middle class remains narrow, the upper class extremely thin.

By the time of the first free elections in May, 1990, Romania had 75 registered parties and by 1996 there were 200. Some of the new parties were in fact revivals of the old historical parties, but times and conditions had changed; agrarian parties were weaker than before. The programs of all the parties stressed the importance of moving toward a market economy, political democracy, integration in the international community, the provision of similar benefits to various groups in the electorate, and the elimination of corruption. Datculescu dismisses the idea of separating them into "left" versus "right" and prefers "National Conservatives" (those that favor increased state control over the economy and are more nationalistic) versus "Cosmopolitan-Liberals" (those desiring rapid progress toward capitalism and stressing cosmopolitan values). The parties in the latter group do significantly better in elections.

The emotional divisions between the two camps run deep, says Datculescu, citing data demonstrating how each side gives itself a favorable image and demonizes the other. Furthermore, although their programs are similar, differences among them do exist on certain issues: the treatment of former communists, the possible restoration of the monarchy, national stability and inter-ethnic relations, and issues related to economic reform.

The first three issues, however, appear to be more divisive for the parties than for the voters, most of whom are interested first and foremost in the straightforward and compelling question of social and economic conditions for themselves and their compatriots. It is in this domain that the sharpest divisions arise among the people themselves, particularly around the question of *pace*. The young, intellectuals, professionals, and well-trained workers in successful companies would like to see faster progress toward a market economy. Older citizens, rural inhabitants and broad masses of wage earners in less successful companies want change to proceed at a slower pace, preserving jobs and ensuring steady wage increases. Seeking to win support from both sides, the parties do not take sides unambiguously, and thus it is no surprise that there is little evidence of strong partisan attachment among the voters. Although in each election there may be identifiable differences by group, particularly between rural and urban and between younger and older voters, these differences do not translate into partisan loyalty and cross-class voting is the rule. The performances of the parties do not vary greatly from election to election, but Datculescu shows that the aggregate results conceal sometimes "massive" shifts of individual allegiances.

Thus, very much like their counterparts in the other nations, Romanian voters are broadly agreed on the importance of certain basic issues and on the position they expect the parties to take on them: improve the economy, raise salaries, keep unemployment down, fight corruption. The parties can do little to distinguish themselves from one another except to insist on their ability to meet such goals better than their competitors, and weak partisanship and voter fluctuations are therefore likely to continue.

Uncoupled Democracy: The Disconnection of Cleavages, Parties, and Voters

We may now claim to have found the answers to our questions. Although there are many important differences from case to case, certain generalizations may be made. It is possible to identify clear-cut cleavages in the earlier histories of all these nations, although most of these received only limited partisan representation and did not endure. There has been little or no freezing effect: the hot blasts of twentieth-century war and totalitarian conquest destroyed the earlier parties, eliminated many of the cleavages they responded to, and crushed the institutional structures that supported both. Nor has there been what might be called a deep freezing effect: post-totalitarian thaws have permitted the restoration of democratic institutions, but have not brought the old parties or the old divisions back to life.

Nor is it easy to identify new and contemporary cleavages. The one division that seems to exist everywhere, unambiguously, and that appears to be assuming the guise of a true cleavage, is that between the *minority* who are doing well in the post-communist struggle and want to do better, faster, and the *majority* who are doing poorly (or are deeply concerned about the plight of the poor) and want to slow things down and maintain or reestablish some measure of pre-revolutionary social security. The parties seek to reassure the majority but in office tend to follow, out of faith in its eventual efficacy or hope of personal gain or a combination of both, the will of the minority. Eager to differentiate themselves in the voters' minds, they adopt positions on other issues, some of which are of minimal interest to the voters (for example, attitudes toward the past, decommunization). Although voters' ballot choices sometimes suggest an ability to link their own views to those of appropriate parties, they have been repeatedly disillusioned by the performance of the winners once in power. There is a strong tendency to shift from party to party and candidate to candidate, hoping for a better response to the socioeconomic issues that trouble them the most.

On the face of it, then, classical cleavage theory does not stand up well to post-totalitarian realities. The parties have formed not in response to structured cleavages but to the chance for gaining power. The major cleavage shapes neither the party system nor the parties' program in or out of power. Voters for whom their position vis à vis that cleavage is paramount have no clear-cut partisan home.

Nevertheless, there are important advantages to be gained by looking at the political histories of these five nations through the cleavage lens. First, this focus permits us to bring a greater depth of understanding to the politics of nations whose histories have been broken and disrupted time and again by forces beyond their control. It is important to know what cleavages existed in the past, to recognize their absence in the present, and to grasp the reasons for this lack of continuity.

Second, when we cannot find the old, we naturally look harder for the new, and these authors tend to agree that an important new division is emerging, one that is based on socioeconomic factors, but not necessarily on the class identification of those who are taking sides. Calling this new division simply "winners versus losers" is too simplistic. If that is all it is, then it is not *not* about class; it describes the transition of whole populations into a new lower class and a new (and increasingly narrow) upper class. On the other hand, it is equally simplistic to see this cleavage only in class terms, given the number of those who appear to be winners but urgently seek political solutions for the plight of the growing body of losers. The new classes surely exist, and are continuing to form. But the political argument is not between them; it is between free market liberals and economic populists.

Having taken us this far the cleavage perspective forces us also to recognize that the connections we have for so long presumed must necessarily exist, connections between cleavages and parties, and then in turn between parties and their voters, do not in fact always exist. Contemporary parties in Eastern and Central Europe are often reluctant to respond to existent cleavages, taking one side or the other. They try to substitute other divisive issues and/or they try to take both sides of those that exist. They see no political advantage in representing a strictly minoritarian point of view, not when modern communication techniques seem to permit all things to be said, at all times, to all the listeners. Once in office, party representatives are not constrained by commitments they may have appeared to have made. Socialists jump to join the global economy, traditionalists forget their promises to be kind. Personal ambition cathects with international design and IMF-type adjustments are made with little hesitation.

Voters, too, are capable now of independent action. A choice may have to be made among existent parties, but that choice now seldom reflects a strong partisan commitment, nor even a certainty of agreement with a party's program. More and more often, voters make their choices based on a combination of candidate preference and sheer hope that that which seems least bad may actually prove somewhat good. When elected candidates disappoint and hopes are blasted yet again, voters move on.

This *uncoupling of the forces of electoral democracy,* of parties from cleavages and of voters from parties, is a phenomenon that is not limited to East and Central Europe. The forces at work—the impact of the global economy, the ever more open pursuit of political power as an instrument for controlling the distribution of a nation's wealth, and the developments in modern communication—are forces that are presently changing the nature of cleavages, party politics, and voter responses across the globe. The cleavage between free market liberalism and economic populism may well be becoming the dominant new cleavage for all of us. The readiness of parties to sidestep that cleavage, to try to substitute issues that matter to citizens less (however important some of them may be), or to pretend to take one side while adopting the other in practice are not political phenomena with which voters in the rest of the world are unfamiliar. And partisanship is in decline almost everywhere, while abstention and voter disillusionment are on the rise.

There are differences, of course. In these new democracies, the parties are newer and more plentiful, the voters have had long and bitter experience in sorting out political substance from chaff, and the need to effect change is more desperately felt than in most western democracies. Furthermore, there are numerous differences between the cases themselves, differences which we have not chosen to highlight here, but which are amply apparent in the individual chapters. Nonetheless, it is not unreasonable to expect that when outsiders explore the politics of this part of the world one result may well be a clearer understanding of what is going on at home, and the need to adapt our party research strategies accordingly.

NOTES

1. The Workgroup is a subgroup of the Committee on Political Sociology of the International Political Science Association and the International Sociology Association. The first two volumes were Lawson (1994) and Ignazi and Ysmal (1998).

REFERENCES

Appadurai, Arjun. 1997. "The Research Ethic and the Spirit of Internationalism." *In* Items, vol. 51, No. 4, Part 1, New York: Social Science Research Council, 59–60.

Ignazi, Piero, and Colette Ysmal (eds.). 1998. *The Organization of Political Parties in Southern Europe*, Westport, CT: Praeger.

Lawson, Kay (ed.) 1994. *How Political Parties Work: Perspectives from Within*, Westport, CT: Praeger.

Part II

Cleavages and Parties prior to 1989

3

Between Democracy and Authoritarianism in Bulgaria

Georgi Karasimeonov

Bulgaria is a latecomer to the community of national states in Europe, gaining independence in 1878 in the aftermath of the Russo-Turkish war.

The liberation of Bulgaria from Ottoman domination in 1878 and the subsequent establishment of an independent Bulgarian state were part of the vast historical process of creating national states in Europe. For all its uniqueness, the Bulgarian case was marked by a number of characteristics and features that were determined by the historical conditions prevailing in the Balkan region during the nineteenth century. Those conditions were a component part of the ill-famed Eastern Question—that is, the fate and very existence of the Ottoman Empire—by that time in a deep and incurable crisis that had begun in the late eighteenth century.

There were two principal factors underlying the evolution of the Eastern Question: (a) the attitude of the European Great Powers, and (b) the struggle of the Balkan and other non-Turkish nationalities in the Ottoman Empire for political emancipation and the establishment of independent states of their own. In the course of the historical process these two factors were closely intertwined and interacting, assuming multifarious and sometimes paradoxically bizarre combinations and proportions. One specific feature of the Christian nationalities on the Balkans was their dual identity. After the Ottoman conquest, they were forcibly made part of a politically, economically, and culturally backward system that delayed their normal development by centuries. However, the Ottoman yoke failed to suppress the Balkan nationalities' awareness of spiritually belonging to the European civilization. The ideas of the Renaissance, the Enlightenment, and especially of the French Revolution penetrated among the conquered Balkan nationalities and, depending on local circumstances, powerfully influenced the development of the national-liberation movements in the region.

By the nineteenth century, the disintegration of the Ottoman Empire had become an irreversible process. The first among the Balkans to break away were the outlying parts of the empire; this was followed by a successive formation of a number of national states: Serbia, Greece, Romania, Montenegro and, finally, Bulgaria. In each case, the establishment of a new state was the result of national or national-revolutionary effort combined with Great-Power intervention after Russia's victories in its wars against Turkey.

The liberation of Bulgaria was accomplished in one of the historically most unfavorable variants. Because of the proximity of the Bulgarian lands to the heart of the Ottoman Empire—Istanbul—the political regime in the area was particularly fierce, and military and political control was unabating and strict. For these reasons the climax of the Bulgarians' revolutionary efforts—the April 1876 uprising—failed, while the geographic conditions made it impossible to wage continuous guerrilla warfare and await the outbreak of a Russo-Turkish conflict, as was possible elsewhere on the Balkan Peninsula (for example, in Serbia, Greece, Montenegro, and Albania). The uprising was suppressed with unprecedented brutality.

In the Russo-Turkish war that followed, the Bulgarian nation, though represented by a volunteer force and supporting Russia's war effort in every way, did not have the status of a full-fledged participant in its own liberation. This automatically guaranteed the Russian government's unconditional political and psychological advantages in the affairs of the newly liberated Bulgaria. Had these advantages been ill-understood and clumsily used, they could have brought discord to the relations between liberators and the liberated. However, in the beginning of Bulgaria's life as a free nation, nothing of this sort happened. On the contrary, largely with Russia's help, Bulgaria began its existence as a free state at a level which, far from being lower, was in many respects *higher* than that of the other Balkan states.

Unlike the other Balkan nations, the Bulgarians had the unique chance, even in a European context, to choose and elaborate the principles of their state system themselves. The 1878 Treaty of Berlin stipulated nothing more than Bulgaria's turning into a vassal principality of the Ottoman Empire. Its liberation was accompanied by a painful dismembering of its initially granted territory by the San Stefano treaty. This fact became a central focal point of political life of independent Bulgaria and had a major influence on the political parties and their policies.

The Constituent Assembly was convened in Veliko Turnovo on February 10, 1879, its principal aim being to adopt Bulgaria's first Constitution. The draft submitted to the delegates' attention had been prepared in Russia. Against the background of Russia's strained relations with the Western governments, which were seeking ways to supplant the overwhelming Russian influence in Bulgaria, Russia's tsarist government demonstrated tact and a careful approach to the needs, feelings, and yearnings of the Bulgarians, laying at the core of its draft the principles of constitutional monarchy, the system of government that the other Balkan states already had.

It was during the debates on the orientation of the future constitution that Bulgaria's first political parties, the Liberals and the Conservatives, were born. The Conservatives spoke for the interests of the few town and village well-to-do. Compared with Conservative parties elsewhere in Europe, the Bulgarian Conservative Party had a limited social base; it was not linked to any sociopolitical structures of the past. The Conservative Party justified its name mainly by its views in the area of state organization and government. It sought to secure a ruling position for the propertied elite, limiting the influence of the common people in government affairs: It proposed electoral barriers and supported a strong monarchy, with a bicameral structure of parliament with a Senate and a State Council.

The Liberals represented the vast majority of smallholders. They sought to apply the democratic values of the French Revolution, refracted through the parliamentary principles of the British Liberals' political philosophy and maximally attuned to Bulgarian conditions. The Liberals won a difficult but decisive victory in the Constituent Assembly. As finally adopted, the Constitution differed considerably from the original Russian draft, which made it one of the most democratic constitutions in Europe.

While proclaiming the principles of a democratic state administration, the Constitution could not guarantee by itself the prescribed balance of power among monarch, government, and Parliament within the triangle of power. It depended on the concrete social and political conditions whether the monarch would enjoy unchallenged supremacy, whether in the presence of a very strong political party the government would turn into a parliamentary dictatorship, and whether the country would have a two-party or a multiparty system in which the monarch would act as arbiter of the classical parliamentary type. In the course of time, Bulgaria gave examples of varying relationships among its governing institutions.

September 1885 saw the unification between the Principality of Bulgaria and Eastern Rumelia, which was the first phase of the national unification of the Bulgarians in a single state after the Liberation.

There were *several historical periods* that determined political life and its party configuration after liberation and the initial establishment of the constitutional order. Each of these periods had its specific lines of conflict and cleavages that determined to a great extent the formations of political parties and their policies. Their mobilization capabilities were limited by the lack of democratic traditions and the backward nature of society, but Bulgaria had a small but well educated elite, part of it under the influence of radical democratic ideas. At the same time, patrimonial conditions of life determined by the domination of the peasantry and smallholders, with no significant social, economic and religious polarization, centered social and political conflicts around two major dominant issues: first, the national question and especially the liberation of the Bulgarian population in Macedonia, and second, the relationship between the major institutions, the monarchy and the parliament—more precisely, the scope of the monarch's prerogatives. The latter was part of a larger conflict regarding who should determine national priorities—the foreign-born king or the Bulgarian political forces and their parliamentary institution. At a later historical period this conflict grew into a sharp political division between the proponents of a republican form of government and a limited role for the king, and those who supported a strong monarchy and were closely associated with its policies.

The first period (1879–1894) began with the establishment of the new Bulgarian state and the new constitutional order and ended with the fall of the Stambolov regime in 1894.

This period was marked by the establishment of the first parties—the already-mentioned Liberals and Conservatives—and was followed in the next years by numerous internal divisions and periods of disruption of normal activity by authoritarian rule, the most notorious being the period after 1889 when strongman Stefan Stambolov established a one-man rule and banned most parties.

The Stambolov regime was a direct challenge to parliamentary democracy. Elections were marked by violence and low voter turnouts. A number of grossly anti-democratic laws were adopted, as were constitutional amendments that gave the government control over Parliament (for instance, the number of deputies was reduced and the procedure for adoption of laws was modified). Nonetheless, the Turnovo Constitution was preserved.

The Stambolov regime also restricted the monarch's role. However, the ambitious King Ferdinand would not be content with being nothing more than a figurehead, and the Stambolov regime was marked by continuous rivalry between the Monarch and the Prime Minister.

The imprint of the Stambolov regime on Bulgarian politics was felt for many years after its fall. Political rudeness and intolerance accompanied and discredited democracy in Bulgaria. Election violence became a common practice. The manner in which subsequent cabinets treated the Parliament was also part of the Stambolov heritage. The role of the parties in it seldom corresponded to their real influence among the electorate. The more "indisputable and convincing" a party's election victory, the more violent the methods by which it had been achieved. Conversely, the few instances of fair elections during Ferdinand's reign led to a certain parity in Parliament and to the formation of minority governments. The Parliament lost much of its real weight in Bulgarian politics compared to the first years after the country's liberation from Ottoman domination in 1878.

The major cleavages were mostly cross-cutting, leading to divisions and to the formation of parties that spun off from the first two: the Liberals and the Conservatives. They were typical clientelist parties clustered around major political figures.

The national question and the way it should be solved created two major political camps very early. One was for unconditional support of Russia and its dominance in Bulgarian affairs. The other had a more sober attitude toward the Liberators and opted for a pro-European orientation. The division into

Russophiles versus Russophobes determined to a major extent the party formation and their internal struggles in the first period.

The second period (1894–1918), beginning after the fall of the Stambolov regime, led to a major restructuring and revival of party activity. New conflicts and cleavages, a result of capitalist development, made their appearance. The new bourgeoisie had to face a growing working class which was reflected in the rise of left-wing socialist and populist parties. In 1891 the Socialdemocratic party was established, followed in 1899 by the Bulgarian Agrarian Peoples Union, representing the interests of the small landowners.

By the turn of the century, the Bulgarian economy had acquired an increasingly modern capitalist image. Starting in 1904, it entered a phase of rapid growth that continued uninterrupted until the Balkan wars of 1912–1913. The socioeconomic changes complicated the country's political structure. By and large, however, it remained more sensitive to the influence of political factors.

It was under those circumstances following the fall of Stambolov that the gradual establishment of a mode of government known as "Ferdinand's one-man regime" began in Bulgaria. King Ferdinand did not mount a direct attack against the foundations of parliamentary democracy; he abolished neither the Parliament nor the Constitution and, in comparison with other monarchs on the Balkans, he leaned to a much lesser extent on special constitutional prescriptions to restrict parliamentary democracy. The one-man regime in Bulgaria was not autocratic rule in the full sense of the word; it was personal control over the key sectors of power. Ferdinand succeeded in enlisting the support of the national bourgeoisie, even though it remained politically fragmented.

The fall of the Stambolov regime was followed by a process of internal and external stabilization. The international recognition of Prince Ferdinand came as a result of the restoration of Bulgarian-Russian relations in 1896. The reasons for the fierce conflicts between the country's political forces on the basis of pro- and anti-Russia were partly eliminated, democratic parliamentary rule was restored, former political parties were revived, and new ones were formed. Between the turn of the century and World War I, Bulgaria had an extremely diverse political spectrum, partly marked by the classical division into left, right and center. There were four parties with a leftist orientation—namely, the two social-democratic parties better known as Left Wing and Right Wing Socialists, the Bulgarian Peoples Agrarian Union, and the Radical Democratic Party—and six bourgeois parties, not clearly differentiated between right and center.

In the sphere of domestic policies, there were no fundamental differences between the platforms of the bourgeois parties. The significant progress that Bulgaria made during the first decade of the twentieth century was also a result of the activities of all the governments during that period, with continuity in the major aspects of internal policy. Despite the existence of quite a few bourgeois parties, there were no dominant ones. More often than not, personalities, rather than guiding principles, kept the different parties united. In common parlance, the different parties were usually referred to by the names of their leaders. The Bulgarian bourgeoisie had proved unable to provide economic independence for the political intelligentsia; in fact, a career in politics was often seen as a means for personal enrichment. Partisanship and corruption went hand-in-hand, poisoning the Bulgarian political atmosphere.

Foreign-policy factors also contributed to the lack of unity among the bourgeois political forces. The unresolved national question devoured much of the resources and political energy of the Bulgarian nation. Different views regarding what policies to follow with regard to the Great Powers, the Ottoman Empire, the other Balkan countries, and the national-liberation movement in Macedonia and Andrianople Thrace, created major controversies among the parties.

Until World War I at least, there was no political party in Bulgaria with a stable influence among the electorate, or within a given social layer, for that matter. Government instability was due to the fact that no party stood any chances of winning a clear majority of seats; coalitions in Parliament were no less difficult to achieve.

The extreme fragmentation of party life, full of intrigues, was further fueled by the general tendency of parties being formed around influential politicians, many of them of dubious personal and public morality, rather than around clearly formulated ideas, principles, and values. Even parties with a pronounced ideological and social image of their own—for example, the Bulgarian Peoples Agrarian Union and the Bulgarian Social Democratic Party—failed to act as a corrective of political morals and practices: The former's term in office was a period of parliamentary anomalies, while the latter made it understood that if it came to power, it would not hesitate to strip all its opponents of their constitutional freedoms.

For all its imperfections, the early introduction of a multiparty system of government nevertheless gave a powerful impetus to the expansion of political involvement. The functions that the state performed in the sphere of the economy and finance—incidentally, quite "modernized" by the standards of a preindustrial society—worked in the same direction. The proportional system of representation and the introduction of a universal voting right for men, even though falling short of automatically institutionalizing civil liberties in the form known in Western Europe, provided conditions for organizing party and political structures on a national basis. The pluralistic parliamentary system and the modernized functions of the state, coupled with all the nonpolitical transformations that were linked with the increasingly intensive integration of the Bulgarian economy into the world market, provided the frame within which it became possible for personalized parties and their clientele networks to be contested by "new" elites appealing for the involvement of much broader social strata in politics. This is the explanation for the emergence and rise to power of the Agrarian Union.

As to the ordinary voters, insofar as they could be persuaded to go to the polls at all, they usually gave their support to whatever local party group held power in its hands at the moment, for it could give everything—and take it away. As a rule, they did not care which party was in power, owing to their general political illiteracy but also to the striking similarity between party platforms which left little room for real choice.

The third period (1918–1944) reflected the consequences of the deep crisis after World War I. Bulgaria was severely punished by the victors of the war. It not only did not achieve national reunification, but lost new territories to Greece, Serbia, and Romania. This fact, combined with the deep economic crisis, stimulated radical political attitudes that resulted in the dominance of left-wing parties in the early twenties. Its high point was the absolute majority received by the radical populist Bulgarian Peoples Agrarian Union at the elections in 1921.

Actually it was not until after World War I that Bulgaria faced the freedom-or-modernization dilemma. Under the circumstances of postwar radicalism and despair, the Agrarians came to power in the name of a populist, anti-urban, anti-industrialist and, consequently, anti-modernization platform. The main political conflict was between the peasant masses and the urban elite. The urban elite twice decided that conflict in their favor by violent means, that is, by coups. In 1923, with the help of the army and the monarchy, the populist regime of the Agrarians was brought down and a brutal authoritarian rule was established, lasting until 1929. After a temporary revival of democratic procedures, the 1934 coup was followed by the imposition of a dictatorial monarchic regime that remained in power until World War II. Its markedly protectionist, proindustrial policies, coupled with the social mobility accelerated by the Great Depression, enabled the economy to gain a dominant position over politics and ideology. It was a period where authoritarian options won over parliamentary rule.

World War II created new divisions, confronting the pro-Fascist and pro-German forces with the semi-legal democratic opposition and the radical Fatherland front supported by the Communists, Russia, and the Comintern. The latter were the winners, especially the radicals which took power in 1944.

This marked the beginning of *fourth stage*—from limited pluralism to communist dictatorship. The main cleavage was provoked by a major issue: communist rule or democracy. From 1944 until 1947 the Communist Party with the support of the USSR was able to eliminate all opposition parties and establish its power monopoly.

The communist regime that lasted until 1989 provoked cleavages of a brand new nature based on the radical reformation of society. It eliminated the market economy and private property as well as democracy. On one side, old cleavages were subdued; on the other, new ones appeared.

The postwar totalitarian regime, which was also guided by modernization ambitions, was an antithesis of sorts: Its aim was full control over all institutional spheres; under it political power reached its apex, permeating society at all levels;

the existence of any independent organizations, even purely nonpolitical ones, was inadmissible; the social groups, communities, and classes inherited by it were left without their own political representatives and replaced with state-controlled formations; there were no opposing social forces, because formally there were no conflicting interests; atomized and isolated, the individual was left alone in the face of the vast guardianship of the state from which alone he expected any satisfaction of his needs and ambitions.

The communist regime attempted to control and regulate all conflicts in the name of creating a "harmonious" and classless society. It tried to eliminate old cleavages by forcefully transforming the economy from a market to a planned one, eliminating all alternate forms of property on the basis of private ownership. By subduing any autonomous "civil society" it tried to eliminate all forms of independent activity of social, political, and professional groups—in other words, all potential forms of resistance to the encompassing power of the party-state.

This "grand historical experience" of radical transformation did alter the conflict lines in the society. While pushing to the periphery and "extinguishing" old cleavages like those between labor and capital, or those based on the national question or external alliances, it nourished new ones reflecting the evolution and later crisis of the communist economic and political system.

One such cleavage was a result of the new social structure that replaced the old one based on private property. The new class structure was based on access to the control of the power resources in the party-state system. The so-called "new class," or nomenclatura, developed with time into a specific social group facing the great mass of the citizens and, given the growing problems and challenges facing "real socialism," became a parasitic group focused on safeguarding its own privileged position in society.

This new type of class division reflected the growing conflict and cleavage between a nascent civil society composed of various groups versus a nomenclatura retaining the power monopoly. This widening cleavage became the determinant factor in the emergence of opposition to the regime and thus its downfall in the late 1980s.

Ethnic conflict in the 1980s, provoked by the policy of forceful assimilation of the Turkish minority, further deepened the rift between the nascent civil society and the regime, leading to the latter's growing isolation.

The late 1980s sharpened the conflict between the modernizers, the pro-western-oriented groups, on the one hand, and the traditionalists, tightly linked to the Soviet regime, on the other. This cleavage determined the conflicts between the reform communists and the hardliners in the Communist party as well as between the "new opposition" and the communist party machine.

The communist society was not a cleavageless society, although the regime tried to subdue the expression of conflicts. Formally "hidden" cleavages manifested themselves in a specific way and appeared in the various internal party struggles and the attempts to oppose the regime and its repressive acts. In

Bulgaria they did not have the same scope as in other Central European countries where the resistance to the regime did reach large proportions, but were nonetheless a major factor in the later changes to democracy.

REFERENCES

Bell, John. 1993. "Bulgaria." *In* S. White (ed.), *Developments in East European Politics,* 83–96. London: Macmillan.

Crampton, Richard. 1987. *A Short History of Modern Bulgaria.* Cambridge: Cambridge University Press.

Moser, Charles. 1994. *Theory and History of the Bulgarian Transition.* Sofia: Free Initiative Foundation.

4

Cleavages and Parties prior to 1989 in the Czech Republic

—————————————— Lubomír Brokl

THE CONCEPTUAL FRAME OF REFERENCE

In every society the articulation and institutionalization of current political relations, conflicts, and cleavages are simply the most recent layer of political reality, built upon layers of the past. Through a system of collective symbols, which normally covers the memories of about three generations, the past affects the articulation of political problems in any present time. Thus cleavages which may seem to have been "historically solved" can be remobilized, rearticulated, rationally or irrationally legitimized, and can function again as significant conflicts or even as full-fledged cleavages.[1] It is with this understanding that we examine twentieth century Czech politics, and seek to apply Stein Rokkan's model of developmental linkages to our understanding of contemporary cleavages (Rokkan, 1968: 26–65).

In 1968 Rokkan declared,

The developmental model to be explored posits clear-cut time limits to its operation: *in terminus a quo* is the conflict over the cultural-religious identity of the emerging nation-state in the sixteenth century; *in terminus ad quem* is the establishment of universal and equal electoral democracy and the "freezing" of party alternatives, in most countries during the 1920s. This limitation in the span obviously also defines the geographical focus of the model: it only applies to the territories and the polities which were immediately affected by the clashes between the Reformers and the Roman Church and the consequent strains between secular and religious powers . . . all these countries can point to long histories of competitive parliamentary politics. By the early 1920s they all had extended the right of political citizenship to all adults. (Rokkan, 1968)

He adds, "In our attempt to explain the variations in the structuring of partisan polities we . . . first identify four 'critical junctures' in the sequences of nation-building; we next identify the principal cleavage lines generated by the decisions taken at each critical juncture, and we finally generate from each of the possible cleavage structures the core system of parties and test these predications against the historically given cases" (Rokkan, 1968: 51). By this method, Rokkan produced the model of developmental linkages in Table 4.1 (Rokkan, 1968: 54).

In a separate volume, Lipset and Rokkan claimed that two major revolutions in the Western world had produced four sets of structured cleavages which had, in turn, determined the creation and mutation of the political party systems during the era under consideration. These revolutions—and the sets of cleavages each produced—were as follows (Lipset and Rokkan, 1967):[2]

Table 4.1
Rokkan's Model of Development Linkages

1 *Critical juncture*	2 *Critical issues*	2 *Resultant cleavages*
1.1 Reformation: the 1648 settlement and the nineteenth and twentieth century secessions	1.2 Consolidation of territorial state	1.3 Peripheries vs. center: ethnicities/language groups against central dominance; moralist/ religious rejection of central culture
2.1 National Revolution: post-Napoleonic nation building	2.2 Control of territorial standardization media, primarily mass education	2.3 Church versus secular State
3.1 Industrial Revolution: 1850s onwards	3.2 The primary economy: protection versus modernization (tariff). The secondary economy: freedom of enterprise vs. state control; rights of owners/employers vs. right of workers/employees	3.3 Rural/agricultural vs. urban/industrial interests; Worker-Owner cleavage
4.1 International Revolution: Russian Revolution and after	4.2 Integration of underprivileged strata in national community	4.3 Communism vs. Socialism; Pacifism neutralism vs. commitment to nation/larger alliance

1. National revolution:
   a) functional cleavages: church versus state, Christian versus secular
   b) territorial cleavages: center versus periphery, centralist versus autonomist
2. Industrial revolution:
   a) functional cleavages: worker versus owner, capital versus labor
   b) territorial cleavages: urban versus rural, feudal (landlord) versus peasant

For reasons that will become clear as we proceed, the creation and evolution of cleavages and parties in the Czech and Czechoslovakian case does not permit a simple and unmodified application of the Lipset-Rokkan model. However, the terminology and the general approach, particularly the notion that critical periods produce critical issues that result in structured cleavages and concomitant party systems, *are* useful, and will be employed.

HISTORICAL BACKGROUND (1618–1848)

By 1618 the division between Catholic and Protestant powers in the Czech lands led to military battle and the defeat of the Protestants, an event of great importance to the future of the Czech political system. In the period following this defeat, Protestants were forced to adopt Catholicism or emigrate, and the properties of non-Catholics were expropriated by the state.[3] By 1650, the population of the Czech kingdom had been reduced from 3 million (in 1618) to 800,000, and some 2,170 villages and 138 towns had disappeared (Zdrahal, 1921: 87–88).[4] German colonists moved into the abandoned space and set up a system of oppressive rule over the remaining Czech population. This period, which came to be known as the Second Serfdom, took place during the same time that Western Europe was experiencing the growth of capitalism and the consolidation of the nation state.

A new social structure, from which the former Czech nobility had been expelled, now emerged, and a new set of cleavages crystallized, to wit: serfs (Czechs) versus feudal barons (foreigners, usually German); periphery (Czech) versus town (Germanized); and center (German Vienna; a union of Catholic and state powers; the German language) versus periphery (clandestine and dissident Protestantism; the Czech language). But these cleavages had no organized political manifestation; they made their appearance in peasant rebellion and in religious, moral, and literary protestant dissidence. Nevertheless, the system of collective symbols that emerged in response to these cleavages has shaped Czech political culture to the present time, and thus has had an impact on the present political system.

The development of capitalism, accompanied by the abolition of serfdom (in 1781) and of religious tolerance, gave rise to a social mobility of labor from the Czech countryside to the Germanized towns, and had the effect of renewing Czech identity. By 1846, the Czech lands had 6.5 million inhabitants, and the use of the Czech language was growing rapidly. By 1880 Czech was to be the mother tongue of 5.2 million people; by 1900, of 5.955 million.[5]

THE BEGINNING OF PARTIES (1848–1879)

The period from 1848 to 1879 can be seen as the next critical period for the emergence of the Czech parties, a period when the quest for greater Czech autonomy began to be taken more seriously by all concerned, and when the articulation of political interests began to be undertaken by political organizations, including parties. In 1861 the Hapsburg monarchy transformed itself into a a constitutional monarchy. However, Czech response to the new constitution was suspicious and recalcitrant: The period from 1863 through 1879 was a period of passive resistance, when most Czechs refused to participate in either the imperial institutions or the new parliament. The conflict-ridden Czech-German cohabitation of power—and with it the underprivileged condition of the Czech population—remained in effect, and the struggle for decentralization, liberalization, and democratization, a struggle led by members of the bourgeoisie and intelligentsia fighting on behalf of the underprivileged classes, continued.

An important development in this struggle was Bismarck's policy unifying the Prussian and Austrian Germanies (1871), a step which made it possible for the Czechs to imagine breaking free of the Austrian Germans and possibly establishing a connection with rebellious Hungarians against the Hapsburg monarchy (Traub, 1926: 78). However, the Hungarian situation was different. Hungarians had already obtained federal status within the empire as of 1867, with local rule divided between Germans and Hungarians. Ethnically, socially, and economically, the Hungarians were more compatible—and thus more "trustworthy"—as semi-equal partners within the empire than were the Czechs. Ethnically, the Czechs represented the Slav majority in the monarchy. Socially, the Czechs lacked the notion of status; they did not have a national aristocracy and they preferred western liberal values. Economically, three-quarters of all industry within the empire was located in the territory of the Czech kingdom. For all these reasons it was unlikely the Czechs would be granted a similar degree of civic/legal equality; it was also unlikely that they could build a separate pact with the Hungarians. Furthermore, most of the new industrialists within the Czech lands were opposed to separation: The empire provided them with an extensive market, and they much preferred internal democratization to absolute separation.

Thus this became a period of intense debate regarding issues of nationhood, decentralization, and autonomy. A wide range of economic and political interests were articulated by associations, self-help and education organizations, interest groups, specialized chambers, and the Czech newspapers.[6] And now political ferment was reflected in organized political life, which took the form of the following four distinct political movements:

- A moderate national liberal movement, composed of the national bourgeoisie (in particular the catholic and conservative large landowners), a significant portion of the intelligentsia, and various politicians cooperating with the historical aristocracy. From 1860 to 1890, under the name of "National Party" (Old Czechs-Staročeši), it became the leading Czech party.
- A radical democratic movement, first found in the liberal democratic wing of the National Party after its defeat in the elections of 1848. This movement was composed of that part of the bourgeoisie and the intelligentsia that was oriented more democratically than nationally. In 1874, this current broke off from the National Party and became the "National Free-Thinking Party" (Young Czechs-Mladočeši). Its demands included freedom of religion, but also universal suffrage, positive relationships with social democrats and socialists, and an end to passive resistance.
- The conservative, catholic-oriented movement. Composed of members of the higher classes (especially the aristocracy) and the clergy, this group articulated its interests in the terminology of territorial patriotism, and favored a state religion. (In general, the members of the landed nobility, some of whom were of Czech nationality, were catholic, loyal to Viennese policy, and did not believe in the future of the Czech nation.)
- A socialist movement. In the 1860s, as the conflict between labor and capital became politically significant, a growing labor movement made its appearance, and became institutionalized in 1874 with the founding of the international Social Democratic Workers' Party of Austria. This movement focused on conflicts regarding nationhood and on creating national solidarity.

All four groups presented themselves as anti-feudal and anti-government, that is, as liberal and democratizing. In Lipset/Rokkan terms, they were by-products of the nascent national revolution, producing territorial cleavages: center versus periphery, centralist versus autonomist. The debate focused on how best to resist the domination of the German minority. However, the lines of division between Czechs and Germans were not clear-cut politically; there were still cross-alignments, as German entrepreneurs and workers had many interests in common with their Czech counterparts. Nevertheless, the cleavages were becoming sharper. Germans living in Czech lands and fearful of Czech emancipation became more intensely opposed to measures of liberalization.[7] At the same time various socialist movements were becoming ever more nationalist in focus. The National Social Democratic Party was based in the Czech-speaking masses, and increasingly expressed their interests as a national interest.

Although divided as to how best to achieve true national autonomy, the Czech population was remarkably unified during this period in other respects. The Czechs were not divided by sub-national social barriers, nor by religion. Eager never to repeat the violence and disruption occasioned by the forced violent re-Catholicization of the seventeenth century, both Catholics and Protestants could be characterized as "soft" on religious questions, and in contrast to surrounding nations there was a significant level of secularity in Czech society. The main legacy of Protestantism was an ethic; that of Catholicism, a culture.

Finally, although the industrial revolution was moving rapidly forward, this was not a period of strong cleavages between worker and owner nor between capital and labor: The lower classes and the bourgeoisie had many interests in common in the process of capitalization. The political focus was on issues of nationhood.

CLEAVAGES AND PARTIES RELATED TO INDUSTRIALIZATION AS WELL AS TO QUESTIONS OF NATIONAL IDENTITY (1879–1918)

The period from 1879 to 1918 was one in which political divisions shifted to the functional dimension of the industrial revolution, articulated by the workers' movement and by the Social Democratic Party, and then moved back again to the territorial dimension of the national revolution.

The Czechoslovak Social Democratic Party was established in 1878. Within this party liberal and radical democratic currents of the middle class articulated the new divisions between worker and owner and between capital and labor, and sought wide-ranging democratization, which they favored extending to the working class. The party developed an ever wider base and achieved significant influence.

From the mid-1870s to 1906, the political articulation of the cleavage based on nationhood was given its strongest voice by the National Free-Thinking Party (Young Czechs), which grew steadily stronger and became the leading party of the Czech bourgeoisie from 1891 to 1906.

However, socialist parties were also becoming more representative of this cleavage as well, especially as the Social Democratic Party was becoming more and more internationally oriented. In 1897 the unified international Social Democratic Workers' Party of Austria divided into six national parties in the German part of the empire, and the Czech National Social Party was established. It included many skilled workers, the petty bourgeoisie, white-collar workers, and some members of the intelligentsia. It was a party of political practice, combining a middle-class understanding of socialism with a commitment to strong nationhood. It rejected the idea of class struggle and supported the humanism of Tomáš Guarrigue Masaryk (later to become the first president of the Czech Republic). Marsaryk led a group of "realists" who did not choose to establish a party of their own. Composed of Czech intelligentsia and scientists, this group sought to minimize Czech national euphoria and put nationalism on a rational basis, stressing antifeudalism, liberalism, and democratization.

In 1899 another important new party, the Agrarian Party, was formed. Although composed largely of small peasants and farm workers, the broad-based agenda and identity of this socially reformist, Christian, and nationalistic party, as well as its appearance at a time of such steady migration toward the towns, prevent our identifying it as a sign of a deepening rural-urban cleavage in Czech society.

Meanwhile, the social homogeneity of the Czechs deepened, as progress was made across class lines: By 1900 the Czechs had the highest literacy rate of the nine nations of the Hapsburg monarchy, and the highest proportion of professional employees (except in the domains of energy, trade, and transportation, where Germans still dominated).[8] This was a period of emancipation and rapid modernization of Czech society in all sectors.

THE CZECHOSLOVAK REPUBLIC (1918–1938)

The explosion of blocked and intertwined cleavages during the First World War did not provide a solution to them; it only created a new situation, in which they could continue to function. The Czechoslovak Republic (1918–1938)[9] was a multinational state, which now included the most backward parts of Austria-Hungary, their conflicts, and their crystallizing new cleavages. The worker versus owner, bourgeoisie versus labor, urban versus rural, and center versus periphery cleavages became economic conflicts to be solved by political means and negotiated with unions or other representative organizations. These divisions were complicated by Czech-German cross-national working-class solidarity as well as by the conflicts and the solidarity of the Czech-German capitalist class.

The Republic abolished feudal privileges and titles, carried out a land reform, introduced civil liberties (including the vote for women in 1920), and mandated the equality of all nationalities. In the new democratic political environment, it carried out national and industrial revolutions in Slovakia and Sub-Carpathian Ukraine. Throughout this period, the state emphasized the *civic* principle rather than a *collectivist* one, as a prerequisite for the creation of a nation. As cleavages crystallized, processes of co-alignment and of cross-cutting alignments both took place. It was a complex and volatile period, rich in political feeling and action.

One of the serious difficulties encountered early was the inability of many of the Austrian Germans living with the borders of the former Czech kingdom to accept the fact that they now lived "against their will" in a different state, one which they blamed on the "anti-Revolutionary Imperialism of the Alliance" (German Social Democracy) and of the Versailles system. The abolition of their aristocratic and church privileges and of the advantages of the German language was experienced as a deprivation, even though German was given an equal status and was an official language of the Czechoslovak parliament and German capitalist dominance was not touched. As a result, they sought to reattach the border region of the Czech state to Austria, and part of Slovakia was occupied by Hungary (1918–1919).

However, the Czechoslovak army rapidly renewed the integrity of the state, and economic prosperity, far greater than that in postwar Germany or Hungary, softened the strong national antagonism.[10] Czechoslovakia's standard of living after the war was very high (among the ten highest in the world) and this fact alone led many to hope for the end of co-aligned Czech versus German cleavages capable of polarizing the political system and for the crystallization of cross-cutting cleavages that would tend to promote a stable democratic system.

Although such hopes foundered after the Nazi takeover of Germany, democracy was maintained in Czechoslovakia until the Second World War, and was fully destroyed only by German occupation.

Another cause for hope in the early years of the democratic republic was the virtual disappearance of the religious cleavage. The Catholic Church was no longer favored by the state, and was struck by a decline in the number of believers. Protestant churches emerged. As already noted, Czech society tended toward the secular, and there was little hostility among the faiths, despite the fact that the reluctance of Slovak politicians prevented full implementation of the constitutional provision for total separation of church and state.

Out of the fabric of cleavages brought together in the new republic, twelve significant parties emerged. Seven were nationwide parties, Czech and Slovak, and participated in all elections; four German parties and one Hungarian party participated in three of the four elections and also won seats.

The Social Democratic Party was the winner of the 1920 election, having campaigned on the cleavages separating worker from owner and labor from capital. It took 26 percent of the votes, more than twice that of the second strongest party, the Czechoslovak People's Party, which gained 11.3 percent. It was later supplanted as the leading worker's party by the Czechoslovak Democratic Party.

The Agrarian Party took only 9.7 percent of the vote in 1920, but became the strongest party of the republic once the socialist movement had been divided by the Communists.[11] The AP favored reform, but was opposed to socialism as well as to large capital interests. It was supported by unions, cooperatives, and economic organizations, some of which had been founded in the days of the Austro-Hungarian empire. As a party spearheading agrarian reform, it controlled the countryside, while the other parties shared representations of the interests of the other half of the population. (As of 1930, 34.6 percent of the Czechoslovakian people worked in agriculture; 34.9 percent in industry.) It no longer hesitated to exploit the cleavages urban versus rural and feudal (landlord) versus peasants, and it was the leading party in most of the coalition governments. In the 1930s it maintained a positive relationship with the German Nazi parties in their common struggle against the Social Democratic Party (a development which prevented its reemerging after the war and permitted the Communists to include agrarian reform as a major issue in their own propaganda).

The Czechoslovak People's Party was a state-forming, moderate, catholic party. Since its support was concentrated in the secular Czech lands, it did not seek to exploit the cleavage of church versus state, preferring to work for a compromise solution on this issue. The Slovak People's Party, another catholic party, was readier to take up the issue of church versus state, working on behalf of the clergy in Slovak lands where catholicism prevailed. This latter party also supported Slovak autonomous and nationalistic tendencies and, later, the idea of an independent Slovakia allied with Nazi Germany. It was not reestablished after 1945.

The Czechoslovak National Socialist Party was radically socialist, stressing the elimination of exploitation, a fairer wage system, and both political and social equality. It represented the Czech political/cultural tradition of noncollectivist socialism, insisting on the Protestant ethics of John Hus. It sought not socialism but rather a social and just republic, with a powerful presidential office and a Slavonic political orientation. It did not seek to exploit worker-owner cleavages.

The Czechoslovak Communist Party broke away from the Social Democratic left wing and established itself as a separate party in 1921, an echo of the Russian Leninist revolution. In 1929 it purged reformists advocating a Czech way to socialism and became Stalinist. It participated in three elections with an average return of 11 percent of the votes, and was the first party to gain seats in a parliament that represented the disloyal opposition, the radical class party alignment. Its electorate was drawn from the working class and left-wing intellectuals.

Four German parties also represented the disloyal opposition. The Czech-German ethnic cleavage had been toned down during the first decade of the republic owing in large part to the fact that Germans in Czechoslovakia were living better than Germans in the German Reich, had better opportunities for investment, and were strong participants in the government. However, once the Nazis gained power in Germany, Germans in the Czechoslovak Republic began to identify themselves with the idea that they too were "Herrenvolk," the "Übermenschen." They accepted the idea that some Czechs could be "Germanized," and that the rest would be resettled somewhere beyond the Ural mountains.

The menace to Czechoslovakian democracy represented by the Communists and the German parties had the effect of strengthening the consensual character of the democratic forces in the republic. Governments changed by changing coalitions of these forces, not by alternating power between governing and loyal opposition teams. The need to focus on the survival of democracy became more important than the representation of particular cleavages and the quest for solutions to the problems they represented. However, this change of focus was self-defeating; the failure of democratic elements to address the problems that had produced the cleavages contributed to the establishment of wartime and postwar totalitarian governments.

TOTALITARIANISM RIGHT AND LEFT (1938–1989)

By the final years of the Czechoslovakian Republic, it was possible to see signs of the international revolution posited by Rokkan (see Table 4.1), and its consequent cleavages. The cleavage between Czechs and Germans now took the form of a struggle between democracy and right-wing totalitarianism. By the end of the 1940s a new cleavage with international dimensions had emerged: communism (left-wing totalitarianism) versus democracy (Talmon, 1965). For fifty years totalitarianism of one form or the other triumphed over democracy, as the political elite in Czechoslovakia recognized and legitimized these developments attempting to deal with the structural cleavages whose solutions the interwar democracy had failed to find.

The postwar elections (1946) were won, in Czechoslovakia as in other Eastern European nations, by the Communists.[12] The party's score was 38.12 percent nationally, 38.5 percent in the Czech lands, and 30.37 percent in Slovakia. This election was subject to serious manipulation by the Communists: A lowered age limit, combined with the absence of elections between 1935 and 1946, meant that anyone born later than 1915 was going to the polls for the first time. Such voters were both inexperienced and radical. The Communists were also the last to submit their election program, permitting them to include the most impressive parts of other parties' programs. Their program, stressing a democratic and nationalistic plan of modernization, reconstruction, and social reform, was less socialist than that of the Social Democratic Party. And finally, although the Soviet army was not on Czechoslovakian land, it was known to be poised for intervention in Hungary and Germany.

Despite these conditions, the election victory did not provide the three-fifths majority required for constitutional change, leaving the Communists dependent on coalition with other parties. The united National Front, a coalition of government parties, was therefore formed.[13] The Communists took the most important posts in the government and dedicated themselves to securing further positions in the state apparatus, the army, and the police. The other coalition parties were thoroughly infiltrated by Communist agents.

The Communists gained the confidence of the lower classes by adopting a favorable social policy, including agrarian reform, the nationalization of industry, and the distribution of property confiscated from the Germans under the terms of the Potsdam Agreements of the Allies. The struggle for power came to a head in 1948, when the armed party militia were in the streets and the Communists were able to take over the state by parliamentary means. There was no need to bring in the Red Army. The new government promised to solve all accumulated cleavages in a "war on the [effects of the] war" (Patočka, 1990: 134).

For the first twenty years of Communist rule, the still scarcely touched industrial potential of the nation was turned to the uses of the Soviet Union and preparation for war with the West. The general mobilization during World War II had provided structures, organization, and planning capacities, which the Communists could now take over for new purposes. However, although nationalized industry operated at full capacity, it was neither developed nor modernized, and went steadily downhill. It may be possible to characterize the period of the rule of the Communists in other nations as a period of modernization, but in Czechoslovakia and particularly in the Czech lands, it was a period of stagnancy and regression. The emerging cleavages between the state directive system and the needs of manufacture did not officially exist. They were explained away as sabotage by class enemies or at best as "objective growth problems." In practice, they manifested themselves as a drop in productivity, poor quality of products, and limited selection.

During this period more traditional cleavages were eliminated, often by drastic means, or simply denied. The national cleavage between Czechs and Germans was "solved" by transferring all Germans (except those who had been openly anti-Nazi) and many Hungarians to Germany and Hungary. The existence of a cleavage between Czechs and Slovaks was denied, although in fact many Slovaks were deeply disappointed to be denied an autonomous state and both peoples were at best ambivalent about having to accept the control of Czechoslovakian institutions. The traditional cleavage between workers and owners was addressed by nationalizing private ownership of means of production and land. The cleavage between rural and urban populations was minimized by dedicating great skill and technical equipment to the development of cooperative farming, bringing the rural peoples' standard of living to a level as high as, and sometimes higher than, that of towns. Eventually, cooperative farms even began to manufacture nonagricultural products. The cleavage between church and state was resolved by nationalizing church property, liquidating religious orders and monasteries, and turning former church buildings and lands over to the army or to large-scale agricultural production. While it carried out this program, and distributed atheistic propaganda, the government also provided free access to state-controlled churches, thereby minimizing popular resistance.

Any possibility of political resistance was eliminated from the beginning by means of mass reprisals and executions, and heavily guarded frontiers prevented emigration. The institutional structures of political democracy (parliament, president, government) were formally preserved, albeit in the hands of a single party. The National Front united the Czechoslovak Communist Party, the People's Party (traditionally addressing the interests of the rural population and of Catholics), the Czechoslovak National Socialist Party (the former middle class and the intelligentsia), the Slovak Freedom Party, and the Slovak National Revival Party. All the individual parties, except the Communists, suffered steadily declining memberships and in effect lost their separate identities during the following years. The Social Democratic Party merged with the Communist Party in 1948. All political space was occupied by the single totalitarian party.

By the end of the 1960s, however, economic development was stagnating and it began to be apparent to many that change was essential. Widespread discussion and expert analysis led a new generation of pragmatic managers both within and outside the party to believe that serious reform was essential, including the transformation of the political system as well as of the social and professional structures (Machonin, 1969).[14] The 1968 Prague Spring became a national movement, with the general public demanding political democracy and a market economy, demands the dominant and reformist wing of the Party was eager to meet. Free competition of political parties was one point of the Action Program adopted by the reform Czechoslovak Communist Party.

Soviet armed intervention brought the reform movement to a screeching halt and deepened the social crisis. Approximately one million citizens—party members as well as nonparty members, family members as well as actual participants—were punished by dismissals from work and the imposition of wage ceilings for future employment. Such state-imposed downward mobility paralyzed performance in a number of expert and managerial professions and ruined worker morale. Police blockades checked cars and notified employers of the names of suspected shirkers.

The purges and persecution were largely concentrated in the Czech lands. Slovakia was almost untouched by these reprisals and Slovaks were appointed to the empty posts in central offices in Prague, a procedure which led to the establishment of a Slovak community in the capital.

The suppression of the Prague Spring was severe. After twenty years had passed, Václav Havel described what had happened in poignant terms:

The singing of enthusiasts and the screaming of martyrs have ceased . . . the revolutionary methods and terror have been replaced by stolid motionlessness, buck-passing canniness, bureaucratic anonymity and unimaginative stereotypes . . . it is . . . not true that there is no war and killing here. The forms of war and killing are only different: from the sphere of observable life and social events they have been moved to the gloom of unobservable inner destruction. [Witness] the unique, absolute and classical death of stories (of the fifties) that, despite all their horror, were somehow mysteriously able to give meaning to human life . . . [it is] as if this death has been dispelled by the slow, bloodless, but dreadfully omnipresent death of non-events, non-life, and non-time. A sort of collectively deadening, social and historic nothingness.[15]

However, even as Havel wrote, a new generation of pragmatic managers, joined again by some of the party apparatchiks and encouraged by Soviet perestroika, was beginning to struggle once again for change. This time they did not ask, but simply acted: They carried out private business activities within the framework of the system and at the expense of the state, beginning the formation of the newly arising entrepreneurial class whose activities and structures were legalized after November 1989.

The substantial social cleavages that remained unsolved and unrecognized under Communist rule inevitably reappeared immediately after the revolution had taken place. The totalitarian state had refused to establish democratic institutions capable of addressing these problems. The new state did not have time to do so before one of them—the nationalistic divisions between Czechs and Slovaks—achieved such severity as to cause the breakup of the state.

NOTES

1. For the purposes of this chapter, cleavages are defined as long-term, structural conflicts that are politically articulate, giving rise to opposing positions, and which competing political parties propose to solve. The objective character of certain cleavages, particularly in historically complicated Central Europe, is not always certain, unless we apply Thomas' theorem: If people consider a certain fact to be real, even if it is not, it becomes real in its consequences, as people act as though it were real. The conditions of Central Europe and

the use of a proportional representation electoral system sometimes make it particularly difficult to define the borders of division.

2. Daniel-Louis Seiler developed the model further in *La politique comparée* and in *De la comparaison des partis politiques*.

3. The victors allowed a six-week period of "ad conversionem vel emigrationem" during which non-Catholics must either convert or leave. Among those exiled were J. A. Komenský-Comenius and V. Hollar-Bohemus, the latter one of the founders of English graphic arts.

4. According to other sources it was 900,000 inhabitants out of 1,700,000 (see Kavka et al. 1956: 220).

5. Přehled Československých dějin II-1, Nakl.ČSAV 1960, p. 562.

6. The only association officially permitted by the monarchy was the Jenota for the Encouragement of Industry in the Czech Lands, founded in 1933. The Chamber of Commerce and Industry was established in 1850, but was controlled by the German liberal bourgeoisie until the 1880s. One of the organizations established during this period was the radical secret organization Repeal, named after the Irish political resistance and founded in 1847.

7. In 1886 German members resigned from the Czech regional assembly when the Czechs refused to recognize German-speaking territories inside Czech lands.

8. Czechs: 93.8 percent ability to read and write, 1.9 percent only read, 4.3 percent illiterate; Germans: 91.8 percent ability to read and write, 1.3 percent only read, 6.8 percent illiterate; Italians: 81 percent, 2.45 percent, 16.4 percent. The other nations followed quite far behind (for instance, Slovenians, later part of Yugoslavia: 68.5 percent, 7.5 percent, 23.9 percent; Poles: 47.5 percent, 11.7 percent, 40.8 percent, and so on). Source: Živanský, T. 1906. "Národnostní statistika Rakousko-Uherska (National Statistics of Austria-Hungary)," in V. Tobolka, ed., *Česká politika I (Czech Politic I)*. Jan Laichter, p. 270. German dominance over Czechs in certain areas is reflected in the following:

	Agriculture	*Industry/Transport*	*Commerce/Army*	*Administration*
Czech	2,560,100	2,167,570	552,100	656,820
German	3,068,123	3,514,185	1,232,870	1,356,435

Data for 1902. *Source:* Živanský, T. 1906. "Národnostní statistika Rakousko-Uherska (National Statistics of Austria-Hungary)," in V. Tobolka, ed., *Česká politika I (Czech Politic I)*. Jan Laichter, p. 273.

9. In this section, I draw heavily on Broklová, 1992.

10. The so-called Legions were formed during the war by Czech fugitives from the Austrian army. They fought on the Southern and Western fronts against the Austrians and the Germans, and on the Eastern front the Legions were used against the Bolsheviks (taking and holding the railroad line between Moscow and the Far East). This army of more than 50,000 men from a state not yet existent, fighting side by side with the democratic powers, gave the creation of that state international credibility.

11. The Agrarian Party supported the formation of the Communist Party in 1921 in order to weaken the Czechoslovak Democratic Party.

12. Broklová, Eva and Lubomír Brokl. "Od politické democracie k totalitarismu, Volby 1946—projev vůle lidu?," in *Sociológia*.

13. The idea of such a coalition had been mentioned as early as 1943 in negotiations between President Beneš and representatives of the Moscow-led Czechoslovakian Communist Party. And even earlier, the Nazi occupation had united the nation's parties in the National Unity Party, before silencing political life completely.

14. See also the study of made by a team of economists under Professor Šik and the interdisciplinary team of Professor Z. Mlynář.

15. Havel, V. Příběh a totalita, Svědectví 1897, p. 81, P. Tigrid, Pa fae.

REFERENCES

Broklová, E. 1992. *Czechoslovak Democracy, the Political System of the Czechoslovak Republic from 1918 to 1938.* Prague: Slon.

Kavka, F., J. Polišenký and F. Kutnar. 1956. *Přehled dějin Československa v epoše feudalismu III (1526–781).* Praha: SPN.

Lipset, S. Martin and S. Rokkan. 1967. "Cleavage Structures, Party Systems, and Voter Alignments: An Introduction." In Seymour Martin Lipset and Stein Rokkan, *Party Systems and Voter Alignments: Cross-National Perspectives.* Glencoe: The Free Press.

Machonin, P. et al. 1969. *Czechoslovak Society in 1967, an Analysis of Social Stratification.* Bratislava: Epocha.

Patočka, J. 1990. *Kacířské eseje o filozofii dějin.* Praha: Academia.

Rokkan, S. 1968. "The Structuring of Mass Politics in the Smaller European Democracies: A Developmental Typology." In Otto Stammer (ed.), *Party Systems, Party Organizations and the Politics of New Masses,* 26–65 Beiträge zur 3. Internationalen Konferenz über Vergleichende Politische Soziologie, Berlin 15–20 January 1968; Berlin: Institut für politische Wissenschaft an der Freien Universität Berlin.

Seiler, D.-L. 1982. *La politique comparée.* Paris: Armand Colin.

———.1986. *De la comparaison des partis politiques.* Paris: Economica.

Talmon, J. L. 1965. *The Origins of Totalitarian Democracy.* New York: Praeger.

Traub, H. 1926. *Naše politické dějiny v 19.stoleti.* Prague: Stanzí Nakladatelstuiu.

Zdrahal, F. V. 1921. *České stavovské povstání 1618 a následky jeho porážka na Bilé hore.* České Budějovice: J. Přibyl & J. Zelenka.

5

Hungarian Cleavages and Parties prior to 1989

——————————— *György G. Márkus**

INTRODUCTION

Although their original analysis did not include Eastern Europe nor the territorial consequences of two world wars, the theoretical work of Stein Rokkan and Seymour Martin Lipset permits us to put Hungarian regime change into a broader historical and territorial perspective and arrive at a better understanding of the changes that have taken place, the nature of past and present cleavages, and, most important for our present purposes, the party systems that have evolved (Lipset and Rokkan, 1967; Flora, 1983: 19).[1]

The successive collapses of the Ottoman, Austrian, and Russian empires brought about major changes in the conditions of state- and nation-building in the region east of the Germanic territories (Flora, 1983: 19). Territorial consolidation, external boundaries, the administrative and cultural penetration of territories have all become open problems in a context of huge socioeconomic dislocations, deprivation, inequality, and ideological vacuum. Following the collapse of the Soviet dominated Eastern bloc and of the Soviet empire, in a geographical space where the fit between state and nation has traditionally been unstable, the struggle between center and periphery has inevitably become the dominant cleavage linked to conflicting cultural, linguistic, religious, ethnic, and economic claims, and exacerbated by economic collapse.

It is important, however, to distinguish between Eastern Europe 'proper' and the countries of the interface periphery or buffer zone caught in cross-pressures between major state-building centers (Flora, 1983: 19). Thus we come to the distinct category of East Central Europe, a region where structural traits reflect a

*The author thanks NATO for the research grant provided supporting his work on parties and cleavages in Hungary.

historically changing mix of West and East European components (Szücs, 1990; Bibó, 1986). In Eastern and South Eastern Europe, the emerging political landscape is characterized by a center-periphery cleavage between "we" and "they" groups of primordial identities, and ruling Communist parties did not hesitate to take up ethnonationalist and/or imperialist issues. In (East) Central Europe *cultural politics*[2] evolved as a key factor in the cleavage between center and periphery, as parties formed around the question of territorial and national response to the gravitational attraction of "the Western world" or global "triad capitalism." In response to the universalist standardizing traits of democratic capitalism adopted by the center, the political actors of the periphery have become culturally divided between those ready to make a radical adjustment and those determined to defend separate national identities.

The domestic political landscape of post-communist societies is further complicated by the fact that the ruling national and multinational political institutions of the West have failed to develop an adequate strategy for responding either to the region as whole or to the individual countries, a situation in sharp contrast to the clear and material commitment of the allied powers for the democratization and reconstruction of West Germany, Italy, and Japan after World War II. The major cause of this failure is "bad timing"—that is, the fact that the changes in the East have taken place during an era when the Western world is facing a deep and painful process of transformation, due to the emergence of a postindustrial civilization, of postmodernity, and of a general trend to globalization undermining the traditional role of the nation-state. The prevailing and dominating neoliberal monetarist paradigm had special disruptive effects for Eastern countries.

The decline of industrial society carries with it the decline of the centrality of the class cleavage. Territorial and cultural cleavages become ever more dominant. A centralizing system of standardization comes into conflict with the protection of cultural distinctiveness and the autonomy of individual countries and regions. Universalism wars with particularism (Rokkan, 1982; Touraine, 1992). At the same time, an urban-rural (center-periphery) cleavage coinciding with a federalist versus anti-federalist cleavage is gaining strength at the level of Europe and within the E.U. member nations (Andeweg, 1995).

In East Central Europe these changes bring with them two seemingly contradictory consequences for party systems. The construction of capitalism generates class-formation processes, and the Europeanization of parties and party systems strengthens adjustment to the established—but now questioned—Western party structures, from which questions of class are largely excluded.

These contemporary complications arise out of a yet more complicated past. Nowhere is the past more complex and more powerfully significant in explaining contemporary cleavages and parties than in Hungary, as we seek to explain in this chapter.

THE EVOLUTION OF CLEAVAGES

The location of Hungary in a geopolitical buffer zone or interface periphery has resulted in a permanent instability in the processes of state-formation and nation-building, and these discontinuities and disruptions have had their impact on collective memory. Conquered by the Ottomans—then subject to Hapsburg rule, then defeated (in 1848–1849) in the revolutionary quest for independence—Hungary did not achieve even semi-independence until 1867, when a compromise solution gave the Hungarian polity a measure of autonomy within the Hapsburg monarchy.

The party landscape prior to World War I was characterized by the division between those who accepted the Austro-Hungarian compromise and those who continued the quest for national independence. As in other regions with a history of absolutist feudal regimes constraining bourgeois and civil development, national identity preceded the nation-state, and brought with it early forms of cultural politics. Those who aspired to national emancipation became often opposed to socioeconomic modernization, perceived as something alien. As early as the rule of Joseph II (1780–1790)—when a program of enlightened absolutism coupled social modernization with cultural Germanization, and continuing during the first years of the nineteenth century—the two ideas became ever more clearly opposed, however diligently the slogan "Fatherland and Progress" may have been brandished about. As Count István Széchenyi, the great reformer of the nineteenth century, pointed out, anyone who tried to cooperate with "Vienna" in the interest of national bourgeois development, the "*de facto* politicians of the Vienna air," were labeled traitors by "the *ex principio* patriots" of the Hortobágy puszta (steppes east of the Danube) (Kulcsár, 1989). The cleavage between modernization and nationalistic traditionalism expressed a real development, rooted in the very substance of modernization as a historical, social, and cultural process, "a process of social change whereby less developed societies acquire characteristics common to more developed societies" (Lerner, 1968). The question was how best to combine the universal with the particular, the past with a vision of the future, the patterns provided by tradition with the blueprints offered by others, the existent dependence and the hoped-for sovereignty (Gerschenkron, 1962). The cleavage has not always been sharp and clearly defined. At some points of history, as in the "reform age" preceding 1848, and again during the bourgeois and national revolution of 1848–1849 itself, modernist and patriotic forces could ally or even merge. Traditionalists have sometimes supported a type of modernization which, as an alternative to catch-up adjustment, focuses on preserving national cultural values and identities, as in Japan. Moderate traditionalists both prior to and after 1989 have claimed to seek to "select those techniques of modernization which correspond to our awareness of tradition, our experience of identity" and may "relate to external models with obligatory suspicion" (Kulin, 1995).

Traditionalists stress Hungarian nationhood above all, and favor strong authority, a strong church, and the community. Traditionalism has not been confined to a single class, nor to the clergy. Populists (or narodniks) as well as all those who favor Gemeinschaft over Gesellschaft, those who are inward-looking, and those who draw their arguments from history and poetry are all traditionalists. Traditionalists were traumatized by the Versailles treaty of 1920 (the "trauma of Trianon") and have never abandoned the dream of bringing all Hungarians back together. Westernizers, on the other hand, have been more likely to favor catch-up modernization and individualism, multicultural diversity, a secular state, and human rights. They have been outward-looking, drawing their arguments from sociology and seeking the development of the civil society. Westernizers have been readier to accept given (imposed) boundaries and treat the problem of Hungarians living elsewhere as a human rights problem.

In contrast to party stabilization on the basis of structured cleavages in the West, party formation in Hungary was an enterprise of elite networks. In this tradition parties have emerged as intellectual "milieu parties" in which the collective memory, the common language, and the aesthetic taste of the relevant subculture were more important than the substantive content of party programs. Two characteristic features arise from this type of party formation. The first is "premodern": party struggles have a "tribal" character, with strong emotionalization. Psychological factors—in particular, subjective prejudices and sympathies—are permanently entrenched. The second trait can be seen as "postmodern": parties have unclear profiles and do not offer clear-cut policy alternatives; instead, they sell themselves to the electorate by marketing their distinct aesthetic images through the mass media.

Thus the Hungarian party landscape was characterized by the dominance of cultural politics. The central cleavage of traditionalism versus westernization was, to be more exact, a cumulation of cultural and territorial cleavages. Yet the Hungarian citizens themselves consistently maintain overwhelmingly materialist value orientations, and socioeconomic issues have consistently been both urgent and central. This is clearly demonstrated in the table in Chapter 9. How has it been possible for cultural politics to assume such primacy? How can we explain the weight of history in shaping party formation and party competition?

The Prolongation of the East Roman Empire

As we learn from the work of Stein Rokkan and S. M. Lipset, the political history of (Western) Europe with its critical junctures of the national and industrial revolutions is the consequence of the collapse of the Roman Empire, more precisely of the *West Roman Empire*. Rokkan identifies Europe with the domain of the Roman Catholic Church after the schism of 1054. This excludes the Eastern areas in the domain of the Orthodox Church—above all, the Russian Empire, which was economically isolated from the Western city belt and culturally encapsulated through the subjugation of the church by the state. We are inclined to believe that the Russian Empire was in fact the successor supranational colonial power of the East Roman Empire.[3] Thus the formation of the Soviet Union, and its eventual formal takeover of Eastern and Central Europe at the end of World War II, was the continuation and strengthening of Russian hegemony in the area. But this hegemony, however powerful, never established itself smoothly over the eastern territories of the former Roman Empire. Territorial consolidation, changing external boundaries, and administrative and cultural penetration of constituent territories were always problematic; ever-increasing socioeconomic dislocations, deprivation, and inequality made them more so. In a geographical space where the fit between states and nations has always been unstable, conflicting claims of cultural, linguistic, religious, and ethnic rights—cultural politics—quite naturally assumed ascendancy. Hungary has had a history that has inevitably heightened consciousness of ethnic vulnerability and fear of extinction. The nation began as a medieval imperial state, with large territories falling to the Turks, after which the whole country came under Hapsburg rule, leading to a long string of failed uprisings and revolutions. After World War I Hungary was severely truncated, losing a third of its population and two-thirds of its territory. Allying with Nazi Germany during World War II, out of revisionist aspirations, led only to occupation and, after the war, the long period of Soviet domination, which included the cruel repression of the national uprising in 1956. But the fears produced by such a history do not constitute a "collective memory." Such anxieties have been largely restricted to one part of the cultural elite and have been in sharp contrast to the pragmatic-materialistic attitudes of the population.

Exogenous Modernization and Dualist Social Structures

In Hungary, ever since the days of Joseph II, the enlightened Hapsburg emperor, the response to the advance of the West has been divided along cultural lines. The division between those giving priority to "the Fatherland" or to "Progress" in the beginning, between tradition and modernization in the more recent past, has always been a cultural division. From Germany to Russia, cultural and political currents—Slavophiles and Zapadniks, adherents and opponents of a Sonderweg (a special national development path deviant from the universal "Western"-type of development)—emerged along this cleavage. This remained true even throughout the communist era. Opposition to Communism was naturally organized and divided according to these complementary and contradictory principles: human rights activist Sakharov and the writer Solzhenitsyn in Russia, the Polish Committee for the Defense of Workers (KOR) and Church in Poland, and "urbanists" and "populists" in Hungary.

This centuries-old Kulturkampf along the lines of territorial and cultural cleavages is rooted in a particular (Hungarian and regional) type of social structure in the course of (semi-)exogenous modernization. Hungarian sociologists and historians describe this pattern by the term "dualist social structures," meaning the coexistence of functions between a feudal traditional sector (including "historical" upper and middle classes, "historical" cultural elites) and a bourgeois sector (capitalist upper and middle strata, urban intellectuals, and cultural elites) mainly recruited from ethnic subcultures (Erdei, 1987). This kind of dualist society is typical of backward societies facing external challenges of capitalist development. As S. M. Lipset has shown, cultural or ethnic minorities outside the national "core group," groups of "sociological deviants" who have not been fully integrated into society, often play a strong innovative role when such challenges must be met, particularly when the dominant group is itself dominated by traditional values that contradict the requirements of economic, cultural, and political modernization. This type of "nonorganic modernization" is, however, "extremely vulnerable to political attacks from those who maintain traditional values" (Lipset, 1969: 98).

In Hungary, the Jews first of all, then the German-speaking population and, to some extent, smaller cultural-ethnic minorities such as the Armenians and the Greeks became the equivalent of the innovative "sociological deviants" described by Lipset. The preconditions of the special role of Jewry in all fields of modernization were given in their inherited cultural traditions conducive to embourgeoisement, in their presence in the spheres of finance and commerce and in the "free professions"—as a result of their exclusions from the feudal and estate-centered society—and in their linguistic and cultural assimilation. Their many contributions to Hungarian culture and science were also important. Even more apropos was the consistent involvement of so many Hungarian citizens of Jewish origin in radical progressive and leftist thought and political movements, especially manifest in the heavy "Jewish overrepresentation" in the failed Soviet type Council Republic of 1919, continuing into the Communist Party leadership between 1945–1956, and evident also as a very significant weight in the later anti-regime opposition.

THE EVOLUTION OF THE PARTIES

Parties of the Dualist Period (1867–1918)

The formative period of a party system in Hungary can be dated to the years around 1867, after the completion of the Austrian-Hungarian compromise following the defeat of the 1848–1849 Freedom Fight. The period between 1867 and 1918 (the end of World War I and the collapse of the Dual Monarchy) can be characterized from the point of view of our investigations as that of "constitutional politics." The parties that emerged were neither ideological nor class parties. The centuries-old cultural and territorial divide between adherents of inward-looking identity based on national traditionalism and those favoring outward-looking pro-Western catch-up modernization reappeared, dressed up as the "constitutional struggle" of parties over the issues of the standing of Hungary in the Monarchy and of maintaining, restoring, and/or extending statehood.

In this struggle, the years themselves came to stand for partisan identities: 1867 meant standing for the status quo of the compromise; 1848 stood for the initial stage of the freedom fight and bourgeois revolution as an organic continuation of the reform age of the thirties and forties; 1849 indicated the second and final year of the national struggle escalating to the dethroning of the Hapsburgs.

Thus, the original fault line separated the governing Deák Party (led by Ferenc Deák, the architect of the compromise) from the pro-independence opposition defending the principles of 1848 and 1849. However, as a political divide, "1867" was not a realistic cause for opposition, inasmuch as no viable alternative was or could be proposed. On the one hand, the Hungarian Parliament had neither the right nor the power to bring about change. On the other hand, given first the geopolitical situation of the country in a buffer zone between a German eastward drive and an emerging Russian-led Pan-Slavism, plus the presence of increasingly secessionist ethnic minorities, the preservation of the dualist Monarchy was the optimal (and perhaps the only) way to maintain the territorial unity of the country and the power of the Hungarian historical ruling classes. This situation inevitably led to contradictions in party politics and to schizophrenic attitudes on the part of party politicians.

The first major cleavage-related modification of partisan identities and of the party system took place in 1875. Taking advantage of an internal crisis in the Deák Party, Kálmán Tisza, leader of the moderate "center-left" 1848 opposition party, now established the Liberal Party. This reorganized party, supported by liberal nobility committed to economic modernization, took over the constitutional stance of the Deák Party with the party itself, and won—or, to be more exact, continued—control of the government.

With the emergence of this first state party, a kind of one-party system evolved in a period in which a number of unsettled issues remained on the political agenda: the power conflict between Austria and Hungary in a context of the decline and crisis of the Hapsburg monarchy itself; the divisions among the nationalities within Hungary itself; the issue of church versus state; and the intensifying divisions between labor and capital. The ruling party's approach to all these problems was to insist that modernization was to be accomplished without civil society, that the dismantling of feudal structures was to be steered from above, namely, by a group of the nobility possessing the privilege of engagement in public life; that, particularly in a society in which bourgeois attitudes and lifestyles were most strongly represented by Jews and other ethnic minorities, there was a need to reaccentuate liberal values as patriotic. Furthermore, given the 1867 compromise (between a weakening absolutism and a partly liberal mobility), certain aspects of absolutism remained unchallenged, and there was a continuing strong attachment to an essentially feudal center (Gerö, 1995).

This last point implies serious consequences for democratic development including the "normalcy" of representative multiparty Parliamentarism with the rotation of executive power. Thus we find the persistence of anti-liberal politics even in this period of "national liberalism." Specifically, anti-liberal traits were manifest in

- the extremely limited selective system of suffrage. The proportion of voters in the population was between 5.6 percent and 6.8 percent (in the Austrian part of the monarchy, 27 percent of the population had the right to vote). (Sources of these and all following data in this chapter: Rudai, 1936; Földes and Hubai, 1994; Bertényi and Gyapai, 1992);
- an open (nonsecret) ballot;
- the demarcation of electoral districts favoring the governing party;
- the regularity and frequency of frauds and bribery;
- the one-party-system regime of government.

This antidemocratism was legitimized by the political philosophy of the historical ruling class, according to which Parliamentarianism, not popular representation, constituted the essence of national sovereignty.

The practice of single-party dominance continued: The ruling party (first the party of Deák up to 1875, then the Liberal Party of Tisza, reorganized by his son István Tisza in 1910 under the name of the National Labour Party) was reelected in twelve of the thirteen elections held between 1867 and 1914. The governing party was always strongly controlled by its leader(s) and always had a more than comfortable majority ranging somewhere between 60 and 80 percent. Furthermore, the majority maintained by the pro-compromise governing parties strongly contradicted the overwhelming nationalist mood of the Hungarian population. These parties appealed only to modernist, pro-bourgeois segments, to urban groups and, paradoxically, to non-Hungarians. Geographical location had a clear impact on voting attitudes, but the most decisive explanatory factor was nationality (or ethnicity), which is why the ruling "national liberals" created, whenever possible, districts in which ethnic Hungarians were in the minority.

The opposition Independence Party—heavily divided into rival factions— normally won between 15 and 25 percent of the seats in Parliament. Political catholicism appeared in the 1890s with the birth of a conservative People's Party which enjoyed 3 to 7 percent support. Earlier, a single-issue Anti-Semitic Party also appeared on the scene; its program demanding the deportation of Jews won it from 2 to 3 percent of the vote.

From 1905 on, progressive and pro-Western "bourgeois radical" political thinking was represented only by the Democratic Party with a single MP, and by the leftist wing of the Independence Party. Six years after its formation in 1908, the Association (later renamed "Party") of Smallholders, a pro-independence plebian farmers party, won four seats in Parliament.

From the end of the 1880s, a moderate national conservative formation, known first as the Moderate Oppositional Party, and then the United Oppositional Party, was also present with oscillating support, eventually dropping to 4 percent, at which point it joined the Liberal Party, and then, somewhat later, the Independent Party. The only genuine mass party, the Social Democratic party—a party that emerged from the Party of Nonvoters established in 1878 and which was under the ideological influence of the Austrian Socialists—acquired ever more political influence, and played an ever more active social role. However, the struggle of the masses for political power remained rooted in a relatively strong trade union movement and was excluded from Parliament even though a political alliance based on the demand for universal suffrage was forged with the Independence Party in 1905. National and agrarian issues were not included in the social democratic agenda and thus the expression of radical agrarian socialism took place only in dissident movements outside the Parliamentary party system.

Parties in the Counter-Revolutionary Period (1920–1944)

The defeat of Austro-Hungary in World War I was followed first by the peaceful bourgeois democratic revolution symbolized by Count Mihály Károlyi, formerly the leader of the left wing of the Independence Party and, after 1913, leader of the party itself. The revolutionary government consisted of leftist pro-independence politicians, bourgeois radicals, and social democrats. Unable to cope with external military pressure, the terms of the peace treaty, a catastrophic economic situation, escalating popular demands, an ever-intensifying right wing counter-revolutionary movement, and tensions within the new political bodies, the government soon ceded power to the "Socialist Party of Hungary"—that is, to the Communists joined by the Social Democrats, now dominated by their own left wing. The Leninist-type Hungarian Council Republic formed by this alliance was crushed in mid-1919. Under foreign pressure the 1920 elections were the first to be organized on the principles of the secret ballot and universal suffrage. They were held in a traumatic emergency situation, in an occupied, shrunken, and ethnically now rather homogenous country. This was a transitory period, and the election was openly negative in content: Campaigning was focused on attacking the Communists, the Social Democrats, and the "cosmopolitan Liberals," who were deemed responsible for the crushing defeat of the country and the nation. Positive campaigning was limited to the abstract, the cultural, and the ideological, and consisted largely of calling for the creation of "a Christian and national Hungary" with the overarching priority of territorial revisionism.

The Social Democrats chose to boycott the elections, permitting other kinds of political groups to dominate the transition: Christian (mainly Catholic) and agrarian (smallholders) organizations, each gaining approximately equal shares of parliamentary seats. Following the one-party-system tradition, a merger soon took place: a Christian Smallholders' Agrarian and Bourgeois Party, referred to and abbreviated as the United Party, came into being. Political life and partisan identities were adjusted to the spiritual climate of the so-called "Christian-national course" tied to the personality of Admiral Miklós Horthy, Regent of Hungary. Core elements of this orientation were

- national sovereignty, integrity and revisionism;
- patriotic Christian thought with a historic mission to suppress revolutionary ideas, liberalism, bourgeois radicalism, Marxism and last, but not least, Jewish "penetration"; and
- "St. Stephen's Thought," meaning Hungarian national and cultural supremacy in the region of the Carpathian Basin.

Count István Bethlen, the new head of the United Party and the prime minister as of 1921, was committed to a moderate version of the "Christian-national course," to the restoration of historical Hungary under the leadership of the aristocracy, with a strong role for the traditional civil service, addressing the interests of large landowners and big capital, and to a lesser extent those of the nationalistic middle classes including smallholder components. To prevent destabilization by racist and populist radicalism, he limited the suffrage and reintroduced open ballots outside big cities. Thus transformed, the United Party gained 143 out of 245 seats in the 1922 elections. The left-wing opposition, represented by the Social Democrats and by the Liberals, won only 10 and 8 percent of the vote, respectively; racists and "genuine Christians" on the far right made similar scores. Leading an authoritarian party in an authoritarian regime, Bethlen succeeded not only in political, but also in economic, consolidation.

Economic crisis reached Hungary in 1931 and led to a crisis of the United Party. Gyula Gömbös, formerly head of a small racist party and subsequently the leading figure of the rightists within the United Party, became the Prime Minister and announced that Hungary would adopt a corporatist National Working Schedule based on Mussolini's model. Deviating from Bethlen's partly pro-British, partly pro-Italian orientation, he brought Hungary ever closer to Nazi Germany. Following Gömbös's death in 1936 the reintroduction of secret ballots speeded up tendencies of aggressive revisionism and racism resulting in anti-semitic legislation and the partial reannexation of Northern territories under Hitler's patronage.

The 1939 elections reflected this trend. The radicalized "state party," now under the name "Party of Hungarian Life," took a majority of 72 percent of the seats with 49 percent of the votes. Parties of openly fascist orientation, first of all the Arrow Cross Party, collected 30 percent of the votes but only 19 percent of the mandates.

The major factor explaining this ultra rightist breakthrough was the ability of the fascist parties to combine elements of social demagoguery with racist and nationalist propaganda. Many ruling party MPs sympathized with Arrow Cross ideas. The biggest losers of the left-wing opposition were the Smallholders, who lost eleven of their twenty-six seats. The Social Democrats dropped from fourteen seats to five. The Liberals—supported mainly by the Jewish bourgeoisie of Budapest—kept their five seats.

The progressive involvement of the country in World War II in the hope of territorial gains split the governing party into pro-Nazi and antiwar factions. This development was reflected also in actual policies and led to German occupation in March 1944. Following a declaration of armistice in October by Regent Horthy, the Arrow Cross Party with German support took over the government and outlawed opposition parties. The Smallholders, the Social Democrats, the Communists, and the small left-wing Peasant Party, cooperated in an anti-fascist Hungarian Front in an effort to organize resistance.

The Transition to Communism (1945–1948)

This constellation of resistance movements provided the basis of the postwar party structure from which the former governing state party and pro-Fascist formations were excluded. The basic political divide in the period between 1945 and 1948 was between forces more or less accepting the geopolitical status quo of the country in the Soviet sphere of influence and those attempting to bring the country closer to the Western allied powers.

The trauma of Fascism and of the holocaust—plus the fact that the country was liberated and occupied by the Red Army—brought about a situation in which originally and potentially pro-Western social groups, welcoming the liberation of the country, defined themselves as leftists supporting either the Communists or the Social Democrats. At this initial stage the leaders of these movements did not question the reality or the desirability of the Yalta arrangements, accepting Soviet influence although disagreeing, of course, regarding the exact measure of Hungarian autonomy and dependence.

The Smallholders emerged in this bipolar framework as the right-wing catch-all party of the majority of decidedly anti-Soviet and noncommunist voters, attracting support on an ideological basis of patriotism, clericalism, and traditionalism. They were, paradoxically, the party of the modern (noncommunist, that is, free) capitalist West, of private property, of pluralism and, at the same time, the party of premodern values, identities, and structures.

In the municipal elections of Budapest in October 1945, the Smallholders won an absolute majority of 50.5 percent against the United List of Workers (Communists and Social Democrats), which won only 43 percent of the vote. This trend escalated a month later in the national parliamentary elections, at which point the Smallholder vote rose to 57 percent; the Communists took only 17 percent of the vote, the Social Democrats 17.4 percent. The pro-Communist Peasants' Party, with a combination of anti-semitic/anti-German nationalism and populist democracy, gained 6.9 percent, while the only authentic pro-Western party, the Bourgeois Democrats, won 1.6 percent.

The following years paved the way to Communist takeover. Relying on the presence of the Red Army, holding leading administrative positions, including the control of the police and the Army and having their own agents in the first ranks of the coalition parties, the Communists undermined and split all alternative forces. In the manipulated 1947 elections, they emerged as the winning party with 22 percent. The role of the weakened and disorganized Smallholders' party was partly taken over by the Democratic People's Party, a formation in the political tradition of Catholic parties emerging as a second force. The emergence of this Catholic formation was a consequence of the famous "salami" tactics (slicing up of rival parties into ever thinner parts) practiced by the Communists, a major object being the Smallholders—weakened and fragmented, softened up, put under pressure, assaulted. Thus the People's Party came into being as an attempt to strengthen the anti-Communist opposition, and took nearly a fifth of the vote. Overall results (in seats) were: Communists, 100; Smallholders (part of the CP lead "alliance"), 68; Social Democrats, 67; Peasant's Party, 36; National Christian Alliance, 4; Democratic People's Party, 60; Independence Party (right wing national), 49; Radical Party, 6; Independent Hungarian Democratic Party (agrarian, clerical), 18; and Bourgeois Democratic Party, 3. Altogether, the coalition (including Smallholders) won 271 seats and the opposition won 140. In spite of massive frauds, restrictions, and an increasingly oppressive climate, the Smallholders, the People's Party, and the other minor anti-communist opposition parties together won 55 percent of the vote.[4]

Reflecting the change in Soviet politics and the start of the cold war, the "salami tactics" of the Hungarian CP were now replaced by the violent liquidation of the multiparty system. The first target was the "fraternal" Social Democratic Party in June 1948, when the forced fusion of the two parties was accompanied by the expulsion of so-called "right wingers." The Party of Hungarian Workers was created. With the Communist takeover, "other parties" were not banned formally, but rather simply withered away, and for awhile one could even find them in the telephone book. Within a year the Stalinist one-party dictatorship was fully established.

The Dualism of Market Socialism

As has been shown previously, the defeat of the Hungarian fight for national independence from Austria in 1849 was followed first by terror and then, from the middle of the sixties, by a compromise resulting in the dualist structures of the Austro-Hungarian Monarchy with limited sovereignty, a measure of political pluralism, and the introduction of capitalist modernization. Something similar happened after the anti-communist national revolution of 1956. Terror and retaliation were followed by concessions. From the mid-sixties on, a compromise emerged, resulting in a special type of dualism. The main characteristics of this Kádárian compromise were

- a bargain with the great majority of the population in which the party leadership offered (1) a kind of consumer socialism with modestly improving living standards (2) a socialist welfare state with social security and full employment (3) a certain measure of infor-

mal administrative pluralism; (4) a restricted and manipulated cultural autonomy (5) noninterference in private lives and (6) a limited degree of personal freedom (first of all, in granting permissions to travel). The price demanded—and generally received— was simple: noninterference in politics, and respect for, and at least a degree of lip-service to, the "rules of the game";
- the introduction of economic reforms without changing the political structures of the one-party system: market socialism; and
- shifts in the composition of economic and political elites: a diminishing weight and role for ideological leadership; the emergence of an ever stronger and more influential pragmatic and technocratic managerial elite in the economy, in public administration, and within the party itself (Szalai, 1997).

Under these conditions, the political attitudes—and, later, voting patterns of the population—remained determined by paternalism and by consumerist and welfare statist expectations, and the scope for mass scale political mobilization remained narrow. At the same time, however, the relative autonomy and continuity of cultural life contributed to the preparation and the emergence of a bipolar party system built around the carriers of two distinct and conflicting cultural traditions: the "populists" and the "urbanizers" (later to become the core components of the initial hegemonic parties of post-1989 cultural politics, the Hungarian Democratic Forum and the Alliance of Free Democrats).

Emerging political dualism was matched by economic dualism. One sector of the economy of the 1970s and 1980s was rooted in (post)totalitarian bureaucratic central planning, while another was tied to the emerging market economy. Statist political redistribution was complemented by market-based distribution. (Bernhard, 1996). The emerging dualism was reflected as well in the differences between the values, lifestyles, and attitudes deeply rooted in late Kádárism and those shaped by the gradual shift to capitalism.[5] This dualism has remained a strong cleavage, creating a division in post-1989 politics; it explains the strength of the post-communist Socialist Party rooted in both sectors of society.

The Contemporary Relevance of the "Populist"–"Urbanizer" Debate

The basic cleavage between identity-based traditionalism and Westernization, a product of the contradictions in Hungarian state-formation and nation-building under the pressure of exogenous modernization in a semi-peripheral buffer zone, determined party structures and party competition between the 1860s and the 1940s as well as the absence of mass democracy and the weakness of civil society. The special type of single-party system, the geopolitical context with its fatal threats for the country, and the continuing accumulation of territorial and functional cleavages did not, however, allow for a clear expression and translation of this fundamental divide in the party system. In the initial stage of party formation on the threshold of regime transformation around 1989, oppositional forces defined their distinctive identities by reaching back to the tradition of a confrontation that was primarily cultural but carried and expressed the basic historical cleavage most clearly. They revived the debate of populists versus urbanizers that had surfaced in the 1920s and 1930s when both sides opposed the "official" ideology and policies of the "national-Christian course" standing for the continuity of so-called "gentlemanly Hungary," that is, for the continuing supremacy of the upper classes in social and political life. On the populists' side in this debate, carried on among poets, writers, and sociologists, three basic ideas had emerged:

- plebian (peasant) radicalism
- agrarian reform, meaning "the elevation of the peasantry into the body of the nation"— that is, making the peasant the core of the national community
- a collectivist "third road" for Hungary (implying for some a federation of East European peoples) (Lackó, 1992)

Given the fact of a dualist structure with a traditionalist feudal sector and a pro-Western modern bourgeois sector with a high share of Jews in dominant positions, the populists had represented the peasantry as an underclass outside both sectors and had insisted on the utmost priority of the survival of Hungarianhood, which they saw as jeopardized by a modernization dominated by ethnically, racially, and culturally foreign elements.

On the other hand, the urbanizers, Jewish and non-Jewish intellectuals, had defended the applicability of the universalist Western-type social model, and were supported by radicals, bourgeois democrats, and social democrats. In the early 1930s, Prime Minister Gyula Gömbös, with his pro-Nazi and pro-racist inclinations, tried to ally with the populists. Later, Communist politicians similarly, but with more success, also flirted with populist thinking.

The human rights-centered Democratic Opposition from the late seventies on may be regarded as the reincarnation of the Western universalist urbanist tradition (even though the core of this current of dissident intellectuals arose from among the school of Georg Lukács). This is the historical background of the Alliance of Free Democrats, which was to become the hegemonic party of the Westernization block in the post-1989 party landscape.

The leading post-1989 party of the traditionalist side and of the national-Christian government coalition (1990–1994) was to be the Hungarian Democratic Forum (MDF), a party founded in 1987 from the milieu of the populist writers and intellectuals. Its evolution, however, was strongly influenced by party leader and prime minister József Antall, who tried to combine the West European ideal of a German-style Christian Democracy with the moderate Hungarian "national-Christian course" tradition of István Bethlen of the twenties. The inherent tension between radical populism and national modernization not only helps us to understand the decline of this party from 1993 and beyond; it also helps explain the present (early 1998) division of the national opposition into a half Euro-Skeptic, half pro-Western pole represented by the Young Democrats in alliance with a weak MDF and a pole of populist "social nationalism" represented by the Smallholders in alliance with the actual leadership of the divided and weakened Christian Democrats (not to mention the minor anti-Western and anti-semitic parties outside the Parliament). These developments, and others following the fall of Communist rule, will be further discussed in Chapter 10.

NOTES

1. The author thanks the North Atlantic Treaty Organization for a research grant supporting his work on parties and cleavages in Hungary.
2. Here Lipset describes cultural politics as "the relative dominance of cultural or value factors and the superimposition of these factors on others." (Lipset, 1969: 93)
3. Idea put forward by P. Bakka (Bergen University).
4. If we compare this figure with the 57 percent of the smallholders in 1945 and the results of the national traditionalist parties in the 1990 parliamentary elections—that is, 54 percent of territorial lists and 59 percent of the seats—one might interpret this as a remarkable constancy of traditionalist vote potential over forty-three years.
5. This type of situation prevails in a number of other post-Communist countries and creates a social and political cleavage that we may call the post-socialist cleavage, or, in Hungary, the Kádárian cleavage. One side of this cleavage is represented by post-(reform)-communist parties preserving old "specialist" values and attitudes while defending the vested interests of the old-new ruling elite of emerging capitalism. This explains the divisions, the identity crisis of the Hungarian Socialists, but also the strength of this party: its embeddedness in both sectors of the present dual society.

REFERENCES

Andeweg, R. 1995. "The Reshaping of National Party Systems." *West European Politics* 18 (3): 69.
Bernhard, M. 1996. "Civil Society After the First Transition," *Communist and Post-Communist Studies* 3 (29): 301–30.
Bertényi, I. and G. Gyapai. 1992. *Magyarország rövid története*. Budapest: Maecenas.
Bibó, I. 1986. *Válogatott tanulmánipk,* 1–4. Budapest: Magvetö.
Erdei, F. 1987. *A magyar társadalom*. Budapest: Gondolat.
Flora, P. 1983. "Introduction—Stein Rokkan's Macro-Model of Europe." In P. Flora et al. (eds.), *State, Economy and Society in Western Europe 1815–1975.* Frankfurt: University of Frankfurt.
Földes, Gy. and L. Hubai. 1994. *Parlamenti képviselöválasztások (1920–1990)*. Budapest: Politikatörténeti Alapitvány.
Gerö, A. 1995. *Modern Hungarian Society in the Making*. Budapest: Central European University Press.
Gerschenkron, A. 1962. *Continuity in History and Other Essays. Economic Backwardness in Historical Perspective*. Cambridge: Harvard University Press.
Kulcsár, K. 1989. *Magyar Nemzet*, 23 Dec.
Kulin, F. 1995. *Magyar Hírlap*, March 18.
Lackó, M. 1992. "Népiesség tegnap és ma." *2000* 10: 3–10.

Lerner, D. 1968. "Modernization: Social Aspects." In D. L. Sills (ed.), *International Encyclopedia of Social Sciences*, vol. 14. New York: MacMillan.

Lipset, S. M. 1969. *Revolution and Counter-Revolution: Change and Persistence in Social Structures*. London: Heinemann.

Lipset, S. M. and S. Rokkan. 1967. "Cleavage Structures, Party Systems and Voter Alignments: An Introduction." In S. M. Lipset and S. Rokkan (eds.), *Party Systems and Voter Alignments: Crossnational Perspectives*. New York: Free Press.

Rokkan, S. and D. Urwin. 1982. *The Politics of Territorial Identity*. London: Sage.

Rudai, R. 1936. *Politikai ideológia, pártszerkezet (1861–1935)*. Budapest: Atheneum.

Sartori, G. 1968. "Political Development and Political Engineering." *Public Policy* 17: 261–98.

Szalai, E. 1997. *Az elitek átváltozása*. Budapest: Central European University Press.

Szücs, J. 1990. *Die drei historischen Regionen Europas*. Frankfurt: Verlag Neuekripik.

Touraine, A. 1992. *Editions du Dialogue*.

6

Parties, Party Systems, and Cleavages in Poland: 1918–1989

Hieronim Kubiak

Today Western and Central-Eastern Europe appear similar from at least one perspective: while, here and there, a majority of old (especially left-orientated) parties disintegrate or search for a modified identity, new parties (extreme right-wing, in particular) are mushrooming. However, an observer of today's political life should not be misled by this analogy. Changes registered in the West have occurred mostly within otherwise stable and functionally effective multiparty systems, whereas the countries of Central and Eastern Europe, escaping from demophilic political order (Sartori, 1987: part 15.5), have only recently begun to remodel their political systems.

Moreover, the collective actors of the emerging systems have not yet established a strong relationship between themselves and the cleavages existing within society. Yet there is nothing strange in this. The process of creating a new society on such a magnitude is never free of tensions or abrupt turns. Neither can all of them be predicted. While today's transitions are producing dramatic cleavages of their own, the social memory maintains records of the old, often rooted in a nineteenth-century reality. Political and economic systems come and go, but problems that they did not manage to solve, or in fact created, remain. History lives on in this part of Europe mostly through problems not solved at the right time. The past, often mythologized, serves as a salve for today's wounds. This is seen at a personal level as well as in collective behavior.

Transforming the present multipartism into an effective multiparty system will be neither a short nor a painless process. Democracy requires virtues and competences that are only *in statu nascendi* in Central and Eastern Europe. Although hundreds of parties (or quasi-parties) have already emerged, there still seems to be nothing between the micro-level of primary groups and the macro-level of the state (Nowak, 1979: 122–45). This "social vacuum," as the phenomenon was named by S. Nowak in the seventies, exists partly due to the legacy of state socialism, when it was generated by a deficiency of internal sovereignty. However, many large segments of society feel lost in the new emerging political system and, after a short period of mass mobilization in 1989–1990, are withdrawing again into privacy. As opinion poll data revealed in December 1995, 65 percent of Poles consider that none of the more than 270 political parties existing represents their interest. These problems, by no means unknown to East-Central European and Western scholars, are apparent in Poland as in the other East-Central European states.[1]

Modern parties became permanent actors of political life in Central European countries in the second half of the nineteenth century. From the very beginning there were parties of all types: liberal (Hungary after 1867), conservative (Bulgaria between 1879 and 1881), labor (Hungarian Universal Labor Union, 1869) and peasant (Bulgarian Peasant Union, 1899). However, parties developed in a different manner in those countries which had already—before World War I— attained sovereignty within their own nation-states (Romania after 1877, Bulgaria after 1879), within an empire (Hungary after a compromise of 1867), and in those countries that gained sovereignty only after the end of World War I (Czechoslovakia and Poland). In the first group of countries, the majority of parties could operate legally from the very beginning and thereby give rise to a party system in which it was possible to construct effective governments. However, in the second group, for lack of independence, parties could accumulate these kinds of political experiences only after 1918.

Although the populations of these countries did participate in parliamentary elections at the end of the nineteenth century, these were not elections for their own political institutions, and their consequences for the formation of a modern political culture were therefore limited. At the time of the partition of Poland, for instance, Poles had elected deputies to the Wien Reichsrat from so-called Galicia after 1864, to the Berlin Reichstag from the Prussian partition beginning in the 1890s, and to the Moscow Duma after 1905. In the first Duma there were 55 Polish deputies, mostly representing the National Democratic Party.

The interwar period (1918–1939) successively brought Central Europe years of prosperity and a proliferation of multi-partism in the 1920s. Dozens of parties emerged in practically every country. While some of them did well, others collapsed quickly or merged with other similar political entities. Coalitions and blocs were concluded and broken. This cauldron of political passions was heated again and again by class, ethnic, religious conflicts, and/or by different interpretations of Raison d'État. This multidimensional process of social and political fights created the frame of reference for the forced homogeneity which existed after 1945, as well as for beginning of the systemic transformation after 1989.

Jürgen Habermas is no doubt correct when he asserts that "in Poland, Hungary, Czechoslovakia, Romania, and Bulgaria, where state, socialist society, and the political regime did not come into existence through revolution but as a consequence of war and the presence of the Red Army, the abolition of so-called people's democracies meant a return to the old national symbols, and a continuation . . . of prewar political traditions and known party systems" (Habermas, 1993: 38). Regaining sovereignty (internal and external) does not automatically extinguish open and latent conflicts, and a collapse of one way of solving problems does not simultaneously remove these problems from the public concern. On the contrary, sovereignty and freedom of action make cleavages more visible.

The history of modern Polish political parties began in the last quarter of the nineteenth century. It is important to remember this not merely for the sake of historical accuracy but also because old symbols are still valid in politics and many collective actors fight for the right to use them. Several of today's parties consider themselves to be the successors of old parties. Some of them even see this as the source of legitimization of their political aspirations. Among the first Polish mass parties were two left parties (the Polish Socialist Party, PPS, founded in 1892 after unification of earlier socialist movements, and the Social Democratic Party of the Polish Kingdom and Lithuania, SDKPiL, founded in 1894); several centrist or left-centrist parties (among others, the Peasant Party, SL, founded in 1895 and transformed in 1903 into the Polish Peasant Party, PSL); and several right-wing parties (the most important of which for the future political scene became the National Democrats, ND). The roots of ND reached back to the Polish League, founded in 1887. The history of all these parties illustrates the main Polish problems and cleavages of that time: national and social.

The parties of the left were divided over the priority of these issues. While the PPS opted for national liberation as a prerequisite for other demands, the SDKPiL saw things in the opposite way. The first choice symbolized the view of Józef Piłsudski, the second of Rosa Luxemburg. Later this developed as the difference between the Polish socialist point of view and the communist, taken by the Polish Communist Party, KPP, founded in 1918, and to some extent the Polish Workers Party, PPR, founded after 1942. Centrist parties introduced the peasant question to Polish politics, focusing on problems of agrarian reform, and prepared peasant leaders, such as Wincenty Witos, to become politicians at the national level. The National Democrats opened a further strand in Polish politics: ideological and political nationalism. From the perspective of Roman Dmowski, the most influential member of the ND, the nation was perceived as a "physical unit whose definition needed yet to be forged." For him, "minorities, whether based on caste, religion, or ethnic differences, were alien bodies within the nation." Instead of tolerance, a "healthy national egoism" was needed. Any other way was "not conducive to building a state that could survive in the modern world" (Zamoyski, 1987: 329). Yet the Poland of the Jagiellonian Commonwealth was and remained multiethnic. The sensitivity of the national question for Poland was obvious at the time of the Versailles peace negotiations[2] and as the Second Republic of Poland came into existence. The first ethnic party emerged on the Polish political scene even before 1918, in the shape of the Jewish Socialist Union Bund, founded in Wilno in 1879.

Yet another cleavage stemming from that time was related to Poland's external environment. A pro-Russian orientation, represented before 1918 by the National Democrats and, for different reasons, the SDKPiL, came into collision with an anti-Russian orientation, represented by Józef Piłsudski and his PPS.

POLISH PARTIES AND PARTY SYSTEMS IN THE YEARS 1918–1939

The legal foundation for party activities and a multiparty system in independent Poland was created by the March Constitution of 1921. Based upon the French constitutional tradition, it established a parliamentarian political order and cabinet government structure in Poland. Clearly, political parties constitute the *conditio sine qua non* of such a political order. Thus, article 108 of the 1921 constitution guaranteed to all citizens the right to "establish coalitions, to assemble and to form associations and unions." Parties were understood in this tradition as "voluntary associations of citizens of similar political views and common programs of actions" that tend to influence the political life of the country. They were considered to be an "emanation of society and, at the same time, the necessary mechanism by which the 'social will' of different segments of society could be transferred into the 'state will'" (Burda, 1983: 41).

The rights of minorities and their political representation were secured by the principle of proportionality introduced to voting regulations in 1922. Distribution of seats among parties and coalitions of parties (electoral blocs, unions, camps, and so forth) was based on the Hare system (a form of proportionality adopted again in 1946).[3]

Polish multipartism was a consequence of cleavages and also produced further cleavages, many of which were reproduced in the postwar Republic of Poland. Similar to the situation today following the collapse of communism, the "Promised Land" looked "like a disappointment to those who viewed it from afar. . . . The Poles had dreamed of their Arcadia individually, and had to live in it collectively" (Zamoyski, 1987: 340). The art and practical skills of operating within a modern polity had to be learned by citizens from scratch through everyday interactions and this required more time than writing and enacting a constitutional law.

What type of a society was Poland when it regained its sovereignty? First, it was highly diversified internally. Cleavages and conflicts jeopardized not only its stability, but also the actual existence of the country. Positioned between a Germany rebelling against the limitations of the Versailles Treaty and an ideologically aggressive Soviet Union, there was little room for experiments. And yet Poland had the features of an experiment on a large scale.

Post–World War I Poland reemerged on the international scene as a multiethnic political entity, but with a unitarian state structure. As Table 6.1 shows, one-third of the citizenry of the Second Republic was not of Polish ethnic origin, lived in regional concentrations, and had several of its own problems related to language, religion, and cultural distinctiveness that had to be addressed. Jews, for instance, about 10 percent of the total population of Poland after 1918, sought recognition of their minority rights during the preparations for the Versailles Conference. Backed by American but opposed by French and British Jewish representatives, some Eastern European Jewish leaders demanded that their group be given a special status and be recognized as a national entity entitled at least to proportional representation in parliament and other political institutions, as well as to linguistic and educational autonomy. The Polish-Jewish controversy of this time is well documented in the reports and correspondence[4] of Hugh Gibson, the first American minister to Poland.

Ukrainians wanted at least to preserve the rights they already had in the last decades of the Hapsburg empire. Lithuanians found themselves in an uneasy situation, especially after military conflict over the status of Wilno. Relations with the German minority were also far from cordial. Under pressure of events in revolutionary Russia in the Ukraine, Lithuania's drive to independence and other developments, Józef Piłsudski's original idea of a Poland as a federal

Table 6.1
Ethnic Composition of Polish Society in 1931

National identity	1931 Census (on the basis of language spoken at home)		Jerzy Tomaszewski's estimation (on the basis of religion)	
	Thousands	*Percent*	*Thousands*	*Percent*
Total population	31,916	100.0	31,916	100.0
Polish	21,993	68.9	20,644	64.7
Ukrainian	4,442	13.9	5,114	16.0
Jewish	2,733	8.6	3,114	9.8
Belarus	990	3.1	1,954	6.1
German	741	2.3	780	2.4
Russian	139	0.4	139	0.4
Lithuanian	83	0.3	83	0.3
Czech	38	0.1	38	0.1
"Tutejsi" regional identity	707	2.2	—	—
Others	11	0.1	11	0.1
No information	39	0.1	39	0.1

Source: 1931 census data: *Mały Rocznik Statystyczny 1937 (1937 Statistical Yearbook).* 21–24. Warszawa: GUS.

Jerzy Tomaszewski. 1985. *Rzeczypospolita wielu narodów (Republic of Many Nations),* 35. Warszawa: Czytelnik.

Commonwealth of Three Nations had to be abandoned. After the victorious 1920 war with Red Russia, Poland had to learn how to live with its minorities. Between 1922 and 1928, ethnic parties won, as Table 6.2 demonstrates, more than 20 percent of seats in the Seym and became an important factor in politics.

The formation of the party system had a dramatic impact on social and regional cleavages. The Polish social structure, as can be seen in Table 6.3, was full of potential conflict. When state independence had been achieved, the unifying patriotic euphoria soon became overshadowed by partisan interests. Economic crisis and slogans of the October Revolution added further fuel to the fire.

While existing parties were undergoing the process of adaptation to the normal conditions of legal political life, new parties were being created. As if this were not enough, ethnic and social cleavages were intertwined with regional and religious issues. All three parts of former partitioned Poland, now joined as a single sovereign entity again, demonstrated exactly how much they had become different from one another during the nineteenth century. Galicia was very poor and underdeveloped, but, due to relative freedom in the Hapsburg empire, very Polish. Great Poland, with its most advanced agriculture, tradition of pragmatic work, and well developed educational system, was characterized by strong anti-German feelings. The central and eastern part of the country, formerly under Russian control, was characterized by a mixture of agricultural backwardness, ethnic and religious conflicts, and illiteracy, with rebellious attitudes of workers who had previously produced goods for the Russian market and had established relations with Russian revolutionary movements. Although one-third of Polish society was non–Roman Catholic, composed of people with an Eastern Orthodox, Uniate, Jewish, or Protestant background, Catholicism effectively became the state religion after the Concordat was signed with the Vatican in 1925.

Ethnic and religious cleavages again overlapped and reinforced each other. Poles were generally Roman-Catholic, Ukrainians were either Eastern Orthodox or Uniate, Germans tended to be Protestants, and the Jewish minority was of the Mosaic confession. All these cleavages were represented in the shape of thirty-one political parties in Seym of the first postwar term (see Table 6.2).

The Polish multiparty system flourished especially from 1918 through 1926. Later, after J. Piłsudski's coup d'etat (May 1926), this system was attacked for "seymocracy" and factionism ("partyjniactwo")[5] by devotees of "strong state" and "strong hand" and was gradually dismantled. This occurred not only by legal, but also illegal means and actions (such as restricting freedom of the press and limiting or even suspending the rights of the legal opposition during the so-called "Brest election" of 1930[6] and, between 1934 and 1939, interning thousands of party activists at the Bereza Kartuska camp[7]).

After the coup of May 1926, the powers of the president were strengthened. Step by step, a type of authoritarian regime was formed, with a single major political bloc. Yet in May 1926, the majority of Polish society, exhausted by problems of everyday life and political battles, legitimized Piłsudski's action.

Table 6.2
The Second Republic of Poland. Elections and Political Fragmentation of the Sejm (Polish Parliament)

Type of institution, term and years	Number of party lists	Turnout (percent of all eligible voters)	Number of seats	Number of parliamentary clubs	Number of MP's representing the main political orientations (blocs, camps, groupings)				
					political				
					left	centrist	right		national minorities
Constitutional Assembly 1919–1922	21	60–94.4	340–432	10–19	106	87	134		13
Sejm of the first term 1922–1928	25	67.9	444	15–20	98	132	125		89
					political				
					left	centrist	right	governmental bloc	national minorities
Sejm of the second term 1928–1930	34	78.3	444	20–22	137	52	37	125	83
Sejm of the third term 1930–1935	17	75.0	444	13–16	83	14	63	249	33
				groupings: general, professional, regional	governmental bloc	nonpartisan			national minorities
Sejm of the fourth term 1935–1938	1	46.5	208		170	16			14
Sejm of the fifth term 1938–1939	1	67.3	208	5	164	21			23

Sources: Ajenkiel, A. 1989. *Historia sejmu polskiego (History of Polish Sejm)*, 265–353. Warszawa: PWN; Zieliński, H. 1985. *Historia Polski 1914–1939 (History of Poland)*, 72, 144, 198, 212, 242. Wrocław-Łódź: Ossolineum; *Mały Rocznik Statystyczny 1939 (Small Statistical Yearbook)* 335. Warszawa: GUS. part. XXI. Sejm i Senat (Sejm and Senate), tables 1–3.

Notes: 1. Election to the Constitutional Assembly took place on 26 January 1919, and additionally eight times in the years 1919–1920. In March 1922, deputies from Wilno region jointed the Assembly. Therefore, turnout and number of deputies were different in successive years.

2. Constitution of 1935 changed the number of seats in Sejm from 444 to 208.

3. "Governmental Bloc" denotes Bezpartyjny Blok Współpracy z Rządem (BBWR) in the years 1928–1935 and Obóz Zjednoczenia Narodowego (OZN) after 1935.

Table 6.3
Social Structure of Poland in 1930s (estimation)

Main structural units (all family members included)	Thousands	Pct.
Land aristocracy	179,000	0.4
Owners of big and middle factories, business, banks and etc.	763,000	2.4
Intelligentsia: scholars, teachers, free professions, clerks and etc.	750,000	2.3
Small owners (including shopkeepers and craftsmen)	3,536,000	11.0
Peasants, foresters, and gardeners etc.	18,927,000	60.0
Workmen (farm workers not included)	6,000,000	18.6
Others	1,700,000	5.3

Source: Szczepański, Jan. 1965. "Zmiany w strukturze klasowej społeczeństwa polskiego (Changes of Polish Society Class Structure)." In A. Sarapata (ed.), *Przemiany społeczne w Polsce Ludowej (Social Transformations in People's Poland)*, 5–79. Warszawa: Państwowe Wydawnictwo Naukowe.

It was popularly accepted that an effective government based on Piłsudski's personal charisma could, and should, stop further political fragmentation of society.

The political composition of six terms of prewar Polish Seyms is shown in Table 6.2. Some observers of the Polish political scene concluded that the multipartism seen in Poland from 1918 through 1926 was a direct consequence of a form of anarchism endemic in the Polish national character, or, expressing the same conviction more euphemistically, evidence of a deficiency of political skills among Poles ("not a society, but a great nation"[8]). But the facts contradict such easy generalizations. Polish multipartism of those years was first of all a product of cleavages, conflicts, and antagonisms which characterized the historical process of the development of this nation-state. The rebirth of Poland was by no means a painless event. Contradictions present in the decline of feudalism mixed with social tensions caused by underdeveloped capitalism. Ambitions of the old elite (land aristocracy and gentry) and ideologies conflicted with the aspirations of the new social forces and their beliefs. Centralizing drives of the dominant Polish national group collided with centrifugal tendencies of national/ethnic minorities. Multipartism also led to the manifestation of regional interests and asymmetrical aspirations of different churches and denominations. Using Talcott Parsons analytical categories, it could be said that Polish multipartism collapsed because political cleavages were not balanced by supraparty consensus, not "checked by a set of mechanisms that operate *below* the level of party division as well as by the more general national consensus that operate *above* that level" (Parsons, 1967: 245).

THE YEARS 1945–1989

Although the post–World War II history of Poland is seen by many observers as a singular period of communism, for analytical purposes it has to be divided into five phases. The first lasted from 1945 until 1947. It was, for many reasons, a time of a dramatic passage from the political system of the Second Republic of Poland to the rigid order of the People's Republic of Poland. Its main characteristics were owing less to the internal composition of Polish political forces and the competition between them and more to the broader consequences of the agreement reached during the Yalta Conference between the governments of the USA, UK, and USSR. The final document of that Conference, signed on February 12, 1945, stated that the Polish Provisional Government of National Unity had an obligation to undertake a free and unrestricted election, based on a common and secret ballot, as soon as possible. According to this agreement, all democratic and anti-Nazi parties should be granted equal rights to participate in the election. The second phase, from 1947 to 1956, was shaped by Stalinism and the complete destruction of what remained of the original Polish political tradition. In the third phase, which began in October 1956, attempts were made to remodel the system and make it more democratic. This phase lasted until the December 1970 crisis. The initial passion for reforms were cooled down at the beginning of sixties by so-called "small stabilization." The March 1968 events signaled a new crisis. The fourth phase, Edward Gierek's "opening to the West" or "goulash communism," encompassed the entire decade of the 1970s. The last, and fifth, phase began with the August 1980 Gdańsk-Szczecin agreements and the founding of the "Solidarity" movement. It passed through the years of Martial Law, followed by ineffective attempts to regain control over social attitudes and the Round Table agreement, and culminated with the parliamentary election of June 4, 1989.[9]

Poland emerged from World War II changed not only politically, but also in terms of its ethnic and religious composition. The Holocaust and the loss of 47 percent of the territory of the Second Republic, populated to a large extent by national and religious minorities, transformed a formerly multiethnic society into one with a 95 percent majority. This change had a direct consequence for the denominational structure. Polish society since 1945 has become predominantly Roman Catholic, with up to 96 percent membership in the church. Ethnic cleavages were occasionally highlighted, sometimes tragically as in the case of the Kielce pogrom and "Wisła Action," but generally they disappeared from everyday life.

After the agrarian reform, nationalization of industry, banks, and business, social cleavages were also reshaped. Moreover, what remained of the old cleavages was soon overshadowed by those new-born: national imperatives versus Soviet domination, social forces oriented toward the Second Republic legacy versus an ideological system installed by "revolution from abroad," the Church versus the Party, rising civilizational expectations versus inefficient economic system, and, generally, society contra state. In the years following the war, Poland was torn between two contradictory tendencies. On the one hand, "the workers wanted a system which recognized their needs, the peasants wanted land, the young intelligentsia wanted a fresh start, and everyone wanted peace and bread" (Zamoyski, 1987: 373). On the other hand, about 30,000 people from both sides of the ideological barricade (up to 16,000 were former soldiers of the

Home Army and political opposition) were killed in a postwar civil war, and thousands were imprisoned up to 1956. The system, not being able to fulfill its promises, fell into the trap of every revolution. As early as June 1956, the state found itself in a bloody confrontation with blue-collar workers in Poznań. The same occurred in 1970, 1976, and in the 1980s. Gradually, the normal channels for the articulation of social and citizen dissatisfaction were all blocked, with the exception of the Church. All such channels fell under party-state control, and the state became the main opponent of every conflict. Reforms, usually initiated under the pressure of mass unrest and never carried out to their planned end, were able to remove many of the Stalinist limitations, but were not able to change the overall nature of the system.

Nevertheless, from 1945 through 1947, at least seven political parties acted legally. According to the March Constitution of 1921, all had the right—even if not all could use it freely—to participate in parliamentary elections.[10] All linked themselves to prewar traditions, although none of them was identical with any prewar organizations or political movements. They often emerged following breaks (quite often provoked) within larger entities and represented mostly leftist sprinter groups. The growth of some of them, especially of the Polish Socialist Party (PPS) and the Polish Workers Party (PPR), was striking. By the end of 1944, the reborn PPS had some 5,000 members; by April 1945, about 140,000; by December 1946, approximately 283,000; and by September 1947, nearly 713,000. However, several months later, at the time of its amalgamation with the PPR, PPS membership had dropped to 599,000. The PPR case was quite different. It had grown from 20,000 in mid-1944 to 39,000 in December of the same year, to 235,000 by December 1945, to half a million one year later, to more than 800,000 by September 1947, and to almost a million members by June 1948 (Czubiński, 1976: 852–53). Until 1947, the most powerful party of all, with about 600,000 members, was Mikołajczyk's Polish Peasant Party (PSL).

Other symptoms of forthcoming Stalinization could be observed. The most evident were the privileged position of the Polish Workers Party in the state institutions, growing pressure on other parties not to compete but to create one bloc at the parliamentary election of 1947, the fate of noncommunist political leaders (such as S. Mikołajczyk and K. Popiel) and of other activists of parties that lost the 1947 election, and the forced unification of heretofore independent parties. The official results of the 1947 election to the Constitutional Assembly are shown in Table 6.4.

The process of consolidation continued inexorably. In December 1948, the PPR and PPS were merged to create the Polish United Workers Party (PZPR), in which the PPS traditions and leaders were immediately marginalized. A year later, in November 1949, the United Peasant Party (ZSL) resulted from the unification of the Peasant Party (SL) and an anti-Mikołajczyk faction of the Polish Peasant Party (PSL). In June 1950, when a leftist group from the declining Labor Party (SP) joined the Democratic Party (SD), the new scene was set. The main actors were

Table 6.4
The Republic of Poland and People's Republic of Poland. Elections and Political Composition of the Seym (Polish Parliament)

Type of institution, term and years	Number of seats	Political composition (percent and absolute numbers)				
Constitutional Assembly, 1947–1952	444	Bloc of Democratic Parties 80.1 (394)	Polish Peasant Party (Mikołajczyk) 10.3 (28)	Labor Party (Popiel) 4.7 (12)	PPP "New Liberation" 3.5 (7)	Others 1.4 (3)
		PZPR	*ZSL*	*SD*		*Independent*
Seym of the first term, 1952–1957	425	64.2 (273)	21.2 (90)	5.9 (25)		8.7 (37)
Seym of the second term, 1957–1961	459	52.0 (239)	25.7 (118)	8.5 (39)		13.7 (63)
Seym of the third term, 1961–1965	460	55.6 (256)	25.4 (117)	8.5 (39)		10.5 (48)
Seym of the fourth term, 1965–1969	460	55.4 (255)	25.4 (117)	5.5 (39)		10.6 (49)
Seym of the fifth term, 1969–1972	460	55.4 (255)	25.4 (117)	8.5 (39)		10.6 (49)
Seym of the sixth term, 1972–1976	460	55.4 (255)	25.4 (117)	8.5 (39)		10.6 (49)
Seym of the seventh term, 1976–1980	460	56.7 (261)	24.6 (113)	8.0 (37)		10.7 (49)
Seym of the eight term, 1980–1985	460	56.7 (261)	24.6 (113)	8.0 (37)		10.7 (49)
Seym of the ninth term, 1985–1989	460	53.3 (245)	23.0 (106)	7.6 (35)		16.1 (74)

Sources: Topolski, Jerzy (ed.) 1976. *Dzieje Polski (History of Poland)*, 861. Warszawa: PWN; *Mały Rocznik Statystyczny 1986 (Small Statistical Yearbook 1986)* Table 1/22. Warszawa: GUS; *Sejm PRL. Stan na początku kadencji (Seym of People's Poland. Data for the beginning of the term)*, 21.

now the PZPR together with the ZSL and the SD. But the dominant role had clearly been assigned to the PZPR. The period of single-party rule began in 1947 and lasted, although with some modifications after 1956, for nearly forty years (Wiatr, 1967: 108–23). (In the sixties, after discussion with Giovanni Sartori, this system was named by Jerzy J. Wiatr as "the hegemonic party system".)

The essence of this political arrangement in Central Europe was that other existing parties, as well as voluntary organizations, had no choice—if they wanted to exist—but to accept the leading role of the PZPR, with important consequences for the Polish political culture, consequences that continue to have an impact today. These are (1) the lack of well-established patterns of legal opposition; (2) the obliteration of the bonds between the ruling party and state (under these conditions the state transforms itself into a "party state" and may be seen as analogous to H. D. Lasswell "garrison state"); (3) the politicization of police and military forces; (4) the blockage of normal channels of élite selection and exchange (normally founded at least to some extent on open competition); (5) the substitution of strong belief in an argument of power and "barricade mentality" ("we" or "they," *tertium non datur*) for negotiating techniques of conflict resolution, the skills of living in a pluralist society, and the ability to perceive one's own reality rationally; and (6) the atrophy of a "political instinct," which under normal conditions forces politicians to continuously seek social acceptance.

Under these circumstances, the need for legitimacy and trust is replaced by a strong conviction regarding one's own historical mission and the absence of any reasonable alternatives.[11] The absence of promised (or desired) effects can always be justified by pointing to a syndrome of limited sovereignty ("we certainly would if we only could").[12]

It would not be true to assert that the PZPR, and its reformist wing especially, did nothing to limit the dysfunctions of the single-party system. However, the most far-reaching steps, taken in the summer of 1981 during the IX Extraordinary PUWP Congress, were already too late. Yet even then one thing was still excluded from consideration: the loss of dominant power. A transformation of the single-party system and its voting regulations was desirable, but not to the point where the system could be changed to its prerevolutionary form by ballot. Even as late as the Round Table negotiations the party leaders were ready to share, but not to lose power totally.

Although voting regulations evolved throughout the whole period, and after 1956 especially, toward a more democratic ideal, their function was nevertheless always the same: to assure the reproduction of the hegemony of the ruling party. Such regulations ensured that the final results of a ballot were always known before the election. The whole procedure was ritualistic, and only rarely assumed an unmistakably plebiscitarian character. For decades, authorities appealed for participation in voting without allowing a real election to take place.

Under such conditions, turnout achieved an additional political meaning. High turnout was interpreted as a sign of legitimacy; lower turnout, even if only by one or two points, was always treated as a sign of growing frustration. The parliamentary election to the Seym of the tenth term of June 1989 differed dramatically from earlier elections, but, as a result of the Round Table contract, it maintained the numerical ascendancy of the ruling coalition (PZPR, ZSL, SD) over others.

However, in a changed international milieu and under pressure from an awakened society, a contract between élites was no longer enough. The voting regulation, which allowed for "1/3 democratic election" to the Seym and 100 percent free election to the Senate, had in fact opened the way to a new experience for most Polish citizens. Events were moving out of control of the hands of politicians, old as well as new. The 1989 election brought an explosion of multipartism, but not an institutionalized multiparty system. After passage of the law of 28 June

1990, permitting any group of fifteen citizens to register in the tribunal as a political party and have all the political and legal rights such registration implied, parties began to bloom. By April 1995, the number of parties had reached 270; by March 1996, they had surpassed 300. There were dozens of parties, but the ideas of a nonpartisan common goal, of the public interest, and of developing a set of principles to ensure system stability, had not yet emerged. There was a parliamentary opposition, but the rules of the democratic game had not yet been learned. There were representatives of different political forces in state institutions but there was no capacity for cohabitation. In sum, cleavages and partisan approaches were still not balanced by a supraparty consensus on the norms and rules of the system, and a workable multiparty system was still impossible to create.

CLOSING REMARKS

Although numerous differences exist between individual countries, the current political systems of Central and Eastern Europe are generally composed of the remains—beliefs, norms, fears, procedures, institutions, and so forth—of a system that no longer exists, plus characteristics of a system that has not yet been fully realized. The landscape, therefore, is full of contradictions. The most striking, at least for Poland, are

1. While the number of parties and quasi-parties is growing dramatically, the total membership of parties is shrinking. The attitude of Poles toward political parties seems to be somewhat ambivalent. On the one hand, they accept parties as indispensable components of parliamentary democracy, but on the other hand, they are satisfied neither with contemporary politicians nor their parties.[13]

2. Although the number of parties continues to grow, the number of voters participating in successive parliamentary elections remains low. As Adam Michnik observed as early as 1991, "problems are generated not by the number of parties, but their quality." Although voter turnout remains low, parties are viewed as being still preoccupied with themselves or, from the point of view of strategic segments of society, with issues of secondary importance. Opinion polls make clear that most Poles believe today's conflicts are caused not by social cleavages, but rather by competition within the political class.

3. Although a substantial part of Polish society looks for "nonpolitical politics" and a pragmatic program, many parties still battle over yesterday's problems and/or eschatological values.

4. Although the necessity of creating political coalitions—parliamentarian and governmental—seems obvious to many leaders, a clear-cut concept of nonpartisanship has yet to emerge.

Maurice Duverger stated some years ago that political parties age. For today's observer of the political scene this assertion is not enough. One has to ask a further question: What gets old? Does this observation refer only to some types of parties or, more generally, to the phenomenon of political parties? It was a rather common conviction not so long ago that nation-states were the last word of a historical process. An international community without these entities was simply not conceivable. Only some utopian thinkers thought otherwise. Yet how it is today? Is European integration possible without questioning the old axioms? Is, *mutatis mutandis,* an understanding of Central and Eastern European political processes possible today without challenging the old concepts of parties and party systems? New and difficult questions must be asked; hard and honest answers must be found.

NOTES

1. As evident in the writings of, among others: Kenneth, Janda. 1995. *Restructuring the Party System in Central Europe.* Paper presented at Manchester Conference on Party Politics in the Year 2000, 13–15 January 1995; Lewis, Paul G. 1994. "Development in Post-Communism Poland," in *Europe-Asia Studies*, vol. 46, no. 5: 779–99; Ágh, Attila. 1994. "The Hungarian Party System and the Party Theory in the Transition of Central Europe," in *Journal of Theoretical Politics*, no. 6: 217–38; Smolar, Aleksander. 1994. "The Dissolution of Solidarity," in *Journal of Democracy,* no. 5: 70–84; Wiatr, Jerzy J. 1994. "From Communist Party to Socialist-Democracy of the Polish Republic," in Kay Lawson (ed.), *How Political Parties Work,* 249–61. Westport-London: Praeger.

2. As evident even from the so-called "Small Versailles Treaty," signed between the Allied Powers and Poland (28 June 1919). Article 93 obliged Poland to protect the interests of those citizens who differed from the majority by "race, language or religion."

3. Norms of the March Constitution (1921) and of voting regulation (1922) were already changed in prewar time by the April Constitution, enacted in 1935. Article 32 of that Constitution defined suffrage as: universal, secret, equal and direct, but not, as it was in the case of the March Constitution, proportional. Instead, the voting regulation of 1935 introduced the majority system, one voting list, and so-called nonpartisan "regional assemblies," which monopolized the process of selecting candidates. Paradoxically, the voting regulations of People's Poland (from 1952 until 1985) were much closer to the law of 1935 than that of 1921.

4. Kept at the Hoover Institution on War, Revolution, and Peace. See: Kapiszewski, Andrzej. 1991. *Hugh Gibson and Controversy over Polish-Jewish Relations after World War I.* Kraków: 'Secesja'.

5. Both terms used by, among others, Józef Piłsudski. "Seymocracy" means ascendancy of legislative authority over executive authority. "Partyjniactwo" means a style of parliamentary activities dominated by a partisan approach to questions under debate. Both terms are pejorative.

6. The label given by the opposition to the parliamentary election of November 1930. Just before the election, state authorities arrested and kept in custody at the Brest-Litovsk Military Prison a substantial number of the leaders of the political opposition. Those arrested were accused of preparation for conspiracy against "members of the government." About 5000 activists were arrested, including 84 former MPs and senators.

7. A camp established in 1932 for Ukrainian nationalistic leaders and for political prisoners generally. They could be detained there on the basis of an administrative decision, without an investigation or a trial.

8. A bitter statement by Kamil Norwid from the 1850s. See: Norwid, K. 1985. *Myśli o Polsce i Polakach (Thoughts on Poland and Poles),* 23. Białystok: KAW.
9. The Round Table negotiations were discussing between the Polish United Workers Party and the forces composing Solidarity held from February 6, 1989, to April 6, 1989, and resulted in the first legal political opposition in the history of state socialism.
10. These were Polska Partia Socjalistyczna (PPS, Polish Socialist Party), Polska Partia Robotnicza (PPR, Polish Workers' Party), Stronnictwo Ludowe (SL, Peasant Party), Stronnictwo Demokratyczne (SD, Democratic Party), Polskie Stronnictwo Ludowe (PSL, headed by S. Mikołajczyk, Polish Peasant Party), and Polskie Stronnictwo Ludowe 'Nowe Wyzwolenie' (PSL-NW, Polish Peasant Party "New Liberation"). There were also small Catholic groupings, which won three seats in the January 1947 election.
11. From this type of wishful thinking emerged the constitutional legalization of the PZPR's political role. Article 3, part 1 of the constitutional amendment enacted in 1976 stated that the PZPR is the leading political force in the country.
12. I discussed this phenomenon in Kubiak, Hieronim, 1994, "Social sciences and the challenge of transition: the Polish case," in *AS/Science,* no. 7: 6–7.
13. Data from Research Center on Public Opinion (June 1994 survey) show that Poles consider the parliamentary democracy as the "best form of rule" (70 percent of investigated) but at the same time are not satisfied with existing parties (53 percent) and politicians (87 percent share the view that the "majority of politicians care only for themselves"). A 1995 survey demonstrates that Poles prefer political blocs to political parties.

REFERENCES

Burda, Andrzej. 1983. *Konstytucja marcowa. Dokumenty naszej tradycji. 1921 (The March Constitution. Documents of Our Tradition. 1921).* Lublin: Wydawnictwo Lubelskie.
Czubiński, Antoni. 1976. "Główne etapy i kierunki rozwoju Polski Ludowej (The Main Phases and Directions of the People's Poland Development)." In J. Topolski, ed., *Dzieje Polski (History of Poland).* Warszawa: PWN.
Habermas, Jürgen. 1993. "Nachholende Revolution und linker Revisionsbedarf. Was heisst Sozialismus heute?" Quoted from the Polish translation: *Dziś,* vol. 3.
Nowak, Stefan. 1979. "Przekonania i odczucia współczesnych (Convictions and Feelings of Contemporaries)." In M. Rostworowski (ed.), *Polaków portret własny (Pole's Self-Portrait),* 122–45. Kraków: Wydawnictwo Literackie.
Parsons, Talcott. 1967. *Sociological Theory and Modern Society.* New York: The Free Press.
Sartori, Giovanni. 1987. *The Theory of Democracy Revisited.* Chatham: Chatham House Publishers.
Wiatr, Jerzy J. 1967. "The Hegemonic Party System in Poland." In J. J. Wiatr (ed.), *Studies in Polish Political System,* 108–23. Wrocław: Ossolineum.
Zamoyski, Adam. 1987. *The Polish Way. A Thousand-year History of the Poles and Their Culture.* 329. London: John Murray.

7

Romania: Cleavages and Parties before 1989

Petre Datculescu

ORIGINS AND HISTORY OF THE ROMANIAN PARTY SYSTEM

The crystallization of cleavages and the development of the Romanian party system are to be understood in the context of four sets of political conditions characteristic of Romania between the early nineteenth century and the beginning of World War II. They are

1. External pressure
2. Internal social structure
3. Limited and fragile integration of the political community
4. The national debate over the country's model of development

External Pressure

In geopolitical terms, Romania has always been at a point of confluence. A small country, its options on the international arena have been limited. Throughout history, powerful states have repeatedly occupied or threatened it.

External factors have been decisive in shaping Romania's economic life. The political elites have copied the ideas and political institutions of the more developed nations in Europe. The economy has been under foreign control. In referring to the period before World War II, Eugen Weber noted: "Between five- and six-sevenths of industrial capital investment was owned or made available by foreigners. Foreign capital owned two-thirds of the oil industry, dominated the insurance business, controlled the banks" (Weber, 1966: 529).

Social Structure

Toward the mid-nineteenth century, 85 percent of the Romanian population lived in the countryside, while merely 15 percent lived in towns and cities. Almost a hundred years later, in 1944, the rural population still prevailed, representing 66 percent of the total number, as against the 34 percent of urban population.

During this period, three-quarters of the country's active population made their living by working in agriculture, but the peasantry could not be characterized as a homogeneous class. Some owned land, others worked as farm hands, and still others were agricultural proletarians. Whatever category they were in, their lives were far from easy. According to Keith Hitchins, for all the categories of rural population, income was insufficient to cover the cost of food, clothes, and expenses for church services, school, and health services, to say nothing of taxes (Hitchins, 1996: 365–66).

The masters of rural Romania were the landowners. In the early twentieth century, about two thousand of the major landlords held about 38 percent of the total surface of arable land (Rosetti, 1908: 577–580). Romanian landlords did not reside in the countryside, they lived either in Bucharest or abroad. They did not manage their estates on their own and were not concerned with introducing new technologies in agriculture. The administration of these estates was delegated to leaseholders, who represented a very limited social stratum placed between the landlords and the peasants.

The development of industry started out with difficulty after 1870 and gained speed after 1886, when the Liberal Party introduced a law for protective tariffs and direct state support to industrial enterprises. But the working class represented only 10 percent of the active population in the early twentieth century, before 1939 (Hitchins, 1996: 387).

The urban middle class included merchants, civil servants, professionals, and entrepreneurs. This small class represented the Romanian petty bourgeoisie. Although small, this segment counted more members than the industrial and banking bourgeoisie.

From an ethnic and religious point of view, the population of Romania was quite homogeneous. In 1930, out of a total population of more than 18 million, 71.9 percent were Romanians, while 28.1 percent belonged to different ethnic groups. Even in Transylvania, where a potential for ethnic conflicts did exist, 57.8 percent were Romanians, 24.4 percent were Hungarians and Szeklers, while 9.8 percent were Germans (Bulei, 1996: 115). These proportions did not change significantly until after the end of World War II.

Limited and Fragile Integration of the Political Community

Kenneth Jowitt rightly considers that the Eastern European national states existing in the interwar period, to the extent they had been established by that time, evinced an extremely limited and fragile capacity for the political integration of all the individuals formally contained within their territorial boundaries (Jowitt, 1971: 89). In reference to the interwar period, Jowitt wrote: "In particular, in most of these countries, the absence of a set of national publics in possession of politically relevant resources, articulating their interests and aspirations, and capable of offering sustained support for political programs led to the development of political systems as in Romania—whose intense nationalism may in part be viewed as an index of their fragile political-social identity" (Jowitt, 1971: 90).

During the formation of modern Romania, peasants and workers never benefited from effective representation and were totally excluded from political life. They were mere spectators. Political action was the monopoly of personalities, of politicians holding important offices, of small groups of officials concentrated in the capital. Public organizations or institutionalized parties had little or no involvement in such action.

The National Debate on the Country's Model of Development

After World War I, the new Romania included Transylvania, the Banat, Bessarabia, and Northern Bukovina. The country's territory increased from 137,500 sq. km. in 1914 to 295,049 sq. km. in the early '20s.

The task of organizing the new Romania led to a heated debate over the model of national development. Two conceptions clashed. Those with European aspirations wanted Romania to follow closely the path of economic and social development taken by the Western world. They saw no difficulty in implementing in a predominantly rural Romania a model of industrial capitalism which had proved to be viable in the conditions of urbanization and industrialization characteristic of Western Europe.

Traditionalists, on the other hand, saw Romania's agrarian character as a specific context that could not be overlooked. In their opinion, development had to be based on the unique cultural, social, and national heritage of the country.

A third alternative was added by those who believed in the necessity of combining political democracy and Western technology with the unique agrarian structures of Romania (for a detailed analysis of the national debate see Hitchins, 1996: 315–58).

The First Political Parties

When the first political parties appeared in Romania foreign pressure and the characteristics of the social structure were the two major issues dominating the political scene.

During the early nineteenth century, Romania was under Turkish domination, while its economy and trade were controlled by Greek landlords. The small Romanian landlords felt frustrated and tried to acquire the local privileges held by foreigners. In the beginning, they enjoyed the political support of large landowners. The cleavage between the Romanian nationalist landlords and the Greek landlords was the first major political cleavage in Romania. The landlords' revolt generated a political movement that proved to be relatively successful.

The movement directed against foreign domination was called the national party. Two factors influenced the movement in a decisive way: the ideas of liberty and equality of the French Revolution, and the early forms of disobedience of the oppressed peasantry. The social character of the movement gradually came to prevail over the national one. Small landlords supported action taken to relieve peasants from the excessive duties they were made to pay to their masters, the large landowners. No peasant revolt followed, but the ever more obvious social character of the movement led to the splitting up of the landed gentry into two rival and enemy factions after 1821, the small landlords animated by liberal ideas of reform and the large landowners holding conservative views. The national movement against foreign rule was thus divided, and the two factions were to be the bases for the Conservative and the Liberal Party created later on.

The Conservative Party was the party of large landowners. But as early as the mid-nineteenth century the political base of this party had begun to disintegrate, as the number of large landowners declined, owing to land reform, which meant a successive allotment of land to the peasants, and the introduction of universal suffrage. Another element that contributed to the total disappearance of the Conservative Party was its pro-German attitude during World War I.

The Liberal Party started out as the party of small landlords in the cities, as early as 1849. Later it also penetrated the countryside. Between the accession to the throne of King Carol I (in 1866) and 1933, Romania's political life was dominated by the Liberals. They represented the interests of the middle class of traders and industrialists who were theoretically in conflict with the large landowners.

The National Party in Transylvania and the Socialist Party were also among the first political parties in Romania. The establishment of the National Party of Transylvania in 1869 was a consequence of the mobilization of Romanians in Transylvania against the annexation of this province by Hungary. The Socialist Party was founded around 1879. Soon after, it became the Social-Democratic Party (in 1893) as a consequence of the more intense political activity of Romanian socialists. The slow pace of industrialization and the small number of proletarians prevented the socialist movement from acquiring wider support, organizing itself politically and playing a significant role in Romania's parliamentary life.

CRYSTALLIZATION OF CLEAVAGES AND PARTY DEVELOPMENT BEFORE WORLD WAR II

On Sunday, December 20, 1937, Romanians who showed up at the polls had no way of knowing they were casting their votes in the last free parliamentary elections in a great while and that soon Romania was to embark upon a long totalitarian night that it would only be able to leave behind half a century later, in 1989.

The results of the 1937 elections, shown in Table 7.1, are interesting to analyze from the perspective of crystallization of cleavages and party development in Romania before World War II (Enescu, 1937: 12).

In 1937, the National Liberal Party (and its allies), although ranked first, did not manage to fulfill the 40 percent quota that could have entitled them to the electoral bonus stipulated in the Election Law of 1926, which would have meant victory and a majority in the Parliament.

In the interwar period, the Liberals had been the strongest party. But their power was based more on authority and political maneuvering than on their capacity to mobilize the electorate in the context of social cleavages or in favor of dominant social problems.

The model adopted by the Liberals was the Western world. But the liberalism of Romanian Liberals was nothing like Western European liberalism. The Romanian bourgeoisie was far too weak to become a vehicle of social change as the bourgeoisie had been in Western Europe. Consequently, the Liberals used the state to create in Romania a Western-type financial and industrial infrastructure. But the state was dependent on foreign capital. The self-reliant support of industrialization generated profits that benefited only a few members of the financial

Table 7.1
Results of the Romanian Elections Held on December 20, 1937

Parties	*Number of votes*	*Percentage*
The National Liberal Party	1,103,353	35.92
The National Peasant Party	626,612	20.40
The Party "Totul pentru Țară"*	478,368	15.58
The National Christian Party	281,167	9.15
The Hungarian Party	136,139	4.43
The "Gh. Brătianu" National Liberal Party	119,361	3.89
The Radical Peasant Party	69,198	2.25
The Agrarian Party	52,101	1.70
The Jewish Party	43,681	1.42
The Party of the German People	43,412	1.42
The Social Democratic Party	28,840	0.94
The People's Party	25,567	0.83
The Work Front Party	6,986	0.23
Other independent groups and lists (53 in all)	11,145	0.36
Total number of votes	3,026,140	98.52
Cancelled bulletins	45,555	1.48
Total number of voters	3,071,695	100.0

* In literal translation, "Do Everything for Your Country."

and industrial oligarchy. On the other hand, it generated an increase in prices, which dealt a decisive blow to the large agricultural masses and the civil servants in towns and cities. The Liberals realized they would be unable to raise sufficient political support in the elections. Hence they made a last attempt to attract the peasantry by elaborating a new agricultural policy. But their Manifesto to the country, made public at the very last moment in November 1937, came too late to prevent electoral disaster for the Liberal Party.

The peasant parties were no more successful in attracting the masses to the political life of the country and in representing the interests of the rural population effectively. The most important peasant party, which was the most important opposition party as well, was the National Peasant Party established in 1926, following the fusion of the venerable Romanian National Party of Transylvania and the Peasant Party established in 1918. The National Peasant Party was honestly concerned with the undemocratic aspects of interwar political life and the difficult situation the peasantry was in. But they failed to perceive and find solutions for the urgent needs of the peasantry. They believed that the consolidation of democratic political institutions would eventually lead to a free and prosperous economy that would also be beneficial for the peasants. Sensing their lack of social support, the Peasant Party concluded an electoral alliance with the fascist party "Totul pentru Țară," which came in second in the 1937 elections. In accepting this alliance, the National Peasant Party made a substantial contribution to the failure of the fragile Romanian democracy.

Leftist parties had almost no influence on political life in the interwar period. They tried to obtain the support of urban workers and represent their interests. But their electorate was extremely reduced in numbers, and the capacity of leftist parties to mobilize this electorate was even weaker.

Beginning in 1921, the left was divided ideologically into communists and social-democrats. The initial membership of the Communist Party amounted to 2,000, with this figure decreasing to less than 1,000 just before the war. The Communists had been banned by the government because they had accepted the anti-national and anti-state theses dictated by Moscow. They supported ideas that fundamentally contradicted religion, traditions, and dominant values of the Romanians. The Communist Party could therefore play only a minor role in interwar politics.

The social-democratic movement was no more effective. The socialist ideas were neither well enough known nor accepted to the full by the Romanian working class, and the social-democratic parties had never managed to obtain a significant improvement of the situation of the working class. Therefore it came as no surprise that in the 1937 elections, the Romanian Socialist Party obtained only 0.9 percent of the votes and no seat in Parliament.

The most striking gains in 1937 were made by the extreme right.

The fascist organization "The Iron Guard," established by Zelea-Codreanu (1899–1938), had managed to become a mass movement in the '30s, leaping from an electoral support of one percent in 1931 to 15.58 percent in 1937, when it entered the elections with its legal party, "Totul pentru Țară."

The best explanation for the rise of the extreme right can be found precisely in the low degree of integration of the Romanian political community. In particular, as Eugen Weber pointed out, there were sections of the young and the peasantry that were either unattended to by the existing political organizations or mobilized, that is definitively uprooted from their social-political settings" (Weber, 1937: 101–27).

The Romanian fascist movement managed to pull together vast segments of the population from all social strata that had been neglected by the democratic political forces. Besides the young and the peasantry, the movement also included urban workers, segments of the urban petty bourgeoisie, the rural clergy, and individuals at the periphery of society. The message of the movement was ultranationalist and anti-semitic, pigmented with elements of orthodoxy, revised in a fanatic manner. In a destructively violent way, the movement condemned what it called the hypocrisy of those in power, but also the values of European liberalism, rationalism, and industrialism. The party promoted the cult of the Romanian peasant, who was defined as a personification of purity and a model of national revival.

SOCIAL AND POLITICAL CLEAVAGES DURING COMMUNIST RULE

The interwar political community and party system were weakened by two successive authoritarian regimes, which were later crushed by the communist dictatorship. Yet it is also true that the traditional parties contributed to a great extent to the establishment of King Carol II's dictatorship between 1938 and 1940 and that of Marshall Ion Antonescu's dictatorship between 1940 and 1944. Later, in August 1944, before the imminent establishment of communist dictatorship, the National Peasant Party enjoyed a sudden and strong popularity, because it had promoted a democratic program and was perceived as a force that could prevent the ascension of the Communists. However, quite inexplicably, the National Peasant Party did not mobilize the masses or seize power. Consequently, a power void emerged which the Communist Party was able to fill (Georgescu, 1992: 246).

The Years of Communist Dictatorship

The over 40 years of so-called socialist development of Romania proved to be a total failure in all its aspects. The system generated an overcentralized and rigidly planned economy. It led to inefficiency and the stifling of any initiative. The founding ruler of communist Romania was Gheorghe Gheorghiu-Dej, an old-time communist appointed as head of the country by Stalin. In the late fifties, Gheorghiu-Dej picked Nicolae Ceaușescu to become his favorite within the party. Ceaușescu, who was born in 1918 to a poor village family, had been in the communist movement since he was fifteen. When Gheorghiu-Dej died in 1965, Ceaușescu replaced him with the help of the influential Prime Minister Ion Gheorghe Maurer and continued the earlier drive toward nationalism and full industrialization.

In the early '70s, Ceaușescu tried to force economic growth by irrationally boosting industrial development, with a stress on heavy industry. It was a Stalinist obsession, which came into severe conflict with the resources available and the unfavorable context in the world market. Unavoidably, industrial production started to decrease as early as the '70s, while the country's foreign debt increased.

The problems of agriculture remained unsolved. The investments made to make agricultural production modern and effective were anemic. Collective farms were under government control. Agricultural producers lacked motivation and the quality of life in rural areas was no higher than it had been in the interwar period.

A tyrannical regime based on repression and the secret police took hold of all the structures of society: economy, culture, politics, the family, and the private sphere. The very "unmodern" and unprecedented cult of Nicolae Ceaușescu's personality and that of his wife, Elena, lay at the very heart of this system. In his book "Modern Tyrants," Daniel Chirot explains the causes of modern tyranny. They include (a) "the presence of nationalist ideologies that stress resentment of the outside and blame external forces for perceived domestic failures"; (b) "a worldview that believes in the inevitability of conflict between races or classes"; and (c) "a strong association between anti-individualistic, communal ideologies, and acceptance of regimes that consider individual rights insignificant" (Chirot, 1994: 264). All these causes were apparent in the establishment of tyranny in Romania by Ceaușescu.

The End of the Dictatorship. Dominant Problems and Cleavages in the '80s

During the '80s the problems of the Romanian society had become so serious that some analysts started wondering whether the system would be able to endure for long.[1]

There were two dominant aspects in the '80s that generated massive social cleavages and eventually led to the collapse of the communist regime: (1) a dramatic decrease of the living standard, combined with deliberate attempts by political elites to demodernize Romanian society, and (2) stricter control and domestic ideological repression associated with the attempt to isolate Romania from the influence of international social, political, technical, and scientific changes.

Since the late '70s it had become obvious that the communist state was no longer in a position to fulfill its social functions. Gradually the Romanians became the poorest people in Eastern Europe. Imports were almost totally discontinued. Agricultural production was exported, while the population had access to only minimal food rations. Food stores were out of supplies most of the time. Even bread was rationed.

Energy consumption was drastically reduced, both for economic and household consumption. Heating was insufficient and the supply of electrical energy was interrupted for long periods and over extended areas, both in the urban and rural communities.

Investments for the construction of new apartment buildings, for health services, education, and culture were in constant decline. The income of the population decreased constantly while prices rose. Jobs were relatively stable, but industrial workers were obliged to discontinue work for longer or shorter periods, due to the energy and raw material shortage. Production plans set unrealistically high targets that could not be attained for objective reasons, yet the workers were penalized with reductions of up to 50 percent of their monthly wages for what was called their "failure to fulfill the plan."

The intention to make Romania regress to a form of neo-underdevelopment was becoming ever more obvious. Technological improvements were no longer made. The political elite and Ceaușescu himself discouraged the introduction or utilization of computers in industrial processes. In agriculture, fuel shortage was a chronic problem, while peasants were advised to return to the use of animals for traction and to manual work. Gas was also rationed for private-car owners, while under the pretext of weather problems, the use of personal cars was prohibited during winter and a part of spring.

In many households, electrical appliances became useless or were irrecoverably damaged due to frequent power shortages. The population was invited to reduce the number and power of the bulbs used and to refrain from using electrical appliances, including refrigerators and heating devices. An "energy" police checked houses and apartments to make sure the population conformed to the measures requiring the suppression of excessive natural gas and electricity consumption. During the night, the streets were dark and restaurants closed at 9 P.M.

Economic decay and social demodernization were accompanied by an anti-intellectual campaign and more intense domestic ideological repression. The control of the Communist Party and the secret police in all the spheres of intellectual activity hardened. Nicolae Ceaușescu's interminable discourses were declared models of supreme wisdom, offering solutions for all the domains and problems in the country. The number of newspapers, magazines, and books published was drastically reduced. Political, artistic, social, and scientific information from the Western world was censored to the maximum. The broadcasts of the national television station were reduced to two or three hours a day, being limited to patriotic programs commending the communist regime and the "beloved ruler." Scholars, scientists, social researchers, and journalists were under constant supervision through a multitude of means. Those who owned typewriters had to take them to a police station every year to have a sample of their characters taken. Thus citizens were discouraged from typing texts that were not acceptable to the regime. If they were bold enough to do so nevertheless, the police could easily locate the typewriter the texts had been written on. In ideological institutions typewriters were locked with ordinary padlocks at the end of each day, to prevent them from being used by the "enemies of the socialist order." Telephone contacts with foreigners were limited and under full supervision. Any form of dissidence was repressed more severely than in any other Eastern-European communist country.

In the background of these dominant issues, two major cleavages appeared in the Romanian society: (1) the cleavage between the political elite—that is, the leadership of the Romanian Communist Party—and the working class, and (2) the cleavage between the political elite, on the one hand, and the technical and cultural elite, on the other.

The Political Elite versus the Working Class

Between 1948 and 1980, Romania's urban population increased from 23.5 percent to about 45 percent. Urbanization was achieved through industrialization. In 1985, the percentage of people employed in industry was 46.8 percent, as compared to 38.3 percent of in 1950. Most of them were workers.

This massive social mobilization was more important from a qualitative, rather than a quantitative, point of view. Massive industrialization did not imply the modernization of the Romanian society. On the contrary, the social mobilization generated by industrialization allowed the Communist Party to penetrate social life in an effective manner and created the conditions for the establishment of a new political community based on the integration of vast segments of the population.

Indeed, the Communist Party elevated the working class to a leading position in the society, and the industrial worker with a rural background became the social base of the Communist Party. For the peasants-turned-workers, the change brought a profession that required higher education, an improved social status, better wages, and higher political recognition. In return for all these, they agreed to be subordinated by the Communist Party.

Silviu Brucan claims that technological progress threatened to spoil the cohabitation between the Communist Party and the working class, as it led to a decrease in the numbers, status, and social prestige of manual workers and to an increase in the importance of intellectuals. Brucan demonstrates that both Nicolae Ceaușescu and Leonid Brezhnev deliberately prevented the assimilation of technological progress in civil industry to avoid sacrificing industrial workers, who constituted the social base of the Communist Party (Brucan, 1992: 158–159).

Until the '70s, the Communist Party lived up to its commitment made to the workers, while the workers accepted the leading position and the self-assumed objectives of the Party. The economic deterioration in the '80s led to a crisis and a major cleavage between the workers and the communist political elite. The workers no longer received their full salaries, jobs were less secure, and the difficulties of everyday life were unbearable.

The first signs of the incipient cleavage appeared in 1977, when 35,000 miners in the Jiu Valley went on a strike that could be stopped only by promises made personally by Ceaușescu to the miners and after the strike leaders had been arrested. But the most dramatic illustration of the cleavage that separated workers and the political elite was the revolt of the workers in Brasov on November 15, 1987. Two years before the collapse of the communist regime, more than ten thousand workers initiated an actual rebellion that went beyond social claims and that insisted on the overthrowing of Nicolae Ceaușescu's communist dictatorship.

Technocracy versus Political Elite

Nicolae Ceaușescu's policy oriented against the intellectuals was extremely tough for two reasons. In his effort to preserve the loyalty of the working class, Ceaușescu tried to glorify manual work by granting it a higher social importance than that of intellectual activity. On the other hand, Ceaușescu had always feared that intellectuals were more interested in their freedom of thinking and expression than in their salaries and material advantages, although before 1971 material privileges had been quite effective in winning over the opportunistic support of intellectuals. The anti-intellectual policy materialized in lower pay for intellectuals in comparison with qualified workers in top industries and the reduction of their share in the social structure. Between 1961 and 1985, the number of high-school graduates decreased by 14 percent, while that of higher education graduates decreased by 13 percent. Meanwhile, the number of vocational school graduates increased by 44 percent.

The most important tension, in this author's opinion, was that between the technocracy and the Ceaușescu regime. The technocrats—that is, the technical and managerial staff in the economy—had all been integrated into the Communist Party. Yet they were submitted to double pressure. On the one hand, Ceaușescu required them to produce and fulfill their plans without having the necessary energy, raw materials, spare parts, high-performance technologies, or salary funds. On the other hand, they were under the pressure exerted by workers, who refused to be held accountable for an economic inefficiency for which they were not responsible and who also had to face growing social problems. Managers were forced to distort production statistics to avoid being considered saboteurs. They were forced to accept economic orders from the center that they knew could not be satisfied locally. They had to approve with admiration the aberrant economic and technical instructions that Ceaușescu and his wife would "bestow" on them on the occasion of their frequent visits in factories, or at the just-as-frequent meetings managers had to attend in Bucharest. During the 1989 revolution, the technocratic industrial superstructure sided with the workers who went out in the streets. This fact, insufficiently studied in the political analyses of the Romanian revolution, contributed to a great extent to the overthrowing of the dictatorship in Romania.

DOMINANT ISSUES INHERITED BY POST-DICTATORIAL ROMANIA AFTER THE COLLAPSE OF THE COMMUNIST POWER ELITE

On the morning of December 22, 1989, the population started their decisive assault on the headquarters of the Communist Party in the center of Bucharest. Around noon, the Ceaușescus climbed on the roof of the building and left in an overcrowded helicopter. Some minutes later, the crowd stormed the building. By then, the army and a part of the dreaded Securitate had sided with the people. Soon after his flight, Ceaușescu was caught and taken into custody by the army. On December 25, 1989, after a hasty trial, Nicolae and Elena Ceaușescu were shot in the yard of the barracks in the town of Târgoviște.

What were the dominant issues inherited by the Romanian society after the downfall of the Ceaușescu clan? Many analysts consider that the major cleavage was the conflict between those who were supposedly the supporters of the communist regime and those who had declared themselves to be anti-Communists. More specifically, they consider that the former members of the Communist Party were fundamentally separated from those who had not been party members.

However, the almost four million Romanian communists did not actually represent the political elite and were in no way the pillars of stability for the communist regime. Most of them had become party members out of opportunism or in order to be able to hold a better professional and social position, which presupposed Communist Party membership. The real political elite, the "central nomenklatura," was about ten thousand people (Georgescu, 1992: 311). This was a rather primitive elite, recruited among workers and peasants in a proportion of 80 percent, poorly educated, and animated by the ambition to earn higher salaries, social privileges, and a higher status as party officials. Although they were obedient executors, most of them had not managed to acquire the communist ideology by the '80s, did not feel at ease when they had to promote the unpopular measures of the regime, and were not at all persuaded of Ceaușescu's infallibility or of the "glorious" perspectives of Romanian communism. They had no doubt that Ceaușescu was out of touch with reality and that the socialist human and social structures were in ruin. Yet they had adopted Ceaușescu's exalted nationalism and xenophobia and were using them as a grotesque legitimation of their support for a lost cause. It came as no surprise, then, that after the December revolution, the former political elite made no gesture in support of the communist regime and made no attempt to restore it, although many continued to point at an invisible enemy and tried to mobilize the population against the presupposed danger of communist restoration.

Another element that seemed to express a deep cleavage was the relationship between the Romanians and the Hungarian minority in Romania. From a demographic standpoint, Romanians represented about 89 percent, while the Hungarians represented about 7 percent of the total population. Most Hungarians live in several counties in Transylvania. The popular revolt against Ceaușescu started in Timisoara in the form of a spontaneous civic protest against the forced eviction of the Hungarian priest Laszlo Tökés from his home. Tökés became a symbol for the revolt. In a speech aired on December 20, and later on, during his trial on December 25, Ceaușescu suggested that the Romanian revolution was nothing but an international plot for the dismemberment of Romania. These details, but more than that, the violent interethnic conflicts in the former Yugoslavia and Transnistria, increased the fears of the public concerning the possibility of Hungarian secessionism in Transylvania. But the tensions between Romanians and Hungarians for real or imaginary, rational or irrational causes, were the consequences of postrevolutionary political evolution rather than the sequels of the communist regime. At the time of Ceaușescu's overthrow, the Romanian-Hungarian relationships did not contain any conflictual, and even less explosive, charge. Although the communist political elite had engaged in a nationalist rhetoric and tolerated or encouraged xenophobic attitudes, including anti-Hungarian, anti-Jewish, and anti-Russian feelings, Ceaușescu himself had been obsessed with the idea of social and national homogenization, and attempts had been made to reduce the political influence of the Hungarian minority of Transylvania, nonetheless there had been no program of systematic suppression of ethnic groups nor had ethnic minorities had a poorer life than the majority.

Thus although subsequently the Romanian and Hungarian nationalistic drive managed to mobilize important sections of the public belonging to the two ethnic groups, the confrontation between Romanian and Hungarian nationalists was not based on a major interethnic cleavage. The dominant issues that Romania was to inherit immediately upon the fall of the communist political elite were related to economic survival and were almost identical for all social strata because of the nature of the social structure shaped by the communist society.

At that moment, 60 percent of the active population was employed in industry, and industry was fully state-owned. About 30 percent worked in an agriculture organized in cooperatives; only 10 percent of the workforce was employed in services. The former social base of the Communist Party—the workers, and partially the peasants—had been deceived and pauperized economically. These categories were employed in state-owned structures that had to start a difficult journey toward a market economy. They could be neither destroyed nor made more effective overnight from an economic point of view.

Industrial workers were interested in keeping their jobs, higher salaries, the fulfillment of their needs (such as food and thermal energy), and their individual liberties. These were extremely urgent interests, shared by other social groups.

Moreover, after the traumatic experience of the revolution, *all* citizens wanted Romania to be protected from instability and the reproduction of violence.

The new political parties established after the Revolution were faced with the problem of mobilizing these segments of the population. The extent to which they would succeed and integrate the national community politically depended on the extent to which they recognized the real interests of the social categories they intended to represent.

NOTE

1. Vlad Georgescu was among the first analysts who, in the mid-eighties, predicted the imminent fall of the Romanian Communist regime: Georgescu, Vlad. 1992. op. cit, p. 302.

REFERENCES

Brucan, Silviu. 1992. *Generaţia irosită: Memorii.* Bucharest: Universul & Calistrat Hogaş.
Bulei, Ion. 1996. *Scurta istorie a românilor.* Bucharest: Merovia.
Chirot, Daniel. 1994. *Modern Tyrants: The Power and Prevalence of Evil in Our Age.* New York: The Free Press.
Enescu, Constantin. 1937. Semnificaţia alegerilor din decembrie 1937 în evoluţia, politică a neamului românesc. *Sociologie românească,* II (11), 512–26.
Georgescu, Vlad. 1992. *Istoria românilor de la origini pân ă în zilele noastre.* Bucharest: Humanitas.
Hitchins, Keith. 1996. *Romania: 1866–947.* Bucharest: Humanitas.
Jowitt, Kenneth. 1971. *Revolutionary Breakthroughs and National Development: The Case of Romania, 1944–1965.* Berkeley and Los Angeles: University of California Press.
Rosetti, Radu. 1908. *Pentru ce s-au răsculat ţăranii.* Bucharest (unpublished).
Weber, Eugen. 1937. "The Men of the Archangel." *Journal of Contemporary History 1* 1: 101–27.
———. 1966. "Romania." In Hans Rogger and Eugen Weber (eds.), *The European Right.* London: Wiendenfeld & Nicholson 501–75.

Part III

Cleavages and Parties after 1989

8

Past and New Cleavages in Post-Communist Bulgaria

Georgi Karasimeonov

THE NATURE OF POST-COMMUNIST CLEAVAGES

The post-communist Bulgarian political system did not inherit a structurally responsive democratic party system nor had there ever been, even in the pre-communist era, conditions favoring the "freezing" of a relatively stable party system.

Cleavages reflect deep and permanent conflicts and divisions in society. In a society undergoing a period of radical transformation, a period of "liminality" in Dutch anthropologist Arnold van Gennep's three-stage scheme (Bauman, 1994: 15), there can be no cleavage structure which in Lipset and Rokkan's sense determines stable party formation.

Historical time is needed in which divisions and conflicts characterizing postcommunism will motivate more or less permanent political behavior and transform into cleavages that will determine the new party structures and systems. The new cleavages will on one side be a product of irrational, chaotic formation of new societal relations, and on the other side of rational decisions by the new democratic power structures. Some of their contours can be observed today; others will appear in the future, determined by the process of reformation of society. (This gradual process was understood by Stein Rokkan; in a later work on Norway he formulated six steps in the process of translating cleavages into political and organizational structures [Rokkan, 1990: 140].)

The party subsystem of a nascent new society and political system will scarcely reflect any stable political and party identification and preferences on the basis of cleavages typical for established democracies. Thus, there is room for enriching Lipset and Rokkan's cleavage theory, and developments in Central and Eastern Europe give us such a chance. In this chapter I introduce a new typology of cleavages that could help us to understand the appearance and disappearance of cleavages and political parties in that region of the world.

Post-communist societies reveal at least four types of cleavages: residual (historic), transitional, potential (emergent), and actual.

Residual or *historic cleavages* are those inherited from the pre-communist past that manifest themselves anew in the post-communist reality. *Transitional cleavages* are those that determine party formation and divisions at the initial stage of transition, but later disappear or are "swallowed" by new cleavages typical for the period of consolidation of post-communist society. *Potential (emergent) cleavages* are those major issues and conflicts in post-communist society that are in the phase of appearance and might become actual cleavages as a consequence of the development of the new economic and political system. And *new (actual) cleavages* are those that are a product of the post-communist society and are permanent enough to determine party formation.

All these cleavages are present in the nascent democracies in a different proportion depending on their historical and more recent developments, their traditions, and their culture.

Conflicts in nonconsolidated democracies of a post-communist type differ radically from the classical four dimensional type of cleavages analyzed by Lipset and Rokkan. Political parties find themselves at the initial mobilization phase (Lipset and Rokkan, 1967: 136) and have to establish their identities and links with a stable electorate. This process finds itself in flux because parties need enough time to experiment with their policy orientations and test them in several election rounds until a certain stability of party-voter relationship establishes itself.

Bill Lomax observes that in East-Central Europe the "political identities and cleavages they do represent are based neither on social interest, nor political programs, nor structured belief systems . . . to the extent that such cleavages exist . . . they cut across the parties almost equally . . . each party has its liberals, its nationalists, its conservatives, its social democrats, its populists, its radicals" (Lomax, 1995: 185).

Most of the new parties are spiritual communities very often based on affect and emotions rather than on interest or reason. They reflect not so much societal divisions, as clashes among elites, personal sympathies, and animosities.

Similar observations cause Bernhardt Wessels and Hans-Dieter Klingemann to introduce the concept of "flattened societies" where the citizens are unable to define their political interests in relation to their location in the social structure. To a great part this is a result of the fact that the location of individuals in the societal structure is determined by the state as the largest and practically only employer (Wessels and Klingemann, 1994: 12–13).

Parties in post-communism not only reflect conflicts but are also agents of conflicts. Their policies influence the formation of cleavages more than those of parties in any established democracy. Their political role and the type of relations between parties (confrontational or more tolerant, consensus oriented) can become a major factor for the transformation of certain conflicts and issues into cleavages. In other words, parties not only reflect cleavages, but because of the fact that "politics" dominates the "economy" at the initial phase of changes, they are a major factor of the radical restructuring of society. On their political involvement and their role as parties in government depends which conflicts and issues will have a major impact on the new societies and how they will or will not be resolved.[1]

In communist societies, old "historical" cleavages were subdued or swallowed and "replaced" by radical new types of divisions and conflicts that have no or very little resemblance to pre-communist historical and societal circumstances. This was particularly true in societies with underdeveloped capitalism that lacked pre-communist stable democratic political systems and culture such as Bulgaria, Romania, and Albania. Consequently, post-communist societies did not inherit the traditional cleavages and their recent party development reflects primarily the clashes and contradictions of the last phase of the communist regime before its downfall.

The class cleavage and urban-rural cleavage reappeared in Bulgaria more as a psychological phenomenon for part of the older electorate than as a reflection of a real conflict. The "new working class" that emerged in socialist times was a privileged group compared to other social strata in the communist regime, and never experienced the contradictions inherent in the class conflicts that marked advanced capitalist countries in their historical development, not to mention the lack of "class consciousness" or solidarity.[2] Similar is the case of the rural community of the past which had been transformed by speedy urbanization processes over the last forty-five years and today encompasses mostly older people favored by socialist transformation and modernization of the agrarian economy.[3]

Communist Bulgaria was a highly atomized society where social links of a solidaristic type were limited to certain subgroups of a patrimonial type (family) or to intellectual circles. The class or social group feeling was missing. Their reactivation will be a question of time with the establishment of market economy and civil society.

PARTY PLURALISM AT THE INITIAL STAGE OF TRANSFORMATION

The formation of party structures in Bulgaria reveals two major periods after 1989, each of which is characterized by a different set of conflicts. These divisions may later transform into cleavages and become more or less a determining factor in the establishment of the post-communist party system.

The *first period* is characterized by the initial transformation and democratization of the political system. In most post-communist societies, as well as in Bulgaria, this first period was dominated by one major division and conflict, or transitional cleavage revealed in the struggle between two major political blocks.

On one side were the supporters and the driving political forces of the reform movement united in the Union of Democratic Forces (UDF), and on the other, the representatives of the old system grouped around the Communist party. The conflicts and political struggles between them determined the initial party formation. The political alignments were mostly psychologically motivated, based on ideological confrontation. Wessels and Klingeman write of a "super issue"—reform-communism versus liberal democracy, which has structured the merging party systems in the first phase of democratization (Wessels and Klingemann, 1994: 12).

The major issue behind that ideological confrontation was the redistribution of power resources between old and new elites. The center of the struggle was the elimination of the power monopoly of the communist party which had its roots in all layers of the party-state structure.

Although the anti-communists and the reform-communists had similar views on the necessity of change, the struggle for the redistribution of power resources put them into different camps. The latter were the main target of the newly established opposition which faced them at the Round Table talks, where some of the major decisions paving the road for democracy were set (Verheijen 1995: 105–16).

Both blocs were socially and ideologically heterogeneous, although the UDF much more so, and this heterogeneity was the cause for the later differentiation and divisions of both major blocs.

The proponents of radical reforms were assembled in the new parties that sprang up in the months after the downfall of the old regime which had formed the UDF. They included three major political groups. First, there were those that were led by some of the surviving members and leaders of the old "historical parties" like the Socialdemocratics, the Agrarian "Nikola Petkov," the Democratic party, and the Radical-Democratic party. Former dissidents in the Communist party who had taken part in various protest actions preceding the downfall of the communist regime constituted a second group. Most prominent among them were the Ecoglasnost movement, the Club for Glasnost and Democracy, and the Trade Union Podkrepa, whose leaders and members were mostly former members of the Communist party.

The third group consisted of newly created parties or organizations (for example, the Republican Party, the Christian-democratic Party) that joined the newly formed opposition—the coalition Union of Democratic Forces (UDF).[4] The supporters of the Union of Democratic Forces could be subdivided into *two major sub-groups:* the *restaurationists* (the representatives of the old privileged classes marginalized by the communists), who were longing for a "return to the past," and the *modernizers* from the newer generation opting for the westernization of society. The UDF was also divided between the *radicals*, supporting revolutionary "decommunization" and no compromises with the communists, and the *moderates*, who accepted the rules of parliamentary democracy and evolutionary change. At the initial stage the radicals and the moderates, the restaurationists and the modernizers, were recruited in one camp. Their lack of organization and financial and other resources (such as media) brought them together into a coalition facing a most powerful opponent, the ex-communists, renamed a few months after the regime change as the Socialist Party.

The convergence of these various sub-groups in the UDF was motivated by a one-dimensional policy and ideology: removal from power of the former communists. All their inner differences were subordinated in the name of the "liberty myth" and anti-communism. Their main characteristic was that their political activity was for the greater part value-determined, especially in the case of the young, the intellectuals, and the purely opportunistic by the goal of gaining power, a typical phenomenon for "outsiders" or political "turncoats."

The parties in the UDF were clientelist and charismatic elite-centered, more like friendly circles and cultural-milieu parties than authentic parties. They had a very heterogeneous electorate that caused internal differentiation and divisions as soon as the major task, eliminating the communists from power, had been achieved.

That the old cleavages had lost their relevance was revealed in the fact that the historical parties lost their initial advantages very quickly and were marginalized. This was the case for the socialdemocrats and the agrarians, who, in the past, had reflected the labor-capital and the center-periphery, rural-urban cleavages respectively. These cleavages had lost their significance and now played almost no role, as became even clearer at a later stage when they opted for a more moderate policy, defying the radical anti-Communists. Consequently, their initial influence dwindled drastically.

In the *communist camp* there were also two major groups present: the *supporters of reform* and the *conservatives*. The supporters of reform also had their radical and moderate wings. The radicals wanted a definite engagement with democratic change and break with the past, while the moderates stressed the need to keep the party together and were keen on preserving as long as possible their hold on the power structures.

In the conservative camp were the representatives of the "old guard" fighting to survive and keep their privileges and the political "hardliners," the Marxist ideologues.

Compared to other ex-communist parties, the Bulgarian one evaded serious splits between these groups and kept its relative strength and cohesion through the founding elections and into the period thereafter. It witnessed an erosion of its membership, but was able to transform gradually into a parliamentary party, preserving the core of its organizational structure and keeping a balance between the various wings.

The first period of party formation was characterized by a harsh confrontation between both major camps determined by the radicalization of the UDF after the founding elections and its attempts to implement a policy of extreme "decommunization," which reached its high point after the second round of parliamentary elections in November 1991.

At the same time, the radicals in the UDF lacked the necessary majority in parliament, and with time underwent internal divisions that weakened their political influence and undercut their efforts at marginalizing the ex-communists who remained powerful opponents.

The Bulgarian Socialist party (BSP) was able to use the internal divisions in the anti-Communist camp and "allow" the integration in the political system of moderate representatives of the UDF even though it retained its absolute parliamentary majority after the 1990 elections, thus lessening the pressure of the radicals. The policy of "appeasement" was most clearly demonstrated in the support the reform communists gave to the election of the leader of the UDF, Jelju Jelev, to the presidency in the summer of 1990. It showed the desire of the communists to compromise on the power question in the name of avoiding a radical "decommunization" and achieving a consensual relationship with the opposition.

Although the confrontation between the UDF and the BSP determined the political landscape for the following years, the "flexibility" of the communists and the internal instability and relative weakness of the UDF kept the political process on peaceful grounds, although at the same time it deterred the reform process and blocked the political dialogue between the major political forces. This was accentuated by the fact that the November 1991 parliamentary elections left the parliament without a clear majority and the key to any government formation in the hands of the small ethnic Turkish party—the Movement for Rights and Freedoms (MRF)—which used this unique opportunity to play with both sides so as to keep its leverage possibilities.

The integration of the MRF into the political system represents an interesting case of a peaceful and constructive resolution of the ethnic tensions that had reached their apex in the late 1980s as a consequence of the policy of assimilation initiated by the communist regime. Ethnic tensions remained a factor in the post-communist landscape, but they did not escalate into major conflicts endangering the democratic process.

Although the struggle between the UDF and the BSP was reflected in various political clashes, the main dividing line between them was who should have the initiative in the reform process and, following from that, who should be its main beneficiary. There was in reality no irreconcilable divergence between the elite of both blocks, as was clearly demonstrated in the activity of the Popov government (December 1990 through October 1991), a de facto coalition government that initiated the start of the reforms.

The divergence that sharpened the conflict was clustered around the question of who should control the levers of power in a society dominated by an all-powerful bureaucratic state. The lack of a private sector and the presence of a weak civil society, especially at the start of the reform, concentrated the political struggle in the state bureaucracy that detained the major decisionmaking resources. The power question overshadowed all other policy differences. Radical decommunization for the UDF meant mostly the marginalization of the communists in the main state structures.

As long as a normal balance between the public and the private sphere is not established and civil service laws do not create the necessary guarantees against political appointments and reprisals against public officials, the state bureaucracy will remain a major area of conflict between the political parties, a condition accentuated by the patronage tradition typical for Southern Europe. Those who keep the command of the state bureaucracy retain enormous resources to determine who the beneficiaries of the reform process will be, as is clear in the example of privatization.

The relative balance of power between the UDF and the BSP, and the unresolved "power" question until the parliamentary elections in 1994, blocked not only the reform process, but kept other issues and conflicts in the "shadow," preventing them from becoming a motivating factor for electoral behavior and party identification. It was the basis for the persistence of a bipolar, confrontational party "system" and determined government formation which was marked by instability and the lack of stable parliamentary majorities.

At the same time, the first transitional years brought major changes in the social, economic, and cultural situation of the country, which determined a new set of conflicts and potential cleavages that will, to a great extent, determine future party development and party identification.

The *second period* of the transition that started following the third parliamentary elections in December 1994 was characterized by relative consolidation of democracy and marked by the peaceful rotation of power between the major protagonists. The confrontation between the two major blocs, although hampering the effective work of the democratic institutions, had not endangered the democratic system itself.

The electoral results, which gave a resounding victory to the socialists, could also be seen as a defeat for the extreme anti-Communists in the UDF and their policy aimed at radical "decommunization." The majority of the population had expectations that the socialist government would stabilize the economic situation and guarantee their well-being. Quite the opposite happened. The BSP leadership was reluctant to start the painful, but urgent, reforms and by the end of 1996 it had lost most of its former support. On one hand, it succumbed to the interests of the nomenclature capitalists, who were not ready to lose positions in the state-run economy and accept a real-market economy based on competition; on the other hand, the social base of the BSP was not disposed to accept the new social differentiation that the reforms would have created. Pressed between those two poles, the BSP lost control of the situation and was unable to stop the deterioration of the economy, which led to internal party confrontations and anti-government rallies during January 1997. Afraid that its policy could cause serious civil unrest, the government resigned, leading to preterm elections in April 1997. They gave a resounding victory to the UDF, which was once again able, after its short-lived stay in power in 1991–1992, to form the government and initiate the delayed reforms. On its success depends the success of the march toward democratic consolidation. This will also determine the "fate" of new and old cleavages.

CLEAVAGES, PARTIES, AND THE CONSOLIDATION OF POST-COMMUNISM

In post-communist Bulgaria, compared to other countries in Central and Eastern Europe, residual (historic) cleavages have a very limited effect on party formation. One reason is that communist rule had a much more radical effect on society than in some other countries. However, new cleavages are now emerging and are likely to have an effect on the party system in the course of future developments.

Socioeconomic Cleavages

The chaotic and, in many ways, irrational, transition from a centrally planned economy to a market economy leads to fundamental changes in the social structure of the post-communist society. Its major features are the radical polarization between a fast growing "class" of social marginals and poor, and a small caste of an affluent oligarchy, in its greatest part the heirs of the "red bourgeoisie" that amassed its riches from hidden privatization of the old state property. This process leads to the formation of a society where the great majority are the "losers" and a small minority are the "winners" in the transition to market economy.

This cleavage is clearly different from the class cleavage typical for the early development of today's capitalist countries because it is not based on a capital-labor conflict. Its roots are in the massive impoverishment of great masses of people in all social, professional, and age groups and the melting away of the "leveled" society and the socialist "middle" class which had a certain stability in living conditions and security in the patronage state.[5]

Another potential cleavage will derive from the conflict between the interests of the national capital represented in the major economic groups and the state bureaucracy which holds in its command great resources in the dominant sectors of the economy. The process of privatization, leading to an enlargement of the private sector of the economy, undermines the decisionmaking perimeter of the state and its representatives in the various structures. This loss of resources is met with resistance in the state bureaucracy, which is losing part of its privileges and material benefits (including from corruption), especially in the lower levels of the state machine.

On another level, this contradiction creates a growing gap between the great majority dependent on the state redistributive capacities (especially the salaried state employees and social groups dependent on the inherited centralized social security funds) and the minority which are engaged in the private sector, especially in its most dynamic areas. This contradiction sharpens in the conditions of financial deficits and dwindling state budgets. Free enterprise is facing growing animosity and restrictive policies, especially on the part of left-wing parties.

Another conflict influencing party politics is that between the criminal capital, which prospers in the conditions of economic anarchy and the absence of laws regulating the market economy, and the "legal" economic groups, who are ready to abide by the rule of law in the developing post-communist market economy. The first amassed its fortunes from speculation, tax evasion, and various criminal activities (drugs, racketeering, etc.) that favor the "feodalization" of the country, weak democratic institutions, the growing "corruptization" of politics. The second will opt for the modernization of the country and be ready to cooperate with those political groups and parties following similar goals.

With the growing integration of the country in the international economic institutions and the opening of the national market for foreign capital, contradictions will arise between the relatively weak national capital looking for protectionist policies and the "foreigners." This cleavage will intertwine with specific cleavages developing because of the foreign policy orientation of the country.

Sociopolitical Cleavages

The establishment and autonomization of a viable civil society, and indeed the whole process of "detotalitarization" of the post-communist society, will dominate party formation and party policies for a long time to come. Its major reflection is the conflict and opposition between the state and all social and professional groups attempting to enlarge their sphere of autonomous activity, the "islands of civil society"—private entrepreneurs, media, universities, nongovernmental bodies, and so on. Politically, it pits all groups and parties that embody the interests of the state bureaucracy and the collectivist, statist-oriented social groups, against the representatives of civil society, from the entrepreneurs to the intellectuals and professional groups trying to escape dependence on the old "socialist" state, that is, those who most passionately represent the values of liberal democracy, freedom, and private property.[6]

National–Ethnic Cleavages

As already mentioned, ethnic conflicts do not have the explosive character typical for other Balkan countries surrounding Bulgaria. The consequences of the assimilatory policies of the communist regime in the '80s were rebuffed by all major political parties and the principle of ethnic and religious freedom was established in the new Constitution.

At the same time, the new Constitution declares the illegitimacy of parties based on ethnic, racial, or religious lines (Art. 11). This article, contested by some constitutionalists, is a reflection of the specific internal and geopolitical situation of Bulgaria and the fears of most political parties that purely ethnic parties (especially of the Turkish minority encompassing around 10 percent of the population) could endanger the sovereignty of the state. That is why the Movement for Rights and Freedoms that originally registered as a "political movement," although socially based mostly in the Turkish population, has declared itself a national party. The later ruling by the Constitutional court allowing the MRF to participate in political life and its willingness to integrate in the political system, plus its actual participation in government formation over the past years, has substantially lowered ethnic and religious tensions.

However, such tensions could be reactivated by the growth of "Bulgarian nationalism" or by religious fundamentalism in the Turkish population, represented in both cases by the activity of marginal political parties and groupings. A change of orientation of the MRF toward a policy furthering ethnic tensions with demands for national autonomy would also exacerbate ethnic division.

Although far from the extent in some Western European countries, xenophobia is on the rise in Bulgaria, provoked by marginal extremist groups. Such sentiments could be exploited by some parties as the economic crisis marginalizes growing numbers, especially among the younger generation.[7]

Religious and Cultural Cleavages

Although religion has never played a dominant role in party formation in Bulgarian politics, in the aftermath of communist ideological dominance and forced atheism, a deep cultural-value vacuum has ensued, leading to growing disorientation in peoples' minds. The role of the dominant Church (Greek orthodox) was greatly weakened by internal struggles that led to a loss of authority and influence.

The cultural-value crisis is sharpened by the educational crisis and destabilization of family life. This has left the field open for a multitude of pseudoreligious groups and sects that "invaded" post-communist countries, including Bulgaria. Their destructive influence, combined with the growth of islamic fundamentalism in parts of the Turkish minority, has led to an undermining of national religious and cultural values, especially in the younger generation. This situation brings to the forefront the issue of safeguarding national identity and culture versus groups and values furthering national nihilism.

Cleavages on International Policy and Orientation

Bulgaria's political life has been strongly influenced by its historical development and geopolitical situation. Foreign policy issues and conflicts have often determined political alignments and realignments and the orientation of political parties.

Post-communist realities reveal similar tendencies. Two major political orientations are influencing party policies—the pro-European, integrationist on one side, and the panslavic, nationalist on the other. In the new international conditions, the issue of NATO reveals to the greatest extent the clash between these two groups as the first represented by the UDF and the other by circles in the BSP, burdened by its past allegiances to Russia. A sharpening of the conflict between Russia and the West will undoubtedly have a great impact on the parties' policies and their internal divisions.

CONCLUDING REMARKS

These major nascent and potential cleavages will undoubtedly have a major effect on the existing or future parties. A typical phenomenon is that most of these cleavages are crosscutting and determine not only differences and conflicts between political parties, but also within the parties themselves, a fact that will lead to internal restructuring and to various, sometimes unexpected, political alliances.

The emergence of potential cleavages is only one prerequisite and factor for creating political motivations and orientations, and party preferences. To become determining factors of party identification they must translate into permanent political interests motivating electoral behavior and attachments toward one or another party. This means that post-communist parties are facing two major challenges. The first is to prove their effectiveness as parties in government which are able to react to conflicts and cleavages so as to satisfy electoral demands and expectations. The first transitional years are too short a period (at the same time marked by instability) to create stable evaluations of the political parties' efficiency as government parties. Although, at the end of 1995, most major parties in Bulgaria did have a chance to accede to government positions and have their short history as parliamentary and governing parties (in local governments as well), it is just not enough to form stable party preferences on the basis of comparative experience. The electorate as a whole still has only vague and superficial perceptions of the governing potential of the major parties.

Several rounds of rotation in power by the different political parties will create more or less permanent political allegiances and transform post-communist cleavages into more determining factors for party identification. The parties' policies as response to the conflicts and issues generated by cleavages will become the major factor in determining electoral behavior and party allegiances in the coming years.

The second challenge they must face is the establishment of linkage networks with all sectors of civil society, which will enable them to absorb electoral demands and political interests and transform them into practical policy decisions. This will mean creating organizational structures and overcoming the clientelist nature typical for many new parties as well the establishment of links with major interest groups (trade unions, nongovernmental structures, civic organizations).

Although there are certain "primary attachments" to one or another political party and coalition (Kitschelt, Dimitrov and Kanev, 1995: 158), it will take quite a long time to establish a structured party system with a degree of firm and predictable linkages between citizens and political parties. In the near future, under the influence of emergent cleavages, today's major parties and coalitions will face further internal restructuring and will have to reaffirm their identity.

The BSP as a conglomerate of at least three wings (socialdemocrats, pragmatists, and marxists) will experience deep internal conflicts mostly between the left wing-oriented members and electorate, and those leaders associated with the new bourgeoisie.

The UDF will move from a coalition of parties to a more homogenous political formation, but in that process it will have to determine its value orientation and overcome its one-dimensional, still-dominant anti-communist confrontational orientation. It will have to react to the new issues and emergent cleavages to achieve political stability and overcome the shrinking of its electoral base. It will face the challenge of the newly established center-left coalition, the Peoples Union, which is trying to project the image of a responsible conservative force exploiting the political inheritance of the agrarian party.

The MRF will detain its ethnic identity, but its role in the new political system will depend to a large part on its ability to counter religious fundamentalism and escape the provocations of Bulgarian nationalists.

NOTES

1. For example, laws pertaining to restitution of property, or privatization laws, or those concerning ethnic questions, are most likely to create, sharpen, or soften certain conflicts and issues that could evolve into cleavages.

2. That is why, in the founding and more recent elections, blue-collar workers voted heavily for the pro-market oriented UDF, motivated by quite other than class-oriented behavior. See chapter 13.

3. That is why the rural population supported heavily the former Communist party and not the traditionally pro-agrarian Bulgarian Peoples Agrarian Union which, in the pre-communist times, had been a major political force.

4. For details see Karasimeonov, Georgi. 1995. "Differentiation postponed: Party Pluralism in Bulgaria." In G. Whightman (ed.), *Party Formation in East Central-Europe*, 154–79. Elgar.

5. This cleavage reveals itself in the findings of the latest national surveys where 77.3 percent of the respondents declared that the conflict between rich and poor is the major contradiction in Bulgaria's society. BBSS Gallup International Yearly Report, 191. Sofia 1995.

6. In the public mind this specific cleavage is demonstrated in the conflict between government and governed which, for 76 percent of the surveyed, is a major contradiction of post-communism. BBSS Gallup Yearly Report, 191.

7. This cleavage is revealed in the fact that fifty-five percent of the respondents in the Gallup yearly report point to contradictions between Bulgarians and minorities as a major conflict in political and social life. BBSS Gallup Yearly Report, 191.

REFERENCES

Bauman, Zygmunt. 1994. "After the Patronage State." In C. Bryant and E. Mokryzky, *The Great Transformation?* London: Routledge.

Kitschelt, Herbert, Dimitar Dimitrov and Assen Kanev. 1995. "The Structuring of the Vote in Post-Communist Party Systems: The Bulgarian Example." *European Journal of Political Research* 27.

Lipset, Seymour and Stein Rokkan. 1967. "Cleavage Structures, Party Systems, and Voter Alignments." In Peter Mair (ed.), *The West European Party System*. Oxford: Oxford University Press.

Lomax, Bill. 1995. "Impediments to Democratization in Post-communist East-Central Europe." In G. Whightman (ed.), *Party Formation in East-Central Europe*. Aldershot: Elgar.

Rokkan, Stein. 1990. "Towards a Generalized Concept of Verzuiling." In P. Mair (ed.), *The West European Party System*. New York: Oxford University Press.

Verheijen, Tony. 1995. *Constitutional Pillars for New Democracies*. 105–16. Leiden: DSWO Press.

Wessels, Bernhard and Hans-Dieter Klingemann. 1994. *Democratic Transformation and the Prerequisites of Democratic Opposition in East and Central Europe*. Papers from Wissenschaftszentrum Berlin, July 1994.

9

Czech Political Parties and Cleavages after 1989

──────── Josef Blahož, Lubomír Brokl, and
Zdenka Mansfeldová

INTRODUCTION

As of the beginning of November 1989 there existed three political parties in the Czech Republic (and six in all of Czechoslovakia): the Communist Party of Czechoslovakia, the Czechoslovak Socialist Party, and the Czechoslovak People's Party. In practice, however, the nation functioned as a one-party system, with all three parties closely associated in a "National Front" led by the Communist Party.

In December 1989, the Federal Assembly of the late Czechoslovak Socialist Republic adopted a resolution canceling the fourth article of the constitution and thereby the leading role of the Communist party. On January 23, 1990, law No. 15/1990 defined basic conditions for the establishment of political parties and movements and on February 27, 1990, a new election law was enacted.

In the following months, popular fascination with newfound freedoms led to an explosion in Czechoslovakian political party life. Old parties were renewed, new parties were formed, and associations and unions of the most distinct nature, whose objectives and functions were often mutually intertwined, confused and mistaken, took the name of party. Associations eager to acquire political power but with none of the other usual attributes declared themselves as parties.

Nearly ten years later, the process of forming and crystallizing the party system continues in what is now the Czech Republic, and the links among interests, class, party, and cleavages are not yet clearly established.

At the time of the revolution, rudimentary structures were already in place for some of the newer parties, and some of the historical political parties quickly revived (for example, the party known as Czechoslovak Social Democracy, later the Czech Social Democratic Party), evoking their history and tradition as grounds for legitimacy. During the first two years of the transformation, the political profile of the new parties was hard to identify. Many were ephemeral in character. All stationed themselves to the right of the Communists, in what can be termed a wide political center. In this chapter we seek to analyze the divisions in popular opinion and describe the emerging cleavages on which the new political party system has been based.

FORMATION OF A NEW COMPETITIVE MULTIPARTY SYSTEM

There were sixty-six political parties registered by the Ministry of the Interior and an additional twenty-seven parties still hoping to be registered for the parliamentary elections of June 1990.[1] In this spectrum it was already possible to distinguish the right, the left, and the center, although the boundaries were not always clear. Right- and center-oriented parties were more plentiful than parties on the left.

When the election took place (June 8–9), sixteen political parties, movements, and election alliances ran candidates for election to the Federal Assembly from within the Czech Republic, and thirteen parties offered candidates for the Czech parliament (Czech National Council).

The new election law abolished the old single-member district system used under communist rule and reintroduced the proportional representation system that had existed in the first Czechoslovak Republic, with party lists. Some politicians and political scientists had argued for a mixed electoral system or a first-past-the-post system, believing that the stronger majority thereby obtained would serve as a barrier against potential future extreme multipartism. But the prevailing view was that proportional representation was essential during a period of strong anticommunistic cleavage.

However, an attempt was nevertheless made to limit political fragmentation and prevent the extreme pluralism that had been typical in the prewar parliament, by establishing 5 percent of the vote as the threshold for a party's entrance into the federal parliament. When two or three parties or movements allied and ran a single list of candidates, the threshold became 7 percent; for alliances of four and more parties, the figure was 10 percent. Similar thresholds obtained at the level of the Czech National Council: 5 percent for one party, 7 percent for alliances composed of two parties, 9 percent for an alliance of three parties, and 11 percent for four and more parties. The setting of thresholds had the desired effect: Only four political organizations succeeded in acquiring sufficient votes to be seated in each of the two legislative bodies.

As Table 9.1 makes clear, the parliamentary elections of 1992 brought the decisive victory of the right-wing, cosmopolitan, civic, and market-oriented Civic

Table 9.1
Results of 1990, 1992, and 1996 Parliamentary Elections: for the Composition of Czech Government, Federal Government, and Federal Assembly after Election (over 5 percent of votes)

Party	Composition of Czech Government							Composition of Federal Government				Composition of Federal Assembly							
	1990				1992				1996				1990		1992		1990				1992			
	Parliamentary seats		Cabinet posts		Parliamentary seats		Cabinet posts		Parliamentary seats		Cabinet posts						House of Nations		House of People		House of Nations		House of People	
	N.	%	N.	%	N.	%	N.	%	N.	%	N.	%	N.	%	N.	%	Mandate	%	Mandate	%	Mandate	%	Mandate	%
OF	127	49.6	10	47.6	—	—	—	—	—	—	—	—	9	56.3	—	—	50	49.9	68	53.1	—	—	—	—
ODS	—	—	—	—	—	—	11	58.0	—	—	8	50.0	—	—	4	40.0	—	—	—	—	37	33.4	48	33.9
KDS	—	—	—	—	—	—	2	10.5	—	—	—	—	—	—	—	—	—	—	—	—	—	—	—	—
ODS	—	—	—	—	76	29.7	—	—	68	29.6	—	—	—	—	—	—	—	—	—	—	—	—	—	—
KDS	—	—	—	—	—	—	—	—	—	—	—	—	—	—	—	—	—	—	—	—	—	—	—	—
KDU/ČSL	19	8.4	2	9.52	15	6.3	4	21.0	18	8.1	4	22.5	—	—	1	10.0	6	8.8	9	8.7	6	6.1	7	6.0
ODA	—	—	—	—	14	5.9	2	10.5	13	6.4	4	22.5	—	—	—	—	—	—	—	—	—	—	—	—
HSD-SMS	22	10.0	1	4.76	14	5.9	—	—	—	—	—	—	—	—	—	—	7	9.1	9	7.9	—	—	—	—
LSU	—	—	—	—	16	6.5	—	—	—	—	—	—	—	—	—	—	—	—	—	—	—	—	—	—
ČSSD	—	—	—	—	16	6.5	—	—	61	26.4	—	—	—	—	—	—	—	—	—	—	—	—	—	—
KSČM	32	13.2	—	—	—	—	—	—	22	10.3	—	—	—	—	—	—	12	13.8	15	13.1	—	—	—	—
LB	—	—	—	—	35	14.1	—	—	—	—	—	—	—	—	—	—	—	—	—	—	15	14.5	19	14.3
HZDS	—	—	—	—	—	—	—	—	—	—	—	—	—	—	4	40.0	—	—	—	—	—	—	—	—
SPR-RSČ	—	—	—	—	6.0	14	—	—	18	8.0	—	—	—	—	—	—	—	—	—	—	6	6.4	8	6.5

VPN	—	—	—	—	—	—	—	—	—	4	25.0	—	—
KDH	—	—	—	—	—	—	—	—	—	2	12.3	—	—
Independent	—	—	8	38.1	—	—	—	—	—	1	6.3	1	10.0
Other parties	200	18.8	—	—	200	19.1	150	11.1	—	—	—	—	—
									18.4	—	16.8	—	26.8	—	25.8

Names of Parties, Movements, and Coalitions: OF–Civic Forum; ODS–Civic Democratic Party; KDS–Christian Democratic Party; ODS-KDS–Christian Democratic Party merged with Democratic Party in 1996; KDU-ČSL–Christian Democratic Union and Czechoslovak Peoples' Party; ODA–Civic Democratic Alliance; HSD-SMS–Self-governing Democracy Movement-Association for Moravia and Silesia; LSU–Liberal Social Union, a grouping consisted of three collective members: Czechoslovak Socialist Party, Green Party and Agrarian Party; ČSSD–Czech Social Democratic Party; KSČM–Communist Party of Bohemia and Moravia; LB–Left Block, a coalition consisted of Left Block and the Communist Party of Bohemia and Moravia; HZDS–Movement for a Democratic Slovakia; SPR-RSČ–Association for the Republic-Republican Party of Czechoslovakia; KDS-Christian Democratic Party.

Democratic Party (ODS) in the Czech Republic. Furthermore, in comparison with the 1990 election results, there were more parties in parliaments after the 1992 election (seven parties in the Federal parliament and nine parties in the Czech parliament), although some of the new parties had taken part in the 1990 election on the lists of other parties (for example, ODA on the list of Civic Forum, KDS on the list of KDU-ČSL). The 1996 elections, which took place after the Czech Republic was no longer linked to Slovakia, brought a drop in the number of parties winning parliamentary representation, now down to six. (More detailed information about the percentage of votes and seats received by all of the parties represented in Parliament is presented in part IV, chapter 14).

By 1997, the governing coalition consisted of the above mentioned Civic Democratic Party, the right-wing Civic Democratic Alliance (ODA) and the only remaining Christian party, the historical Christian Democratic Union—Czech People's Party. The other small Christian party, the Christian Democratic Party, founded in 1990, merged in 1995 with ODS. The strongest opposition party was the Czech Social Democratic Party (ČSSD), situated on the left center of the political spectrum. The only extreme left-wing party represented in Parliament was the Communist Party of Bohemia and Moravia (KSČM).

The Communist Party had not collapsed. Although it had certainly lost members, it maintained its hard core of support and a stable electorate. It had become old and isolated, and occupied a far lesser place in the party system, but it had not disappeared. Other leftist parties (for examples, the Left Bloc, the Party of the Democratic Left, and the Party of Czechoslovak Communists) had broken away from the CP but remained with it in an isolated political ghetto (Mansfeldová, 1996: 8). The divisiveness of the left is one of the new characteristics of the Czech political system.

The extreme right was represented by the Association of the Republic—Republican Party of Czechoslovakia (SPR-RSČ). The SPR-RSČ offered a populist and nationalist (anti-German) program based on xenophobia, not on solving the Republic's relationship with Germans and especially with Sudeten Germans.

There were no significant parties in the center. The only party at all likely to give the center greater significance was the Free Democrats. Prior to the 1996 elections this party was able to co-opt the Liberal National Socialist Party. It makes its appeal to intellectuals and others in the professions (doctors, teachers), but so far with little success.

Except for the weakness of the political center, the range of parties in the Czech Republic was now similar to that in other European democracies (Brokl, 1994: 8). The multiparty nature of the new Republic thus seems well established, although it is likely that the largest parties on the right and left, the ODS and the ČSSD, will continue to grow. The ODS has a fairly stable electorate, while that of the ČSSD is less so. The KDU-ČSL, representing Christian values and Christian solidarity in the formulation of social policy, is also likely to maintain an important role, given its markedly Christian orientation and following.

The ODA had some difficulty distinguishing itself from the ODS. Although this party seeks to stress its differences from the leading party, in fact it seems to vary only in its opinions regarding decentralization (the ODA would prefer decentralization of government, while the ODS urges a strong centralized state).

Although the party spectrum appears to be divided between right and left, with an almost nonexistent center, in practice the policy recommendations of both right- and left-wing parties tend to fall in the center. Although polarization or at least left-right differentiation is apparent in the coalition-opposition system, at the same time moves toward integration are found at both ends of the political spectrum. The general public would prefer to see more parties in the center, but this concern is now felt less intensely than heretofore.[2]

This form of party-system development provides an interesting contrast with that of advanced democracies of Western Europe, and also with that of the United States. The Czech system demonstrates what we may call the "Dazzled with Democracy" tendency of post-totalitarian systems. Under such conditions, those who create new parties are naturally keen to exercise their opportunities for free choice and little tempted to compromise their positions by moving precipitously toward the center. Whether a system fixed in such circumstances will endure must depend largely on its capacity to incorporate existing cleavages, a topic to which we now turn.

CONTEMPORARY DIVISIONS OF OPINION

As it became possible to express political opinions more freely after 1989, it became clear that the Czech people were and still are divided on the following key problems:

Economic Transformation

From the beginning, a key factor in the formation of preferences for political parties in the Czech Republic was the nature of opinions regarding economic reform. Although there has been widespread support for economic reform, for privatization and restitution of property, there have been important differences as to what method of privatization should be followed. Key questions have revolved around the role of the state, the speed of the process, and who should have the right to participate in the process of privatization and restitution (in particular, what should be the rights of the former communist nomenclature and of emigrants). Also of concern has been the role of foreign investment and the degree of participation of foreign companies in the process.

The Relationship between Civic Society and Political System

Modern associations, cooperatives, and organizations of civic society began developing in the Czech lands at the end of the eighteenth century and the beginning of nineteenth century, as the Age of Reason and industrialization came to the Hapsburg monarchy. The emergent civil society, evolving at the local level where self-government was often able to function independently of the state and German domination, contributed strongly to the Czech national revival. This civil society, the counterpart of totalitarianism, was almost entirely destroyed during the years of communism as completely incompatible with its principles; what fragments remained were adjusted to totalitarian principles. Thus, as of November 1989, practically every aspect of life depended on the leading role of the Communist Party.

During the first years after November 1989, a number of original associations and organizations recovered, many organizations were newly established, and the organizations officially operated by the regime changed their subject and orientation. However, in contrast to the past, most of these associations and organizations have lacked the social and economic background to be able to exert a strong influence on policy.

Indeed, some organizations and their initiatives were greeted with widespread mistrust, especially by those whose political opinions placed them on the right. Trade unions, professional chambers, and other nonparty organizations had existed throughout the period of totalitarian rule with the approval of the Communist Party and had tended to serve merely as its instruments. For many of the new democrats, the ideal model of society, and thus of a political system, was a simple one: there would be no place for civic organizations and associations; there would be merely the citizens on the one hand and the state on the other. The main representative of this view was Václav Klaus, the head of the ODS, but other right-wing parties followed suit.

At first, it might seem that the distrust of the Communist party and related associations would automatically extend to parties as well as other intermediary groups, and thereby cause a new interest in the institutions of direct democracy, and in particular in the use of the referendum. Such, however, has not been the case. The referendum is rejected not only because its use might be disadvantageous to the coalition in power (as the opposition claims), but also because of the long and negative experience Czechs have had with the so-called "popular vote" of the totalitarian system, a vote which was never more than a prearranged manifestation of support for those in power. It is quite understandable that most citizens, never having had experience with genuine direct democracy, do not want anything that reminds them of the simplistic and meaningless votes of the totalitarian years. However effective an instrument of democracy the referendum may be in smaller communities, it has not yet won approval in the Czech Republic, because parties are seen as safer vehicles for the expression of the popular will in the new democracy. On the other hand, there is a recognition that for the transformation of society to take place quickly and in a systematic fashion, a measure of centralism is required.

In any case, popular opinion on these questions deserves some attention as the basis for one of the important problems of today. For although over 80 percent of Czech citizens consider it desirable that in a democracy the decisions should be made primarily by elected representatives, it is also true that 75 percent of citizens believe that nongovernmental organizations and the experts associated with them should be invited to help resolve important issues. Three-fourths of those polled believe there should be close cooperation among elected politicians, experts, and civic organizations (Budování států, May 1995: 1).

Social Security

In the pre-Munich Republic, as well as in the Austrian Hungarian Empire before it, the Czechoslovak social security system was classified by Gosta Esping-Andersen as corporate and conservative (Esping-Andersen, 1991: 27). In the period of communist rule the paternalistic system was in force. After 1990, and especially after the 1992 election, there was extensive discussion concerning social security and the redistribution of resources, and of the conflict between political redistribution with a paternalistic role for the state, supported by left-wing parties, versus the application of market principles in social policy, as supported by the right-wing coalition. In 1995 the ruling coalition, after considerable intracoalition dispute, agreed on the introduction of what Andersen has termed the liberal model, based primarily on the responsibility of the individual (Esping-Andersen, 1991: 26). The purpose of such a system is, of course, to reduce social expenditure. Recognizing that this kind of system is unusual for this nation, the government has been careful to introduce it slowly, step by step. This approach has reduced social tension over this issue, but it remains a question on which opinion is divided.

Ecology

The devastation of the country as a consequence of communist ecological and industrial policy was extreme, and indeed even before 1989 the ruling regime was constantly under attack for its failings in this regard. There were some ecological groups and initiatives before 1989 but little progress was made. After the fall of communism, the economic and political transformation of the society acquired primary importance, and the catastrophic ecological situation still has not been effectively addressed.

An interesting phenomenon has been the level of support for the Green Party. There is an apparent connection between the vote for the Greens and the size of a municipality: the bigger the municipality, the higher the vote for the Greens. However, the generally positive relation between the Green vote and the size of the municipality does not apply in areas where the environment has been heavily damaged in the effort to meet other needs; the Greens received more votes in small villages than in cities of over 20,000 inhabitants (Jehlička, Kostelecký,

1995), particularly in Northern Bohemia. In any event, how to handle the problem remains an issue on which Czech opinion is divided.

Human Rights

Spontaneous popular enthusiasm for human rights was one of the prime movers of the revolution, but ebbed considerably in the succeeding years. Perhaps it is always the case that when the demand for human rights becomes a significant instrument of political struggle, establishing those rights ceases to be the goal after political victory: If the totalitarian system has been defeated in the name of human rights then one assumes that *eo ipso* the rights have been attained. On the other hand, even the best codification of human rights in a nation's constitution and laws will be insufficient if there is no strongly rooted consensus for their support. Unfortunately, such a consensus is still absent in Czech society, to the point where some have argued the position of *ombudsman* is needed to ensure that basic rights will be protected (Blahož I, 1994: 36 ff.).

Decentralization

Today there is a strong tendency to see decentralization of the state as the key element in the organization of democracy (Elcock, 1982: 45; Rokkan, Urwin, 1982: 60 ff., 165 ff., 152 ff., 433 ff.). The functions and services of the state must be placed nearer the citizens, their effectiveness must be improved, and citizens must have greater control over their exercise and expense. However, although all these postulates would appear to have been substantiated theoretically and demonstrated practically in the political life of advanced democracies, the issue remains one of the significant division of the Czech political scene, at least for the political parties. Ordinary citizens are, however, notably less interested in the issue, and appear to be becoming even less interested as time goes by (IVVM 94–01). Nonetheless, it has proved important for the parties to work out compromises on this issue in order to be able to form the governing coalitions after both the 1992 and the 1996 elections.

The German Question

Although Czech nationalistic fervor is relatively low as compared to other post-communist countries, the German question is a delicate one, and its insensitive solution could raise that nationalism to dangerous new heights. As Maurice Duverger has pointed out, ideologies and myth create the system of values in a society, and in the Czech Republic as elsewhere nationalistic values are replete with myths (Duverger, 1976: 96 ff.).

The years of Nazi aggression and occupation from 1938 to 1945, and the subsequent period of German expulsion in the early years of the communist takeover, provide historical fodder for a wide range of myths and opinions. The divisions relevant to this issue are not only left versus right, but across the political spectrum, and, even more importantly, across the generations. Older citizens are more likely to respond emotionally, on either side, whereas for most of the younger generation (those up to about forty-five years of age), the question is one of history, especially with regard to the earlier period of Nazi domination. There is, however, a danger that the issue will be given new life among the youngest voters, particularly if it is exploited in connection with socioeconomic tensions as the new society takes shape.

Assurance of Security of the Czech Republic

Once the new Republic was established in 1989, it was necessary to assure the security first of Czechoslovakia, and then of the Czech Republic. The first phase of this endeavor can be characterized as the establishment of the closest possible contact with developed Western democracies and the generation of certain guarantees of security in the framework of the so-called Visegrad Three (Poland, Hungary, and Czechoslovakia).

The second phase, beginning with the split of Czechoslovakia on January 1, 1993, is characterized by the individual endeavor of the Czech Republic to be admitted to the European Union and to the North Atlantic Treaty Organization. The earlier idea of strengthening security by intensifying cooperation in the framework of the Visegrad Three or, later, Four, has been explicitly abandoned, as the Czech people seek to guarantee their security by joining the European Community and NATO. Popular support for joining the EC was originally strong and unambiguous; while that for membership in NATO was more reserved. Recently a measure of euroscepticism has evolved. The data of the Central and Eastern Eurobarometer show that the number of those with a positive impression of the aims and activities of the European Union declined from 45.4 percent in 1992 to 26.4 percent in 1995 (Commission of the European Community).

HOW PARTIES INTERPRET AND ADDRESS CONTEMPORARY DIVISIONS OF OPINION

The principal parties of the Czech party system address the new divisions in the following ways:

Economic Transformation

The parties of the ruling coalition—that is, the ODS, the ODA and the KDU-ČSL—are in general agreement regarding the pace, the methods to be used, and the scope of privatization to be achieved in achieving the economic transformation of the nation. This consensus no doubt helps explain the fact that privatization has proceeded more rapidly and extensively in the Czech Republic than in other post-communist countries. According to the OECD report of 1995, 70 percent of Czech property is now in private hands (Ekonom, 1996: 28).

Differentiation of the political parties within the right-left spectrum was and is still dominated by the economic dimension. As noted earlier, all the parties in the political spectrum promote privatization of the economy; the differences of opinion develop regarding the return of property and the method of finding the correct owner. The Communist Party does not agree with the idea of returning state property. Other parties disagree over the method of doing so, particularly over whether or not the voucher methods should be used. Right-oriented parties unanimously promote the voucher method, while those on the left insist on the sale of shares to employees. Only the ČSSD has endorsed the idea of combining the two methods (Brokl, Mansfeldová, 1993: 12–13).

The opposition also urges a slower pace and different methods of implementation. So far, however, Social Democracy has failed to present a cohesive model of economic transformation, despite its assertion that its team of experts would manage the economy far better than those now in power.

Decentralization

The question of whether a political system should be confined to the narrower meaning (state plus political parties plus citizens) or extended to its broader sense (state plus parties plus civic initiatives and interest organizations plus citizens) has gradually become the object of political disputes among Czech parties, within the Government coalition as well as between that coalition and the opposition.

While the ODS takes the narrower view of the concept, the ODA and the KDU-ČSL, as well as the democratic opposition (ČSSD), favor the broader approach. They support wider participation in collective decisionmaking and believe decentralization must be accompanied by self-governing democracy. Prime Minister and ODS Chairman Václav Klaus has repeatedly refused to acknowledge interest groups and civic initiatives as legitimate players in the political system, saying, "Those who stress civic initiatives, self-governing democracy, and civic society are not fostering decentralization but simply expressing their mistrust of the state" (Klaus I, 1994: 5). On the other hand, those who advocate the broader approach often tend to do so for the wrong reasons, imagining that the involvement of civil society is something that can be achieved "from above," in some sort of Government or Parliamentary transformation of society (Dahrendorf, 1994: 12).

On the whole, this division is not a particularly dramatic or serious one. Some civic organizations and civic initiatives will, indubitably, gradually assert and achieve influence in the political system. To seek to accelerate their development excessively and artificially, granting them a space in the political arena, which they have not earned in open democratic competition, would probably be as harmful to democratic society and to the state as would be the administrative restriction of their origin and actions.

Social Security

The new codification of social security mentioned above has provoked considerable criticism from the opposition, as well as from within the ruling coalition on the part of the KDU-ČSL, which continues to express its reservations. Again, however, the opposition has thus far failed to propose a coherent alternative, despite the fact that this may be one of the issues on which the governing coalition is—or at least was—most vulnerable in public opinion. The ODS lost a part of electoral support after adopting the new system, and the beneficiary was the ČSSD, which steadily gained electoral support, becoming the second-strongest party in the Parliament in the 1996 election with 26.44 percent of the vote, only 3.18 percent less than that gained by the winning ODS.

Ecology

Division in public opinion on this issue has not yet been addressed effectively by the parties. Environmental problems have not been salient for most of the political parties. Long-term underestimation of the severity of ecological problems has not changed, either within the government or within the opposition, despite the patent seriousness of the situation. Although proenvironmentalist positions were taken by the Free Democrats (SD) and the Moravian-Silesian regionalists (Czech Moravian Union of the Center—ČMUS), these parties steadily lost electoral support, taking only 2.05 percent and 0.45 percent of the vote, respectively, in the 1996 election. The Green Party did not take part in the 1996 election. At the other extreme is the ODS with a vigorously anti-environmental position (Markowski, 1995: 36). The parties' continued neglect of this issue is likely not only to have a serious effect on the health of the population but may also cause undesirably intense activities by ecological organizations determined to bring about change, even if to do so means violating the laws.

Human Rights

Overall, the Czech party system has made a strong response to the issue of human rights. From left to right, the parties have made the implementation and guarantee of human rights cornerstones of their programs and party manifestos. The Bill of Fundamental Rights and Freedoms passed in 1991 and now a part of the Czech constitution is an impressive sign of the determination of all parties to make significant change in this domain (Blahož II, 1992: 32 ff.). At the same time, there are differences among the parties on this issue.

The parties of the Government coalition, and in particular the ODS and ODA, place their emphasis on personal and political rights and see social, economic, and cultural rights as qualitatively different. They argue that the inclusion of the latter rights in the Bill of Fundamental Rights and Freedoms was owing to the need to simplify the process of establishing the new Constitution; they should not be considered the same level of importance. The opposition parties, on the other hand, and in particular the ČSSD, believe that social, economic, and cultural rights are of equal importance. Nongovernmental organizations such as the Czech Helsinki Committee take the same position (Palouš, 1995: 9).

In point of fact, the bill fully complies with the International Covenant on Economic, Social and Culture Rights and the International Covenant on Civil and Political Rights (United Nations, 1970: 1 ff., 13 ff.). The Czech dispute on the relative value of the different rights is, of course, a division found between the democratic right and the democratic left on a global scale.

Decentralization

In advanced democracies the present tendency is for parties of the democratic right and center to make the strongest arguments for decentralization (Summers, Seovik, 1979: 187 ff., 197 ff.). In the Czech Republic, however, the situation is somewhat more complex.

Decentralization was, not surprisingly, the most important issue for the Moravian party, the Czech Moravian Union of the Center. The party sought serious decentralization and the creation of regional bodies freeing Moravia and Silesia from the administrative organization of the state (Kroupa, 1994: 3).

The strongest party in the government coalition, the ODS, hesitates to recommend the addition of a new administrative division of State territory, such as regions, to the present division into districts and communities, although it made electoral promises to foster decentralization. This reluctance, criticized both by the opposition, especially ČSSD and ČMUS and its coalition partners (in particular the ODA), is no doubt owing to the strong influence the Government is able to exercise over the districts, particularly their executive component, the District Offices, as well as to the concern of the ODS that adding a new tier of local government would weaken the power of the center.

In addition, however, it is necessary to be realistic about the qualifications, as well as the political and legal culture, of those who would assume the new managing positions at the local level. The ODS argues that the speedy introduction of a higher tier of administrative territorial units without careful preliminary study and the formation of qualified professionals would be risky and unwise. Its circumspection and caution, particularly considering that as the strongest Government party it bears the greatest responsibility, is therefore understandable (Klaus II, 1994: 5; Stráský, 1994: 6).

The German Question

The parties of the ruling coalition and the opposition parties agree in insisting that the postwar decrees of President Eduard Beneš regarding the immediate renewal of a democratic system must remain in place. These decrees include regulations against nazi crime, crimes against humanity, and nazi occupation.[3] However, although these measures could entail complications regarding issues of property, in practice the efforts made to achieve closer and friendlier cooperation between the Czech Republic and Germany in the future are of far greater significance. The governing coalition has encouraged the joint work of German and Czech historians attempting to make an objective evaluation of the period 1938–1948, and this work has been closely connected with the preparation of a Czech-German declaration addressing some unresolved historical issues. The Social Democrats support this activity of the government.

Meanwhile, the extreme parties on both the left (KSČM) and on the right (SPR-RSČ) try to extract the maximum response from the public by the use of vociferous nationalist propaganda—an effort which makes finding a positive solution that much more important for the future stability and security of the Czech republic (Havel, 1995: 3).

Assurance of the Security of the Czech Republic

The "Partnership for Peace" offered by the West to Central and East European nations has been adopted by all parties in the Czech ruling coalition. At the same time, the government emphasizes that this must be seen as a short-term measure which must be replaced by full membership of the Czech Republic in NATO, the only realistic guarantee of the external security of the nation. Social Democracy (ČSSD) agrees fully with this approach (Havel, 1995: 3). Only the parties of the extreme right (the SPR-RSČ) and the extreme left (the KSČM), as well as other minor left-wing parties, argue that the Czech Republic should not join either the European Union or NATO.

Although a referendum will have to be held, the issue of how to protect the external security of the nation is not an issue of cleavage between the ruling parties and the most important opposition party; it is rather an issue unifying all democratic forces.

CONTEMPORARY CLEAVAGES IN THE CZECH REPUBLIC

Our analysis of contemporary divisions of opinion leads us to two questions: first, which are cleavages?; second, which of Rokkan's types of cleavages seem not to exist in the Czech Republic?

Economic populism versus market liberalism emerges as the strongest structuring principle in the Czech Republic (Markowski, 1995: 33). It is sufficiently strong for us to speak of a *socioeconomic cleavage*. The main question now is the role of the state in the economy. Closely connected to this issue are the divisions regarding issues of social security and the redistribution of resources, that is, the conflict between those favoring a political redistribution with a paternalistic role taken by the state and those who would adopt market principles in social policy.

We may also speak of a *cosmopolitan versus nationalist cleavage,* revolving around attitudes toward membership in the European Union and NATO, toward neighboring countries (especially Germany), and toward the advisability of accepting foreign influence and foreign capital. Attitudes toward ethnic minorities and asylum policy can be assimilated here as well.

Arguments about the role of civic society do not, however, qualify as a structural cleavage in the contemporary Czech Republic. As the political sphere and civic society develop simultaneously, it is natural that the role of various interest organizations and of intermediary organizations in general will be debated. Whether or not the decisions of professional chambers prove decisive in granting licenses is an important question which must and will be resolved but which should not be expected to produce an enduring division in Czech society.

Other, more traditional cleavages appear not to exist at the present time in the Czech Republic:

Rural versus urban. The period of totalitarian rule in fact succeeded, through etatization, leveling, and modernization, in keeping this traditional division to a minimum for forty years. So far the process of restitution of land and agricultural property does not suggest the creation of a significant layer of private farmers, especially as a large part of the land continues to be operated by cooperatives. The negative impacts of economic reform and governmental agricultural policy on farmers and rural people are reflected in the parties, but do not lead to the revitalization of the rural-urban cleavage. The effort to establish agricultural parties has not produced an organization with the power of the Agrarian Party in the prewar years. The Agricultural Party, as a part of the coalition, won parliamentary seats in the elections of 1992 but did not succeed in reinforcing its positions or gaining a stable electorate; it terminated its operation in 1995. The interests of its potential electorate are represented by the left-wing parties and the KDU-ČSL. Instead of the traditional cleavage we find rather a set of conflicts of interests resulting from restitution, competition, and the removal of subsidies.

Owners versus workers. This cleavage is latent, but not yet crystallized. We will recognize its distinct articulation, manifestation, influence, and shape only after completion of privatization and the concomitant change in ownership conditions. At the same time, new mechanisms are in place to articulate and resolve conflicts between employers and workers' organizations.

The government decided at the beginning of the transformation process to cooperate with trade unions as well as with emerging entrepreneurs and employers' unions, in order to mediate interests and prevent or solve conflicts. This corporatist approach undoubtedly slows the emergence of a traditional owner/worker cleavage. None of the parliamentary or more powerful off-parliament parties addresses this set of problems directly, none places itself solely on the side of the workers or solely on the side of the employers.

Church versus state. The land reforms of the anti-feudal revolution had already greatly weakened the power of the Church by the origin of the republic in 1918, and the communist regime completed the process of destruction. After November 1989, the Catholic Church proved unable to capitalize effectively on a brief period of positive public inclination. Rather than take advantage of this temporary abatement in the strongly secular, if not anticlerical, bias of the Czech public, the Church focused on its internal problems and on how to obtain the largest possible property through the process of restitution.

In 1995, 21 percent of the Czech people declared themselves to be "believers," 31 percent accepted the existence of God, and 48 percent were atheists (IVVM 95–06). By 1994 the figures had become 24 percent, 31 percent, and 45 percent, but by 1989 the tide had turned again and the respective figures were 16 percent, 24 percent, and 60 percent (IVVM 94–12). According to 63 percent of the Czechs as of 1995, churches are useful only to care for mental life, whereas only 18 percent would give them opportunity to influence political life, 12 percent do not know, and 7 percent are not interested in the question (IVVM 95–07). The single Christian party among Czech political parties, representing a relatively small and elderly electorate, won 8.08 percent of votes in the 1996 election.

CONCLUSION

The question of continuum or discontinuum of cleavages in the Czech Republic can be answered in favor of a continuum and an overlapping of old, emerging, or resolved contradictions and conflicts. Real cleavages as structural conflicts, more or less obviously represented by some actors of the political life, are perhaps only now developing.

As a result, we can state that classical structural cleavages were articulated in Czech society only after division of the state in 1993. The contradictions related to the social transformation under way in the Czech Republic, which are interpreted, manifested, and represented by individual parties, do not polarize or break up the established horizontal structure of political parties. The overall picture is one of continuity. The internal structure of contradictions reflecting current social problems is dynamic, unstable, and changeable, and results from the fact that individual contradictions overlap and complement each other at many levels. An example may be the real (as opposed to the declared) policy of the strongest party, ODS, which often changes its positions to absorb the more centrist part of the electorate. Internal tension results, but the party does come out ahead of its opposition in this way. Thus, to the extent that cleavages are developing and having an impact in the present Czech system, they are more likely to manifest themselves in divisions over policy within the ruling coalition (be it of the left or the right), rather than among the parties in general.

NOTES

1. Krejci enumerates sixty-six registered parties in his book, "Who will win the elections," 1992, Prague, Echo, p. 62.

2. In March 1993, 53 percent of citizens were concerned by the absence of a political middle; in March 1996, it was only 43 percent (*Public Opinion Research Institute IVVM 96–03*).
3. During the provisional situation after World War II and up until the 1946 election, presidential decrees had the force of law. More than three million Sudeten Germans were expelled from Czechoslovakia after World War II.

REFERENCES

Blahož, Josef I. 1994. "Human Rights Law in Czechoslovakia, Hungary and Poland." In Forsuthe David (ed.), *Human Rights in the New Europe. Problems and Progress.* Lincoln and London: University of Nebraska Press.
Blahož, Josef II. 1992. "Human Rights, Their Guarantees and the Constitutional Judiciary in CSFR." In *Austrian Journal of Public and International Law* 43: 31–71.
Brokl, Lubomír and Zdenka Mansfeldová. 1993. *Political Parties and Their Programs. East Central Europe 2000 (background study).* Institute of Sociology, Academy of Sciences of the Czech Republic, Prague.
Brokl, Lubomír. 1994. "Politická kultura a politický prostor (Political Culture and Political Space)." *Lidové noviny*, November 11: 8–9.
Budování státu (Building the State): International Politological Institute, Faculty of Law, Masaryk University, Brno, May 1995.
Česká republika očima OECD. Ekonom (newspaper), 1996, No. 36, p. 28.
Commission of the European Community, *Central and Eastern Eurobarometer* (Brussels: European Commission, 1993, 1994, 1995, 1996).
Dahrendorf, Ralf. 1994. "Stát bude muset v budoucnosti zeštíhlet (The State Will Have to Slim Down in the Future)." *Lidové noviny*, March 15: 12.
Duverger, Maurice. 1976. *The Study of Politics.* Nelson: Sunbury on Thames.
Elcock, Howard. 1982. *Local Government, Politicians, Professionals and the Public in Local Authorities.* London and New York: Methuen.
Esping-Andersen, Gosta. 1991. *The Three Worlds of Welfare Capitalism.* Oxford, Cambridge: Blackwell Publishers.
Havel, Václav. 1995. "Novoroční projev prezidenta Václava Havla (New Year's Address of President Václav Havel)," *Lidové noviny,* January 2: 3.
International Covenants on Human Rights. 1970. New York: United Nations, Office of Public Information, April.
IVVM 94-01, 15.1. 1994 No. 930. (Public Opinion Research Institute).
IVVM 94-12, 29.12. 1994 No. 969. (Public Opinion Research Institute).
IVVM 95-06, 2.8. 1995 No. 998. (Public Opinion Research Institute).
IVVM 95-07, 3.9. 1995, No. 1008. (Public Opinion Research Institute).
Jehlička P. and T. Kostelecký. 1995. "Czechoslovakian Greens in post-Communist society." In Dick Richardson and Claris Rootes (eds.), *The Green Challenge. The development of the Green parties in Europe,* 208–31. London: Routledge.
Klaus, Václav. I. 1994. "Pohled na naši zemi zvenčí (Look at our country from the outside)." *Lidové noviny* August 8: 5.
Klaus, Václav II. 1994. "Znovu regiony (once again: regions)." *Lidové noviny* June 13: 5.
Kroupa, Aleš. 1994. "Decentralizace a efektivita státní správy." *Data & Fakta*, no. 8, Sociologický ústav AV ČR.

Mansfeldová, Zdenka. 1996. *Political Parties in the Czech Republic in the Process of Social and Political Changes.* Paper presented at a conference organized by Friedrich Ebert Foundation, Prague.

Markowski, Radoslaw. 1995. "Political Competition and Ideological Dimensions in Central Eastern Europe." *Studies in Public Policy* 257: 154–77

Novák, Miroslav. 1997. Systémy politických stran. úvod dojejich srovnávacího studia. Praha: Slon.

Palouš, Martin. 1995. "Zpráva o stavu lidských práv v České republice (Report on the State of Human Rights in the Czech Republic)." *Czech Helsinki Committee Newsletter* 1: 2–10.

Rokkan, Stein and Derek Urwin. 1982. *The Politics of Territorial Identity, Studies in European Regionalism.* London: Sage Publication.

Seiler, D. L. 1982. La politique comparée, Paris: Armand Colin.

Stráský, Jan. 1994. "Obce, okresy, regiony (Communities, Districts, Regions)." *Lidové noviny* March 30: 6.

Summers, Gene F. and Arne Seovik. 1979. *Nonmetropolitan Industrial Growth and Community Change.* Lexington: Lexington Books.

10

Cleavages and Parties in Hungary after 1989

──────────────── György G. Márkus*

Nineteen eighty-nine was a critical juncture in the history of East Central and Eastern Europe, and Hungary was no exception. As Seymour Martin Lipset has pointed out, none of the new nations had effective civil societies in place, and it was difficult to institutionalize pluralist policies. The need to form parties arrived suddenly and without preparation (Lipset, 1993).

Party formation in Hungary began from the existence of small illegal or semi-legal dissident networks on the one side and the former state party (divided into a reformist and an orthodox wing) on the other. Reformers—renaming their party "Hungarian Socialist Party" in late 1989—were in key positions, actively preparing the transition to democracy and the market economy; "genuine" Communists—carrying on under the old name "Hungarian Socialist Workers' Party," by now, just "Workers' Party"—lacked not only support, but the will and the means to control the transition. The weakness of the Communists meant that the regime issue soon lost its primacy; the central cleavage became the value-based division between the oppositional forces. In the formative period of the new parties, the nationalists sought a compromise with some of the reform communists, while liberal parties sought a radical change of elites—although, in 1994, the ex-dissident liberal Free Democrats formed a coalition government with the Socialists facing a national and anti-communist opposition. The new ascendancy of the cleavage between two elite groups within what had been the opposition permitted the reemergence of a central and historically rooted cleavage, the cleavage between Traditionalists and Westernizers.

The two dominant parties from the intellectual milieu, the Alliance of Free Democrats (SZDSZ) and the Hungarian Democratic Forum (MDF), were direct descendants of these two parallel and competing currents as they had manifested

---

*The author thanks NATO for the research grant provided supporting his work on parties and cleavages in Hungary.

themselves in the opposition of the past ten to fifteen years. The MDF originated in a movement of national "populist" writers, historians, and social scientists, held together by their anxiety about the "destiny problems of nationhood"—by which they meant the consequences of the Versailles/Trianon peace treaty—the Hungarians in the diaspora, demographic decrease, cultural and ethnic vulnerability, and "national diseases" such as suicide, mental stress, and the loss of moral values and solidarity. The original political orientation was a kind of plebian, quasi-leftist, "national third road" concept, an orientation somewhere between "Eastern" Communism and "Western" Capitalism. In the first year of its formation in 1987, this movement was joined by many members and descendants of the former Christian traditionalist middle classes. Following party leader József Antall (later, prime minister), traditionalist and Christian conservatism emerged as the dominant force in party politics, although in bitter rivalry with radical populism.

On the other side, the SZDSZ was the direct continuation of the Democratic Opposition of the 1980s, with the ethos of moral resistance against the regime (in contrast to the semi-peaceful symbiosis of populist writers with nationally oriented Communist party leaders). The milieu of the hard core of the SZDSZ typically consisted of Budapest intellectuals who had started their ideological careers as committed Marxists. Some of them had been followers of Georg Lukács, making their long march to become human rights activists, revisionists and, finally, radical liberals. Many of them came from *nomenklatura* families; many were of Jewish origin.

Parties like the SZDSZ and the MDF, led by intellectuals and drawing from subcultural elites, quickly became dominant in the new regime, and parties based on parties from the past, such as the Christian Democrats, the Social Democrats, and the Smallholders, were forced to adjust. The reformist wing of the former state party, now the MSZP (the Hungarian Socialist Party), also acquired the traits of what we may call the milieu party type. These parties each drew from specific cultural milieux. Their members shared analogous life experiences and socialization patterns, had similar sociocultural backgrounds, and similar aesthetic tastes. Although they often shared vague overarching value orientations, the specific political priorities and programmatic ideas of members could and often did vary. This aestheticization of politics, looked upon as a typical postmodern development in the West, has been present from the very beginning of multipartism in post-communist Hungary (Harvey, 1994).

As a result, contradictory processes emerged as the parties, party alignments, and the party system took shape. On the macropolitical level, the trend of crystallization and selection along the cultural cleavage of Westernization versus traditionalism was accomplished in a short time. Of the 160 or more protoparties registered, only six were able to overcome the threshold of 4 percent in 1990 and of 5 percent in 1994 (the same six in both elections: the ex-reform-communist Socialists; the Hungarian Democratic Forum, the Smallholders, the Christian Democrats on the "national" side, the Alliance of Free Democrats on the

Westernization side, and the Alliance of Young Democrats, originally on the Westernization side, by now on the opposite side of the major cleavage). However, inside the parties, severe conflicts have been evident from the beginning between those whom we may call *movementists*, eager to preserve the loose coalition character of the organization, and *partitocrats*, those favoring a more bureaucratic and professional party organization, as well as between groups and personalities linked to divergent political and ideological currents. As a result, party leaders, as is typical in pre-mass parties, seek to hold themselves "above party" (Sartori, 1968: 261–98).

In contrast to the heterogeneity of the individual parties and the prevailing pragmatic, materialistic, and consensus-oriented citizenry, the new party system thus emerged as the confrontation of two value-based camps. The MDF won the 1990 election on the basis of its presentation of itself as the "Quiet Force," promising stability and a nonradical approach to the problem of regime transformation, and became the hegemonic party of the traditionalist camp (comprising also the Christian Democrats and the Smallholders, although the latter, becoming a radical and populist protest party, soon left the coalition). The Free Democrats—together with the Young Democrats—were the key parties of the radical, liberal, antitraditional Westernizing camp, which also included the mainstream of post-reform-communist Socialists. The two political camps manifested the age-old division between those for whom the supreme value was the maintenance of national identity and the survival of Hungarian nationhood and those who made making a radical sociocultural adjustment to the West and the pursuit of catch-up modernization the central goal of political life: in short, Hungarianhood versus civil society. On a continuum of values, the traditionalist parties focused on organic solidarity, ethnocentric collectivism, cultural distinctiveness, homogenizing state authority, clericalism, and looking inward; the Westernizers believed in individualism, multicultural diversity, rewarding performance, autonomy, the free market, secularism and looking outward (Márkus, 1994: 154–70).

Although all the neotraditionalist parties demonstrated an emotional preoccupation with the "trauma of Trianon," they mainly treated the issue more as an issue of symbolic politics than as an issue requiring revisionist action. Representative of this was the comment by Prime Minister Antall in June 1990: "I am a prime minister of fifteen million Hungarians—in soul and in emotions." (Hungary proper has a population of ten million.) The stance of the Westernizing parties was that of *Realpolitik*: accept the administrative status quo and treat the question of Hungarian minorities abroad as a human rights problem. The issue was aggravated by nationalistic policies in neighboring Rumania, Slovakia, and Serbia. As in the past, the Hungarian nationalist elite could be interpreted as threatened by others, or as threatening *to* others; this historical dilemma became a component of post-communist cultural politics.

Parties, however, are not just prisoners of existent cleavages. They play an independent role in cleavage translation, in policymaking, in structuring the political space, and in shaping one another (Sartori, 1968). While in many consociational democracies of Western Europe political elites have been successful in overcoming divisive heterogeneity, the opposite has been the case in Hungary, where political elites have tended to superimpose their own subcultural divisiveness, based on latent or past cleavages, on a much less divided electorate. In the period between 1990 and 1994, during the rule of the national-Christian *Lager* (the German term for "camp," denoting a partisan bloc in the context of "pillarizing" cultural politics), the intensification of these cleavages, by the elites, led inevitably to the neglect, or at least the inadequate treatment, of economic issues.

In addition, there was a striking ambiguity in the personality of Prime Minister Antall. On the one hand, conscious of a historic mission, he regarded himself, his party, and the national-Christian ideological community as forces destined to restore the organic identity of the Hungarian nation, and its continuity all the way back to the eleventh century nation-building efforts of Saint Stephen, the first king of the country, who converted his people to Western Christianity, established a strong centralized state, and made Hungary a part of "Europe." He pled for a spiritual community of the nation as a whole. On the other hand, he also viewed his historic mission as requiring that he do his best to foster Europeanization, the capitalist social market economy, the rule of law, and the integration of Hungary into the EU and NATO (Révész, 1995). This dualism contained not only the contradiction between a history-rooted veneration of nationhood and the supranational postmodern construction of Europe, but also the incompatibility between the ideals of a spiritually united Christian national community and a Western-type pluralist and multicultural democracy and its concomitant readiness to accept different ideologies as legitimate (Lipset, 1959).

POST-COMMUNIST KULTURKAMPF

The first years of post-communist Hungarian pluralism were thus characterized by a political discourse, both within and outside of Parliament, overloaded with symbolic issues and questions of national identity and historical continuity. The central theme became, "Who is a genuine Hungarian?" The elites of the governing party were convinced they had not just won a simple electoral victory but had been legitimized as a metaphysical entity, as representing the fundamental nature of the nation (Révész, 1995: 121).

Opposing forces, whether political, journalistic, or academic, were consequently regarded as threatening the survival of the nation. Using the German term *Kulturkampf* (cultural struggle), originally coined to describe the conflict between state and church for the control of education in Western Europe around the turn of the century, we can point to three central areas of party and public policy competition in Hungary during this period.

The Control of the Educational System

The identification of national curricula, the role and place of religious education, the restitution of schools and universities as Church property, and the question of secular education were "classical" Kulturkampf conflicts both on the central level and on the level of local communities.

The Control of the Media

The existence of independent and often critical public and private media was interpreted as the effort of "media intellectuals" to damage the cause of the nation by both the moderate conservatives and the radically nationalist currents of the governing parties fighting for the "occupation of the media" and seeking to purge public television and radio of undesirable components. The radical nationalists gaining—at least, temporarily—leading positions in public television and broadcasting went so far as to interpret the struggle as one of "cosmopolitan liberal-bolshevik" intellectuals versus a "genuine" Hungarian and Christian media, thereby adding a distinctly anti-semitic edge to the debate.

The efforts to control education and the media as means of indoctrination produced a number of problems. The principles of the rule of law and of checks-and-balances via the counteracting forces of pluralist institutions were put at risk. Instead, an effort was being made to impose a kind of social pillarization on the Hungarian citizenry, a pillarization which could be found among the cultural elites, but not within the de-ideologized public. Initiatives were undertaken—with relatively little success—to establish parallel, culturally distinctive civil society networks, including professional organizations, especially (but not exclusively) on the side of the traditionalists. "One has to work constantly to change the soul, the mentality of a people," Antall declared. According to his confessor, the Prime Minister's final words on his deathbed in December 1993 were, "I wanted a Christian Hungary, only this has a future" (Révész, 1995: 120). His success may be measured by noting that only one-sixth of all Hungarians claim to live according to the teachings of the churches.

The Control of Foreign Policy

Foreign policy was an area in which the conflict between modernist and traditionalist (western and nationalist) tendencies were particularly marked. Although the ruling elite was strongly dedicated to leading Hungary into the communities of Western European integration and NATO, they constantly indulged in rhetorics of national sovereignty, drawing on a nineteenth-century style of nation-state romanticism and displaying a passionate preoccupation with ethnic solidarity. Two events of 1993 illustrate this almost schizophrenic ambivalence. In May, the "Basic Treaty" between Hungary and Ukraine was to be ratified by Parliament. The treaty prepared and negotiated by the government was a piece of Realpolitik and the compromise it made with a view to the Euro-Atlantic integration of Hungary soon became a kind of prototype. While the Hungarian side acknowledged the existing post-Versailles state boundaries, the other side accepted the responsibility for granting minority rights to ethnic Hungarians. In September, however, Admiral Horthy, the prewar Governor (Regent) of Hungary and the embodiment of revisionist policies responsible for leading Hungary to Hitler's side in the hope of restoring Great Hungary, was given a quasi official reburial.

Furthermore, the ratification itself was a contradictory process and led to a split between radicals and moderates in the traditionalist camp, not only on the intraparty level (Democratic Forum versus Smallholders), but also within the ruling party, resulting soon in the split of the radical rightist groups from the MDF and in the establishment of the Hungarian Truth and Life Party by István Czurka, former MDF vice president. In this context, it was no surprise that the Parliamentary ratification of the treaty could succeed only with the votes of the "modernist" opposition parties. (After the change of government following the 1994 elections, the new governing parties extended the "basic treaties" to Slovakia and Romania, under fierce attack from the national opposition.)

Ambiguities in Cleavage Translation

In other areas of policy, the conflict between the traditionalist ideological bias and the determination to accept the requirements of capitalist transformation was more subtly, but nevertheless strongly, at work, producing profound ambiguities. Three examples illustrate this tendency:

First, the process of de-etatization collided with centralizing, statist tendencies in public administration and with political interventionism in economic and cultural domains. The tendency of the MDF (and later the MSZP) to seek to establish itself as a state party was, of course, in direct contradiction to the commitment to decentralization (Ágh, 1994).

Second, any hopes for a free and spontaneous development of the privatization process were seriously dampened by statist efforts to recreate a "national-Christian middle class." Political patronage, including partial restitution and massive compensation to selected groups, in spite of the influx of foreign capital, had unforeseen and often destructive effects, both socially and economically. The anti-collectivist bias in culture resulted in the creation of a mass-scale small peasantry lacking the means for efficient farming. The formerly successful sector, a combination of cooperative and household farming, became a branch in permanent crisis.

Third, the practice of clientelist redistribution and growth-induction, disregarding equilibrium, also made it impossible to set a clear-cut public economic policy pursuing the radical structural reform and deregulation that all agreed were necessary. Ministers of finance came and went, and there was a constant confrontation between a monetarist approach and a growth orientation within the government.

Overall, the political record of the MDF government is a complex one. Certainly real progress was made in key areas: the maintenance and consolidation of the general framework of the rule of law and of the institutions of multiparty parliamentary democracy, the steady progress toward a capitalist market economy, and the steps taken toward integration into West European and North Atlantic supranational organizations. Regime change became irreversible, no mean accomplishment.

On the other hand, with respect to socioeconomic public policies the performance of this government can best be described as muddling through. The economy did gain in relative autonomy despite attempts at political control. The most serious deficit was in establishing effective political linkage between citizens and government—what we may call the *failure of cleavage translation.*

The language and style of communication resulting from elite consciousness of having a historic mission were alien to the ordinary citizen. The vast majority of the population had been effectively socialized in the years of János Kádár's "goulash communism." They were strongly materialist, committed to the welfare state, and de-ideologized. These attitudes and value preferences did not change overnight. Ideological distances and fragmentation characterized the parties and their elites, producing a kind of "polarized multipartism" in Sartori's terms: "a political system characterized by centrifugal drives, irresponsible opposition and unfair competition [which] is hardly a viable system" (Sartori, 1968: 261–98). But these differences were not reflected in the general public. The parties did not simply translate existent cleavages; they imposed their own. There was not simply a noncorrespondence, *but a deep gap between a party system based on cultural politics and an electorate hostile to ideological penetration*—that is, to the centrality of ideology. The evidence is clear in Table 10.1: Priorities of Kulturkampf policies were rejected (see 14, 16, 18), while a programmatic, materialist, and welfare statist attitude (1 to 5) prevailed.

THE ANTI-KULTURKAMPF VOTE AND THE POST-SOCIALIST CLEAVAGE

There were several stages on the way to the crushing defeat of the MDF and the national-conservative parties in the 1994 elections. After the first year of confusion (expressed in the widely supported taxi-drivers' strike and the reversal of votes in the 1990 municipal elections), there was a period of public apathy regarding the parties. Then the FIDESZ, the generation-based, radical and pragmatic Alliance of Young Democrats, an anti-party party, attracted popular support, and subsequently the public turned to the Socialists (in what might be called an evolution from *exit* to *voice*). The sweeping victory of the ex-Communist Socialists in 1994, plus popular support for the coalition they made with the ex-dissident Free Democrats (the second strongest party in the vote), demonstrated popular support for a mix of continuity and change. (In effect, this was what the electorate had sought in 1990, when it accepted the MDF's claim that it would be the "Quiet Force," achieving change peacefully and carefully.)

The vote contained a two-fold message: a refusal of ideologically determined policymaking (by this time the Socialists were seen as "professional" and "pragmatic," not rooting their platform in the cultural cleavage) and moderate support for Westernization. The voters were not interested in making the time-trip back into the twenties and thirties; a shorter trip into the late eighties had greater appeal. The well-known faces and familiar style of the ex-Communists offered a sense of stability and security, after the turmoil of the first post-89 government and its policies. And returning them to power gave the voters a sense of restoration of continuity, a conviction they need not live in shame for having long accepted Kádárian "goulash communism"—their own biographies were relegitimized. The sweeping victory of the Socialists in 1994 revealed the existence of a set of deeply rooted post-socialist cleavages in the society and the economy. The post-socialist cleavage family, "Kádárian Communism versus emerging capitalism," can also be described in the

Table 10.1
Assessment of the Importance of Hungarian Political Objectives (on a continuum from 1 to 5)

	Average
1. Competent people should manage the economic affairs of the country	4.77
2. To improve the standards of health care and education	4.75
3. To ease the burdens on the population resulting from economic transformation	4.69
4. To decrease unemployment	4.62
5. To increase pensions and social benefits	4.62
6. To protect human rights and individual freedom	4.60
7. To struggle against crime with a police having efficient means and authority	4.59
8. To decrease injust inequalities between people	4.49
9. To stop the fall of morality	4.46
10. To protect the environment more efficiently	4.35
11. Efficient representation of Hungarian interests abroad	4.22
12. To grant the right for abortion to women	4.19
13. To promote private enterprise and free markets	3.97
14. To strengthen national feeling	3.71
15. To speed up privatization of state companies	3.22
16. To remove ex-CP members from leading functions	3.19
17. To grant further functioning for nonprofitable enterprises and mines	2.82
18. To increase the influence of religion and the churches	2.73

Source: Kurtán et al. (eds.), 1993. "Median." In *Magyarország Politikai Évköngve* (Political Yearbook of Hungary), 650.

terms of a dual society (or social dualism) split into a sector rooted in state socialism and a sector of capitalism in-the-making. Beginning from the middle of the sixties, a special type of authoritarian regime had emerged, based on the "Kádárian bargain": one-party-rule and external dependence were to be accepted by the population in exchange for improved living standards, social security, economic reforms, a limited cultural and administrative pluralism, and a toleration of "privacy." A technocratic elite assumed increasingly important positions in politics and in the economy. Concomitantly, a process of petty-embourgeoisment of significant strata tied to a market-oriented "second economy" emerged. In preparing the political and economic regime change, the political arm of this technocracy, in the shape of the reformist wing of the state party and later of the ex-communist Socialist Party, played a leading role.

Following the 1990 elections, this "late Kádárian technocracy" was able not only keep, but also decisively to strengthen its dominant positions in the economy. In the political field, however, it was more or less marginalized. It presented itself as a new kind of ruling class, "managerial capitalism" (I. Szelényi: 1994), but a class with a double face. On the one hand, it was the antithesis of bourgeois-type political democracy, favoring informal decisionmaking, nonpublic bargains, and the spread of political patronage. On the other hand, it was committed to capitalist marketization and to radical Westernization.

Discomfort with this situation led the leadership of the MDF to break away in 1993, but the change came too late and too incompletely to save the party. Fear of radical decommunization and of increasing fascist and anti-semitic tendencies mobilized broad segments of the electorate to protest and contributed to the rapprochement of the MSZP and the SZDSZ on the levels both of the party elites and of their supporters. Beginning with the Democratic Charta movement[1] against radical rightism, these developments pushed the FIDESZ, unwilling to ally with the Socialists, over to the nationalist-conservative side of the basic fault line.

By the 1994 elections the majority of the population had become seriously frustrated by the first years of regime change. Neither the introduction of pluralist democracy nor the transition to a capitalist economy had made life easier or more secure. The sweeping victory of the Socialists in 1994 expressed the response of broad segments of the population to the decrease in living standards accompanied by a Kulturkampf neglecting socioeconomic issues. The public believed that if the ideological and cultural issues could be set aside, everyday life would be improved. Demands for social security, welfare, and consumption were thus now channeled into a Kádárian nostalgia and into votes for the familiar faces and styles offered by the ex-Communist party in social democratic colors.

The ensuing alliance of Socialists and Free Democrats represented the opposite sides of the Kádárian cleavage. Combining these two forces meant that at first the tensions in the new ruling coalition were as high as in the predecessor regime, but over time the Free Democrats were slowly compelled to adjust and assimilate, a price for remaining in power which come at serious cost to their identity.

Shock Therapy as Cleavage-creating Policy

The reaction of the socialist-liberal government to the overpoliticization of the previous regime and its efforts to revitalize a fictitious national-Christian middle class was to adopt a conscious strategy of depoliticization, especially of the public media, as well as a technocratic problem-solving approach to public policy. The commitment to rational technocratic calculation and engineering assumed the qualities of an ideology and proved to be an effective way to legitimize the increasing power of the post-communist managerial elite (Szelényi, 1994: 21–29).

Technocratic crisis management became particularly important in March 1995, after nine months of stalemate owing to intracoalition conflict as well to conflicts within the senior coalition partner. At that point the policy package of Lajos Bokros was adopted, and became the very essence of government policy. The most important components in this "stabilization program" were the stimulation of exports by currency devaluation and import duties; streamlining social and health services; giving up universal allowances; introducing residual means-tested transfers; limiting collective and personal consumption; imposing wage restraints; reducing spending and employment in public education, public health, and scientific research; and cutting back the public sector across the board. Thus, a general monetary restriction was pursued with the aim of restoring financial equilibrium as the precondition of growth.

Was this shock therapy related to the question of political cleavages? The answer is complex and multidimensional:

First, the Bokros package as a public policy issue of rational choice had nothing to do with any structural cleavage. It was, rather, a *Sachzwang*—that is, a consequence of exigencies without viable alternative. Hungary's cumulated public debt and the continuing disequilibrium resulting from the economic policies of the Communist past (and, to some extent, of the previous government) left the new government no other alternative.

Second, the package represented a basic act of *economic regime transformation*, and as such could be related to the set of post-socialist cleavages.

Third, the package followed the logic and the necessity of commodification as the basic principle of a capitalist market economy. As Bokros himself pointed out, the purpose was to prevent having secondary income redistribution by the state distort the primary income redistribution by the market. Here we see a basic political division in capitalist systems, the classical *social democratic cleavage* that originated in the conflict between labor and capital. It is the conflict between forces interested in policies of decommodification—that is, in a political redistribution against the market—and forces interested in the "undisturbed" functioning of the market, and the extension of the market logic to society as a whole. On another level, this can be seen as the conflict between *mass democracy* with its objectives of inclusion, popular participation and equality and the *class-based inequalities* of "pure" capitalism in which the functioning of market allocation is allowed to lead to exclusion. The Bokros package adopted an openly Hayekian philosophy, rejecting social citizenship as morally unjust.

Fourth and finally, the Bokros package can be seen in international terms as stemming from a typical *center versus periphery* cleavage. The economic and political penetration by supranational decisionmaking centers is manifest in the interventions they made to ensure that their priorities of economic and social policymaking were respected in Hungary. IMF demands and the impact of the Maastricht convergence criteria were of decisive importance for the government in its resolution to adopt the package even at the possible cost of jeopardizing its legitimacy and its chances of reelection. Furthermore, foreign interference tended to produce a relevant domestic political cleavage: acceptance of dependency ("what is good for the IMF is good for Hungary") versus an anti-colonialist defense of the national interest. This cleavage was apparent in the division between the government and the opposition, but also within the individual parties, and, increasingly, within the general population.

In sum, the introduction of the "stabilization package" shifted the fundamental cleavage in Hungarian politics away from that originally formulated in cultural terms and toward a *pre-class socioeconomic commodification* cleavage. The formal centrality of the cultural divide in party politics is, however, persistent. "Class struggle" is dressed up as Kulturkampf.

The Effects of the Commodification Cleavage on the Party System

The shift in cleavages, as defined by party elites, has had a strong and sometimes surprising effect on intraparty and interparty cleavages, particularly among the out-of-power traditionalists. In response to the Bokros program, the opposition adopted a quasi-social-democratic, even Keynesian and welfare-protectionist line of attack on the government. Ferenc Kulin, a moderate conservative, has sought to justify this change of policy profile by admitting, first, that the central ideas of nationalistic parties and the actual political attitudes of the electorate could not be reconciled: "The national awareness of present Hungarian society is not in a state in which it could be mobilized." On the other hand, fighting against the policies of "adjustment to a world market dominated by multinational companies . . . and globalized media powers" can be, he has argued, a practical way of working against "anti-national policies." He even achieves a nationalistic variant of the decommodification argument prevailing in Western center-left parties: ". . . economic policy which does not measure the far-reaching social effects of each of its steps is anti-national" (Kulin, 1995).

The only party which is unambiguously and whole-heartedly in favor of commodification and, therefore, of the stabilization package, is the Alliance of Free Democrats. Although the program is harmful to the interests of the SZDSZ middle-class clientele employed in or dependent upon the public sector, it is compatible with the liberal ethos and with the radicalism of the party elite on the question of regime change. The nationalist opposition has been quick to seize upon this stance as a further sign that the SZDSZ is the "arch enemy," cosmopolitan, and "non-Hungarian," thereby occasionally seeking to split the coalition. Similar arguments are sometimes made within the MSZP as well.

THE IDENTITY CRISIS OF THE SOCIALISTS

The Socialist Party has become a key actor in Hungarian politics, but at a cost of serious problems of identity, strategy, and maintaining electoral support. The landslide electoral victory of this formerly ghettoised "successor" party—taking 33 percent of party list votes in the first round and winning almost all constituencies in the second—has made the party the first popular *catch-all* party in Hungarian political history. It is the best organized party in the country with a strong, active membership and a reservoir of professional leaders on several national and local levels. Overcoming its quarantine-like isolation of 1990–1991, during which time it was predominantly an urban intellectual party, it succeeded first in attracting blue-collar workers in industrial centers and then moving out to capture support from the whole spectrum of Hungarian social stratification and value orientations.[2] The party has especially strong support in the older age groups.

However, in spite of (or perhaps due to) its broad character as a catch-all party, the MSZP has brought instability to itself and to the party system. As the gravitational center of politics it provides "coalition linkage." It has collected the votes of blue-collar workers and pensioners and of managers, administrators, and the cultural elite; it appeals to winners and to losers, to the urban and to the rural population, to the traditional trade unions, and to international and domestic monetary institutions. But it is unable to offer a single consistent identification.

The mainstream of the MSZP has found its place on the pro-Western side of the basic cultural cleavage of Hungarian politics, although the party is not rooted in that divide. It has a double identity: as the successor party it attracts the votes and sympathies of former members of the Communist Party; as a party committed to the basic values and principles of Western social democracy it attracts the support of social democrats. It is a social democratic party; at the same time, it has the strong organization and technocratic leadership style of the state party of the pre-1989 period. It is a catch-all party along several dimensions—that is, according to sociological criteria (generation, region, profession, milieu), according to pressure group memberships, according to personal ties and networks, and according to ideological rivalries (trade unionist, social liberal, nationalist, Marxist and bureaucratic-technocratic). Not surprisingly, following the electoral victory and formation of the government, tensions within the party increased. Not all the often conflicting electoral expectations could possibly be met, economic and financial constraints limited policy alternatives, and the strategic and ideological options of inner-party groupings and personalities became ever more divergent.

In the first nine months of government the inner-party tensions focusing on economic policy and on the relationship between the coalition partners made decisionmaking on crucial policy issues all but impossible. Since the adoption of the stabilization package, the debate within the party has led to a delicate but fragile balance. This has been expressed by Ferenc Kósa (who belongs to the current of nationalist-minded anti-capitalists), "My sense of justice," he has said, "gives me no peace; a victorious party cannot put its values into a deep freeze" (*Magyar Nemzet*, October 21, 1995).

Freezing and Change

The 1994 elections brought about a normal, regular shift of power between governing and opposition party blocs (although the FIDESZ changed its location in the cleavage structure) and seemed to confirm the position of the six parliamentary parties as central actors in the political game. Has structural consolidation, an *early freezing*, taken place? (Ágh, 1995). We may say so only with substantial qualification. As we have seen, the cleavage base has recently been seriously transformed. The paradox of the present Hungarian party system is that it appears to have frozen in the stage of the dominance of the nonstructural, value-based cultural cleavage and now has to adapt to the structural commodification-decommodification cleavage comprising, in the context of a transformation crisis, the social conflicts between winners and losers. This pattern of evolution and change of identity contradicts the Rokkanian thesis concerning the stability of party alternatives.

The functioning of parties as agencies of linkage in Hungary may also be questioned. There are no organic links between social cleavages, government decisionmaking, and political stability. In contrast to the significant weight of structural determination with low (if recently increasing) volatility in Western Europe, only 20 percent of the Hungarian electorate have a sense of party identification (be it stronger or weaker, unconditional or conditional). Together with an extremely high degree of volatility, however, we have also witnessed the increasing role of leftist economic priorities in shaping the 1994 election results.

Patronage and Dealignment

From late 1996 on, the relative stability of the Hungarian party system has been increasingly questioned by the electorate and by sharpening centrifugal movements in the individual parties. This destabilization was due to the policy record of the government under Prime Minister Gyula Horn and the corresponding changes in public opinion. The government strategy for financial consolidation has been successful, the equilibrium of the economy has substantially improved, public spending has decreased, and the confidence of international financial institutions and of foreign capital appears to have been restored. The social costs of these improvements, however, are considered by some to be too high. Real personal income declined by 15 to 16 percent in the first two years of the new government, income inequalities are growing, the middle strata is losing buying power, and the welfare system, particularly in the domain of health care, is showing alarming signs of financial collapse. By the fall of 1997, very modest signs of a relative improvement in general living standards were apparent, but the trend of growing inequalities continued.

General discontent, manifested by a score of 75 percent "pessimistic" in the 1996 Eurobarometer survey, is aggravated by the issue of corruption. A political patronage scandal involving an individual brokerage fee of eight million DM paid by the State Privatization Agency is seen by many as the mere tip of an iceberg, and the issue is exploited by the opposition parties and important in shaping popular political attitudes. Former SZDSZ leader János Kis has written, "The authority of democratic institutions has touched bottom; in the whole of East Central Europe, it is the weakest in this nation." He believes the "late-Kádárian bargain" has failed and blames the coalition partner. Ex-functionaries promised to maintain basic social security benefits to secure leading positions in which they practice clientelism and corruption to an extent that makes a mockery of their promise. Corruption, the parasitical penetration of a weak state by interest groups, and the interconnections between the public service and big capital are linked to the poor performance of the state and the decay of public services (Kis, 1996: 4–10).

The self-defense of the coalition parties (the Free Democrats having been shown to be involved in the scandal as well as the Socialists) has been to remind the opposition parties they did no better. Surveys indicate that public opinion reacts not only by withdrawing support from the government, but also by questioning the legitimacy of democratic institutions, particularly parliament and the parties. Mass protest against this "pornography of politics" threatens to override and/or distort the significance of social and cultural cleavages as it has in a number of other pluralist nations (Italy, Belgium, Austria, Spain, Iceland, and Japan, among others).

The present crisis of legitimacy strongly affects the parties. Within the MSZP the ability of party leader Gyula Horn to use his personal blend of autocratic leadership and tactical mediation to contain intraparty groups and discourage actual or potential rivals has not however been weakened and his authority has prevailed. Growing international prestige, healthy macroeconomic indicators and the halt in the decline in living conditions seem to restore—at least partially—confidence for the Socialists and their leader. Organizational rivalries among party bodies and ideological confrontations are dampened in the name of discipline and loyalty.

The SZDSZ also faces serious challenges. It suffers from a loss of party identity and autonomy as junior partner in coalition with a party of a very different political culture, yet has not been willing to risk isolation outside the government. A party with a heritage of moral resistance, it has found itself involved in dubious affairs. It must make the difficult choice between the prevailing economic reductionism of liberal policies versus standing up for its declared republican ethos. And finally, its middle-class clientele is being alienated by the restrictive monetarist policies with which the party is now associated.

Thus, as to the cleavage basis of the politics and policies of the now governing—"leftist" and "rightist"—parties, with the Socialists reasserting their dominant position and the Free Democrats losing their authentic and independent identity, we witness a syndrome of mutually reinforcing cleavages. Westernization, resulting from a cumulation of cultural and territorial cleavages is the decisive option. Its social content is externally determined, a logical consequence of the center-periphery relation: It is the victory of commodification representing the actual interests of the economic elites, of the winners of the transformation. However, a considerable number of old and middle-aged "leftist" voters remain loyal to the Socialists, even if their interests are hurt and their values are disregarded in public policies.

On the side of the present opposition we detect two contradictory tendencies. The first tendency is a corresponding cumulation of cleavages, a response to the Westernization bloc: decommodification tied to nationalist-clericalist positions and to anti-communism. An inherent consequence is the radicalization of party competition. The second tendency is an ever-deepening divide between a more militant, demagogic wing and a more pragmatic wing, amounting to a bipolarity. The rivalry between "Torgyánism" as "social nationalism," the program of demagogic anti-liberal populism and social redistributionism represented by József Torgyán, leader of the Smallholders, and the more moderate approach of the Young Democrats (FIDESZ), has led to a crumbling of the other parties of the traditionalist-nationalist opposition. Power conflicts emerged and escalated in the Forum and the Christian Democrats. In January 1996, half of the Parliamentary group of the MDF formed the moderate and pragmatic Hungarian Democratic People's Party (MDNP), in response to the victory of the more populist wing. Things, however, changed very soon. The MDNP has remained isolated and without any significant popular support. The Forum also risks failing the 5 percent threshold. While FIDESZ—according to János Kis, former leader of SZDSZ—is occupying the political space of the MDF of the early nineties (Kis, 1996: 9). MDF (that is, the rest of MDF) has concluded a pact of electoral alliance with the Young Democrats. The struggle for power and for ideological "purity" has been even more self-destructive for the Christian Democrats. The scandalous victory of party leader György Giczy standing even closer to the extra-Parliamentary fascistoid Party of Hungarian Truth and Life than to J. Torgyán was followed by the self-liquidation of the parliamentary group of the KDNP: the moderate majority of Christian Democratic MPs have joined the fraction of FIDESZ.

The "early freezing" thesis thus seems to be losing its relevance in Hungary, where an oscillation between tendencies of apathetic dealignment and more or less radical realignment appears to be the pattern. Meanwhile, party fragmentation is lessened, as the Socialists emerge on one side, and Young Democrats on the other, as the principal actors.

EAST-WEST CONVERGENCE

Central and Eastern European scholars and politicians sometimes tend to idealize Western political systems, failing to see the disturbing contradictions emerging in recent years. There are, in fact, surprising similarities between recent developments in the two regions. Some analysts of the Western party landscape point to an absence of equilibrium. On the one side they find parties to be increasingly irrelevant to the general population. Their role as purposive actors has weakened, they are losing their distinctive identities, and national governments are losing their room to maneuver. Membership declines, and a pervasive sense of disenchantment gains ground. Traditional parties become vulnerable to "anti-party system" assaults. Yet as Peter Mair points out, at the same time that the "parties on the ground" are in decline, "the public face of party, and especially the party in public office, is becoming stronger and enjoying an enhanced profile. . . . This shift can be seen as part of a long-term and almost autonomous process of party adaptation in which their eroding linkages with civil society have been compensated for by an ever-closer linkage with the state . . . highlighted by the patronage question, which depends almost entirely on access to public resources. . . . The state *is* the parties, or the parties *are* the state" (Mair, 1995).

If anything, Mair's thesis is more valid for East Central Europe than for Western Europe. Parties as public office holders are indispensable in the task of providing the necessary political steering of the massive economic transformation. While in the West the transformation of the parties (into state agencies) is taking place at the expense of mass parties with strong roots in civil society, in the East the absence or weakness of such roots clearly facilitates the functioning of the linkage between party and state.

CONCLUSION

Living and working on the threshold of the twenty-first century and entering a new modernity, a postindustrial age of globalized economy and globalized communications, scholars today reasonably question the future of political systems, of parties, and of cleavages. For Alain Touraine the decisive and central conflict in politics today is that between System and Subject, Reason and Identity, universalism and particularism, the world of production and the world of reproduction, the invasion of a homogenizing world market and the preservation of cultural differences stemming from social origins. When universalism linked to global market powers threatens the subject, antimodernizing and even fundamentalist and xenophobic effects and attitudes will result. Rational and aggressive universalism tends to destroy subjectivity and collective memory; the defense of identity may degenerate into racism and ethnic cleansing. The only solution is mediation combining rationalization and subjectification (Touraine, 1992).

Throughout the democratic world political actors look for new roles, new channels of representation. Are the cultural politics of Hungary, representing the age-old rivalry between traditionalists and westernizers but taking different and more modern forms as commodification proceeds apace, really so different from the politics of the West? Is it not possible that the dominant political cleavage in Hungary corresponds to new social realities that are in fact found throughout the world?

NOTES

1. The Democratic Charta, a political movement initiated in August 1991 by PEN President György Konrád (member of SZDSZ) and soon supported by thousands of liberal, social liberal, and socialist intellectuals, was directed against the Kulturkampf radicalization tendencies in the MDF government. Peaking from 1991 to 1994, it served as an umbrella organization to various demands:

- a reawakening of civil society drained by party pluralism;
- an opposition to authoritarian tendencies expressing a democratic consensus;
- an experimental field for a liberal-socialist political alliance.

(see: Bozóki, András. 1997. "The Politics of Movement-Intellectuals after the Regime Change: The Democratic Charta in Hungary." *Politikatudományi Szemle* 1: 237.)

2. This seems to confirm Sartori's thesis that the party system becomes structured in response to the rise of a mass party, although that author's corollary that such a party also contributes to the structural consolidation of the party system has not yet been apparent. (Sartori)

REFERENCES

Ágh, A. 1994. *The Revival of Mixed Traditions: Democracy and Authoritarian Renewal in East Central Europe.* Budapest Papers on Democratic Transition, no. 92.

Ágh, A. 1995. *The "Early Freezing" of the East Central European Parties: The Case of the Hungarian Socialist Party.* Budapest Papers on Democratic Transition, no. 129.

Harvey, D. 1994. *The Condition of Postmodernity.* Cambridge-Oxford.

Kis, J. 1996. "A rendszerváltásnak vége." *Beszélő.* August-September, 4–10.

Kulin, F. 1995. "Mitöl nemzeti?" *Magyar Nemzet,* 19 September.

Lipset, S. M. 1959. *Political Man.* New York: Doubleday.

Lipset, S. M. 1993. *The Social Requisites of Democracy Revisited.* Presid. Address ASA, Manuscript.

Magyar Nemzet, 21 Oct. 1995: 9

Mair, P. 1995. "Political Parties, Political Legitimacy and Public Privilege." *Western European Politics,* 18: 40–57.

Márkus, G. 1994. "Parties, Camps and Cleavages in Hungary." in M. Waller et al. (ed.), *Social Democracy in a Post-Communist Europe,* 154–70. London: MacMillan.

Révész, S. 1995. *Antall József távolról.* Budapest. Sík Verlag.

Sartori, G. 1968. "Political Development and Political Engineering." *Public Policy* 17: 261–98.

Szelényi, I. 1994. "Menedzser-kapitalizmus." *Magyar Lettre International* 19: 21–29.

Touraine, A. 1992. *Critique de la Modernité.* Paris.

11

Political Parties and Cleavage Crystallization in Poland, 1989–1993

Jerzy J. Wiatr

Transition to democracy in the post-communist states faces a peculiar problem which is mostly absent in the democratization processes in post-authoritarian systems. Authoritarian dictatorships, even if they lasted several decades, did not change the fabric of their societies to the same extent as did the communist regimes. Whether the social change that took place under the rule of the communist party was consistent with the party's ideology and with its declared policy goals is beyond this discussion. What is relevant for the study of cleavages and political parties is that the social change that had occurred during the communist regime has made unimportant or even nonexistent many social cleavages of the pre-communist past.

Poland is a good example in this respect, perhaps even more so than other post-communist states. Territorial change after the Second World War, combined with the forcible transfer of population (ethnic Germans to Germany, ethnic Poles from territories lost to the USSR to new homes in Poland) and with the extermination of most of the Polish Jewry during the Holocaust, resulted in the most homogenous structure of the Polish society ever. If in prewar Poland political parties to a large degree reflected ethnic diversity and cleavages resulting from it, this is no longer true now. While political exploitation of ethnic prejudices by some political groupings does take place (for instance, in the form of anti-semitic demonstrations), ethnic cleavages do not constitute sources of formation of political parties.

Along with ethnic cleavages gone also are the religious ones. Polish Roman Catholicism is the dominant religion to such an extent that all other denominations play only marginal roles. While there is tension resulting from the opposition between religious integrism (fundamentalism) and radical anticlericalism, there is strictly speaking no religious cleavage of the type which we observe in many plural societies.

Economic cleavages have been greatly reduced in importance and changed in nature. Economic transformations from the postwar years abolished the once-powerful conflict between the peasantry and the land-owning nobility, since the latter had lost its land under the land reform decree of 1944. Outside agriculture private ownership existed but a powerful bourgeoisie could not emerge due to legal and extra-legal restrictions used against it by the government. There were economic differences between people and some saw the conflict between rich and poor as an important one, but compared to the pre-communist era this cleavage was mostly latent.

It does not follow, however, that the society was undivided or that it felt itself to be undivided during the communist years. Most Poles saw the social reality as dichotomically divided between "us" (the common people) and "them" (those in power or close to them). This was particularly true during the period of the most successful mobilization within the Solidarity movement, 1980–1981. However, genuine class politics did not emerge and are unlikely to reappear until the consequences of dismantling state socialism have been experienced by the Polish people.

One may, therefore, argue that old social cleavages—the one with roots in the pre-communist time—do not play any major role in contemporary Polish politics. They have been replaced by new ones.

TYPOLOGY OF CLEAVAGES

In a paper presented to the international conference on political parties in New Europe, held in Vienna in April 1992, I suggested the emergence of a three-dimensional political space in post-communist Poland (Wiatr, 1993a: 108–21), in which three cleavages were dominant: (a) the economic cleavage, (b) a cleavage of opinion regarding the issue of state secularism, and (c) a cleavage regarding the issue of historical responsibility for the communist period ("de-communization" issue). This interpretation was soon challenged by a more elaborate typology based on five, empirically distinguishable, dimensions, proposed by Krzysztof Jasiewicz (Jasiewicz, 1993: 387–411). His five dimensions are: (a) state protectionism versus free market orientation, (b) secularism versus. religiosity, (c) xenophobia versus Westernization, (d) political authoritarianism versus democracy, and (e) decommunization. Testing empirically the salience of his five cleavages (by the use of survey data), Jasiewicz concluded that all five dimensions reflected political cleavages at the time of the first free election to the Parliament (October 1991), but that only three of them (b, d, and e) were as divisive as hypothetically expected. The issue of secularism versus religiosity turned out in his analysis to be the most divisive of all (Jasiewicz, 1993: 401). The economic dimension, however, had been somehow mixed with the nationalism versus Westernization dimension, leading Jasiewicz to introduce two other dimensions: political and economic liberalism versus populism, and Westernization versus nationalism. Consequently, he has discovered—through the factor analysis of survey data—four political options, correlated with declared willingness to vote for a political party. These four options have been termed liberal-democratic, conservative, populist, and socialist. In addition, the author has identified a certain number of respondents whose declared preferences placed them in a "centrist" position, characterized by diversity and inconsistency of views among those who were classified in such way (Jasiewicz, 1993: 404–5).

In my further analysis I intend to focus on the original of three cleavages suggested in my 1992 paper. This is because of the different nature of my approach, which focuses on political parties, not on individual voters.[1] I look into party platforms and the patterns of behavior of their parliamentarians to identify the most important differences between them. Two dimensions which showed some saliency in Jasiewicz's survey are markedly played down in Polish party politics. The first of these is authoritarianism versus democracy. While some Poles are authoritarian and show such attitudes in the interview situation, political parties carefully avoid looking authoritarian, particularly those which have some stronger political following. Of the parties represented in the 1991 and 1993 Parliaments, only the Confederacy of Independent Poland can to some degree be defined as authoritarian, because of its internal structure and its strong support for a presidential system of government. This is too little (particularly considering the Confederacy's very poor showing in the 1993 election) to consider authoritarianism a major political cleavage in contemporary Poland.

Similarly, the Westernization versus nationalism dimensions do not distinguish political parties strongly enough. All major political parties opt for Poland's integration with the European Union and admission to the North Atlantic Treaty Organization. Some politicians do this with a little bit of reservation but there is much more consensus among the political class than among the general public on this issue. It seems to me, therefore, that it would make little sense to consider this issue as a major cleavage in party politics.

The election of 1993 reduced the number of viable parliamentary parties to six: *Alliance of Democratic Left*, composed of a number of organizations under the leadership of the Socialdemocracy of the Republic of Poland; *the Polish Peasant Party; the Union of Liberty*, formed after the election by the fusion of the Democratic Union and the Liberal-Democratic Congress; *Union of Labour; Confederacy of Independent Poland; and the Non-Party Bloc for Support of Reforms*. A number of political parties received between 2 and 7 percent of popular vote but were unable to get parliamentary seats due to their failure to reach the required threshold for the Seym election. Some of them, however, have single senators. Their position in the political system may change if in the future election they are able to overcome divisive conflicts and to form a coalition. For this reason, in my analysis of relations between parties and cleavages I do not exclude the extraparliamentary parties if they received at least 2 percent of votes in the Seym election of 1993.

SOCIOECONOMIC CLEAVAGES

Economic strategies have constituted major divisions between political parties in post-communist Poland and they played a crucial role in the election of 1993 (Wiatr, 1993b). After four years of radical economic reform, called the Balcerowicz Plan (after the Vice-premier and Finance Minister Leszek Balcerowicz), both positive and negative results of the radical ("shock") therapy have been evident. This is not the proper place to evaluate Poland's economic performance during the first four years of economic reform (1990–1993) and such analysis has been done by many other students of Polish reforms (Przeworski, 1993: 132–98). What concerns me now are cleavages generated by the radical reform and their political consequences.

Such cleavages can be divided in three groups. First, some groups benefited from the economic change, while others lost absolutely or at least relatively, in comparison to the most successful ones. Income differences are markedly greater than under the communist regime and chances of improving one's situation are increasingly uneven. The "haves" are mostly younger, better educated, and living in regions of greater economic activity (therefore, less affected by mass unemployment, particularly in larger cities). The "have-nots" are, first of all, unemployed (who happen to be less well educated), older, living in depressed areas and, to a very high degree, farmers. Among political parties, three cater for the "haves" and have a high number of better-off people in their ranks: the Union of Liberty (particularly after the fusion which brought the Liberal-Democratic Congress into the party), the pro-Wałęsa Non-Party Bloc for Support of Reforms, and the ultra-liberal (in monetarist terms) Union of Real Politics. They oppose higher taxes for the rich and demand reduction of social services. They also argue that high social costs of reforms were inevitable and that they cannot be reduced without jeopardizing the economic reform itself. On the other hand, the Alliance of the Democratic Left, the Union of Labor, and the Polish Peasant Party based their electoral campaign on the defense of the "have-nots," although the Alliance of the Democratic Left did it with some prudence, arguing that marketization of the economy is too important to be tampered with by radical social reforms. The parties of the extreme parliamentary "right," as well as the Confederacy of Independent Poland, campaigned for the votes of the poor strata to various degrees, but—with the exception of the Confederacy—their credibility was negatively affected by the fact that all of them had participated in some governments of the 1989–1993 period, which were considered responsible for the effects of the economic reform.

The second aspect of the socioeconomic cleavage is the opposition between state interventionism and monetarism. In theoretical terms, both are doctrines or policies applied in the economic activities of governments. However, their social implications are markedly different for various groups in the society. Generally speaking, monetarism favors those social groups which are stronger and better able to take care of themselves in free-market competition. Interventionism can have various consequences, some neutral from the point of view of social classes (for instance, investing in the arms industry does not favor any social class as such, although it may have positive consequences for people working in this industry). On the other hand, however, weak social groups, ill-fit for free competition (such as the old, the uneducated, the single-parent families, and the disabled) need governmental assistance which is less likely to come if monetarist policies limit the possibilities of an active role of the state in social policy. Education, health care, and public transportation are also examples of fields in which state interventionism can make a difference. Consequently, this aspect of the economic cleavage tends to organize the political scene in the way analogous to the first one: the liberal Right supporting monetarism, the Left supporting state interventionism and the non-liberal Right taking a middle road (except the strongly interventionist Confederacy of Independent Poland).

The third aspect of the economic cleavage has a different nature: it is the special position of agriculture and the conflict of interests generated by it. Poland has avoided collectivization of her agriculture during the most repressive communist rule.[2] Differently than in other communist states, Polish agriculture remained predominantly in private hands. But most of the farms have been too small and too poor to match the efficiency of Western modern farming. In addition, when Polish currency became commonplace, Polish farmers have been forced to compete with subsidies for Western food products. As the result of all these factors, agriculture suffered more than other sectors of the economy and the farmers" standard of living fell more than that of other classes. This gave an impetus to class-oriented peasant politics. The Polish Peasant Party (PSL) is an old political formation which, in 1995, celebrated the centennial of its beginning. It is now the only class party in Poland in the sense that (a) it can count on the support of the majority of the peasants, and (b) it has very little support among other groups of the society. The originality of the PSL in the Polish party system is it cannot be clearly placed on the Left-Right continuum, but rather follows such policies as it believes to be in the interest of the peasantry. Consequently, the PSL is ready and able to make alliances either with the Left or with the Right. If classified as a "centrist" party, it does not always represent middle-of-the-road policies but is rather "centrist" by its ability and willingness to take part in any political combination that is in the interest of its constituency. No other party is a class party in this sense.

SECULARISM VERSUS RELIGIOUS FUNDAMENTALISM

The collapse of communist rule produced a radical shift in relations between the state and the Roman Catholic Church. Under the communist regime, the

Church played a pivotal role in voicing protest, organizing independent initiatives, and giving shelter to opponents of the regime. Its relations with the rulers varied from open conflict (and persecution) to cooperation (Micewski, 1982). It commanded very high respect among the Polish people.

After the fall of communism, the Catholic Church became the most powerful social institution, aware of its contribution to the struggle against the former regime and willing now to collect the debts incurred by the nation to its spiritual leader. Its strong position was further increased by the fact that most of the leaders of the "Solidarity" movement were active Catholics, demonstrating their fidelity to the Church. Finally, the impact of the Polish Pope John Paul II has been very great, largely because Poles have been proud to have one of their own on the throne of St. Peter.

The Church insisted on reorientation of the state away from the constitutional principle of separation from the churches. The very concept of state-church separation is referred to (by cardinals, bishops, and many Catholic intellectuals) as a product of communist ideology, Western liberal democratic patterns notwithstanding. Catholic politicians have been able to introduce restrictive anti-abortion legislation (January 1993). When the Parliament made an attempt to liberalize it (in 1994, after the victory of the Left in parliamentary election), President Wałęsa successfully vetoed the new law. Religious instruction has been introduced in public schools. The law on radio and television declares that public stations have the obligation to observe "Christian values." Generally, to quote a Western writer, "many observers see the first four years of Solidarity government as a triumph for traditional Catholic moral values" (Heyden, 1994: 166).

However, the triumph of Catholic values in public life during these years was not reflected in a triumph for fundamental Catholic parties. The election of 1993 was to a very high degree contested on the secularism versus fundamentalism issue (Wiatr, 1993b). The Left—particularly the Alliance of Democratic Left and Union of Labour—declared their opposition to religious fundamentalism and committed themselves to policies that would reverse the situation. Right-wing parties either expressed support for the current policies of the Solidarity-based governments or went even further, demanding more concessions for the Church. All of these parties lost in the election and became thereafter the extra-parliamentary opposition. Their only voice in the Senate were isolated senators from the Right (no more than five out of one hundred senators).

The middle-of-the road position on the religious cleavage is taken by four parties. The Polish Peasant Party declines to oppose the demands of the Church, but leaves its parliamentarians the right to vote their conscience. A minority of the PSL parliamentarians support the secularist Left in the critical votes on Church-related issues. The Union of Liberty supports so-called "Christian votes" but avoids taking extreme position on such issues. It tolerated some dissent in its ranks but in 1995 the most vocal secularist of this party, Barbara Labuda, was expelled from its ranks. Two small Rightist parties—the Confederacy of Independent Poland and the Non-Party Bloc for Support of Reforms—generally support the position of the Church but do not make such support the core of their platforms.

The issue is very controversial and divides the Polish society more strongly than any other cleavages. Public opinion surveys show decreasing support for and prestige of the Roman Catholic Church. Nonetheless, religious fundamentalism remains strong and the opposition between fundamentalism and secularism organizes the political scene more strongly than anything else. Some politicians and intellectuals warn that such a situation may lead to "religious cold war" (Michnik, 1993), that is to radical polarization of the political scene along the secularism-fundamentalism divide. I see this possibility as a very serious threat to Polish democracy. In my opinion, a religious "cold war" can be avoided only by adopting Western standards of human rights and religious freedom, combined with neutrality of the state toward churches and religions.

HISTORIC RESPONSIBILITY CLEAVAGE

During the early stages of the transition to democracy the relationship between present and past becomes important. Democracy requires that all citizens are free to vote and to run for public office, unless deprived of these rights by due process of law. It also requires that all political forces are free to organize and to compete. This last principle knows some exceptions. Germany after World War II made it illegal to propagate Nazi ideology and to organize a Nazi party. Finally, democracy faces the problem of how to punish those individuals who violated human rights and committed other crimes under previous regimes.

The question of historical responsibility can be put on three different levels. First, there is a legal aspect. Those guilty of crimes should be put on trial, if it is possible to locate them and to collect evidence. There is no political controversy on this issue in Poland. All political parties support the policy of submitting former state functionaries to the normal process of law.

The second aspect concerns so-called "collective responsibility." Should members of the ruling party, officers of police, army officers, bureaucrats who in various forms and with different degrees of individual commitment carried out the policies of the communist regime, be treated differently from others? Should they, in particular, be deprived of some political rights, like the right to seek public positions? This is the so-called "decommunization" issue. The name has been coined after the "denazification" policy in postwar Germany. On this issue there is a sharp division between proponents and opponents of "de-communization." Both public opinion and political parties in Poland are sharply divided on this issue (Bartkowski, 1993: 80–107). The traditional right-wing parties, as well as the Confederacy of Independent Poland, support in one way or another the principle of collective responsibility and demand that individuals involved in communist policies (even if they individually did not commit any crime) be made to pay a price. The Alliance of the Democratic Left, the Polish Peasant Party, the Union of Liberty, and the Union of Labour oppose the principle of collective responsibility. In the 1993 election these four parties got 53.68 percent of the total vote for the Seym, while the parties which favor "de-communization" received 35.12 percent of all votes. The division is clear but asymmetrical, with the majority of voters voting "de-communizers" out of office.

The third aspect concerns historical responsibility proper, that is, the general evaluation of the communist past. No political party in Poland claims that all was fine during the communist regime. All express criticism of it. But the tone and intensity of criticism differ. For the parties of the post-Solidarity current as well as for the Confederacy of Independent Poland, the forty-five years of communist rule were lost years and should be condemned. For the Alliance of Democratic Left and for the Polish Peasant Party, the past demands more nuanced evaluation, reflecting the international conditions of Soviet hegemony, as well as discriminating between what calls for condemnation and what was good in the policies of the communist regime. In electoral terms, this aspect of the historical responsibility cleavage puts the critics of the communist past, in a somewhat stronger position. Parties that condemn this period won the majority of votes (but not of seats), while 35.81 percent of voters cast their votes for the two parties that defend the record of the communist regime against total condemnation. Around 60 percent voted for parties that condemn the communist period totally. It is the sharp fragmentation of this camp that has made it impossible for it to transform this cleavage into an effective instrument of collective electoral politics.

There is, however, another question connected with this cleavage. How important is the question of historical responsibility for the voters? Who does care? How much? Survey data suggest that the saliency of this cleavage depends to some degree on education (better educated, care more), but mostly on previous political engagement. Those who were actively involved—in the opposition or on the side of the regime—tend to consider the issue more important for contemporary politics. Others are more likely to vote on the basis of current divisions, rather than on the basis of past differences.

CONCLUSIONS

The existence of three main cleavages deepens the fragmentation of the Polish party system. Moreover, the fact that the economic cleavages do not correspond to the two noneconomic ones results in the difficulty in describing the political scene in terms of Left-Right continuum. Some scholars and politicians have even suggested that these terms are irrelevant in the Polish conditions (Wasilewski, 1994: 32). Such argument was particularly popular in the early period of democratization, when it served as the justification of policies aimed at constructing the political scene around the central, ideologically undefined pillar: solidarity.

However, such an argument ignores the saliency of the three cleavages. It is true that each of them defines the political scene differently. But it is possible to discover the main dividing lines. They do not cut simply along the Left-Right division, because there is more than one Right in Poland.

While the Left can be easily defined by the combination of economic platforms serving the "have-nots," secularism and opposition to "de-communization," the Right is divided between its liberal and its conservative wings. The Liberal Right is characterized by economic platforms favoring "haves," moderate pro-Church position and moderate support for "de-communization" (but more in terms of condemnation of the communist past than in terms of collective responsibility of individuals involved in the communist politics). The Conservative Right, on the other hand, is characterized by middle-of-the-road economic programs, religious fundamentalism, and radical "de-communization." The only party that does not fit such a typology is the Union of Labour which is leftist on the first two cleavages, but strongly condemns the communist past (without, however, supporting the idea of collective responsibility). This is because it is the only leftist party with some affiliation with the democratic opposition to the communist regime (particularly among party leaders).

The distances between the Left, the Liberal Right, and the Conservative Right differ depending on the cleavage concerned.

On the economic cleavages, the Left is most strongly opposed to the Liberal Right, and less so to the Conservative Right. On the religious cleavages, the sharpest differences exist between the Left and the Conservative Right, with the Liberal Right standing somewhere in the middle. The same is true for the historical responsibility cleavages. Since the last two cleavages explain the major part of political differentiation in Poland, one may put this in somewhat different terms. Combining all three cleavages one can arrange parties along a continuum defined by the sequence: Left–Liberal Right–Conservative Right. Such sequence corresponds quite well with the actual behavior of parties during the parliamentary terms 1991–1993 and the one begun in 1993. Behavioral observation of the parties suggests that the analysis of their ideological profiles produces not just an abstract typology but a typology reflecting a real life situation.

NOTES

1. My analysis combines two approaches. First, I have studied programs and electoral platforms of all major political parties. Second, as member of Parliament (from Alliance of Democratic Left) since 1991 and member of the National Council of the Socialdemocracy of the Republic of Poland, I have had various opportunities to observe the behavior of party leaders and parliamentarians. This can be called a "participant observation method," in the past widely used in sociology.

2. The failure of Polish collectivization is usually explained as resulting both from the strong resistance of the peasants and from the lack of zeal among party leaders and members (Koboński, 1965). The collectivization was finally stopped immediately after

the Central Committee meeting in October 1956, which marked the peak of destalinization in Poland.

REFERENCES

Bartkowski, Jerzy. 1993. "Public opinion and 'decommunization' in Poland." In Jerzy J. Wiatr. (ed.), *The Politics of Democratic Transformation: Poland after 1989*, 80–107. Warsaw: Scholar Agency.

Heyden, Jacqueline. 1994. *Poles Apart: Solidarity and the New Poland.* Dublin: Irish Academic Press.

Jasiewicz, Krzysztof. 1993. "Polish Politics on the Eve of the 1993 Elections: Toward Fragmentation or Pluralism?" *Communist and Post-Communist Studies* 26 (4): 387–411.

Korbonski, Andrzej. 1965. *Politics of Socialist Agriculture in Poland: 1945–1960.* New York and London: Columbia University Press.

Micewski, Andrzej. 1982. *Kardynał Wyszyński, prymas i mąż stanu.* Paris: Editions du Dialogue.

———. 1987. *Kolścioł wobec Solidarności i stanu wojennego.* Paris: Editions du Dialogue.

Michnik, Adam. 1993. "Kolścioł–prawica–monolog." *Gazeta Wyborcza* 27–28 March.

Przeworski, Adam. 1993. "Economic reforms, public opinion, and political institutions: Poland in the Eastern European perspective." In Luiz Carlos Bresser Pereira, José Mariá Maravall and Adam Przeworski, *Economic Reforms in New Democracies: A Social-Democratic Approach,* 132–98. New York: Cambridge University Press.

Wasilewski, Jacek. 1994. "Scena polityczna w postkomunistycznej i postsolidarnościowej Polsce." In Jacek Wasilewski (ed.), *Konsolidacja elit politycznych, 1991–1993.* Warszawa: Instytut Studiów Politycznych Polskiej Akademii Nauk.

Wiatr, Jerzy J. 1993a. "Fragmented Parties in a New Democracy: Poland." In Jerzy J. Wiatr, *Wybory parlamentarne 19 września 1993: przyczyny i następstwa,* 108–121.Warsaw: Scholar Agency.

———. 1993b. *Wybory parlamentarne 19 września 1993: przyczyny i następstwa.* Warsaw: Scholar Agency.

12

Romania: Parties and Issues after 1989

―――――――――――――― *Petre Datculescu*

INTRODUCTION

This chapter attempts to analyze the extent to which the new Romanian political parties are a translation of true divisions and conflicting interests in the social structure and in national political life.

A number of specific questions arise in this context: Are the new political parties in Romania actually based on distinctive social strata? Are there left and right issues in Romania that dominate politics and are related to basic divisions of interests between classes or social groups? Do the parties differ in their stands on these issues and in their "distance" apart? And finally, is there any sign of an emerging social division that will eventually polarize the Romanian political parties across structural cleavage lines?

In attempting to answer these questions, I first look at the development of the Romanian social structure after 1989. Subsequently, I briefly describe the present Romanian party system, assessing the current strength of the parties and the issues they stand for. Thirdly, I present the major issues and controversies in the Romanian national community and discuss the ways in which parties respond to them.

DEVELOPMENTS IN THE SOCIAL STRUCTURE AFTER 1989

The figures in Table 12.1 show that the developments in the Romanian social structure have been extremely slow-moving. Six years after 1989, workers and peasants still constituted the most numerous social groups in Romanian society and, as a result of the deprivation suffered during the Ceaușescu regime and the slow pace of economic reform, social and economic homogeneity persisted.

Table 12.1
Economically Active Population in Romania (percent in various branches)

	1990	1991	1995
Agriculture	28	29	34
Silviculture, forestry, and hunting	1	1	1
Industry	37	35	29
Constructions	6	5	5
Trade	5	6	9
Hotels and restaurants	2	2	1
Transport	6	6	5
Post and communications	1	1	1
Financial, banking and insurance activities	0	0	1
Immovable dealing and other services	4	4	3
Public administration and defense compulsory social assistance	1	1	1
Education	4	4	5
Health and social assistance	3	3	3
Other branches of the national economy	2	3	2

Source: National Commission for Statistics–Romanian Statistical Yearbook. 1996. Bucharest, p. 141.

Public property still prevails. At the end of 1994, fixed assets were still in state property in a proportion of 89 percent. The remaining 11 percent were not fully in private hands either. At least half of them were owned jointly by the state and private owners (Pasti, Miroiu and Codiță, 1997: 81–82).

While it is true that in 1994 the private sector accounted for 35 percent of the GDP, it actually is a poor sector which is represented mainly by trade activities. More than 90 percent of the small- and medium-sized enterprises employ four people at the most. Only about one-fifth of all employees work in the private sector, and their salaries do not differ significantly from those of public sector employees.

The overwhelming majority of private entrepreneurs are farmers. They are small landowners in an almost fully privatized agriculture. Privatization, however, has resulted in nothing more than a restoration of the traditional peasant households that existed between the wars and in the creation of a class of landowners that lack resources, know-how, farming equipment, and irrigation systems, have no access to credits, and are unable to trade their products independently.

The difficulties encountered by small landowners also stand in the way of the modernization of rural areas, and 52 percent of Romania's population lives in these areas. There is at present an enormous gap that is likely to become even wider in the future between the rural world and the urban centres. The stratification according to living standard—presented in Table 12.2—suggests that there is a low degree of social polarization and the middle class is hardly a majority.

Table 12.2
Stratification of Romanian Households according to Living Standard (in percent)

	Total	*Urban*	*Rural*
Poor	19.9	11.6	30.0
Less than average but not poor	44.2	44.8	43.5
Average	24.3	30.1	17.2
More than average but not rich	7.7	9.3	5.7
Rich	3.9	4.2	3.6
Total	100.0	100.0	100.0

Source: Social Stratification Research Data. IRSOP Market Research. 1997. Bucharest.

To sum up, the analysis of the Romanian social structure reveals a large working class depending on their jobs in a declining state-run economy, a massive private peasanty economically immobilized in small farms, a narrow middle class, and a thin section of upper-class families.

THE NEW PATTERN OF ROMANIAN POLITICS

Revival of the Multiparty System

On the evening of December 22, 1989, the Romanian state TV announced the disintegration of the monolithic communist party and its replacement by a proto-party movement called The National Salvation Front. In many respects, the NSF wanted to be like the Forums in Hungary, the former GDR, and the former Czechoslovakia—movements that had been trying to mobilize people with the most diverse political conceptions directed against totalitarian systems and for the peaceful transformation of dictatorships into democratic civic societies.

As in other East-European countries, many NSF members would have liked to keep the movement as an expression of democracy in its broadest sense or as a political premise for identifying paths for development between socialism and capitalism, or between East and West.

The origin of the NSF and its leaders, headed by Ion Iliescu, is surrounded by a certain mystery (Călinescu and Tismăneanu, 1992), which has not yet been clarified. The NSF was accused of trying to confiscate the Romanian revolution, of being a refuge in disguise for former communists, of trying to preserve power in the long run. The NSF was also said to be a mere continuation of the former communist party. However, most Romanians did not share this view.

In fact, the Front leadership was the one to abolish the one-party rule and to allow the emergence of multiparty democracy. New parties appeared on the political scene without delay. At this point, the NSF could no longer remain a movement without running the risk of splitting up. On the other hand, the leaders who were still directing the transition were not delighted at the idea of dissolving the Front or moving on to other political parties. Consequently, they transformed the Front into a party that participated in the first free elections of May 20, 1990.[1]

Huntington points out that a long period of party suppression is usually followed by an outburst of political forces and political participation (Huntington, 1968: 107). The Romanian case offers an example. Only a few months before the elections of May 20, Romania had seventy-five registered political parties. In the second democratic elections in September 1992, seventy-nine parties and alliances entered the race for the Chamber of Deputies, and sixty-five competed for the Senate. On the eve of the elections in November 1996, the total number of registered parties amounted to almost two hundred, although only fifty-two participated in the elections.

Broadly speaking, the parties emerging in post-totalitarian periods fall into two categories: new parties, and parties that present themselves as continuations of parties that had existed before the one-party dictatorship. As in other East-European countries, the political community in Romania also felt the need to revive the old historical parties that had been destroyed by the communists shortly after World War II. Unfortunately, for a rather long time the new variants remained true to their original prototype while both the social structure and the dominant issues of political life had significantly changed. This may be one of the reasons why in the first democratic elections in all East-European countries new parties or movements performed better than the so-called historical parties.

Thus, in the 1990 elections in Czechoslovakia, the new Civic Forum swamped the "old" Christian Democrats and Social Democrats. Peasant parties were among the strongest parties after the Second World War in Hungary, Bulgaria, and Romania. But in 1990, Bulgaria's Agrarians got 8 percent, Hungary's Smallholders received 12 percent, and Romania's National Peasant Party, 3 percent.

The Current System of Party Oppositions

Romania has today what may be termed a "pluralist" political system. Political parties are free to organize and compete for power. In addition, pressure groups and interest groups of many kinds may also compete for influence upon political decisionmakers. Ancestral political loyalties have disappeared during the last fifty years and voters feel fairly free to switch from one party to another. Therefore, parties must compete for support and cannot yet firmly count on many constituencies for consistent support.

In a political community with more than fifty legally registered parties, an important distinction is necessary. When I say "political parties," I do not refer to the names of invisible entities with a legal status, empty bank accounts, and a small leadership without followers. I mean real parties with organization, records, and constituencies that have had a tangible impact on the Romanian political life since 1990. The following list of the most significant political parties with their Romanian acronyms provided may help the reader find his way in the volatile Romanian political landscape. (The parties are presented in alphabetical order based on their Romanian names.)

Civic Alliance Party	PAC
Romania's Agrarian Democratic Party	PDAR
Democratic Party	PD
Party of Social Democracy of Romania (Former National Salvation Front Party, FDSN)	PDSR
Romanian Ecological Party	PER
Liberal Party '93	PL '93
National Liberal Party-Quintus	PNL-Quintus
National Liberal Party–Democratic Convention	PNL-CD
Christian-Democratic National Peasant Party	PNȚ-CD
Greater Romania Party	PRM
Romanian Social Democratic Party	PSDR
Socialist Party	PS
Socialist Labour Party	PSM
Romanians' National Unity Party	PUNR
Democratic Alliance of Hungarians in Romania	UDMR

Placing these parties along the classic Left-Right continuum is not an easy task. There are left and right issues in Romania that dominate politics and party rhetoric, but they can hardly be related to basic divisions of class interest. Consequently, neither parties nor the electorate can be divided sharply into left and right, have-nots and haves. Pasti, Miroiu, and Codiță, who examined the political programs of all Romanian parties, have found a number of striking similarities (Pasti, Miroiu, and Codiță, 1997: 135). Basically these programs all contain:

A. A set of commitments towards the general orientations of East European communities:
- Transition towards a market economy
- Political democracy
- Integration into the European Community
- Integration into NATO
- Encouraging foreign investors to invest in Romania

B. A set of promises addressed to distinctive sections of the electorate:
- Credits with subsidized interests for farmers
- Salary indexation for employees
- Lower taxation for private entrepreneurs
- Old-age pensions and allowances for senior citizens, women, children, and disabled persons

- Jobs and credits for buying a home granted to young couples
- Eliminating corruption and a new system of public administration for everybody

In these circumstances, the notions of "left" or "right" are of limited value. However, I believe that the current Romanian parties can be divided into two broad categories with emerging underlying ideological value orientations. One group includes parties that favor the maintenance of an increased state control over the economy and place more emphasis on nationalistic issues. I shall call them "National-Conservatives." A second group comprises parties that favor a faster move towards capitalism and place higher emphasis on cosmopolitan values. I will refer to them as "Cosmopolitan-Liberals." Both groups of parties are equally populistic in their economic promises to the electorate. Within each group, individual parties differ in terms of the strength with which they advocate either state intervention or liberalism on one side and nationalism versus cosmopolitan attitudes on the other. But overall, National-Conservatives are more concerned with redistributionism, egalitarian doctrines, and slower change toward a market economy to allow the formation of domestic capital and a national bourgeoisie. The Cosmopolitan-Liberals are, quite distinctively, more centered on fast social change, private property, free competition, and creating conditions for the penetration of foreign capital to Romania.

An indication of the relative strength of the two groups is provided by the results of the general elections on November 3, 1996 (see Table 12.3).

As can be seen in the table, the "Cosmopolitan-Liberals" are at present clearly stronger than the "National-Conservatives." Their main actor, CDR,[2] is a conglomerate of parties including the National Peasant Party (PNȚ-CD), the National Liberal Party (PNL), another Liberal Party (PNL-CD), and a small Ecological Party (PER) together with numerous other civic alliances and associations. Within the Convention, the strongest party is the National Peasant Party (PNȚ-CD), which considers itself a continuation of the prewar Peasant Party. For reasons of party modernization and international affiliation, the party has adopted

Table 12.3
Relative Strength of the Main Romanian Party Camps (in percent)

National-Conservatives		*Cosmopolitan-Liberals*	
PDSR	23.0	CDR	30.7
PUNR	4.2	USD	13.1
PRM	4.5	UDMR	6.8
PSM	2.0	ANL	1.5
Total	33.7		52.1

Source: Results obtained in the vote for the Chamber of Deputies and communicated by the Central Electoral Bureau, "Curierul Național," November 12, 1996, p. 4. PSM and ANL did not reach the 3 percent threshold to enter the newly elected Parliament.

the suffix CD and announced its commitment to the family of Western European Christian-Democratic Parties. The leaders and core members of this party are former activists and sympathizers of the prewar Peasant Party, some of whom spent many years in communist prisons and were brutally persecuted during the communist regime. However, the Peasant Party managed to attract a number of outstanding Romanian intellectuals who are respected opinion leaders and supported University Professor Emil Constantinescu for nomination as the candidate of the Democratic Convention for the presidential elections in 1992 and 1996. Constantinescu was defeated by Ion Iliescu in 1992 but scored a strong victory in 1996, replacing Iliescu as the president of country.

Considerably less strong than the Peasant Party is the National Liberal Party (PNL), also a member of the Democratic Convention. The PNL is one of at least four liberal parties that claim to be a continuation of the prewar Liberals. The liberal factions more or less originate from one single National Liberal Party which was established in 1990 but disintegrated mainly because of weak leadership and strong internal rivalries. The current PNL appears to be more viable than its brother factions. Quite similar to the old Liberals, the current PNL seeks to serve the private business community. But for the time being, the Romanian private business sector is weak and its members are a clientele of various political patrons.

The second player in the camp is USD, an alliance of the Democratic Party (PD) of former Prime Minister Petre Roman and the small Social Democratic Party (PSDR). Within the USD, Petre Roman's Democratic Party (PD) is definitely the leading force. An ally of Ion Iliescu, Petre Roman became Prime Minister in 1990. But his term ended abruptly in September 1991, when a raid of miners ravaged Bucharest and forced him to resign. Roman retained his second job as a national leader of the government party, the FDSN. But very soon the FDSN broke into a group headed by Roman and a group supporting Ion Iliescu. Basically the two groups differed regarding the pace of economic reform. The Iliescu group was advocating a slowdown of the reform and reinvigoration of existing national potentials by centralized economic control. Roman and his supporters demanded more emphasis on creating national wealth by free market mechanisms rather than strengthening state intervention to redistribute wealth. After the breakdown of the FDSN in March 1992, the two groups became two parties, referred to as the Iliescu party (PDSR) and the Roman Party (FSN and later PD). Despite its liberal-reformist attitude, the PD calls itself a social-democratic party with an eye on have-nots. The party would like to represent both the interests of private business and wage earners of all social strata. As a result of this dual ambition, the party has no clear and stable constituency. Its relative success in attracting supporters is based on a dynamic party activity and charismatic leadership rather than ideology or response to particular social issues.

The UDMR is the party of the Hungarian ethnic minority, while the ANL is an alliance of liberal-oriented parties, including the so-called "Young Liberals"

(PL '93) and a party of intellectuals (PAC) which emerged from a civic movement called The Civic Alliance.

In the "National-Conservative" group the leader is the former government party, the PDSR, headed by former president Ion Iliescu. The PDSR is a continuation of the National Salvation Front, which became a party in 1990 under the name of the Democratic National Salvation Front (FDSN) and later changed its name to the Party of Social Democracy (PDSR).

Originally, this party integrated second-line members of the former communist bureaucracy. But the real core of the party was composed of technocrats who ran the economy and the administration during the communist regime.

Between 1992 and 1996 the PDSR governed in alliance with three "leftist" parties, sometimes also referred to as "nationalist" or even "extremist" parties: PUNR, PRM, and PSM. The Romanian National Unity Party (PUNR) is the counterpart of the Hungarian ethnic party (UDMR). Its social base is located in the region of Transylvania where the party is mobilizing Romanian nationalists against Hungarian nationalists. Another more extreme and chauvinistic nationalist party is the Greater Romania Party (PRM). The leaders and initiators of this party are intellectuals from the vanguard of the former communist system, mainly writers and historians, formerly related to top communist party leaders, also including retired members of the army and the former Securitate. The group glorifies the past and strives to convince the electorate that Romania faces great dangers coming from Hungary, the Jews, Moscow, and the big Western powers.

In many ways the "Greater Romania" nationalists are similar to the Socialist Labour Party (PSM), which is regarded as the true follower of the old Communist Party. Headed by seventy-two-year-old Ilie Verdeţ, once Prime Minister of Nicolae Ceauseşcu, the PSM praises the achievements of the former communist regime, while at the same time distrusting the West and advocating a slow pace of change toward market mechanisms.

An internal split weakened the PSM in 1995 and prevented the party from achieving 3 percent of the votes in the national elections in 1996 and from reentering the Romanian Parliament.

Emotional Divisions and the War of Party Imageries

The leaders, activists, propagandists, and sympathizers of various parties seem to have clear differences in their minds when comparing their party to other parties. Emotional divisions run deep, particularly between the National-Conservatives and the Cosmopolitan-Liberals. But even within the same alliance, parties often find themselves deeply divided on emotional grounds.

Images are vague measures of true party politics. Yet they provide a good indication of party allegiance and current party divisions in Romania. We shall take a quick look at the image war between the National-Conservatives and the Cosmopolitan-Liberals. What image does each party camp have about itself and what image does it have about the other party camp?

The National-Conservatives pride themselves on being the party of the people, those who are most concerned with distributing the fruits of economic reform and market economy widely among all classes and social groups. They flatter themselves as being the ones who gave the country a new course toward a market economy and democracy. A clear self-image of the National-Conservatives is their claim to be the true patriots and safeguards of national stability and territorial integrity. They also pride themselves on being the parties of professionals in economics, politics, and administration.

To the Cosmopolitan-Liberals this image appears as a caricature of reality. They usually begin their assessment of the National Conservatives by defining them as former communists, anti-reformists and anti-democratic. National Conservatives are portrayed as enemies of freedom and accused of economic populism, corruption, demagogy, plunder, and disastrous economic management of the country.

The colorful and flattering self-image of the Liberal Conservatives is sharper because they had not been in the government for seven years after 1989 and only assumed power in November 1996.

They praise themselves as the advocates of real economic reform toward a market economy, defenders of democracy, anti-communist, and Western-minded. They like to present themselves as "European," "modern" champions of free enterprise and of a merciless struggle against crime and corruption. To the National Conservatives, the Cosmopolitan Liberals appear as unprofessional demagogues and political amateurs, lacking any care for the needs and sufferings of all ranks and callings. They are also strongly accused of being unpatriotic, serving foreign powers, unreliable in foreign affairs, and determined to sell the country to foreign capital.

Image wars are interesting in themselves.[3] Yet more interesting to analyze is the extent to which party positions are related to conflicting interests and attitudes of the voters.

SOCIAL ISSUES AND PARTY RESPONSE

For many years one of the most striking characteristics of the new Romanian political pattern was the difference between what parties thought were the dominant issues of the electorate and what the electorate expected from the parties.

Time and time again, parties addressed issues that they thought were indicating large rifts within the electorate and failed to respond adequately to issues that were of central importance to the people. They even insisted at times on mobilizing voters against or in favor of issues that they knew very well were not related to any significant social and political cleavages. After 1989, four major groups of issues dominated Romanian political life: (1) the issue of communism versus democracy; (2) the Monarchy; (3) national stability and inter-ethnic relations; and (4) issues related to living standard and economic reform. These issues gave birth to many conflicts and controversies among social groups and competing parties. But no matter how deeply we dig into the individual issues we will not find any structural conflicts capable of polarizing politics, in the sense of the Lipset-Rokkan model of cleavage development in national communities (Lipset and Rokkan, 1967).

Communism versus Democracy

Beginning in January 1990, the Cosmopolitan Liberal parties campaigned vigorously to mobilize the electorate against what they termed as the crypto-communists and the assumed attempts of communist restoration by President Ion Iliescu and his National Salvation Front Party. There were a number of developments that appeared to justify their anxieties and the anti-communist campaign. The Securitate was still in place, although under parliamentary control. State television was firmly in the hands of President Iliescu and his government. The violent actions of miners in June 1990 and September 1991 were rightly considered as setbacks to the democratic process. During national and local elections, opposition parties felt they were discriminated against in their access to television and funding for effective campaigns.

However, political diversity was becoming a reality. Parties were freely competing for power. Within seven years, three general and two local elections were held. Despite some organizational irregularities and sporadic intimidations, they were generally considered free and fair. A new democratic Constitution had been passed by the Parliament and approved in a national Referendum. Press censorship was abolished. The borders were open for Romanians to travel to other countries. Freedom of religious faith was guaranteed. Despite occasional allegations by journalists or political leaders no reported case of political surveillance or persecution could be documented.

After 1990, IRSOP polls consistently revealed that over 80 percent of the electorate perceived political freedom as an established fact of the Romanian national community, only 3 percent longed for the restoration of the communist regime, and less than 10 percent feared that the communists would be able to assume power again in Romania. But some parties thought they knew better. A central campaign issue of the Liberal Cosmopolitan parties in 1990 and 1992 was the fight against people perceived as having been involved with the former communist party. At the beginning no distinction was made between former communist power holders and ordinary party members. It was only two years later that the Liberal Cosmopolitan parties realized that ordinary members of the former communist party amounted to four million people and that, together with their families, they probably accounted for more than half of the total electorate. Consequently, the 1992 electoral platform of the Democratic Convention included a paragraph "rejecting any kind of blame or accusation directed against the millions of members of the former communist party, including unpaid party leaders. . . ." (Platforma-Program a Convenţiei din Romania, 1992: 4). However, this did not prevent the Democratic Convention from listing emancipation from communism as "the essential objective" of the same platform (Platforma-Program a Convenţiei din Romania, 1992: 4). It is true that stimulating the economy and providing social security were indicated as routes to communist emancipation. But most people felt that communism had been defeated and they would rather have economic well-being as "the essential objective" of a governing force. Because of the social and political changes that had already occurred, the heavy anti-communist emphasis of Cosmopolitan Liberal parties failed to effectively mobilize the voters and caused these parties to score poorly in the national elections in 1990 and 1992.

The Monarchy

Although Romania has a Republican Constitution, many people and parties believe that for historical reasons the country is still at the stage of choosing between being a republic or a monarchy.

The former King of Romania, Michael I of Hohenzollern, was born in 1921 and was forced by the communists to abdicate and leave the country in 1947. His current residence is in Switzerland but in 1997 he announced plans to resume living part-time in Romania. The royal house has no governing program, only the desire to regain the throne. Royal supporters believe that the restoration of the monarchy is justified by the illegal ousting of the king. They also feel that King Michael can help maintain social stability, and pave the way for Romania's access to the Western World exactly as his royal ancestors had done for Romania in the nineteenth century.

But over the last years polls have found that more than two-thirds of the population does not want the former king to return to the throne of Romania and that only about 15 percent favor a restoration of the monarchy; others say they are undecided. The National Conservative parties are fiercely anti-monarchist, while the Cosmopolitan Liberals are divided on this issue. Some highly influential leaders of the Cosmopolitan Liberals genuinely believe that they may be able to widen popular support for the Monarchy. But until this happens these leaders ought to be prepared for losing, rather than gaining, popular votes for their parties.

National Stability and Interethnic Relations

Immediately after 1989 it became clear that controversies related to national security, territorial integrity, and interethnic relations would become a major issue in Romanian politics. Occasionally such controversies turned into ethnic conflicts but only one violent outbreak was registered: in March 1990 between Romanian and Hungarian ethnics in the Transylvanian city of Târgu Mures. There were no deaths but the outbreak left two people severely injured. Since that episode, no violent ethnic conflict has been registered but both the Romanian and the Hungarian nationalist rhetoric sometimes creates the impression of imminent war between the 1.6 million Hungarians and the overwhelming Romanian ethnic majority. Romanian nationalist parties accused the Hungarian ethnics of wanting to dismember Romania and turn Transylvania into an autonomous region, while Hungarian nationalists claim they lack basic rights for preserving and developing their cultural identity in Romania.

There is evidence that some of this nationalist rhetoric is penetrating the minds of both Romanians and Hungarians. Polls show that fears of ethnic war and secession run high among Romanians. Also IRSOP surveys found that the percentage of Hungarians believing they are subject to discriminations had increased from 52 percent in 1994 to 63 percent in 1995.

Yet there is no indication of a major cleavage among ordinary members of the Romanian and Hungarian ethnic communities. Surveys consistently revealed that interethnic hostility did not increase during 1990–1996. In September 1996, when the long disputed treaty between Romania and Hungary was finally signed, 58 percent of both Romanian and Hungarian ethnics from Romania believed that the treaty would have a positive influence on the relationship between the two ethnic groups. More than two-thirds of the Romanians (68 percent) and three-quarters of the Hungarians (74 percent) saluted the treaty as being equally beneficial for both Romanians and Hungarians (Poll taken by IRSOP, 1996).

Many analysts have stressed the role of political elites in maintaining ethnic tensions for the sake of political self-legitimation. As Gagnon puts it, "violent conflict along ethnic cleavages is provoked by elites in order to create a domestic political context where ethnicity is the only political relevant identity" (Gagnon, 1994: 132). In a comprehensive and polemic analysis of ethnic nationalist rhetoric in Romania, Maria Koroknai concludes that up to 1996, interethnic conflict was largely a result of elite manipulation rather than an outcome of ethnic hatred and real disagreements between ethnic communities (Koroknai, 1996).

Economic Reform and Living Standard

For about twelve months immediately after 1989, Romanians enjoyed a brief period of relative well-being that came as a blessing after a decade of communist misery and starvation. Wage earners kept their jobs. Salaries increased, weekly working hours were reduced, and the market was slowly but steadily filling up with fast-moving consumer goods. In rural areas peasants received 2,500 or 5,000 square meters of land per family for personal use. City-dwellers were promised they would be able to buy their state-owned apartments at very low rates.

As a result of these changes it was hardly surprising that President Iliescu and his newly established NSF Party scored a landslide victory in the first national elections of May 1990. Voters felt as if they were participating in a plebiscite on two alternatives of change rather than choosing among competing parties. The alternative stressed by NSF was moderate change with social protection. The second alternative advocated by the main opposition parties was radical change with individual self-protection. As Seymor M. Lipset has suggested, "Once the lowest strata are broken from their allegiance to traditional values and come to believe that a change for the better is possible, they tend to back a political tendency which offers an immediate and uncomplex solution to their problem" (Lipset, 1958: 187).

In 1990, the "immediate and uncomplex" solution for the overwhelming majority of Romanians was to protect the new order established in 1989 and to press forward with moderate changes preserving social and occupational protection.

It was only in 1991 that the economic reform for creating a market economy produced its first negative effects both on economic performance and on public mood. By 1992 industrial production had decreased to 45 percent of the 1989 level. The budget deficit accounted for 2 percent of the GDP. Inflation reached a 200 percent annual rate. One million people, that is, 11 percent of the nonagricultural workforce, were unemployed. IRSOP polls taken in August 1992 showed that prices, unemployment, and broken promises of politicians were considered the most important problems facing Romania on the eve of the second national elections. During this period, two basic divisions emerged among Romanians. One was related to the pace of economic change; the second was based on the issue of personal property. Both divisions cut across all sections of society and proved to be long-lasting rifts within the Romanian electorate.

Slow versus Fast Economic Change

Since 1989 Romanians have been strongly united in their desire to get rid of economic misery and achieve a higher living standard, at least comparable to other Central European nations. But they have been divided about the way of securing a better life. A small section of the society, mainly composed of younger people, intellectuals, professionals, and well-trained workers in successful business companies feel that faster progress toward a market economy is the answer to quick economic growth and prosperity. Typically, the advocates of fast economic reform will express unlimited faith in the power of private enterprise to relaunch the economy even in the absence of capital investment. They are ready to admit that for some time economic well-being would probably not extend to all sections of the society, but eventually everyone would be able to derive a profit from accelerated privatization.

A larger group, including predominantly older people, rural inhabitants, and broad masses of wage earners from ineffective business companies, believe that economic change should proceed at a slower pace, preserving jobs and ensuring steady wage increases. As a rule, supporters of slower economic change will express great expectations toward the state, which is considered capable of improving the economy and securing a better living standard for everybody.

Sensing this division among Romanian voters, the main opposition parties attempted to represent them in the 1992 elections. Liberal Cosmopolitans, united in the Democratic Convention, stressed the necessity of a faster pace of economic reform, based on a quick start and fast implementation of large-scale privatization. They emphasized private ownership as the most effective way of social protection and minimized the role of state intervention in revitalizing dying business sectors.

In contrast, the FDSN promised slower privatization, greater state intervention, price control, production pick-up, reduction of unemployment, and a comprehensive social security program.

Both parties misjudged the extent of popular support for their campaigns. But given Romania's social structure, the FDSN program proved to be more appealing. Faced with soaring inflation and a declining living standard, voters, who were largely dependent on state-owned enterprises, did not believe that fast privatization and the creation of private property would be able to immediately create jobs and provide social protection against the hardships of economic transition to a market economy. In addition, the large number of private landowners in the rural area depended on state support for survival and economic growth.

Between 1992 and 1996, the four-year term in power of the Iliescu party, renamed PDSR, and of Prime Minister Nicolae Văcăroiu, proved to be exhausting and exasperating to both political enemies and supporters. It is true that the Government had achieved a number of notable successes. Inflation was brought down from 300 percent in 1993 to 30 percent in 1995 and 1996. Economic decline was stopped. Two million new jobs were created. In 1992, Romania had to buy food from the rest of the world. But from 1994 on, Romania started to produce enough food for its own population and even for export. Foreign policy aimed at European integration had made progress. However, the national currency (Leu) had continued to fall against the dollar, the budget deficit remained exorbitant, and the salaries of wage earners were 30 percent lower in 1996 than in 1990. Furthermore, bureaucracy grew suffocating, corruption soared, large ineffective industrial enterprises survived on government subsidies, taxation was the highest in Europe, and current legislation and the business climate were far from appealing to foreign capital investment.

The division between advocates of faster economic reform and supporters of slower economic change was still present. Yet the division was somewhat blurred by two separate developments. The supporters of slow change had to admit that their living standard was not improving. On the other hand, the Democratic Convention redesigned its message, placing more emphasis on achieving a quick rise in material well-being than on implementing a fast privatization program, cutting subsidies, liberalizing prices, and shutting down ineffective factories.

Property as a Dividing Line

A structural conflict took shape in 1992 between former real-estate owners deprived of their properties by the communists on the one hand, and the tenants of nationalized apartments and the new land owners in the rural area on the other. Liberal Cosmopolitan parties clearly favor the interests of the former owners. They support a "restitutio in integrum" policy, including restitution of apartments and up to 50 hectares of farmland to the former owners or their heirs. This policy is viewed with apprehension by the roughly two million tenants living in nationalized apartments and by the new landowners who fear they will have to surrender their newly gained rural property if ownership patterns of 1945 are restored. The interests of these groups are strongly represented by the National Conservative parties, particularly PDSR, which advocate limited property reinstatement associated with financial reparation provided by the state for unrestored property.

CONCLUDING REMARKS

The most important characteristic of the Romanian political community is that for the time being economic issues tend to have a more powerful effect on politics than values and ideology. Economic issues, however, cut across all social strata and generate political polarizations that go beyond social classes or status differences.

Since 1989, the most powerful divisions among Romanians were related to the pace of economic reform and the restoration of private property patterns of 1945. These divisions are enduring and may indicate structural cleavages across all the sections of the Romanian electorate.

Other less powerful divisions are related to left-right ideological confrontations, the monarchy, and interethnic relations. But these divisions have mostly been created by political parties and are only to a small extent the result of different interests characterizing opposing social groups. It seems unlikely that these divisions will turn into real cleavages in the near future.

NOTES

1. For a detailed account of the period between December 1989 and May 1990, including an analysis of the first Romanian post-dictatorial elections, see: Datculescu, Petre and Klaus Liepelt. 1991.
2. Throughout the article I use the Romanian acronyms of party names.
3. For a more detailed analysis of the war of images between political parties, see: Verdery, Katherine. 1996.

REFERENCES

Călinescu, Matei and Vladimir Tismăneanu. 1992. "The 1989 Revolution and Romania's Future." In Daniel N. Nelson (ed.), *Romania after Tyranny*. Boulder, San Francisco, Oxford: Westview Press.
Datculescu, Petre and Klaus Liepelt. 1991. *Renaşterea unei Democraţii: Alegerile din România de la 20 mai 1990*. Bucureşti: IRSOP.

Gagnon, V. P. Jr. 1994. "Ethnic Nationalism and International Conflict." *International Security* 19: 141–57.
Huntington, Samuel P. 1968. *Political Order in Changing Societies*. New Haven: Yale University Press.
Koroknai, Maria. 1996. *Romania —A Candidate for Dismemberment?* Paper prepared at Cornell University's Peace Studies Program and submitted to the SSRC MacArthur Foundation, December 1996 (unpublished).
Lipset, Seymour M. 1958. "Socialism—Left and Right—East and West." *Confluence* 7 (2): 98–114.
Lipset, Seymour M. and Stein Rokkan. 1967. *Party Systems and Voter Alignments: Cross-National Perspectives*. New York: The Free Press.
Pasti, Vladimir, Mihaela Miroiu and Cornel Codiţă. 1997. "România—Starea de fapt." *Bucureşti* 1.
Platforma-Program a Convenţiei Democratice din România. România Liberă, 18 august 1992, p. 4.
Poll taken by IRSOP for the dailies "Curierul Naţional" (Bucharest) and "Magyar Hirlap" (Budapest). "Curierul Naţional," September 13, 1996, p. 1.
Verdery, Katherine. 1996. *What Was Socialism and What Comes Next?* Princeton, New Jersey.

Part IV

How the Voters Respond

13

How the Voters Respond in Bulgaria

Vladimir Shopov

EVOLUTION OF THE MAIN POLITICAL FORCES IN THE BULGARIAN ELECTORATE

The formation and evolution of the two main political forces in post-Communist Bulgaria, the Bulgarian Socialist Party (BSP) and the Union of Democratic Forces (UDF), reveals the early emergence of a "bi-polar" party configuration after the regime change in 1989. (See Tables 13.1 and 13.2.)

The BSP was the ex-communist party and the UDF was a coalition of more than ten anti-communist parties and organizations. Their electorates were assumed to mirror each other—that is, it was often stated that the structure of these electorates is more or less similar with insignificant differences. However, closer examination of empirical data shows the differences to be rather important. Certain kinds of voters were drawn to each side: Bulgarian voters' response to the political offer has in fact been mediated by socioeconomic and ideological factors.

In demonstrating the importance of such factors, I rely mainly on three national surveys completed in September 1991, September 1993 and a third survey, the BBSS Gallup yearly report, a summary of twelve monthly surveys covering the whole of 1994. I will also use the results of some other surveys conducted by other established agencies for the study of public opinion. The National Center for the Study of Public Opinion (NCSPO) published the first survey on October 1, 1991, on the eve of parliamentary elections. This survey provides a relatively clear picture of the way in which the electorates of both major parties and coalitions are structured.

Table 13.1
Bulgarian Parliamentary Elections of 1990, 1991, 1994 (percent of vote)*

Parties (coalitions)	1990	1991	1994
BSP (Bulgarian Socialist Party)	47.15	33.14	43.50
UDF (Union of Democratic Forces)	36.20	34.34	24.23
MRF (Movements for Rights and Freedoms)	6.03	7.55	5.44
BAPU (Bulgarian Agrarian People's Unions)	8.03	3.86	–
BAPU (Nikola Petkov)	–	–	3.44
UDF–Center	–	–	3.20
UDF–Liberals	–	–	2.81
BBB (Bulgarian Business Bloc)	–	1.32	4.72
CKB (Confederation for Kingdom Bulgaria)	–	1.82	1.41
PU (Peoples Union)	–	–	6.50
DAR (Democratic Alliance for the Republik)	–	–	3.79

*Threshold for parliamentary representation is 4% of the electoral vote.

One very important indicator, which explicitly points to a dividing line between the parties is place of residence. People living in villages were much more likely to vote for the socialists (25 percent of them declared their preference for the BSP, whereas only 14 percent were for the UDF). The picture changes slightly in small towns and in towns with municipal importance. In small towns the UDF has the support of 22 percent of the electorate, while BSP has 17 percent; both parties get 25 percent support in towns with municipal importance. The UDF's share of the vote increases significantly in towns of regional importance

Table 13.2
Bulgarian Parliamentary Elections of 1994 (Results in Seats)*
Turnout 5,263,418 (75.21%)

Party (Coalition)	Total Votes	(in %)	Seats	(in %)
BSP (Bulgarian Socialist Party in coalition with BAPU "A. Stamboliiski" and PK Ecoglasnost)	2,262,943	(43.50)	125	(52.15%)
UDF (Union of Democratic Forces)	1,260,374	(24.23)	69	(28.8%)
Peoples Union	338,478	(6.50)	18	(7.5%)
MRF (Movement for Rights and Freedoms)	283,094	(5.44)	15	(6.3%)
BBB (Bulgarian Business Bloc)	245,849	(4.72)	13	(5.4%)
DAR (Democratic Alternative for the Republic)	197,057	(3.79)	–	–
BKP (Bulgarian Communist Party)	78,606	(1.51)	–	–
New Choice	77,641	(1.50)	–	–
Patriotic Union	74,350	(1.43)	–	–
Confederation for Kingdom Bulgaria	73,205	(1.41)	–	–

* Results for parties which received over 1% from 48 registered.

and in the capital city. In the former, the UDF attracts 29 percent of the vote while the BSP attracts only 22 percent. The gap is even wider in the capital city Sofia where the UDF attracts 43 percent of the vote with the Socialists receiving only 19 percent. Thus, in 1991, voters in big towns and in the capital were more likely to vote for the UDF, while voters in smaller towns and villages were more likely to support the BSP.

The differences in the electorates of the two parties become more visible when one examines the social structure of the voters. The gap between the two parties is widest among the youngest group of voters (which includes pupils from the last grades of high school, and college and university students), with 38 percent declaring that they would vote for the UDF and 14 percent supporting the BSP. This gap narrows somewhat for the group of industrial workers, where there is 32 percent support for the UDF and 19 percent support for the BSP. The BSP enjoys more support among employees in the agricultural sector than does the UDF (18 percent for the BSP and 13 percent for the UDF). The two parties find almost equal support among the groups of the intelligentsia and the white-collar workers, with the UDF having a slight advantage (26 percent of the intelligentsia declare that they would vote for the UDF with 23 percent supporting the BSP and 28 percent of the white-collar workers supporting the UDF, while the BSP attracts 25 percent of the vote in that group). The BSP finds its widest electoral base among the pensioners, 27 percent of whom declare their intention to vote for the BSP, while only 19 percent intend to support the UDF.

Another indicator that reveals differences between the electorates of both parties is age. The widest gap is to be found in the 18–30 age group, with 30 percent of the voters declaring support for the UDF and only 11 percent supporting the BSP. The dominance of the UDF in the age groups of 31–40 and 41–50 is somewhat slighter—29 percent in the former and 30 percent in the latter—while the BSP receives 21 percent of support in the former and 22 percent in the latter. The picture changes, however, in the age groups of 51–60 and over 60 where the BSP enjoys much greater support—26 percent of the vote in the former and 30 percent in the latter—while the UDF receives 24 percent preference in the former and only 16 percent in the latter. The electorate of the BSP comprises mainly voters from older age groups, while the UDF finds its electoral base mainly among younger voters.

It is also important to note certain differences among the electorates in terms of the educational status of the voters. The BSP enjoys the support of 33 percent of the people with university degrees, while the UDF receives 30 percent of their vote. The UDF is supported by 27 percent of the voters with college education (with the BSP receiving 18 percent support) and by 30 percent of the voters with high-school education (with the BSP receiving 22 percent of their support). It is noticeable that the BSP is supported by 24 percent of the voters who have eighth-grade education, while only 14 percent of them support the UDF (Table 13.3).

Table 13.3
Composition of the Bulgarian Electorate

	BSP and coalition	UDF	UDF-Liberals	UDF-Center	BAPU-United	BAPU "N. Petkov"	MRF	Not Decided	Not Voting
TOTAL	23	25	3	5	6	5	6	17	5
In what area do you live?									
• village	25	14	1	2	9	7	16	16	5
• small town	17	22	3	9	8	7	6	20	5
• middle town	25	25	4	5	5	5	2	18	6
• big town	22	29	4	5	5	3	1	17	5
• capital	19	43	5	5	2	2	–	12	5
Age group									
• 18–30 years	11	30	4	7	4	3	11	15	6
• 31–40 years	21	29	5	8	5	2	7	11	4
• 41–50 years	22	30	4	3	7	6	7	13	4
• 51–60 years	26	30	4	3	7	6	7	13	4
• over 60 years	30	16	1	3	9	7	4	21	6
Education									
• university	33	30	4	7	1	2	–	12	1
• college	18	27	5	8	7	5	1	18	3
• high school	22	30	5	5	6	4	3	14	6
• 4th grade	22	22	2	3	8	6	11	18	5
• lower than 4th grade	24	14	1	1	7	6	12	26	6
Sex									
• male	22	27	3	5	8	6	5	13	5
• female	23	23	4	4	5	4	7	20	5

Ethnicity

• Bulgarian	24	26	4	5	7	5	1	17	5
• Bulgarian Turk	6	6	1	1	2	1	66	13	3
• Bulgarian Gypsy	27	41	–	6	–	5	4	12	4
• Other	7	21	3	10	7	–	17	7	17

Social Group

• pupils, students	14	38	5	14	3	3	3	16	–
• workers	19	32	3	5	6	6	7	13	4
• agrarian workers	18	13	1	2	7	3	38	14	4
• blue-collar	25	28	6	5	6	3	1	16	4
• intelligentsia	23	26	4	10	7	3	1	13	1
• pensioners	27	9	2	3	8	7	3	22	6
• unemployed	19	33	5	4	2	2	10	11	8
• other	12	29	–	3	3	3	6	15	15

Study of public opinion carried out by the National Center for the Study of Public Opinion / NCSPO/ second half of September 1991.

In the case of Bulgaria, it is important to note that the electorate is rather homogeneous in terms of ethnicity, with most Bulgarian Turks voting for the Movement of Rights and Freedoms.

To trace the evolution of the structure of the electorate, I will rely on a survey completed in September 1993 by "Sova-5," a private company for political, social, and marketing surveys. Before studying the empirical data it is crucial to mention that by the time this survey was completed, the UDF had seen its electoral base shrink to a significant extent. Thus, any changes in the structure of the electorates of both parties should be seen against the background of diminishing electoral support for the UDF.

Certain important shifts had occurred by 1993 in voting behavior according to place of residence. The gap between the BSP and the UDF in villages had grown to more than 20 percent (the Socialists getting 33 percent of the support in villages with the UDF getting only 11 percent). The BSP had overtaken the UDF in small towns and in towns of regional importance—the BSP enjoying 26 percent of the vote in the former and 22 percent in the latter, with the UDF receiving 13 percent in both. It is only in the capital city Sofia that the UDF managed to preserve its electoral base—29 percent declaring they would vote for the UDF and only 9 percent for the BSP. As one can observe, the BSP had managed to acquire new support in small towns and in towns of regional importance.

The changes in electoral behavior according to social status are also of interest. The UDF had managed to preserve its support among the youngest voters and among the intelligentsia, leading the BSP by 3 to 10 percent. The BSP, on the other hand, had managed to increase its support among the elderly to 36 percent (with the UDF getting only 9 percent of their vote) and to reverse the trend among workers previously supportive of the UDF; by 1993, 21 percent of the workers supported the Socialists and only 17 percent supported the UDF. The September 1993 survey also shows the UDF slipping further behind among the group of agricultural workers and farmers. The tendency is clear: the BSP was solidifying its position among the groups which decide elections—industrial workers, agricultural workers and farmers, and pensioners—while still preserving its strong position among state employees.

The distribution of the vote in the 18–30 and 31–40 age groups remained more or less constant. The BSP, however, managed to overtake the UDF in the 41–50 age group while solidifying its lead in the 51–60 and over 60 age groups. Thus, the Socialists had acquired a dominant position in the age groups that comprise the greater part of the electorate.

The structure of the electorates in terms of their educational status also remained quite stable. However, the BSP was able to reverse the vote in the group consisting of people with college degrees, thus beginning to dominate in all educational groups with the exception of university degree holders.

The survey completed by BBSS Gallup International in 1994 confirms most of the trends already present in the September 1993 survey. The most important difference, from an electoral point of view, is the withering away of a significant part of the electoral base of the UDF among the youngest voters, state employees, and the elderly. The result of these tendencies is the further widening of the gap of support between the BSP and the UDF, a gap which manifested itself in the electoral results of December 1994, when the Socialists won an absolute majority in Parliament. An October 1995 survey by BBSS Gallup International provides evidence for the argument that the electorate's structure seemed to be stabilizing (Table 13.4). It is, of course, rather difficult to speculate about the degree of that stability, but it is possible to provide a description of the "average" voter of these parties by 1994. People who supported and voted for the BSP at election time were more likely to live in villages and small towns, to be employed in the agricultural and industrial sector, to have an eighth-grade or high school diploma, to be over 50 years of age, and to be spread evenly across the country. On the other hand, voters who supported the UDF were more likely to live in larger towns and in the capital, to be employed in the private sector or to be among the youngest part of the population, to have college and university diplomas, and to belong to the 18–30 and 31–40 age groups whose vote is concentrated in particular parts of the country.

Was there a "hard-core" of voters of the two parties? Various estimations have been proposed, and the most realistic ones put the number of hard-core voters at about 20 to 22 percent in the case of the UDF, and at about 30 percent in the case of the BSP.

LIVING STANDARDS AND VOTERS' PREFERENCES

The response of voters to changes in their financial situation and to transformations in the whole economy are often cited as a clear example of direct cause-effect relationship. The assumption is that should one's financial well-being decline, the government is the first to be blamed and, therefore, voters withdraw their support from the governing party. One would at the very least expect voters to respond in some way when their well-being is at stake.

The reform process in Bulgaria has for many reasons been a rather slow one. A number of crucial decisions were postponed, and no clear philosophy of economic reform has been formulated. The resulting indecisiveness has led to the creation of a situation in which the problems of economic transition were worsened by half-measures, numerous policy U-turns, and so forth. One consequence of this phenomenon was the extreme fall of the standard of living of most Bulgarians, the appearance of mass unemployment, and the growth of social insecurity.

This development has led to a major shift in public opinion where the economic problems of the country have come to dominate in the minds of voters. The NCSPO, in its April 1994 survey, asked people to identify the pressing problems which troubled them. A full 93 percent of the respondents identified "the economic crisis, inflation and further slide into poverty" as their main concerns,

Table 13.4
Structure of the Electorates of the Two Main Bulgarian Political Parties (coalitions)

	People voting for BSP—percent of electorate in the respective groups.	People voting for UDF—percent of electorate in the respective groups.	Nonvoters—percent of non-voters in the respective groups.
Place of residence			
• village	42	12	23
• small town	38	20	24
• big town	32	20	28
• capital	31	31	23
Social group			
• pupils, students	18	25	39
• workers	30	21	27
• blue-collar	27	26	26
• agrarian workers	50	–	50
• private business	39	33	17
• pensioners	54	11	18
• unemployed	31	15	31
Age group			
• 18–30 years	23	20	34
• 31–40 years	24	27	29
• 41–50 years	34	18	25

• 51–60 years	45	20	15
• over 60 years	54	11	19
Education			
• university degree	29	26	18
• college	27	23	31
• high school	37	19	24
• professional school	30	26	26
• 4th grade	45	12	24
• lower than 4th grade	44	6	25
Ethnicity			
• Bulgarian	38	20	25
• Turk	22	10	14
• Gypsy	39	13	34
• Other	50	20	20
• Bulgarian Muslim	26	9	17

BBSS Gallup International, October 1995.

while 65 percent singled out unemployment as their main concern. It is quite clear that these worries cut across party lines and have become problem number one for most voters in the country.

When asked whether their situation has improved or worsened in recent transitional years, voters give the following assessment in a survey completed by NOEMA Agency in February 1993. Asked to compare the present economic situation with that of a year ago, 39.5 percent of the respondents declare that the situation has worsened a great deal and 30.8 percent think that it has worsened somewhat. The people who perceived a significant improvement form only 0.5 percent of all respondents, with 7.5 percent agreeing that the situation has improved somewhat.

One year later the response is almost identical. In the April 1994 survey of the NCSPO, the following question was asked: "Has the financial situation of your household changed over the last 6 months?" 37.9 percent of the respondents declare that the financial situation has worsened significantly, with 33.8 percent of them claiming that their financial condition has worsened somewhat. Only 0.9 percent enjoyed significant improvement, while the situation of 6.4 percent had improved somewhat. These results clearly reveal the dire economic problems which the larger part of the population is experiencing. It is reasonable to suppose, on the basis of such data, that a left-wing party and left-wing politics will be quite attractive to significant portions of the electorate. The advance of the BSP must be assessed against the background of the further deterioration of the financial situation of the vast majority of voters.

This profound uneasiness regarding their future living standard is coupled with persistent egalitarian perceptions and pro-statist attitudes. Asked if the state should ensure that there are no big differences between peoples' incomes, 60 percent of the respondents declared that the state should permanently ensure that such differences do not exist. Another 25 percent thought this to be necessary only at certain times, while only 10.4 percent regarded this not to be the state's business (Table 13.5).

This persistent or renewed longing for the patronage state or some form or another of state intervention and assistance is further illustrated by the data dealing with the overall voters' evaluation of the political and economic changes

Table 13.5
Bulgarian Citizens' Attitudes toward the State

"The interests of the state are more important than rights of the individual."					
	agree completely	agree somewhat	disagree somewhat	completely disagree	don't know
Answer in %	34.5%	14.6%	16.8%	19.6%	14.6%

Noema Agency, February 1993 Survey.

since 1989. Asked if democracy has brought them more social equality, 79.8 percent of the respondents replied with a "No," while only 10.6 percent answered positively. Asked if democracy has brought them a better life 81.2 percent responded negatively, while only 13.1 percent of the interviewed saw their living situation as improved.

These results also help explain the movement to the left during this period. The reasons for this phenomenon are numerous, but most important is the lack of tangible results from the reform process and the inability of the majority of the population to assess the complexity of the radical changes from authoritarian rule and a centralized economy to democracy and market economy. That explains to a large extent the support for the BSP at the parliamentary elections of December 1994, which relied on nostalgia for a past where egalitarian values dominated and which exploited the failure of the UDF to achieve tangible improvements in the living standards of the majority of the population as the parliamentary as well as governing party. Insistence on the values of market economy and private property have created a general negative attitude toward parties that advocate radical changes in the economy while at the same time demonstrating ineffective policies. The financial crisis of the state and its redistributive capacities, especially in the field of social security, has furthered the longing for a stronger role for the state as advocated by the ex-communist Socialist party, which, in the minds of large portions of the population, was associated with the political and economic stability of socialism, while the UDF came to be associated with the chaos and instability characterizing the transitional process.

EVOLUTION OF POLITICAL CULTURE

The development of Bulgarian society since 1989 has posed numerous questions concerning the emerging type of political culture and value orientation. Voices claiming that the prevailing political culture in the country cannot provide the framework in which a democracy can evolve have been often heard. Such abstract assertions are often misleading when one takes into account empirical data, but it is important to acknowledge the fragility of the peoples' attitudes and their ideological perceptions in a period of radical transformation in their life and social status. One-dimensional conclusions are not helpful.

In the Gallup International surveys of 1994 respondents were asked to evaluate both the period between 1944–1989 (of communist rule) and the period 1989–1994. Nearly one-third (32 percent) thought the positive was predominant in the former period, while only 10 percent regarded the period between 1989 and 1994 as a time when the positive outweighed the negative. Only 16 percent of all those interviewed thought that the negative dominated over the positive in the period before 1989, while 29 percent disagreed. And most indicative of all, 12 percent regarded the period between 1944 and 1989 as "lost years," while 34 percent described the period since the beginning of the reforms as "lost years."

It would appear that the past is viewed as a time of opportunity and prosperity in contrast to a difficult and chaotic present.

On the basis of party preferences, 84 percent of the BSP voters considered their personal opportunities in life to have decreased in the post-communist period, while only 3 percent of them thought the opposite. Interestingly enough, even among UDF voters, the percentage of people thinking that their opportunities have increased is not very high—38 percent regard the years since 1989 as years of greater opportunity, while 39 percent think the opposite.

The attitude of the voters regarding the general direction in which the country is heading is always an important indicator. Over the years the number of people who think that the country is moving in the wrong direction has been increasing. The highest figure was reached in July 1994, when 62 percent of all respondents thought that Bulgaria was heading toward a worse state of affairs. While 55 percent of the BSP voters shared that point of view, only about 35 percent of the voters of the UDF think that the country is going in the wrong direction.

The attitude of voters toward the process of privatization is one of the most important problems in terms of emerging cleavages among the voters. It is important to note that close to 40 percent of the electorates of both the BSP and the UDF agree with the need to privatize to some extent. While 53 percent of the voters of the UDF think of privatization as absolutely necessary, this percentage is 20.7 among BSP voters. Despite such differences there is enough empirical ground to conclude that there is a rather stable consensus on the need for privatization. At the same the voters expect that any possible outcome of privatization which will produce inequalities will be offset to some extent by state intervention.

The attitude of the electorate toward democratic changes in the country is certainly one of the most important indicators for the degree of support for a democratic regime. The responses to the question "Are you satisfied with democracy?" reveal the already-mentioned phenomenon of a direct link that many people make between their immediate condition and democracy as a system of government (Table 13.6). But at same time, more concrete questions concerning democratic procedures reveal a much more positive assessment of democratic rules.

Despite a general mood of dissatisfaction with democracy, there appear to exist relatively positive attitudes in regard to democratic procedures (Table 13.7). Another question which tests the degree to which people support democratic procedures is ". . . bearing in mind the situation in the country as a whole, do you think that Bulgaria would develop in a better way without a Parliament?" Here, 47 percent of the respondents disagreed and only 26 percent agreed.

People were also asked to choose one of three possible roads for the political development for the country. A majority (51.3 percent) thought that democracy should be preserved at any price, while only 17.5 percent regarded a strong undemocratic regime as a desirable option. These sets of data can clearly be interpreted as providing grounds for the conclusion that on the whole the Bulgarian population still supports the democratic road of development.

Table 13.6
Bulgarian Citizens' Attitudes toward Democracy

"Are you satisfied with democracy?"

	completely satisfied	relatively satisfied	not satisfied	completely dissatisfied	don't know
Answer in percent	1	9	29	54	7
Voters of BSP	1	6	21	69	3
Voters of UDF	1	19	40	37	3

BBSS Gallup International, Political and Economic Index, 1994.

Table 13.7
Bulgarian Citizens' Attitudes toward Elections

"Do you think that elections are the best way to decide on who will govern the country?"

	Yes	No	Don't know
Answer in %	61	21	18

BBSS Gallup International, Political and Economic Index, 1994.

The attitudes of Bulgarian voters to certain political acts can also be cited in support of this conclusion. Asked to respond if they approved of the refusal to pay taxes as a form of political protest, 75.9 percent stated they completely disapproved of such a practice. Only 3.4 percent of those interviewed agreed completely with this form of protest. Three additional questions, designed to test the degree to which voters would resort to extreme or undemocratic practices of protest, were posed. When asked, "Do you approve of occupying buildings as a form of political protest?," 79.8 percent of the respondents said they completely disapproved of that form of protest. When asked, "Do you approve of blocking traffic, streets, etc. as a form of political protest?," 83.1 percent of the respondents said they disapproved of the practice. Finally, when asked, "Do you approve of damaging property as a form of political protest?," 90.3 percent of the respondents disapproved. This negative attitude to extreme forms of political protest demonstrates the existence of tolerance and patience with more moderate democratic procedures.

THE DIVISION LEFT-RIGHT IN POST-COMMUNISM

The attempt to identify the electorates of both main political parties has involved a thorough examination of voters' opinion on a number of important questions. The empirical data suggests that there exists an electorate with left-wing political expectations and attitudes. These voters expect to live in a significantly regulated economy where the state continues to take care of and provide services to all citizens. The state sector of the economy is expected to dominate economic activity while at the same time keeping taxation low. The positive attitude of most of these voters toward the "socialist period" is also a defining moment for their left-wing identity.

At the same time there clearly exists a large group of voters who express right-wing views and expectations. These are voters supporting private initiative, lower taxation, less state intervention and regulation, greater political rights, and so on. Again, the negative attitude of these people toward the forty-five years of communist rule defines most explicitly their position in the left-right spectrum. At the same time a careful observer of the political and ideological divisions in post-communist societies, in particular Bulgaria, should take the following peculiarities into account.

First, the left-right division developed to a large extent along the axis communism–anti-communism, which, in a sense, continues to provide the essential framework of this division. Second, there is still a large number of voters who incorporate typical left-wing views into a right-wing outlook or vice-versa. Third, Bulgarian voters cannot be treated or analyzed as members of a distinct social group or strata as the process of social stratification has still not produced clearly identifiable social groups with stable electoral behavior. And last, there is still consensus among the elite and the electorate in all major parties on issues which, in established democracies, are a dividing line between left- and right-wing parties, such as the issue of privatization or that of integration in the European community.

CONCLUSION

Empirical studies confirm that there is still high volatility in the voters' behavior and political orientations. There are already some primary attachments to political parties, but it is too early for any definite conclusions. There is currently much more instability in the electorate of the UDF because it is still establishing itself as a political party and lacks a clear identity, while the other major party, Socialist, has a great advantage in that regard. At the time of writing, the BSP government had been only a year in power and it was too early to make an analysis of the consequences of its policies on future electoral behavior, although there were already signs of discontent and internal friction in the BSP concerning the policies of its government. There were growing contradictions among its supporters, mostly between its pro-capitalist, pro-market oriented groups, especially the nouveaux riches, who are part of the former "red" nomenklatura and the lower social classes suffering the most from the social transformations.

The BSP leadership was facing the challenge of trying to preserve its left-wing image while pursuing a right-wing policy oriented toward the market economy and keeping its engagements to the International Monetary Fund and other institutions. The views and values of a great part of its electorate did not coincide with the general policy of the party in government. These growing internal divisions in the BSP confirm that further party realignments are to be expected and that the new cleavages do cross party boundaries. The UDF and other parties faced the same dilemma, as the voters' response to their program is more and more determined by material benefits and economic interests, and less by emotional and ideological reasons.

The general trend to be expected is the shrinking of the hard-core supporters of the political parties and an increasingly unpredictable electorate which will determine its vote on election eve on the basis of rational assessment of the parties' policies and the personal qualities of the candidates for state office.

EPILOGUE (1998)

The fall of the Socialist government in 1997 marked the end of the model of development begun in 1989, a model characterized by the very strong presence of the former Communist party. By the end of 1996 the inability of that government to pursue serious reforms had become the key factor in determining the policy agendas and value orientations of the parties and the electorate. The presidential elections of November 1996 were won by Petar Stoyanov of the United Democratic Forces, who defeated the Socialist candidate by an unprecedented margin of 60 percent to 40 percent. The change was confirmed in the parliamentary elections of the following year (see Table 13.8). Bulgarian voters may now be characterized as having developed a general allergy to great designs, promises and electoral programs. They have a clearer understanding of the nature of the new political elite, and are thus able to make a stronger link between their own attitudes and the vote.

Table 13.8
Results of Parliamentary Elections (April 1997)

Party (Coalition)	*Percent of vote**
Democratic Left (Bulgarian Socialist Party in coalition with Ecoglasnost)	22.17%
United Democratic Forces (Union of Democratic Forces in coalition with People's Union)	52.23%
Bulgarian Business Bloc	4.95%
Euroleft	5.52%
Union for National Salvation (Movement for Rights and Freedom in coalition with Bulgarian Agrarian People's Union, N. Petkov, Confederation "Kingdom Bulgaria," Green Party and New Choice)	7.50%

*Threshold for parliamentary representation is 4 percent of the electoral vote.

REFERENCES

BBSS Gallup International. 1995. Public opinion in Bulgaria, Yearly Report.
Kitschelt, Herbert, Dimitar Dimitrov, and Assen Kanev. 1995. "The structuring of the vote in post-communist party systems: the Bulgarian example." *European Journal of Political Research* 27: 143–60.
National Center for the Study of Public Opinion, Public Opinion, monthly bulletin.
Noema, Agency for social research and marketing, monitor of public opinion.
Sova-5, Agency for social and marketing surveys, monthly and periodical reports.

14

How the Voters Respond in the Czech Republic

Lubomír Brokl and Zdenka Mansfeldová

To understand contemporary voting behavior and the outcome of elections, it is not enough simply to describe how the voters responded. We also need to know what the voters were reacting and responding to. In this chapter, we therefore begin with a review of post-1989 political developments before discussing the results of the elections to the Czech parliament and the Czech senate in 1996, results which surprised most commentators and which, in retrospect, also provide a better understanding of the earlier elections of 1990 and 1992.[1]

THE FIRST TWO YEARS (1989–1991)

After the Communists' fall, the first terms for the new political functionaries were set at two years as a test-trial period. The absolute victor (Table 14.1) of the first elections, June 8–9, 1990, was the Civic Forum (OF), a mass civic movement and the inheritor of the "velvet" revolution in November 1989. A number of political parties and movements were represented by the OF in the elections. For the most part, newly founded and historically established political parties that ran independently[2] were not successful in the elections. The only other successes were the Communists with their stable electorate and the Christian Democratic Union-Czechoslovak People's Party (KDU-ČSL). (The ČSL had been active during the communist period and continued its prewar traditions after the upheaval). A new political party from Moravia–Movement for Moravian and Silesian Self-Government (Hnutí za samosprávnou demokracii–Sdružení pro Moravu a Slezsko, HSD-SMS) declared itself to be representing the interests of Moravia and

Table 14.1
Election Results in 1990 (the Czech National Assembly [Mandate])

	% of votes	Seats
OF	49.5	127
KSČ	13.24	32
HSD-SMS	10.03	22
KDU	8.42	19
Other parties	18.81	–
Total	100.0	200

Note: 96.8 percent eligible voters took part in the elections (Volby, FSú, 1991).

Silesia, but was not a nationalist party.[3] In the beginning this party was carried along by the general disposition toward liberation from "Prague" centralism and the voters' anticipation of local self-government; nonetheless, this party's success in Moravia and Silesia during the elections was surprising. With the advance of democratic transformation the question of local self-government became a universal (and not only a Moravian) issue for this party. However, in the following elections, the HSD-SMS barely crossed the threshold of the required 5 percent and, during the third set of elections, it disappeared from the political scene altogether. None of the political parties that ran in these elections was active in both the Czech and Slovak republics as a federal party, even though some of the parties attempted to establish their organizations in both republics. The Communists came the closest to being a federal party because of the role it had played in the past twenty years, but this same factor limited its success, even though it continued and continues to be a parliamentary party.[4] In Sartori's terminology, it lacks "governing potential" (Sartorí, 1976).

At the beginning of 1991, the Civic Forum split into the well organized right-wing Civic Democratic Party (ODS) and the centrist Civic Movement (OH).

The two-year period between the first and second elections was dominated by the Slovak-Czech dispute about the form of the common state. The decisions made about some fundamental issues in the federal parliament were frequently blocked by the requirement of a "double majority" in the Slovak and Czech parts of the House of Nations. Nevertheless, economic reforms were decided and the program of privatization was launched. The main Czecho-Slovak discourse during the 1990 establishment of the federation became the question of the competence of both republics' governments, under the formula both accepted: "Strong republics, strong federation." The passing of jurisdiction laws in the Federal Parliament in December 1990 caused the federation to be largely purposeless, and more and more issues were now solved by the republics independently. The remainder of the election term was spent by the Czech and federal governments in trying to maintain a basic federation with appropriate functions. At the beginning of 1992 the decision about this issue was postponed until the reelection of new governments in June.

The disputes of the two nations, the Czech and the Slovak Republics, disputes that had been suppressed in the past or, on the contrary, initiated during the communist time, were discussed in the period between elections. In Slovakia these issues led to a national split. The political scene in both federal republics was developing along different lines—even the right-wing/left-wing concept had a different meaning in the two republics. In comparison to the Czech lands, there was almost no right wing in Slovakia except for the VPN, an equivalent to the Czech centrist OF and later OH. After establishing the republics' respective jurisdictions, further differences arose regarding the republics' individual approaches to the transformation of the common economy.

THE 1992 ELECTIONS AND THEIR CONSEQUENCES

In the elections that took place June 5–6, 1992, there were thirty-nine parties on the federal level, twenty-one in the Czech Republic, and twenty-two in the Slovak Republic. In the Czech Republic, all political parties ran for both representative bodies, the federal and the national parliament; in Slovakia, four political parties ran only for the national representative body.[5] (See Table 14.2.)

Of the former members of the Civic Forum, only the Civic Democratic Party (in alliance with the Christian Democratic Party as ODS-KDS) was successful in getting elected into the Czech and Federal parliaments in the June 1992 elections. The Civic Movement (OH), which was the second largest successor to the split-up OF, and which before that point had had a majority in the government, did not win seats in the federal or the Czech national parliament and was pushed out altogether. It was not successful in the 1996 elections, either. From the parties that were part of OF in the 1990 elections and ran independently in the 1992 elections, only the Civic Democratic Alliance (ODA) took seats in the Czech parliament

Table 14.2
Election Results in 1992 (the Czech National Assembly [Mandate])

	% of votes	Seats
ODS-KDS	29.73	76
LB	14.05	35
ČSSD	6.53	16
LSU	6.52	16
KDU-ČSL	6.28	15
SPR-RSČ	5.98	14
ODA	5.93	14
HSD-SMS	5.87	14
Other parties	19.11	–
Total	100.00	200

Note: 85.1% eligible voters took part in the elections (Volby, FSú, 1992).

with more than 5 percent of the vote, thereby winning seats in the federal parliament. The Christian Democratic Union–Czechoslovak People's Party (KDU-ČSL), and the Communist Party of Bohemia and Moravia (KSČM), which was part of the Left Bloc (Levý blok) in the Czech elections of 1992, won seats in both parliaments for the second time. For the last time, the Movement for Self-Governing Democracy–Alliance for Moravia and Silesia (HSD-SMS) made it into the Czech parliament (but was not successful on the federal level). A new addition to the federal parliament was the Liberal-Social Union (LSU), (made up of three independent parties: the Czechoslovak Socialist Party, the Agricultural Party, and the Green Party) which had been founded in December 1991. However, the LSU represented an artificial political center and began to fall apart soon after the elections. Another political party that won seats in both representative bodies was the extremist Union for the Republic–Czechoslovak Republican Party (SPR-RSČ), a party that had not been successful in 1990 and whose program with nationalist and features was seen as improbable and too radical by many. The Social Democrats also had their first success at this time, winning seats in both representative bodies. The political center, represented by the OH, disappeared from the Czech political scene, although as noted earlier positions were taken by the right-wing ODS and later on by the Social democrats as well as the People's party (KDU-ČSL).

Public opinion surveys showed the Czech population moving in the direction of liberal-right values and continuing dissatisfaction with the communist era, while Slovaks were satisfied with the communist period and were now adopting nationalist values (IVVM 92-09; Monitoring IVVM 1992/55).

Election results confirmed these differences in the Czech and Slovak political scenes, and after the elections the composition of the federal representative bodies and the requirement of a "double majority" within the House of Nations meant that action on the most important issues became permanently blocked.

The rapid movement of the two republics toward becoming two independent countries as of January 1, 1993, could suggest the sudden emergence of a deeply dividing structural cleavage that had long been present. But caution is necessary. For one thing, the new democracy, institutionally and legislatively immature, had to solve a number of fundamental problems, which required democratic processes, mechanisms, and institutions that were not in place. If they had been, different solutions might have been found (Brokl, 1992). In addition, public opinion polls indicate that in the early years both Czechs and Slovaks were opposed to separation. It was not until November 1992 that 50 percent of the Czechs and 40 percent of the Slovaks (IVVM 92-11) believed splitting of the federation was necessary (Brokl, Mansfeldová, 1992).

THE ELECTIONS OF 1996 AND THEIR CONSEQUENCES

The 1996 parliamentary elections were exceptional for several reasons. They were the first Czech elections since the splitting up of Czechoslovakia. There were also the first elections for the upper chamber (the Senate). The so-far dominant ODS faced a partner of equal power and a strong competitor, the Social Democrats (ČSSD).[6] Finally, two electoral systems were in effect: PR for the lower chamber and FPTP for the upper chamber (the Senate).

Sixteen parties ran for the lower chamber; each had to reach a 5 percent threshold in order to succeed. There were two rounds of elections for the upper chamber; the first took place November 15–16, 1996, and the second a week later. Senate seats were won by gaining a majority in single-member election districts, by run-off elections where necessary (see Tables 14.3 and 14.4).

The most striking change in the new Parliament was the vastly increased strength of the Social Democratic Party (the ČSSD).[7] Did this development signal the renewal of the labor versus capital cleavage during the transformation process, and the emergence of a class-party alignment? What explains the changing behavior of the Czech electorate?

Table 14.3
Election Results in 1996 (first chamber of Czech Parliament–Chamber of Deputies)

	% of votes	Seats
ODS (coalition)	29.6	68
KDU-ČSL	8.1	18
ODA	6.4	13
ČSSD (opposition - left wing)	26.4	61
KSČM	10.3	22
SPR-RSČ (extreme right-left mixture)	8.0	18
Other parties	11.1	—
Total	100.0	200

Note: 76.4 percent eligible voters took part in the elections (Volby, 96: 8).

Table 14.4
Election Results in 1996 (round 2 for Czech Senate)

	Seats	% of votes for the party
ODS (coalition)	32	49.15
KDU-ČSL	13	10.74
ODA	7	5.19
ČSSD (opposition-left-wing)	25	31.8
KSČM	2	1.96
DEU (extreme right-wing)	1	0.64
Independent	1	0.52
Total	81	100.00

Note: Voter participation: round 1–35 percent, of eligible voters; round 2–30.6 percent of eligible voters (Čsú, 96).

Left-wing-oriented political commentators, politicians, and some specialists in the field of social stratification explain the Social Democrats' success as the result of a return to social class determination of voter behavior. This argumentation in its methodological approach is similar to the ancient ontological evidence about the existence of God: "If we have a concept of God, then something in reality must correspond." However, if we analyze the voters' decisions from the perspective of their social class position we find that this argument is not only not confirmed, but actually rebutted.

(1) During the twelve months before the elections, Social Democrats averaged 17 percent in voter preference surveys. We can consider the voters represented by this number to be their stable and maybe even socially based electorate. However, the Social Democrats' results in the elections were 12 percent higher and were not predicted by any preelection survey. Of the 28.44 percent of the voters who voted for the Social Democrats, nearly half (43.2 percent of ČSSD votes) decided for the party at the last moment before the elections. Of those who voted ČSSD, 28 percent decided during the course of the election campaign and 15.2 percent decided only after the election campaign ended. It is obvious that the Social Democrats' position was not decided by its stable electorate, 17 percent of all voters, but rather by a chance 12 percent vote swing of voters who did not decide until the last moment.

(2) The social class perspective: The ruling coalition parties, or the right, secured 38.9 percent of the voters of "the poor"[8] (26 percent voted for ODS; 8.4 percent for KDU-ČSL; 4.5 percent for ODA), and only 46 percent of the poor voted for the left (24 percent for ČSSD and 14 percent for KSČM). At the same time 25.3 percent of "the rich"[9] and 29.7 percent of business people voted for the left (15.3 percent of the rich and 17.1 percent of business people voted for ČSSD; 3.4 percent of the rich and 4.1 percent of business people voted for KSČM). The ruling coalition parties were voted for by 67 percent of the rich, out of which 49.5 percent voted for ODS, 13.1 percent voted for ODA, and 5.2 percent voted for KDU-ČSL.[10] (Volby, 96: Daily, MF Dnes, 11/6/96: 9; INFAS: 1.6.96/21:35:08). From this data it is apparent that voters' choices were not primarily decided by their social class, but by different factors.

(3) The inadequacy in interpreting the voters' decision-making process due to their social class is also confirmed by the voters' reasons for voting the way they did: "Reasons which led the voters to choose some parties were much more variable [this year] than in the past" (IVVM 96-26/7:3). Reasons that accounted for 83 percent of the answers in 1992, accounted for only 67 percent of voters' decisions in 1996 (see Table 14.5).

Other reasons given in 1996 were as follows: has a good social policy, 4 percent; defends senior citizens' rights, 2 percent; voter wanted to vote left, 2 percent; voter wanted to vote right, 2 percent; other answers, 7 percent.

(4) Finally, voters consider ODS and ČSSD to be parties that are competent in different areas, yet complementary to each other. The ODS has created an image of itself as the party with the best economics program whereas the social

Table 14.5
Voters' Decisions from the Perspective of Their Social Class

	1996 (in %)	1992 (in %)
Good politics	27	31
Good program	21	26
Personages	8	11
Will finish reforms	6	4
Defending voter interests	5	11

democrats, on the other hand, have an image of being able to distribute resources the most effectively. The two parties were rated in the following areas: social care ČSSD–32 percent, ODS–18 percent; housing policy ČSSD–28 percent, ODS–15 percent; health care ČSSD–27 percent, ODS–18 percent, state financing ODS–43 percent, ČSSD–16 percent (Herzmann 10. 6. 1996). Other surveys measuring the popular evaluation of the two parties confirms mixed, not antagonistic, assessments (IVVM 96-25/33).

In reality, then, the Czech voters had diverse reasons for their preferences, and were guided neither by the left-right placement of the parties nor by social class criteria. The theory that the Social Democrats gained through the social class polarization of Czech society in the 1996 elections is not confirmed.

The Psychological Effect of the Required 5 Percent Threshold

The 12 percent vote swing to the Social Democrats, the grand surprise of these elections, may be partially explained by the psychological effect of the PR voting system. A first glance, however, deepens the mystery. The PR voting for the lower chamber had the effect normally associated with the FPTP system (establishing two strong parties and neglecting other parties), while the majoritarian system in the upper chamber elections produced what appeared to be a PR voting system effect. Nonetheless, the swing of votes to the ČSSD in the Assembly appears to be owing to the votes of small party supporters who did not believe that their parties would cross the 5 percent threshold and were afraid that their votes would be redistributed among parties they did not support (Rendlová for MFD and IVVM, 1996; Brokl, 1996; Krejčí, 1996; Novák, 1996). This interpretation is strengthened by a preelection public opinion survey of such small party supporters (IVVM Rendlová, 96-25): Asked if their party could be expected to cross the required 5 percent threshold, Left Bloc voter opinion was as follows: 30 percent said definitely, 46 percent probably, and 23 percent did not think so or did not know. Only 13 percent of DŽJ voters said a definite yes, to their party getting in, 8 percent said probably, and 77 percent did not think so or did not know. DEU's voters said the following: A definite yes, 13 percent; probably, 20 percent; did not think so or did not know, 70 percent. Free Democrats' (SD-LSNS), or the former OH, 6 percent of voters stated a definite yes, 41 percent said probably, while 53 percent did not know or did not think so. Furthermore, in the same poll, 12.8 percent of Czech voters said they preferred small parties which, in the event, did not cross the 5 percent threshold. It seems reasonable to infer, therefore, that the pragmatism of small party supporters played a role giving the ČSSD its strong showing.

The influence of the election formula on the voters' decisions was also a factor in the 1992 elections when the political center, represented by small parties including the OH, disappeared from the political scene. The 1992 elections were not based on the elections of anti-Communism symbols as some authors and journalists have claimed. Communism, which was rejected in the 1990 elections, was not being voted for and neither was capitalism. The 1992 elections were more focused on other issues, such as the progress of political and economic transformation and the Czecho-Slovak disagreements. They indicated a preference for programmatic parties as opposed to vague and uncontrollable movements. In fact, the influence of the threshold can be seen in the first free "anti-Communist" elections of 1990, if we take into consideration the lack of success of the small and also anti-Communist political parties and their leaders' complaints about the OFs "election competition unfairness" when the OF asked voters not to vote for small parties that would not get into parliament and whose votes would be redistributed to the communists.

In sum, the psychological influence of the 5 percent threshold, creating a reluctance to vote for small parties, led to the concentration of votes around the two largest political parties, and produced a majority effect despite the PR voting system. On the other hand, the majoritarian effect of the single member district system in the Senate was dampened owing to the provision for a run-off. Voters more freely chose small-party candidates than they would have with a single vote and plurality election (FPTP). (The final number of parties represented in the two chambers, however, was the same.)

CONCLUSION

Based on this interpretation of results of the parliamentary elections of 1996 we can draw the following conclusions:

1. The number of political parties was reduced as well as their polarization. We can interpret this as a development toward a bipolar party system. It is as if the Czech Republic is expediently taking the path of post-totalitarian Germany: Like Germany in 1949, it is moving away from the great number of parties, not toward a two-party system, but toward a bipolarity of four parties. The condition of maintaining such a bipolar, but not excessively divided, party system will be economic prosperity in the Czech Republic.

2. Voting behavior that significantly influenced the 1996 election results was primarily determined by the psychological factor of the 5 percent threshold (and situational and opportunist factors) and not by social class factors.

3. The elections confirm the continuity of the basic structural axis of transformation.

4. The competitive space of the left and the right is growing, which allows for the fine-tuning of political programs and allows for the peaceful change of governments.

5. The findings strongly suggest the stability of the political régime and the democratic system, which has to be distinguished from government stability.

ABBREVIATIONS OF PARTY NAMES:

ČSSD	Czech Social Democratic Party
DEU	Democratic Union
DŽJ	Pensioners for Life Security
HSD-SMS	The Movement for Self-Governing Democracy–Society for Moravia and Silesia
KDS	Christian Democratic Party
KDU	Christian Democratic Union
KDU-ČSL	Christian Democratic Union–Czechoslovak Peoples Party
KSČM	The Communist Party of Bohemia and Moravia
LB	Left Block, an alliance between the Communist Party of Bohemia and Moravia and the Democratic Left of the ČR
LSU	Liberal Social Union
ODA	Civic Democratic Alliance
ODS	Civic Democratic Party
OF	Civic Forum
SPR-RSČ	Coalition for the Republic—Republican Party of Czechoslovakia

NOTES

1. Based on research carried out by a Czech national team (Z. Mansfeldová [coordinator], Lubomír Brokl, Aleš Kroupa, M. Tuček) within the framework of the international comparative research "The Formation of Party Systems and the Consolidation of Democracy in East Central Europe," led by H. Kitschelt.

2. Some political parties that ran were part of the party list of OF (ODA, The Agricultural Party, The Green Party, and so on) and became independent in the following years. See Brokl and collective, 1994: 8, Brokl/Mansfeldová, 1995; Mansfeldová/Kitschelt, 1995.

3. The Czech lands are made up of Bohemia with Prague, Moravia with the cities of Brno and Olomouc, and Silesia with the cities of Ostrava and Opava. Some political subjects and journalists (namely, German and Slovak ones) understood this party as a representative of the independence-seeking "Moravian Nation" and expected further splitting of the country.

4. Czechoslovakia became a federation consequently to the Prague Spring, but after the Soviet military occupation in October 1968.

5. The election law regulations established the threshold; political parties and movements had to reach a 5 percent level, alliances made up of two or three parties/movements had to have 7 percent, and alliances composed of four or more parties had to secure 10 percent of the vote to enter the Federal parliament. Parties trying to enter the Czech national representative body had the following thresholds: One party needed 5 percent, alliances made up of two parties needed 7 percent, three party alliances needed 9 percent, and four or more parties needed 11 percent.

6. The Czech Social Democratic Party, thanks to the existence of the more left-wing Communist Party (KSČM), could have paradoxically developed as an identical social democratic and not post-communist party.

7. Parts of L. Brokl's "Parliamentary Elections 1996" are used in the following interpretation: See Brokl, L., 1996. *Sociologický časopis*, no. 3, special election issue.

8. Monthly income below 5,000 crowns.

9. Monthly income above 20,000 crowns.

10. This political orientation of part of the Czech petit-bourgeois that feels threatened by excess of economic freedom is common and has been present in the Czech political tradition since the mid-1900s.

REFERENCES

Brokl, L. 1992. "Between November 1989 and Democracy–Antinomies of Our Politics." *Czechoslovak Sociological Review* 28, Special Issue: 23–36.
———. 1996. "Dvě slabiny odhalené volbami–Princip poměrné volby funguje při 5 percent klauzuli jako princip většinový." *Lidové noviny* 6.6.: 9 a ČTV 1, 3.6. 21–22 hod.
Brokl, L. a kol. 1994. "Politický prostor České republiky." *Lidové noviny* 11.11.1994: 8.
Brokl, L. and Z. Mansfeldová. 1992. "Haben wir die Teilung der ČSFR gewollt?" *Ost-West Gegen Informationen.* Sonderheft: 11–15.
———. 1995. "Zerfall der Tschechoslowakei–strukturelle Ursachen und Parteihandeln." In D. Segert and C. Machos, *Parteien in Osteuropa, Kontext und Akteure,* 133–48 Opladen: Westdeutscher Verlag.
Herzmann, J. 1996. "Ředitel FACTUM v rozhovoru s J. Kubíkem." *Mladá fronta Dnes* 10.6.1996.
INFAS, 1.6.96/21:35:08.
IVVM 92–09 a Monitoring IVVM 1992/55 s. 1.
IVVM 92–11: "Názory na rozdělení federace."
IVVM 96–25: "Image politických stran před volbami," otázka 33, Eliška Rendlová, 5. 6. 1996.
IVVM 96–26: "K důvodům volby politické strany," otázka 7, Ján Mišovič, 1.7. 1996.
Kaase, M. and H.-D. Klingemann (eds.). 1983. *Wahlen und politisches System, Analysen aus Anlaß der Bundestagswahl 1980.* Opladen: Westdeutscher Verlag.
———. 1990. *Wahlen und Wähler, Analysen aus Anlaß der Bundestagswahl 1987.* Opladen: Westdeutscher Verlag.
Katz, R. S. 1980. *A Theory of Parties and Electoral Systems.* Baltimore and London: The John Hopkins University Press.
Kitschelt, Herbert. 1992. "The Formation of Party Systems in East Central Europe." *Politics and Society* 20 (1): 13.
Krejčí, O. 1996. "Moc se chovala sebevražedně." *rozhovor pro Ekonom* 24: 11–13.

Lawson, K. (ed.). 1980. *Political Parties and Linkage, A Comparative Perspective.* New Haven and London: Yale University Press.
Lijphart, A. 1990. "The political consequences of Electoral Laws, 1956–85." *American Political Science Review* 81 (2).
Lipset, S. M. and S. Rokkan. 1967. *Party Systems and Voter Alignments: Cross-National Perspectives.* New York: The Free Press.
Mansfeldová, Z. and H. Kitschelt. 1995. *Elite Strategies in Building Party Alternatives, A Process Analyzing of Bulgaria, the Czech Republic, Hungary and Poland.* Paper for the Workshop Public Opinion and Party Formation and Post-Authoritarian Democracies, Duke University, March 24–25.
Martin, W. C. and K. Hopkins. 1980. "Cleavage Crystallization and Party Linkages in Finland, 1900–1918." In Kay Lawson (ed.), *Political Parties and Linkage, A Comparative Perspective.* New Haven and London: Yale University Press.
Nohlen, D. 1990. *Wahlrecht und Parteiensystem, Über die politischen Auswirkungen von Wahlsystemen.* Opladen: Leske & Budrich Verlag.
Nohlen, D. 1992. *Politikwissenschaft 1.* München: Piper Verlag.
Novák, M. 1996. "Volby do Poslanecké sněmovny, vládní nestabilita a perspektivy demokracie v ČR." *Sociologický časopis,* 32, č. 4.
Rendlová, E. 1996. "ODS i ČSSD mohou získat voliče jiných stran," Jiří Kubík (E. Rendlová v rozhovoru s J. Kubíkem). *MFD* 21.5: 2.
Rokkan, S. 1967. "Cleavage Structures, Party Systems and Voters Alignments, An Introduction." In S. M. Lipset and S. Rokkan, *Party Systems and Voter Alignments: Cross-National Perspectives.* New York: The Free Press Glencoe.
Sartori, G. 1976. *Parties and party systems, A framework for analysis (Vol. I.).* Cambridge and New York: Cambridge University Press.
Schultze, R. O. 1987. "Die Bundestagswahl 1987–Eine Bestätigung des Wandels." *Aus Politik und Zeitgeschichte* 37: 3–17.
Volby do Senátu Parlamentu České republiky 1996. Český statistický úřad, Praha, listopad 1996.
Volby do Federálního shromáždění České a Slovenské Federativní Republiky v roce 1990, vol I. a II. Federální statistický úřad, Praha, 1991.
Volby do Federálního shromáždění České a Slovenské Federativní Republiky v roce 1992. Federální statistický úřad, Praha, vol. 1, červen 1992, vol. 2, červenec 1992.
Volby 96, Daily MF Dnes 11/6/96, Mimořádná příloha s. 8.

15

Cleavages and Spaces of Competition in Hungary

János Simon

INTRODUCTION[1]

Lipset and Rokkan explained the development of democratic party systems in terms of the historical condition of socioeconomical and national development (1967). They believed that ideological and partisan divisions sprang from the social cleavages existing in a nation. According to the authors, the differences between competing social groups provided the basis for political conflict, and eventually the voting base for parties. Each nation exhibits its own particular mix of cleavages because of the social and historical composition of the nation and its particular pattern of modernization (Dalton, 1995). Several studies suggest that the proposition of Lipset-Rokkan that "the party systems of the 1960s reflect, with but few significant exceptions, the cleavage structures of the 1920s" is valid (Lipset and Rokkan, 1967: 50).

Is it possible to find long-lasting cleavages in Hungary, or did the four decades of state socialism and a single party system create a "tabula rasa" situation? And, in general, what kind of important social and political cleavages characterize Hungary in the period when it is establishing the institutions of democracy and market economy? One can say in general that cleavages in the Hungarian society are much more structured than some commentators have claimed. With the following study I seek to contribute to a more subtle description of these cleavages by the analysis of the data of yearly time-line surveys conducted between 1989 and 1994, using more than 200 standard questions on a 1000 person country-wide representative sample. (See Appendix One.)

CONTINUITY AND DISCONTINUITY IN THE IDEOLOGICAL CHARACTERISTICS OF THE PARTIES

The Hungarian party system that was formed or formed again in the early '90s seems to substantiate the Lipset-Rokkan theory about the strong historical continuity of cleavages. It is in many ways a continuation of the party system that ceased to exist in 1948, and represents the social values and interests of three great historical periods:

1. The period before the end of World War I. The party of Christian Democracy (Christian Democratic People's Party) and the party of Social Democrats (Hungarian Socialist Party)
2. The period between the two wars. The party of the conservative middle class (Hungarian Democratic Forum) and the party of agricultural smallholders (Independent Smallholders' Party)
3. The two-part period between 1945 and 1948 and in 1988–1989. The party of the social-liberal, traditional city bourgeoisie (Alliance of Free Democrats) and the party of bourgeois liberal-technocrat youth (Alliance of Young Democrats)

All three periods contain a bipolar social cleavage, represented by the attitude toward religion, the duality of the town and the village, and by a generational cut. The oldest cleavage is the one between Christian Democrats and Social Democrats, going back to the last century. Social sensibility is the common feature that helped them to survive a difficult history, and their attitudes toward religion form the sharp cleavage between them.

The conservative national ideology that was represented partly by the upper middle class and partly by the richer peasantry of the villages is from the period between the two wars. The liberal parties that represent modern bourgeois values appeared after the regime change. The Alliance of Free Democrats is representative of an older generation, its lifestyle and ideology is based on the bourgeois traditions of the Hungarian Jews, and its liberal political results were developed mainly after 1945. The Alliance of Young Democrats that was founded in the spring of 1988 represents the younger generation, and its image is in accordance with the pragmatist and technocratic line of the liberals, appearing in national colors. All those values that were born in different historical periods are still present at the same time in different groups of the Hungarian society, but they differ in intensity.

As far as its political system is concerned, Hungary has the image of the most stable democracy in the post-communist region. There were only two parliamentary elections held in the first half of the decade; those cycles were not accompanied by government crises, and extremist, anti-democratic and intolerant political forces were not voted into the Parliament. The balance of forces at the same time brought significant changes among the parliamentary parties. The winner of the 1990 elections, the right-centrist conservative HDF, lost more than

Table 15.1
Election Results in 1990 and 1994 (in percent) (Hungary)

	1st round March, 1990	1st round May, 1994
Hungarian Democratic Forum (HDF)	24.7	11.7
Alliance of Free Democrats (AFD)	21.3	19.7
Hungarian Socialist Party (HSP)	10.8	32.9
Alliance of Young Democrats (AYD)	8.9	7.0
Christian Democratic People's Party (CDPP)	6.4	7.0
Independent Smallholders' Party	11.7	8.8

half of its voters in four years (dropping from 24 percent to 11 percent), and the left-wing HSP tripled the proportion of its voters (see Table 15.1).

The election results in Hungary show us a relatively stable party-system, since the same six parties were voted into Parliament in 1990 and 1994. Deeper analyses show, however, that the profiles of the parties changed between the two elections, and their voters' bases changed significantly, too. The centrist HDF that had the image of the "quiet force" in 1990 moved to the right and became a religious and anti-communist party. The AFD, which had been a right-wing, radical anti-communist party, gradually mellowed and became a centrist liberal party. At the same time, with the aggravation of the economic crisis, growing unemployment, inflation, and citizens' dissatisfaction, anti-communist propaganda lost its credibility, and the Kádár-era, together with the socialist party that grew from the reform forces of that era, gained new respect. This process was accompanied by the "self-cleaning" of the HSP (separations and new alliances), as a result of which it grew from a post-communist party to an internationally recognized Social Democratic one.

CLEAVAGES ON THE VOTERS' LEVEL

The Strength of the Social and Ideological Tensions

The following discussion is based mainly on the data of our survey research of December 1993, a time when the main cleavages had begun to appear and party-preferences represented election results a full half-year before the elections.

It is one of the most important lessons of our research that studies of electoral behavior in Hungary should not rely on only one dimension. We believe that the party-preferences of certain social groups are determined by actual social status and the economic position related to that status, while in other cases the decisive role is played by life experiences, by family traditions, in short, by "cultural socialization." Due to the semi-market circumstances, the voter bases of the particular parties contain strongly divided social groups, which frequently oppose each other. Because the relationships are still plastic and are constantly changing, cross-voting is strong among particular social groups (for example, there is no significant difference between employers and employees; employees vote both for the Left and for the Right, just as employers do) (Bruszt and Simon, 1990; Simon, 1996b).

In our first analysis we studied two questions: In what kind of political field was the competition among parties conducted, and were the 1994 elections decided for the left-wing socialist party by the losers of the developing market economy, who massively voted for the Socialists? Table 15.2 shows what social and ideological problems the citizens considered most important, and how the voters of the parties were organized around those problems.

Hungarians believe that the strongest social tensions are between the poor and the rich, and between those who obey the law and those who break it. The proportion of those who consider political and ideological conflicts, such as government-opposition or Left-Right, strong, is much less. On the level of the citizens, the proportion of those who consider the generation differences or ethnic and religious tensions important is very low. This means that for the majority of society, the everyday-life situation—the fight against poverty and crime—constitutes the mean dimension of the political contest. Thus an important question becomes, "Which party's voter base contains that cleavage in the greatest and the smallest proportions?"

According to Table 15.2, the greatest difference is between the HSP and the HDF in the economic-social field that is considered most important by the citizens. Left-wing socialist voters—probably due to their own market position—consider social tensions between rich and poor the strongest (70 percent of them consider it important), while the voters of HDF, the strongest party of the then-governing coalition, are least likely to see such tensions as high (44 percent). It is not surprising that the economic losers of the regime change backed the HSP with their votes, and the winners voted for the main governing party, the HDF.[2]

Table 15.2
Opinions of Party Supporters Regarding Social and Ideological Tensions in Hungary in 1993 (percentage saying high level of tension)

between	HSP	AFD	AYD	CDPP	HDF	ISHP	n. vote	society
poor/rich	70	53	55	57	44	56	66	60
follow law/lawbreakers	67	55	54	58	53	58	60	58
government/opposition	36	33	31	33	34	44	32	34
left/right	26	18	19	24	22	19	19	17
young/old	21	22	13	21	15	11	19	18
Hungarians/ethnic minorities	18	12	18	15	18	18	19	17
religious/nonreligious	14	13	14	25	15	12	14	15

Economic and Ideological Attitudes of Party Supporters

We consider next some cleavages that the literature considers important for party choices.[3] We created multi-item scales of several statements and then, using variance analysis, checked how they correlated with party choice. We were interested in the main attitudes of the supporters of the parties, and wanted to know whether they differed from one another concerning the main cleavages. We developed the following multi-item scales: attitude toward religion, evaluation of the past, membership in the past state party (Hungarian Socialist Workers' Party), economic situation, market position, and support of a Western orientation (see Tables 15.3a through 15.3g, developed by the ANOVA statistical method).

Our analysis demonstrates that attitude toward religion constitutes one of the most important cleavages in Hungarian society (Evans and Whitehead, 1995). The attitude toward religion among the supporters of the conservative Christian parties that were in power between 1990 and 1994 differs significantly from that of the supporters of the principally materialist Socialist and Liberal parties (see Table 15.3a).

The attitude toward the past, toward "state socialism," is another important political cleavage that spectacularly divides the voters of the parties (see Table 15.3b). It is not surprising that the voters of the HDF are most likely to reject the past regime, and that the voters of the HSP, the party founded by the reform forces of the old state-party, consider the past most positively. But it is a surprise that the voters of the Independent Smallholders' Party are second after the socialists to evaluate the past positively, though the number of ex-party members among them is the lowest (see Table 15.3c). How can the positive image of the past among the Smallholders be explained? To answer that question, one must study the evaluations of the economic situation.

We developed two multi-item scales concerning the economic situation. One of them dealt with the evaluation of the economic situation, the other with the individual market positions according to party-preferences (see Tables 15.3d and

Table 15.3a

Attitude toward Religion (means of scale)		
CDPP	8.576	religious
HDF	7.786	↑
ISHP	7.250	
Nonvoters	6.608	
AFD	6.182	
AYD	6.182	↓
HSP	4.750	non religious
Mean	6.70	

Table 15.3b

	Kádár-era positive (means of scale)	
HSP	18.92	positive
ISHP	17.29	↑
AYD	17.08	
Nonvoters	17.03	
AFD	16.41	
CDPP	15.30	↓
HDF	14.91	not positive
Mean	19.91	

Table 15.3c

	Were not members of Hungarian Socialist Workers' Party (means of scale)
Non-voters	1.955
HDF	1.948
ISHP	1.921
CDPP	1.923
AYD	1.897
AFD	1.884
HSP	1.662
Mean	1.875

Table 15.3d

	Own economic situation is good (means of scale)	
HDF	7.948	winners
CDPP	7.108	↑
AFD	6.568	
AYD	6.308	
ISHP	6.296	
HSP	6.050	↓
Nonvoters	5.973	losers
Mean	6.493	

15.3e). One can see that the losers and the winners of the transition to the market economy are separated in both cases, even if the differences in market positions are not significant. The HSP voters are always at one pole, and the HDF voters at the other, another indication that masses of the losers supported the socialists at the 1994 elections, and thereby determined the results. It is worth mentioning, too, that after the socialists, the smallholders are the second to give a negative evaluation of the economic situation. Undoubtedly, the continuous reduction of

Table 15.3e

Market position is bad (means of scale)		
HSP	12.32	losers
CDPP	12.04	↑
AFD	11.90	
Nonvoters	11.88	
ISHP	11.73	
AYD	11.55	↓
HDF	11.05	winners
Mean	11.85	

Table 15.3f

Free market support (means of scale)		
HDF	7.812	pro-market
AFD	7.361	↑
CDPP	7.351	
AYD	7.248	
ISHP	6.984	
HSP	6.949	↓
Nonvoters	6.657	pro-state protection
Mean	7.120	

state subsidies of the agrarian sector also contributed to the higher evaluation of the past. It confirms our earlier opinion, that the attitudes toward the past should not be reduced to mere ideological explanations, and that they have very real, empirical, economic bases (Simon, 1996a).

Studies dealing with the characteristics of the Hungarian parties and with cleavages always raise the problem of the attitudes of party-supporters toward the market economy and the Western type of development. Table 15.3f indicates that the market economy is supported most by those who feel themselves winners (first of all, voters of HDF), and least by those who see themselves as losers, the voters of the socialists and the smallholders. Although there is no significant difference between the voter bases of the parties concerning the orientation to the West, here also the losers (voters of the HSP and the ISHP) are less supportive of this process (Table 15.3g).

In the first period of the transition (1988–1991), it was mainly the ideological and cultural cleavages that dominated the Hungarian party system. However, six months before the 1994 parliamentary elections, in late 1993, the losers and the winners of the regime-change were already clearly to be seen. Besides the ideological cleavages (such as religion), economic and social cleavages gained more and more importance, and determined several political orientations and attitudes

Table 15.3g

	Support for Western-style development (means of scale)	
AYD	2.867	strong support
CDPP	2.858	↑
HDF	2.847	
AFD	2.797	
ISHP	2.750	↓
HSP	2.687	
Nonvoters	2.651	weak support
Mean	2.759	

(for example, the attitude toward a market economy, support for Western-type development, attitude towards the past, and so on).

Differences in the Voters' Bases of the Parties According to Cleavages

We turn now to the question of to what extent are cleavages able to create party-preferences—that is, to distinguish between the voters of the parties. If we do not find serious differences in the voter bases of the parties, it would mean that the Hungarian party-system is still unformed and plastic. But if we can find cleavages that characteristically divide parties from one another, that would suggest the party-system is stabilizing. We used logistical regression to measure the strength of the differences, and compared the voter base of other parties with that of the Socialist Party, the party that won the absolute majority in the 1994 parliamentary elections (see Table 15.4).

Table 15.4
Ideological and Attitudinal Responses of Party Supporters (differences between the HSP and the others—logistic regression)

	Hungarian Socialist Party					
	CDPP	HDF	ISHP	AYD	AFD	Nonvoters
ex-HSWP member	1.3320	1.5861	1.1317	1.0531	1.1863	1.8802
religious	.5805	.3329	.2888	1406	.1809	.2268
Western orientation support	.5784	.0250	.0356	.5407	.2412	−.2809
Kádár regime positive	−.3306	−.2907	−.2056	−.1926	−.2050	−.2603
left/right position	.2679	3701	.2278	.4427	.3152	.2959
economical situation good	−.0209	.2631	.1146	−.0713	.0380	−.1164
free market support	−.0611	−.0788	−.0245	.0370	−.0009	−.1594
political efficacy bad	−.0081	−.0579	.0992	−.0176	−.0794	.1047

Table 15.4 shows the main dimensions of the political contest concerning the most important cleavages, in relation to the socialists—that is, in what dimensions the characteristics of the HSP voters differ from the voters of other parties, and in what dimensions they do not. Socialists differ from the supporters of all the other parties concerning their membership in the past party, as well as in their evaluation of the past and their position on the left-right dimension. Ex-members of the previous state party support the socialist party, evaluate the old regime positively, and consider themselves and their party as left-wing. These differences decisively distinguish and separate socialist voters from all the other parties.

There are cleavages that separate socialist voters only from one other party, and others from two or more. The sharpest divisions between the Christian-Democrat voters and the socialists are the attitudes toward religion and the support for Western orientation.[4] The voters of the HDF are separated from the socialists the most, along four dimensions: right-wing orientation, religion, evaluation of the past, and evaluation of the economic situation. ISHP and HSP voters differ in the dimensions of religion and Left-Right, but there are also several similarities between them.[5] The Western orientation and the Left-Right dimension constitute the greatest differences between the voters of the AYD and the socialists. There are no significantly sharp differences between the voters of the AFD and HSP, but the strongest is in the Left-Right dimension.

We have seen that each party is separated from the others by one, two, or more cleavages. This demonstrates, on the one hand, that the parties developed their independent images, and that citizens see them separated in certain dimensions. It shows, on the other hand, that there are not only one or two cleavages in the society, but rather a network of cleavages of different strength.[6] This means that the political competition is going on not only in one field, but in several fields and dimensions at the same time.

Types of Party Voters

We study here the main attitude-dimensions the voters are grouped in—that is, the main attitudinal position of party supporters. We grouped our eighteen multi-item scales using factor-analysis. Table 15.5 shows how many dimensions the Hungarian voting age citizens are grouped in according to their political orientation and attitudes, and what kind of attitudinal factors shape the dimensions.

According to Table 15.5, Hungarian voters are grouped in six attitudinal dimensions. In all factor-groups, the attitude toward two problems is represented: to economic and political changes, that is, to market economy and democracy. We group the Hungarian voters according to their attitudes on those two change processes, naming the six types as nonvoters, great winners, powerless, technocrats, authoritarian, and indifferent (see Table 15.6).

Table 15.5
Factor Analysis by 18 Scales

I. factor		II. factor		III. factor	
Party efficacy bad	.9286	Government efficacy is good	.7509	Powerless in politics	.7084
Political efficacy bad	.8433	Economic situation is good	.6313	Market position bad	.6211
No HSWP member	.4073	Religious	.6280	Free market support	-.4471
Authoritarian regime support	.4038	Kádár-era positive	-.3811	Kádár-era positive	.4350
Free market support	-.1832	Trust in general	.3519	Authoritarian regime support	-.3733
Economic situation is bad	.1443	No HSWP member	.3124	Economic situation better	-.2433
		Market position bad	-.2142	Political efficacy bad	.2286
				No HSWP member	-.2113

IV. factor		V. factor		VI. factor	
Western-type development	.7310	Political violence support	.7874	Libertarian-individual values	.7650
Refuse social paternalism	.6531	Kádár-era good	.4396	Left/Right placement	.5152
Free market support	.4300	Left/Right placement	-.3648	No HSWP member	.3619
Trust in general	.3020	Authoritarian regime support	.3544	Western-type of development	.2771
Authoritarian regime support	-.3019	Trust in general	.3030	Trust in general	.2435
No HSWP member	.2096	Libertarian values	.2260	Authoritarian regime support	-.1843
Government efficacy good	-.1822	HSWP member	.2068	Market position bad	.1199
		Free market support	-.1673		

Table 15.6
Voter Types on the Basis of Factor Characters (Hungary)

I. factor: Nonvoters	*II. factor: Great winners*	*III. factor: Powerless*
Pro-authoritarian	Pro-democracy	Anti-free market
Anti-free market	Pro-free market (good market position)	Anti-authoritarian
(they used to be and still are far from politics)	(strongly religious, they feel themselves as political and economical winners of the regime-change)	(defenseless, bad economic position, Kádárist sympathizers)

IV. factor: Technocrats	*V. factor: Authoritarian*	*VI. factor: Indifferent*
Pro-free market	Pro-authoritarian	Pro-democracy
Anti-authoritarian	Anti-free market	Neutral re market
(definitely support Western type of development, had not been members of HSWP, preserved critical attitude)	(support political violence, Leftist, Kádárist, opposing market)	(individualist, Right-wing, used to have and still have loose relation to politics, not very interested in)

How the Ex-members of the HSWP Voted

According to our survey, attitude toward the past constitutes one of the most important cleavages in Hungarian society. This finding supports those researchers who argue that membership in HSWP is an important hidden factor of party choice.[7]

On the basis of the characteristics of the factors produced by the multi-item scales, we are able to answer the question, What is the ex-members' and nonmembers' position concerning the economic regime-change? Is a separate group of the ex-members of the state party formed by the economic winners who preserved their power? Table 15.7 shows how the ex-HSWP members are distributed among the winners and losers.

Table 15.7 shows that ex-HSWP members basically join two groups: the Authoritarian leftists and the Powerless democrats. (In the first group, the correlation with HSWP membership is .2068, and with positive evaluation of the Kádár-era is .4396, while in the second, the correlates are .2113 and .4350, respectively. From those who consider themselves as winners, the Technocrats' correlation with nonmembership is .2096; the Great winners' correlation is respectively .3124. Moreover, their level of rejection of the Kádár-era is also high: .3811. See Table 15.6.) It means at the same time that those of the ex-members of HSWP who have moved into better economic positions, the winners of the regime change, do not form a separate attitudinal group, but are scattered in other attitudinal groups (for example, the Powerless or the Technocrats). There are three possible explanations.

Table 15.7
Economic Winners and Losers according to HSWP Membership (Hungary)

LOSERS	WINNERS
ex-HSWP members	
V. Authoritarian, leftist, support political violence, anti-free market	
III. Powerless but democrats, bad market position but support free market	
	IV. Technocrats: anti-authoritarian, strong free market support
non-members of HSWP	
I. Nonvoters: Authoritarian regime support, anti-free market	
VI. Indifferent, pro-democracy, neutral re market	
	IV. Technocrats: anti-authoritarian, strong free market support
	II. Great winners, support government and democracy, strong free market support

First, the number of those party officials who converted their old political power to economic power might be low. Second, the politics of the Antall-era did not give them the feeling of democratization since it was strongly exclusive against those who have had links to the old regime. Third, the first two explanations are both true and as a result, the majority of the ex-HSWP members saw themselves as losers of the regime-change before the 1994 parliamentary elections (in political or economic terms, or both), and voted for the Socialists.

Support for Democracy and the Market Economy

The Hungarian Socialist Party was formed from the reform-forces of the ex-state party in the process of the democratic transition, so it can be considered a post-communist party. Are democracy and development toward a market economy endangered when the Socialist Party is in power? What kind of voters support that development path and what forces are against it? Generally, how much support is there for a market economy and democracy, and, alternatively, for state paternalism and an authoritarian regime in Hungary? One can answer these questions by taking the two most important organizing principles from all types of voters, and represent market economy and democracy and the voters' attitudes toward them in a two-axes coordinate system (see Table 15.8).

According to Table 15.8 we found voter groups in three (A, B, and C) of the four fields of market-democracy dimensions, and there is no group in field D. Thus, the authoritarian-free market scenario is not an alternative in Hungarian

Table 15.8
Placement of Factors on the Market–Democracy Coordinate System (Hungary)

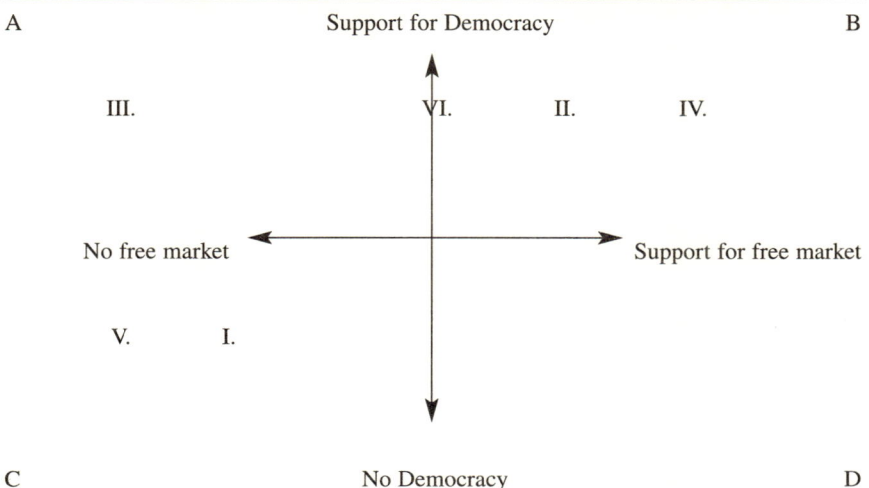

public thinking or in the political field.[8] There are two factor groups against democracy and four that are pro-democracy. But among those that are pro-democracy one group, the defenseless, is against the free market, and another, the group of the indifferent, is economically neutral. Those who are in the best market position support both a market economy and democracy. The main force and supporters of transition in Hungary are Technocrats and Great winners.

CLEAVAGES ON THE LEVEL OF THE POLITICAL ELITE

Parties on the Left-Right Scale

The most important function of the historically always-changing, quasi-mystical Left-Right scale, is that it helps people orient themselves in the field of political parties, and guides their choices. The placement of parliamentary parties on a 10-point scale by the members of the Hungarian parliament is shown in Table 15.9.

Members of the Parliament evaluated the parties in 1996 as citizens did in 1993, except that they saw the two parties of the government coalition, the HSP and AFD, as somewhat closer to each other. The Hungarian Democratic People's Party, which was founded by MPs who left the HDF in 1995, was considered a center party by the MPs themselves, since they put it in between the government coalition and the opposition, but it is still not clear whether the new party is going to act as a link between the two poles or rather separate them in a vacuum. AYD as a bourgeois party moved closer to the center, and ISHP is on the far Right of the scale, as a counterpoint to the socialists. The difference between the two poles is 5.4, meaning that the Left-Right cleavage is a real ideological cleavage for the political elite, although one should not exaggerate this, since it is not stronger than in West European democracies.

MPs associate the positive values of social net, social justice, and antiracism with the Left, while the Right is identified with respect of traditions, defense of national interests, and religiousness.

Tensions and Cleavages

Several analysts have stated that the new political elite in the post-communist democracies do not reflect the real problems of the society.[9] According to West European political scientists, the reason behind this is the weak interest-representation capacity of the historically weak civic society. We believe, however, that in the case

Table 15.9
Parliamentary Parties on the Left–Right Scale according to MPs (Hungary)

HSP	AFD	HDP	AYD	CDPP	HDF	ISHP
3.0	4.2	6.1	6.5	6.7	7.1	8.4

Table 15.10
MP Opinions on Social Tensions by Party (mean–one way, analysis variance)

between	HSP	AFD	AYD	CDPP	HDF	ISHP	MP means
poor / rich	3.513	3.121	3.400	3.400	2.900	3.181	3.373
government / opposition	3.211	3.352	3.500	3.000	3.600	3.800	3.289
follow law / law breakers	3.296	3.151	3.300	2.700	2.700	3.545	3.206
left / right	2.648	2.787	2.800	2.111	2.111	2.700	2.673
Hungarians / ethnic minorities	2.293	2.515	2.100	1.700	2.400	1.818	2.278
young / old	1.888	1.823	2.100	2.000	2.000	2.000	1.910
religious / nonreligious	1.435	1.470	2.200	1.300	1.900	19.09	1.536
Number of MPs	108	34	10	10	10	11	Total: 190*

*49 % of all MPS.

of Hungary, the civic society is not weak, but is strong in a way different from the civic societies in Western Europe or in the USA (Ágh, 1988).

Table 15.10 shows the differences of the opinions on social tensions between the political elite of the parties.

Members of the Hungarian parliament, similarly to the citizens, consider that the tension between the rich and the poor is the strongest. But differently from the citizens, they consider the conflict of the government and the opposition a more important problem than that of crime. A much lower proportion considers the Left-Right tension strong, and similarly to the voters the proportion of those who think that generational differences, ethnic, or religious tensions are important is very small. For the majority of the society, the fight against poverty and crime is the main dimension of the political contest, which is why it is important to see which parties' voter bases contain these views in great and in small proportions. Both the voters and the MPs of the HSP consider the social tensions much stronger than do those of any other party. In the case of three important dimensions regarding the field of political contest as well, the greatest differences can be found between the politicians of the HSP and those of the HDF. The difference is particularly sharp in the evaluation of poverty and crime. In sum, there are no substantial differences between the attitudes of the voters of the parties and those of their political elite.

European Integration and Prejudices

We tested MPs concerning their attitudes toward Europe. According to some theories, the left-wing and liberal parties support European integration, while right-wing conservative ones oppose it. However, 98 percent of the MPs agreed that Hungary must join the European Union. At the same time, we got a very contradictory picture when studying the attitudes of the particular political groups toward integration. MPs evaluated on a 4-point scale to what extent they considered the support of European integration an idea of the policy and the ideology of the Left or the Right.[10] Those who put themselves on the Left-Right scale between 1–4 we coded as left-wing, those who put themselves between 5–6 were coded as centrists, and those between 7–10 were coded as right-wing (see Tables 15.11a and 15.11b).

Tables 15.11a and 15.11b show a paradoxical situation. Left-wing MPs consider the support for European integration mainly as part of the policy of the Left (see Table 15.11a), while Right-wing MPs see it as part of the policy of the Right (see Table 15.11b). At the same time, the Left believes that the Right is not in favor of integration (see Table 15.11b), and vice-versa, the Right thinks that the Left is not (see Table 15.11a). We face here a situation where both the Left and the Right have self-images that considerably differ from the images they have about each other. Representatives of particular poles do not listen to each other, do not consider what the other says or does, but rely upon their own opinions. The other side should obviously represent the opposite opinion, since they are on the other pole. It is probably as a result of "messages" through the press and the lack of direct political dialogue that this situation of "conversation of the deaf" has developed. Our research results dictate that we should give up the black-and-white prejudices that are not supported by any empirical data, but are taken seriously even by some social scientists too, according to which the Left supports European integration

Table 15.11a
Support for European Integration as a Left-wing Value according to MPs (Hungary)

	count	mean	st. deviation
Left	100	3.7100	.47771
Center	30	3.2667	1.0483
Right	52	2.8654	.8863

Random Effects Model—Estimate of Between Component Variance .2233
Homogeneity of variance: Cochrans C Max var. .5202, p = .001 (approx.)
Max/Min. variance 4.816

Table 15.11b
Support for European Integration as a Right-wing Value according to MPs (Hungary)

	count	mean	st. deviation
Left	98	2.8980	.7929
Center	31	2.9677	.9123
Right	51	3.3922	.5321

Random Effects Model - Estimate of Between Component Variance .0685
Homogeneity of variance: Cochrans C Max var. .4772, p = .009 (approx.)
Max/Min. variance 2.939

and Westernization, and the Right opposes it.[11] These theories are not supported by the facts and the data. On the contrary, surveys on the level of the citizens (party supporters), and on the level of MPs definitely contradict them.

CONCLUSION

The Hungarian party system in the first period of the transition (1988–1991) was mainly dominated by ideological and cultural cleavages, but as early as 1993, the winners and the losers of the regime-change were clearly emerging. Economic and social cleavages became more important and determined several political orientations and attitudes (for example, toward market economy, support for Western type of development, and attitude towards the past).

Economic losers of the regime-change supported the HSP during the 1994 elections, and played a decisive role in the victory of that party. Voters of the HSP are separated from the others by their past and by their attitudes toward the past. Members of the past state party support the HSP. HSP voters, unlike the voters of other parties, evaluate the old regime positively and consider themselves and their party Left-wing and mainly nonreligious. These cleavages clearly separate and distinguish socialist voters from all the other parties.

Particular parties have their own independent character, and they are clearly separated in certain dimensions. All the parties are separated from the others by one, two, or more cleavages. There are not only one or two cleavages in the society but a network of cleavages of different strength. Thus the political contest is going on not only in one field, but in several fields and dimensions at the same time.

APPENDIX ONE

We used eighteen scales from different items. An item analysis was conducted, so that in some cases items that reduced overall reliability (as measured by internal consistency estimated using Cronbach's alpha) were removed from the scale. Where possible, the scales were balanced in terms of direction of question wording so as to reduce acquiescence response bias. In some cases, this reduced the internal consistency of the scale, but this was considered preferable because of its beneficial consequences for validity. The effects of choosing one or the other on the strengths of the associations between the scales and other variables are minor.

Multi-item Scales

1. **Religious scale**
    34. People need trust in others for success. I list some groups and institutions, tell me please to what extent you trust them (totally, to some extent, not too much, not at all–4 point scales)
    34.3 The church

34.8 God
(Valid cases 1161)

2. Trust in general

34.5 In fellow countrymen
34.4 In neighbors
34.10 In fellow workers
34.1 In your employer
34.9 In yourself
(Valid cases 683)

3. Libertarian values

Would you support or oppose the following measures?
58.2 To ensure freedom of abortions for women
58.3 To make divorces more difficult
(Valid cases 1171)
(The correlation between the items by Cronbach's alpha was 0.3224)

4. Power in politics

51. Would you be able to do anything against a government decision that violates the interests of people or not?
52. Would you be able to do anything against a local government (municipality) decision that violates the interests of people or not?
63.7 Do you agree that average people are always excluded from power?
(Valid cases 1166)
(The correlation between the items by Cronbach's alpha was 0.553)

5. Political violence support

38. I list some measures of the authorities, tell me please to what extent do you support or oppose each (a 1–4 scale)
38.1 Use of armed force against demonstrators
38.2 Strict punishment of those who do not obey police instructions
38.4 Use of army against strikers
(Valid cases 1160)

6. Authoritarian regime support

40. Do you agree that free elections are the best system of selecting government and leaders?
56.1 Do you agree that parties are needed for democracy?
59.1 Do you think that government based on free elections is better than any other form of government, or are there situations when a non-democratic government is better?
(Valid cases 1161)
(The correlation between the items by Cronbach's alpha was 0.3634)

7. Party efficacy

56. Do you agree with the following statements?
56.1 Parties are needed for democracy
56.2 For me all the parties are the same

56.3 Parties also serve only the interests of their leaders
(Valid cases 1153)
(The correlation between the items by Cronbach's alpha was 0.5680)

8. Tolerance
58.5 Would you support or oppose greater publicity for opinions that differ from the official ones?
66.1 Do you agree or not that some strong-handed leaders would be of great use for the country?
(Valid cases 1156)

9. Economical situation
16. What do you think about the economic situation of Hungary since the present government has been in power—is it better, has it remained the same, or is it worse?
17. Concerning the future: do you think the economic situation of Hungary is going to improve, remain the same or get worse?
18. Has the economic situation of your family improved, remained the same or gotten worse during the last year?
19. Is the economic situation of your family going to improve, remain the same or get worse next year?
(Valid cases 1175)

10. Market position
25. Do you think it is possible that you will become unemployed in the near future?
28. If you lose your job for some reason how easy would it be to find an appropriate job?
119. In case of financial need how easy would it be to find extra work at your present workplace?
53. What do you think, if you lived in a Western country, would you be better off, be on the same level or be on a lower level than in your home country?
(Valid cases 494)
(The correlation between the items by Cronbach's alpha was 0.4047)

11. Free market support
35.1 Do you agree that citizens should pay for medical services?
35.2 Do you agree or not that there should be a maximum limit for the money one person can earn?
35.3 Do you agree or not that people should create the conditions of their living instead of depending on government patronage?
66.3 Do you agree or not that a capitalist economy is the best for Hungary?
49.3 Do you consider it as part of government responsibilities that differences in incomes should be reduced? (4 point scale)
(Valid cases 1154)

12. Government efficacy
21. What do you think about corruption and protectionism under the present government: Is it growing, remaining the same or reduced?

29. How the government uses the money collected as taxes: uses the whole sum properly, partly properly, or they waste most of it?
39. How do you evaluate the present developments in Hungary: are they determined by the interests of a small group, or by the interests of the majority?
(Valid cases 1159)
(The correlation between the items by Cronbach's alpha was 0.4453)

13. State social paternalism
31. Please tell me how important the following things are according to you (4 point scale)
31.3 Medical care
31.4 Standard of living
31.10 Housing situation
31.12 Situation of the elderly
31.14 Reduction of social inequalities
35. Which of the following statements do you agree with?
35.1 Citizens should cover the costs of their medical care and medicines
35.2 There should not be a maximum limit on the money one can earn
35.3 People should create the conditions of their living themselves instead of depending on state patronage
(Valid cases 1176)
(The correlation between the items by Cronbach's alpha was 0.4244)

14. Political efficacy
56.2 Parties are needed for democracy
56.3 All the parties are the same for me
56.4 Parties make it possible to participate in designing politics
63. Tell me please which statement do you agree with?
63.1 I do not care who has power until things are going well in the country
63.2 Politicians are happy if people do not interfere in their business
63.4 It is better not to be involved in politics because sooner or later one gets his fingers burnt
63.5 One should never fully trust in politicians
63.6 Politicians do their best to learn the opinions of the people
63.8 Nowadays only those participate politics who want to make a career
63.9 Politicians are interested in the opinions of the people only when there is a great trouble
68. Many people say that they have completely lost their interest in politics. To what extent do you agree with that? (4 point scale)
(Valid cases 1142)
(The correlation between the items by Cronbach's alpha was 0.6664)

15. Relation to the Kádár regime
36. Which of the following statements do you agree with?
36.1 Hungary saw economic development during that era
36.2 Almost all the Hungarians lived better than now though there were some who got richer than the others
36.3 There was order and social peace
36.4 There was great repression

36.5 No problems were solved
36.6 There was great social development
36.7 There was no freedom
(Valid cases 1157)
(Tine correlation between the items by Cronbach's alpha was 0.7318)

16. Left/Right self placement

2. Many people think that the political opinions of people are differentiated by their being left-wing or right-wing. There is a 10 point scale on this card—please place yourself on the scale (boxes between 0–10)

(Valid cases 1152)

17. Western orientation

54.1 Do you agree or not that our country needs a Western type of development?
(Valid cases 1173)

18. Membership in the HSWP

48. Have you been a member of the HSWP or not?
(Valid cases 1171)

NOTES

1. The author wishes to acknowledge the invaluable help given him by Anthony Heath, Professor of Sociology at Oxford University, Fellow of Nuffield College, and Co-Director of the Center for Research into Elections and Social Trends. Professor Heath provided the guidance and technological assistance necessary for the analysis of the data in this chapter, as well as his constant and kind encouragement.

2. It should be noted that the attitudes of nonvoters are closer to the attitudes of those who voted for the Socialists.

3. The literature that deals with the cleavages in Hungary contains more hypotheses and prejudices than analysis based on empirical data.

4. It does not support—moreover, it is definitely contrary to—the hypothesis frequently cited in political journalism, that socialists support, while Christian-democrat voters oppose Western orientation.

5. According to the scales of self-placement, the Right-orientation of the voters of Smallholders' Party is far from being as strong as could be expected from the statements of the party leadership and their propaganda, and it needs some explanation. We believe that the main reason is the low level of political education of the voters for this party. As a result, they frequently place themselves at one of the neutral central points (5 or 6) on the Left-Right scale.

6. An interesting feature of cleavage theory is that it proposes that democratic systems are actually more stable if their cleavages result in a frustrated system. The reason is that when cleavages are cross-cutting, few people will be completely dissatisfied. For more on this theory see: Thomson, James D. 1967. *Organizations in Action.* New York: McGraw-Hill.

7. See more details on this in: Angelusz, R. and R. Tardos. 1995. "A hidden pillar of electoral behavior." *Politikatudomanyi Szemle* 1: 3, 5–18. It is worth mentioning that the state party had some 850,000 members in the mid-80s, meaning that 15 percent of the

grown-up population were members of HSWP. In the 1994 parliamentary elections the vast majority of ex-HSWP members voted for the socialists.

8. Although some orthodox Marxist groups raised this option in late 1988, HSWP general secretary Karoly Grosz spoke about it in Miskolc. It is not a real alternative in the present Hungarian situation in the thinking of the citizens, but history produced such possibilities several times—for example, in South-Korea in the 70s, and in China in late 80s and 90s.

9. This opinion was expressed, for example, by an outstanding personality, Sandor Csoóri, in late 1993.

10. The question was the following: "People sometimes identify very different concepts with the Left and the Right, and sometimes they are not able to distinguish between them. I list some concepts hereby; please scale them from 1 to 4, depending on to what extent they fall into the categories of the Left or the Right."

11. There were leftist researchers who built a specific cleavage-theory on that black-and-white picture on European integration, according to which Left is for Westernization, and Right opposes it.

REFERENCES

Ágh, Attila. 1988. *The Defensive Society.* Budapest: Kossuth.
Angelusz, Róbert and Róbert Tardos. 1995. "A Hidden Pillar of the Electoral Behavior." *Politikatudományi Szemle* 3: 5–18.
Bruszt, László and János Simon. 1990. *The Silenced Majority.* Budapest: Institute for Social Sciences.
Csepeli, György and Antal Örkény. 1992. *Ideology and Political Beliefs in Hungary.* New York: Pinter.
Csoóri, Sándor. 1993. "The Responsibility of the Intellectuals." *Magyar Nemzet* 27: Nov. 27.
Cusack, Thomas and Bernhard Wessels. 1996. *Problemreich und Konfliktgeladen: Lokale Demokratie in Deutschland fünf Jahre nach der Vereinigung.* Berlin: WZB, FS III 96–203.
Dalton, Russell. 1995. *Political Cleavages, Issues, and Democratic Party Systems.* Paper presented for conference on Comparative Democratic Elections, Kennedy School of Government, Harvard University, May 12–14.
Evans, G. and S. Whitehead. 1995. "Social and Ideological Cleavage Formation in Post-Communist Hungary." *East-Europe-Asia Studies* 47 (7): 1177–1204.
Fábián, Zoltán and István György Tóth. 1996. "Voters' groups and voters" mobility." In E. Sík and I. G. Tóth (eds.), *Social Elevator.* Working Papers No. 7, Hungarian Household Panel. Budapest: TÁRKI.
Heath, Anthony et al. 1991. *Understanding Political Change.* Oxford: Pergamon Press.
Heath, Anthony and Geoffrey Evans. 1995. "The measurement of the left-right and libertarian-authoritarian values: a comparison of balanced and unbalanced scales." *Quality and Quantity* 29: 191–206.
Kolosi, T., I. Szelényi, Z. Szelényi and B. Western. 1991. "Political Fields in the Period of Post-Communist Transition." *Sociological Review* 1: 5–34.
Lipset, Seymour Martin and Stein Rokkan. 1967. *Party Systems and Voter Alignments: Cross-National Perspectives.* New York: The Free Press.

Markus, György. 1994. *Parties, Campand Cleavages in Hungary. Social Democracy in a Post-Communist Europe,* 154–70. London: Frank Cass.
Róbert, Peter. 1994. "Middle Class, Attitudes, Political Preferences." In I. Balogh (ed.), *Cleavages and Elections.* Budapest: Institute for Political Science, HAS.
Rose, Richard. 1991. "Between State and Market." In *Studies in Public Policy,* no. 196, Glasgow: University of Strathclyde.
Schlett, István. "Determinants of Political Divisions in Hungary." In Giovanni Agnelli Foundation (ed.), *Political Culture and the State in the Czech Republic and in Hungary,* 66–79. Budapest: T-Twins.
Simon, János. 1995. "What does Democracy Mean for Hungarians." *Coexistence* 32: 325–40.
———. 1996a. "Citizens' Concept of Democracy in Central and Eastern Europe." In Bruszt-Simon-Bames (eds.), *Post-Communist Political Culture.* Budapest: CEU Press.
———. 1996b. "Politics from Down or How Unemployed Participate in Politics." In Kurtan-Sandor-Vass (eds.), *Political Yearbook of Hungary,* 653–64. Budapest.
———. "The Popular Conception of Democracy in Central and Eastern Europe." In Bruszt-Simon-Bames (eds.), *Post Communist Citizens.* Budapest: CEU Press, forthcoming.
Thomson, D. James. 1967. *Organizations in action.* New York: McGraw Hill.
Tóka, Gábor. 1994. "Parties and Electoral Choices in East Central Europe." In P. Lewis and G. Pridham (eds.), *Rooting Fragile Democracies.* London: Routledge.

16

How the Voters Respond: Poland

Jacek Raciborski

The topic of this chapter is the election behavior of Polish society during the parliamentary elections of 1991 and 1993 and presidential elections of 1995. We are interested not solely in the outcome of the elections to both houses of parliament but also in the phenomenon of election abstention which, in Polish conditions, has been ascribed an essential political significance. It is our intention to show primarily changes in the election preferences of the Poles, and to explain the reasons for these transformations. The realization of this task calls for reference to the political and economic context of the elections as well as to the historical background. I shall not delve into the presidential election of 1990 or the self-government elections (local elections) that took place in May 1990 and June 1994. The reason for this choice is a difference in character which is expressed in particular by the lesser role of "party" in these elections and by a weaker correspondence with basic divisions on the national political scene. True, the political relevance of local elections should not be neglected, but in the face of the main lines of division present in Polish society, an analysis of the pattern of political preferences revealed by Polish voters, conducted from the point of view of this type of an election, would appear to be inadequate.

The elections I shall discuss did not have a political rank comparable with those held in June 1989, whose consequence was the first non-communist government in Central-Eastern Europe. After all, the election of June 1989 did not meet all the criteria which are usually applied to free elections. It was based upon the Round Table contract achieved between the pro-reform Polish United Workers' Party (the PUWP, which ruled uninterruptedly from the end of the Second World War) and the opposition, which appeared under a joint "Solidarity" label. The contract restricted competition to 35 percent of the seats in the Seym (the lower house of the Polish parliament, albeit endowed with decisive competence); this was one of the reasons why the results of this election could not fully reflect the differentiation of civic political preferences. The second, more important, source of the "deformity" of the 1989 election was the fact that despite the anticipation of the government side, it turned into a plebiscite which inquired about support or opposition vis à vis the former authorities. Thus, what is known in literature on the subject as protest votes clearly dominated. The government camp suffered total defeat. All the "Solidarity" candidates to the Seym (with one exception) received their seats in the first round and, on average, won 70 percent of the votes. The PUWP candidates, with few exceptions, did not obtain seats in the first round and the free election to the Seym ended with the spectacular failure of the government camp. Out of a total of 100 senatorial seats, 99 were won by "Solidarity." The division of seats in the Senate did not reflect the actual impact of competing forces owing to the majority vote system. Estimates of support for the PUWP indicate that its candidates for the Senate obtained about 25 percent of the valid votes.[1] The regime was toppled but a significant percentage of the voters supported it to the very end.

The example of the June 1989 election is important from the point of view of theory. It shows the basic limitations of the traditional sociological approach to the analysis of election results. These limitations result from faulty explanations of the results of elections which take place in special historical situations, such as the downfall of authoritarian or totalitarian regimes.[2] In such circumstances, elections are not a routine procedure of democracy; they witness the emergence of a dominant conflict which stifles the appearance of others. This thesis is indirectly confirmed by the observation that in the Polish election of 1989 factors of the voters' status such as their income, profession, education, place of residence (village-town), and age were extremely weakly correlated with voting preferences.[3] Much better results are provided by the application to this type of an election of a historical approach, which concentrates on an analysis of the socioeconomic situation of the country, international conditions, the activity of the foremost contenders, historical resentments, cultural factors and, finally, the events of the election campaign. Subsequent parliamentary elections in Poland (1991 and 1993) were already quite different—they were "normal" and revealed new political divisions in society as well as new determinants of election decisions.

TURNOUT

The turnout of voters is one of the most important indices of political mobilization and of the degree of political alienation of a citizenry. Experiences of the Polish elections show that participation or abstention in elections are also the reactions of the voters to alternatives proposed to them in the course of election campaigns. Literature on the subject, however, proposes a contradictory thesis concerning the reasons and political effects of low polls.[4] Without wishing to resolve this question in more general categories, I would like to formulate the thesis that the particularly poor participation in the Polish parliamentary election in

1991 was caused by the disorientation of the voters which, in turn, was produced by certain features of the political scene, chiefly by the low degree of its structuralization and the circumstances of this particular election campaign.

The parliamentary election of 1991 was attended by 43.2 percent and the election of 1993 by 52.1 percent of eligible voters. The strikingly low poll in the election of 1991 calls for additional explanation. It was as much as 20 percent lower than in 1989 or during the first round of the 1990 presidential election, and almost 10 percent lower than in the election of 1993. A comparison with turnout observed during the first free elections held in other post-communist countries additionally emphasizes the specificity of the Polish election of 1991.[5]

Surveys which I carried out upon two occasions in the course of the 1991 election campaign with the same group of respondents revealed an extremely low level of crystallization of voting preferences. In July 1991, at the very outset of the election campaign, 34 percent of the respondents knew which party they would vote for; in October, three weeks prior to election day, the percentage of respondents with clear cut preferences rose to 41 percent.[6] Differentiations of the level of the crystallization of voting preferences followed a certain pattern: The more a certain group was materially and culturally deprived, the more often were its members unable to indicate which party they would choose. The subsequently ascertained pattern of the differentiation of the electoral turnout was identical. People who are materially and culturally handicapped vote more rarely. This is a well-known universal rule.[7] It does not explain, however, the low level (absolute) of preference crystallization in Polish society. Apart from the group of the best educated and highest-income voters, in whose case the index of preference crystallization exceeded 60 percent, Polish voters encountered basic difficulties in exercising a choice.

The sources of these difficulties were multiple and cannot be reduced to the status features of individuals and groups. They were embedded in the character of the political scene and in the circumstances surrounding the election campaign.

In the 1991 parliamentary elections, the available seats were contested by representatives of 111 parties, associations, and civic groups, the latter being frequently established on-the-spot. More than ten of these contenders came into being as national groups, overcame the initial barriers, and presented their election programs on state television. The ensuing information noise was additionally favored by the brief duration of the activity of all these parties and by their organizational weakness. The parties remained unfamiliar to the voters who misidentified the various programs. My research disclosed that most of the voters were acquainted with only twelve parties. In these circumstances, the election campaign did not lead to the crystallization of those prime issues which were so conspicuously reflected in social consciousness, and polarized the configuration of political parties into two or three dimensions. This thesis calls for further elucidation. It is possible to identify the problems which structured the political scene in Poland by taking into consideration the programs of the assorted parties and the political activity of their leaders. Jerzy Wiatr [1993b] proposed three such issues which, treated jointly, create a model that allows us to describe the "positions" of particular parties on the political stage and to indicate the main dividing lines. I have in mind the following issues: monetarism versus antimonetarism; a lay state and public life versus religious fundamentalism; decommunization (comprehended as the lawful ejection from public life of people connected in the past with the communist party) versus protest against this type of restriction of civic rights. At this stage, we can already formulate the earlier proposed thesis in more precise terms: the voters en masse did not identify the program "positions" of particular parties, nor did they understand what was at stake in the elections.[8] The existing divisions proved to be too complicated to be correctly deciphered by the average citizen, especially since the presidential election had already considerably undermined the heretofore unmistakable division between "Solidarity" and forces connected with the ancien regime.

These were the roots of the mass scale situational disorientation experienced by the voters and having such a negative impact on the level of election turnout. Ultimately, the disorientated voters simply did not go to the polls. Improved attendance in the 1993 election should be connected with reduced disorientation since in the meantime certain parties managed to become a more permanent component of the political scene, and the dividing lines between them grew more marked. Some of the leaders of parliamentary parties also made themselves better known. Two years of the Seym of the first term "clarified" the political scene.

A total of 64.7 percent of the eligible voting public participated in the first round of the presidential elections on November 5, 1995, this figure rising to 68.2 percent in the second round (November 19), the highest turnout since 1989. A certain pattern of Polish voters' reaction to various kinds of elections emerges: The highest turnout was registered in the presidential elections and the lowest in local government elections. This pattern cannot be fully explained by the political impact of various types of elections since, in Polish conditions, the political importance of parliamentary elections is greater than that of presidential elections. Again, this observed differentiation can be explained with the help of an hypothesis regarding the electorate's structural disorientation. When the taking of election decisions offers problems which are greater than normal—(a) greater chaos on the political scene, (b) a greater number of competing political parties who have little-known programs and little-known leaders into the bargain and (c) a more complex procedure for casting votes—then people are more likely to refrain from voting. In the case of presidential elections a much lower level of electorate disorientation appears since the formula is simple, rivalry is personified and the competing candidates are widely known. In the 1995 elections an additional factor which improved the turnout was the high degree of voter polarization which took place before the first round and the intensity of rivalry which was related to this polarization.

THE RESULTS OF THE 1991 AND 1993 PARLIAMENTARY ELECTIONS

Table 16.1 contains the results of elections to the Seym conducted in 1991 and 1993. Only those parties which won no less than five seats (with the exception of the Solidarity of Labour, included for comparative reasons) were taken into consideration for the 1991 election. In 1993 all parties which won seats have been listed. The electoral system also calls for additional explanation. The election of 1991 observed a proportionate system, with a division of seats according to the principle of the largest remainder (the Hare-Niemeyer method). No proviso was applied. This system was altered on the eve of the 1993 election by introducing a

Table 16.1
Results of the 1991 and 1993 Elections to the Polish Seym

Party	1991			1993			
	number of votes	% of votes	number of seats	number of votes	% of votes	number of seats	Evol. index
	1	2	3	4	5	6	7
Democratic Union	1,382,051	12.32	62	1,460,957	10.59	74	0.86
Democratic Left Alliance	1,344,820	11.99	60	2,815,169	20.41	171	1.70
Polish Peasant Party	972,952	8.67	48	2,124,567	15.40	132	1.78
"Motherland" Catholic Election Action*	980,304	8.74	49	878,445	6.37	—	0.73
Civic Agreement Center	977,344	8.71	44	609,973	4.42	—	0.51
Confederacy for Poland's Independence	841,738	7.50	46	795,487	5.77	22	0.77
Liberal-Democratic Congress	839,978	7.49	37	550,578	3.99	—	0.53
Solidarity of Labour/Union of Labour	230,975	2.06	4	1,005,004	7.28	41	3.53
Solidarity Union	566,553	5.05	27	676,334	4.90	—	0.97
Peasant Agreement	613,626	5.47	28	327,085	2.37	—	0.43
Polish Party of the Friends of Beer	367,106	3.27	16	143,82	0.10	—	0.03
Non-party Bloc for the Support of Reforms	—	—	—	746,653	5.41	16	—

* Only a single party—the Christian-National Alliance—appeared as the Catholic Election Union (WAK). In 1993 this party was the main core of a coalition known as the "Motherland" (in Polish "Ojczyzna") Catholic Election Committee. A comparison of the results obtained by these formations is, therefore, quite justified.

** The Non-party Bloc for the Support of Reforms was created upon the initiative of Lech Wałęsa on the eve of the 1993 election.

proviso of 5 percent for parties and 8 percent for party coalitions; this meant that only those parties participated in the division of the seats which nationwide had gained more than 5 percent of the votes (8 percent for party coalitions). Such a change had serious political consequences which contributed to overcoming the fragmentation of the Seym of the second term. However, it would be a grave simplification to explain the reduction of the number of parties which had a parliamentary representation only by referring to changes in the electoral law. Numerous groups in the Seym of the first term had completely lost their voters' support, and no electoral system could guarantee them the continuation of their parliamentary existence.

The 1991 election opened the way to the Seym for representatives of twenty-four election committees. This figure is not only an excellent yardstick of the fragmentation of the Seym considering that politically significant caucuses were created only by nine of the first groups which altogether received 409 seats—that is, 88.9 percent of the seats in the whole chamber. The fragmentation of the Seym is testified to by the fact that even the sum of the seats won by the first four groups did not ensure a parliamentary majority; the same can be said for the fact that the winning party had obtained only 13.5 percent of the seats. Such a parliament had not been elected in any of the other post-communist countries. This state of things must be explained by several factors, of which the most relevant are: (a) delays in the formation of mature and organizationally strong political parties, indirectly caused by the Round Table contract that had produced a single "Solidarity" opposition bloc which competed with the ancien regime and whose unity was upheld for the sake of the effectiveness of radical economic and political reforms; (b) the dispersal of voters' preferences as a result of the multiple lines of division within society and the activity pursued by other factors which disoriented the voters; and (c) the dispositions of the electoral system which did not establish nationwide barriers that would make it possible to discount the "insular" popularity of a group in a national forum.[9]

An interpretation of the election results of 1991, performed in political categories, must draw attention to the following circumstances:

1. The growing disintegration of the "Solidarity" camp which made the joint creation of a government coalition impossible. Nonetheless, treated as a whole, this camp confirmed its domination and enjoyed a relative success (approximately 60 percent of the votes).
2. Parties which had originated in the old order (the Social Democracy of the Polish Republic—SdRP—which was the core of a left-wing coalition encompassing the Democratic Left Alliance (SLb) and Polish Peasant Party (PSL), and which stemmed from the United Peasant Party, a former satellite of the PUWP) once again integrated their electorate and gained a confirmation of the rather universal acceptance of their main program slogans.
3. The elections revealed enormous civic discontent with the former governments of Tadeusz Mazowiecki and Jan Krzysztof Bielecki. The prime reason for this were the

unexpectedly high social costs paid for the implementation of the so-called Balcerowicz plan (the pauperization of the majority of society, rising unemployment, fears for the future).

4. The Catholic Church, which in Poland had exceptionally involved itself in the election campaign, primarily in favor of the Christian National Alliance (a party which for the purposes of the campaign appeared as the Catholic Election Action), suffered a defeat. The party it supported secured a relatively low 8.74 percent of the votes. This outcome showed that the political preferences of the Poles were more loosely connected with their religious preferences than had been believed.[10]

5. The elections were an important stage in the formation of a party system. They eliminated from political life several score groups which aspired to the rank of political parties. They also demonstrated the significance of the organisational factor, namely, that those parties which were capable of creating local member groups and structures which coordinated their activity enjoyed satisfactory results.

6. The election to the Senate ended with a victory for the Democratic Union (UD) which won 21 seats (out of the 100 seats available) as well as for "Solidarity" (11 seats). Eight other groups obtained a significant representation. In this election, voters' preferences did not differ radically from those disclosed during the election to the Seym (see Table 16.2).

COMMENTS ON THE 1993 ELECTION RESULTS

The election held on September 19, 1993, proved to be fortunate for left-wing and center-leftist parties which included the SLD, the UP, and the PSL, whose common feature was their opposition to the government of Hanna Suchocka. In comparison to the results from 1991, the SLD and PSL had now gained twice as

Table 16.2
Results of the 1991 and 1993 Elections to the Polish Senate

Party	1991 number of seats	1993 number of seats
Democratic Union	21	4
Democratic Left Alliance	4	37
Polish Peasant Party	8	36
Catholic Election Action "Motherland"	9	1
Solidarity Union	11	9
Civic Agreement Center	9	1
Confederacy for Poland's Independence	4	–
Liberal-Democratic Congress	6	1
Peasant Agreement	7	1
Christian Democratic Party	3	–
Union of Labour	–	2
Non-party Bloc for the Support of Reforms	–	2
Other parties and independent candidates	18	6

many votes, and the UP, four times as many. A particularly painful defeat was suffered by the Liberal-Democratic Congress (KLD), which had secured 65 percent of the votes won in 1991 despite a campaign professionally organized by Saatchi and Saatchi; the same holds true for the Agreement Center (62 percent of the votes from 1991), and the People's Agreement (a peasant party stemming from the "Solidarity" movement). Another defeated contender was a party coalition known as the "Motherland" Catholic Election Committee in which the main role was played by the Christian National Alliance (ZChN), and which was established thanks to the direct involvement of the Catholic Church (90 percent of the votes from 1991). All these parties lost many more supporters than they managed to attract. The Non-party Bloc for the Support of Reforms (BBWR)—a group created several months prior to the election upon the initiative of President Lech Wałęsa—also did not win an impressive number of votes (5.4 percent).

The chief effect of the election was to overcome the fragmentation of the parliament. Only seven groups obtained parliamentary representation in the Seym, and a coalition of two parties proved to be sufficient to guarantee a decisive parliamentary majority. This situation was the product of an electoral system which contained a number of obstacles, and of a mistaken strategy followed by the right-wing parties which did not manage to achieve pre-election agreements. More than 34 percent of the votes were cast for lists which did not receive a single seat. The distribution of seats in the Seym, therefore, is an inferior indicator of the differentiation of political preferences in Polish society.

The election to the Senate, which was held according to majority rule, also proved to be favorable for the SLD (37 seats) and the PSL (36 seats). The remaining groups and independent candidates jointly secured 27 seats. In a certain sense, these results better reflect the then-prevalent leftist leaning of Polish society and its disappointment in members of the political elite which had emerged after 1989. The similarity of the results of the elections to the Seym and Senate also points to the domination of party, and not personal, voter identification.

The reasons for the election success of the Democratic Left Alliance, the Polish Peasant Party, and the Union of Labor were multiple. Support shown by voters for the opposition parties was, above all, the expression of protest against the economic policy pursued by successive governments created by post-"Solidarity" groups; at the same time, it reflected the belief that a policy which could improve the material situation of the majority of society is feasible. The main election slogan of the SLD, "It doesn't have to be like this anymore," corresponded best to these expectations. The PSL and the UP also severely criticized the government's economic policy. The prevailing social mood was one of despondency. In August almost 70 percent of the respondents asked by the CBOS (Public Opinion Research Center) regarded the general economic situation as poor, and only 5 percent declared that compared with the previous year it was satisfactory. Just as negative were the assessments of the respondents' own material situation and that of their families: 55 percent admitted that it had deteriorated,

11 percent spoke of an improvement, and 33 percent failed to notice any changes. The economic programs of the winning parties supported state interventionism. They placed particular emphasis on the need to assist state-owned enterprises to protect them from bankruptcy, and on the necessity of a similar protection for domestic agriculture, promising a determined struggle against economic crimes and the so-called grey zone.

Note must be made of the fact that voters were not won over by all the opposition parties that condemned the economic policy of the government. The KPN, the Agreement Center and "Solidarity," which called for a vote of no confidence in the government of Hanna Suchocka, in this manner contributing to its downfall, obtained a small number of votes. Populist groups such as Party "X" (2.7 percent) and the Lepper Self Defense (2.8 percent) failed to attract many of the voters. Anti-government opposition and criticism of the official economic policy proved to be insufficient for securing election triumphs.

We agree with those observers of Polish political life whose explanations of the results of the September election ascribe considerable importance to political and ideological circumstances. I share the opinion of Jerzy Wiatr (1993 and in this volume), who maintains that the outcome of this election reflects the voters' resistance not only against the material costs of the transformation of the entire political system but also against a tendency toward the clericalization of public life, decommunization accompanied by a one-sided and negative assessment of the past, as well as against the prevailing style of governing. Each of these reasons requires a brief presentation, a task which I shall tackle on my own responsibility, albeit inspired by Wiatr.

(a) The majority of voters protested against tendencies toward the clericalization of the state. Symptoms of this current included a restrictive anti-abortion law, the introduction of religious instruction in schools, and the signing of the concordat with the Vatican, an act which a considerable part of Polish society perceived as a threat to numerous civil liberties. Those politicians and parties which made the greatest effort to implement such solutions ultimately suffered electoral defeat regardless of whether they were members of the opposition or of the government coalition. On the other hand, persons regarded as leading adherents of a lay state—the opponents of penalties for abortion—enjoyed great personal success regardless of their party origin. Parties which spoke in favor of a secular state included the SLD, the UP, the KLD, and the UD, although in the case of the latter, doubts could be harbored as regards the pro-Church policy pursued by the Hanna Suchocka government. A great majority of UD supporters, however, opted for a lay state. The parties mentioned won 42.2 percent of the votes while their opponents on the other extreme of the political spectrum (the "Motherland," the PSL-PL, the BBWR, and the Coalition for the Republic) won only 16.9 percent.

(b) Most of Polish society disapproved of tendencies to eliminate from public life people who in the past were PUWP members and who held important functions in administration, political life, and the economy. Those parties and politicians who endeavored to introduce lustration and decommunization laws suffered electoral defeat.[11] Parties which favored decommunization and lustration legislation jointly received about 22.4 percent of the votes (they include the Union of Real Politics and the "Motherland"); opponents of the proposed laws (SLD, UP, UD, and PSL) secured 54.7 percent of the votes.

(c) Commentators on Polish political life are nearly unanimous in maintaining that one of the reasons for the election defeat of the "post-Solidarity camp" was its style of governance, characterized by acute conflicts within the elite of the camp, and in particular by the so-called war at the top initiated by Lech Wałęsa on the eve of the presidential election. Its other features included perpetual splits within right-wing parties which reduced to them to the status of obscure groups, the disavowal of leading "Solidarity" politicians suspected of collaboration with the communist political police, nominations of controversial candidates to high posts, and indifference to the prevailing social mood.

These circumstances throw additional light on the defeat of the post-"Solidarity" parties but they do not offer a complete explanation of the success of the SLD and PSL. Both parties attach great importance to organization—they had at their disposal an extensive party structure, numerous activists who became experienced in the course of previous election campaigns as well as the necessary financial means. The ability to refer to the class interests of the rural population was another asset of the PSL, while that of the SLD was the high standard of its leaders. Aleksander Kwaśniewski, Józef Oleksy, and Włodzimierz Cimoszewicz were placed on lists of the top twenty most popular Polish politicians.[12] They were perceived as competent politicians, pragmatic and ready to resolve conflicts. Nonetheless, the popularity of party leaders cannot be overestimated since the above-mentioned opinion poll gave even higher marks to politicians connected with the Democratic Union who did not manage to win over such a large electorate.

1995 PRESIDENTIAL ELECTIONS—RESULTS AND COMMENTARY

Seventeen candidates appeared to compete for the post of President of the Polish Republic, all of whom had fulfilled the condition of collecting 100,000 supporting signatures. Candidates representing marginal groupings and independent candidates who organized and financed their election campaigns on their own appeared alongside candidates nominated by the major political parties. The ease with which a person could gain the status of presidential candidate speaks of the poor degree to which Polish political life is institutionalized and the weakness of the party system. Only four candidates enjoyed the support of relatively strong political parties. These were: Aleksander Kwaśniewski, charismatic leader of SLD (Democratic Left Alliance); Waldemar Pawlak, leader of PSL (Polish Peasant Party) and former prime minister of the coalition government composed of the SLD and PSL (who continued to run the government of the same coalition which had been led by Józef Oleksy); Jacek Kuroń nominated by the Freedom Union (UW), which had been formed by the merging of the Democratic Union (UD) and the Liberal-Democratic Congress (KL-D); and Tadeusz Zieliński, the Ombudsman supported by the Labour Union (UP). Hanna Gronkiewicz-Waltz, president of the National Bank of Poland, enjoyed the backing of less significant parties, among them the ZChN. Lech Wałęsa, still in power, was supported by the BBWR, but that backing had no real impact on his election prospects. The last party candidate was Leszek Moczulski, leader of the KPN, who withdrew a few days prior to the elections. Jan Olszewski, erstwhile prime minister and leader of the Movement for the Republic, also reached for the support of this group but that was not the decisive factor in his relative success.

The election campaign was intense and turbulent, particularly in its closing stages. Election preferences rapidly polarized on two candidates: Aleksander Kwaśniewski and Lech Wałęsa. Kwaśniewski's principal election program tenets were promises of: political stability, continued market reforms, activities to uphold democratic institutions, intensification of efforts to have Poland accepted into NATO and the European Union, liberalization of the provisions of the abortion Act, the introduction of a new Constitution which would, inter alia, ensure the secular nature of the state. Kwaśniewski devoted much time and effort to winning over young voters, presenting them with a vision of a dynamically expanding Poland in which the young would have great opportunities to gain an education, a good job and, in consequence, financial success. He consistently worked to narrow historical political divisions, particularly the division into "Solidarność" and "post-communist" camps. This conciliatory, forward-looking approach was expressed in his principal electioneering slogans: "Let's Elect Our Future" and "One Common Poland."

Lech Wałęsa's campaign was based on patriotic threads. He highlighted what he had done to uproot communism, stressed his commitment to religion and his links with simple people. He stressed that only he is able to lead Poland into NATO structures and the European Union, due to the huge international authority he enjoys (one of his more important slogans was: "The whole world knows Wałęsa"). By electing him, he claimed, the emergence of a post-communist monopoly could be prevented. Wałęsa's principal electioneering slogans were: "Always for Poland" and "Poland must be strong."

As the election campaign drew to its close, the election offices of the principal candidates used the sections of the media which favored them to pursue a negative campaign, leveling personal attacks. Kwaśniewski was accused of not having graduated from university though he had publicly claimed he had. He had not obtained an M.A. degree, so he was accused of lying about his curriculum vitae. An additional accusation was that Kwaśniewski's wife had acquired shares of the "Polisa" insurance company on preferential terms. Wałęsa had to face up to the accusation of not paying tax on the one million dollars he had received from Warner Bros. of the USA for the right to publish his film biography (he had received the cash before being elected president) and also that his election organizing office had worked hand-in-hand with a person with a criminal past. Public relations specialists were agreed that Kwaśniewski's election campaign, shaped to western methods, was the most professional and was managed with the greatest vigor.

The results of the first round of the elections were:

Aleksander Kwaśniewski	35.1%	Hanna Gronkiewicz-Waltz	2.8%
Lech Wałęsa	33.1%	Janusz Korwin-Mikke	2.4%
Jacek Kuroń	9.2%	Andrzej Lepper	1.32%
Jan Olszewski	6.9%	Jan Pietrzak	1.7%
Waldemar Pawlak	4.3%	Tadeusz Koźluk	0.2%
Tadeusz Zieliński	3.5%	Kazimierz Piotrowicz	0.1%
Leszek Bubel	0.04%		

The results highlight the large concentration of votes on the two leading candidates and the poor results of several candidates representing either influential groupings (for example W. Pawlak) or persons enjoying substantial personal popularity among the public at large (for example Jacek Kuroń and T. Zieliński). What had probably occurred was the band-wagon effect—that is, that a number of voters who had initially intended to throw their support behind other candidates, in the final account backed that candidate who, they judged, would win. Preelection polls seem to confirm this observation, displaying sharply rising support for the two first candidates and a fall-off in that for several others. The outcome was that the first round did not correctly reflect all the political divisions within Polish society, though the candidates were of all possible political colours. The major events of the campaign preceding the second round were the TV debates among both contenders, with A. Kwaśniewski making a better impression in the eyes of the TV audience, according to a CBOS public opinion poll.

The results of the second round were:

Aleksander Kwaśniewski	51.72%
Lech Wałęsa	48.2%

Second-round preferences were not sharply marked by sociodemographic features. A. Kwaśniewski commanded the greatest backing among the youngest voters and those in the 40–49 age group; the inhabitants of rural regions and small towns gave him their support notably more frequently. The professional groups in which he won the highest rating were: company managers (55.9 percent), farmers (55.7 percent), office workers (55.1 percent) and the unemployed (60.2 percent). Lech Wałęsa, on the other hand, topped the list among voters above 60 (57.5 percent), and in large cities (52.2 percent). Professionals gave him above-standard preference (55.8 percent) as did business proprietors (57.7 percent) and housewives (54 percent). These features were compiled from an OBOP poll exit analysis on random samples of 57,417 persons.

Very strong regional differences were registered: Kwaśniewski came out well on top in West and North Poland, with Wałęsa dominating in South-East Poland. The pattern of regional differentiation in Kwaśniewski's case was the same as the distribution of SLD votes in the 1993 elections to Parliament. In Wałęsa's case, the pattern was much the same as that of the 1990 regional distribution of results and the differentiation of the results registered by post-Solidarność parties in the 1991 and 1993 elections. The regional differentiation of the voting results reflects the importance of culture factors when elucidating election preferences. These culture differences, it could further be claimed, are the outcome of the differing histories of the various regions of which contemporary Poland is composed.

THE ELECTORATE OF THE MAIN PARTIES IN THE 1991 AND 1993 ELECTIONS

As was earlier stated, divisions within society are better reflected in parliamentary than in presidential elections. Group interests and other structural features of the electorate are much more important in parliamentary elections, hence the need to describe the features of the principal parties.

In 1991, the *Democratic Union* secured the relatively high support of white-collar workers (21 percent), secondary school pupils and students (23 percent), and residents of large towns (20 percent). It successfully bid for the vote of women (17 percent) but failed among farmers (3 percent), and owed its victory predominantly to the white-collar workers.[13] In contrast to the supporters of other parties, Democratic Union voters were adherents of market reforms proposed in the so-called Balcerowicz plan, a plan envisaging a dominating role for the parliament and a state which would guarantee a wide range of social services. The world outlook profile of this electorate was extremely distinct: it openly opposed anti-semitism and favored tolerance and anticlericalism, comprehended as resistance against Church intervention in political life and law-assisted imposition of moral postulates stemming from religious convictions.[14]

Compared to 1991, the sociodemographic features of the UD supporters in 1993 basically did not change. This particular electorate was still dominated by higher-income and, more important, better-educated voters pleased with the current changes and with the functioning of democracy in the country.[15] An examination of the world outlook profile of the UD electorate in 1993 did not show a special attitude towards the Catholic Church and its postulates.[16] This is an essential novelty in comparison with the reconstruction of that profile in 1991, when anticlericalism was vivid. Our finding also justifies the thesis about the loss of a certain number of heretofore anticlerical voters who, presumably, blamed the ratification of the concordat and the introduction of the anti-abortion law on the government of Hanna Suchocka (whom the UD designated for Prime Minister).

In 1991, the *Democratic Left Alliance* won above-average support among old-age pensioners and white-collar workers; on the other hand, it did not manage to make a successful bid for the support of farmers, secondary school pupils, and students. From the point of view of sociodemographic criteria, the SLD electorate proved to be more heterogeneous than that of the UD although it also included an overrepresentation of white-collar workers (approximately 40 percent of all the votes won by the SLD). A conspicuous feature of this electorate was its negative attitude toward the public activity of the Catholic Church, and especially the introduction of the anti-abortion law and religious instruction in state schools; SLD supporters shared a common opinion about the state which they conceived as a guarantor of extensive social services, free-of-charge medical care, and schooling. Their attitude toward the reforms launched by Balcerowicz remained ambivalent; support for the general trend of undertakings performed for the sake of introducing a free market economy was accompanied by reluctance toward privatization and the reduction of the economic functions fulfilled by the state. Probably the most typical trait of this electorate was its resistance to de-communization (perceived as an attempt to eliminate or restrict the participation in public life of people connected with the ancien regime).

The victor of the 1993 elections proved to be the *SLD,* which doubled the number of votes obtained in 1991. The structure of its electorate changed substantially: The increased percentage of workers' votes reduced dependence upon the white-collar voters. The SLD also received the largest number of votes cast by the self-employed (17.5 percent), a veritable paradox considering its socialist character. The rule that the oldest and youngest chose this party less frequently than other voters still applied. Influence among the rural population grew slightly (about 20 percent of the electorate). The distinctive feature of these voters was their antipathy toward the privatization of state industry, accompanied by support for a market economy, albeit with extensive mechanisms of state influence. In the political domain, this electorate favored parliamentary democracy, and expressed its displeasure with a strong presidency and, in particular, with Lech Wałęsa in this post. Next to anticlericalism, the anti-Wałęsa current is the strongest factor which unites the SLD electorate. Another relevant feature is a specific nostalgia: Compared to other voters, the SLD supporters recalled the Polish People's Republic and its accomplishments much more favorably, and in the past were themselves connected with the PUWP more often than any other electorate. In 1993, 40 to 45 percent of the SLD electorate was composed of former PUWP members, a factor which was not, therefore, decisive for the electoral success of this group.

Supporters of the *Catholic Election Action* represent various social and professional milieus: old-age pensioners and housewives provide more than standard support, while self-employed provide the least. The most prominent feature of the political stand of the WAK electorate (and, generally speaking, of ZChN supporters) remains in favor of a state which would offer a privileged position to the Catholic Church and implement an absolute ban on abortion as well as other solutions stemming from the so-called social doctrine of the Church. Some scholars (Dohnalik, 1993; Banaszkiewicz, 1992) perceive in the psychological profile of the WAK electorate numerous traces of an authoritarian and xenophobic-nationalistic attitude. Ballots cast for this party strongly correlated with the religious convictions of the voters.

The coalition, which during the 1993 election went under the name of "Motherland," and which could be regarded as a continuation of the Catholic Election Action, received the support of a similar electorate, but the voting record was much inferior. The national-Catholic option found itself in a clearly defensive position, although it had not yet exhausted its potential. The important reason for this state of things was the belated establishment of the coalition, its organizational weakness, and the absence of truly popular leaders.

The *Polish Peasant Party* is the most class-oriented group on the Polish political scene. In 1991, as many as 74 percent of its electorate were members of the rural population. Every second farmer who voted (including old-age pensioners) supported the PSL. Its adherents strongly opposed the Balcerowicz plan and the privatization of state enterprises; they also counted on the state protection of agriculture. The psychological portrait of this group of voters was dominated by ethnocentrism which, however, is characteristic for the Polish peasantry as a whole and not necessarily connected with elections.

In 1993, the PSL won a spectacular success by doubling the number of votes from the previous election, and by becoming the second most important party on the political scene in Poland. Its electorate remained unaltered. Almost 80 percent were residents of villages and small towns. The party secured a particularly large number of votes in regions dominated by traditional farming where its lower-income and worse-educated supporters are more religious than members of any other electorate, a factor of essential significance in Polish conditions. A large part of the votes cast for the PSL were typical protest votes caused by the deteriorating material situation of the rural population which blamed its plight on successive "Solidarity" governments.

Civic Agreement Center was the name assumed by the Agreement Center (PC) for the purposes of elections. The supporters of this party evade description in categories of their social status. They originated from all relevant sections of Polish society, the only exception being the peasants whose votes were less numerous (5 percent). The Agreement inherited much of the electorate which earlier had picked Wałęsa for President. The main slogans called for a strong presidency and radical de-communization. The economic views remained rather ambivalent and favored market reforms; privatization involving foreign capital was regarded with animosity. The world outlook profile of this particular electorate was composed of authoritarian and anti-semitic leanings.

In 1993, the Agreement Center received 4.4 percent of the votes, a result which was insufficient for obtaining even a single seat. The sociodemographic makeup of its electorate changed significantly. The most numerous supporters included the elderly, with a secondary education, who embodied a radically critical attitude toward the Polish People's Republic and, consequently, opted for de-communization and lustration. The increasingly hostile attitude of the party leaders to Wałęsa ultimately split the electorate: those who voted once again for the Agreement Center shared its opinion about the President, but a considerable number of former supporters now preferred the pro-presidential BBWR.

In 1991, the *Confederacy for Poland's Independence* won an unexpected success. It obtained the largest percentage of votes cast by highly skilled workers (12 percent) and more than 50 percent of its electorate were workers (including the unskilled). It must be noted, however, that workers' votes were exceptionally fragmented (several other political parties each secured around 9 percent of the votes of this particular electorate). Age differentiation was another relevant factor; greatest support was provided by voters aged 26–34 and lowest by voters aged 60 and older. The KPN attracted the most typical protest votes of an anti-communist electorate, which had grown disappointed with the "Solidarity" government and was anxious about the threat created by market reforms for the existence of large state enterprises. The Confederacy had particularly won over the miners whose once-high socioeconomic status had rapidly deteriorated. These determined opponents of the Balcerowicz reforms, rather neutral concerning the question of abortion, regarded themselves as patriots and, above all, as spokesmen for radical de-communization.

In 1993, the KPN lost a large part of its electorate which was not compensated by an influx of new voters. The party became less attractive for workers although an above-standard score was still secured among this group (10 percent). Men offered more support (7 percent) than women (4 percent) or the younger voters. The political profile of the party remained unchanged: the KPN electorate was mainly composed of nationalistic, unwavering opponents of left-wing parties, who accepted populistic slogans pertaining to the economy and principles of division.

The *Liberal-Democratic Congress* emerged after the victory won by Wałęsa, and its election chances were linked with the then–Prime Minister J. K. Bielecki. The party won the relatively numerous support of the self-employed, secondary school pupils, and students. Its voters were radical enthusiasts of market reforms, the reduction of the economic role played by the state, and a secular state. A typical feature, which distinguished them from the supporters of the Democratic Union, was their approval for extraordinary presidential prerogatives.

In the 1993 election, a sizable number of the older electorate left the Congress, a loss which was not made up for by an influx of new supporters. The Congress also ceased to be a parliamentarian party. The group of so-called successful people which it wished to attract no longer recognized it as a reliable representative of their interests. The defeat suffered by the Congress meant that a consistently liberal party representing businessmen was simply unable to stay on the Polish political scene.

The "*Solidarity*" trade union plays a double role in Polish politics: It appears as a trade union, and upon other occasions—especially during elections—as a political party, although it has no such formal status. Already in 1991, the electoral impact exerted by "Solidarity" proved to be unexpectedly small, although it sufficed for forming a parliamentary representation. The majority of those who supported "Solidarity" in 1989 now chose parties which stemmed from the trade union movement; many others grew disappointed in the "Solidarity" movement and simply stayed away from the polls. The union movement also lost the votes of the rural population which swerved toward peasant parties. "Solidarity" managed to retain its influence among the workers (7.8 percent) but it failed to win over white-collar workers.

The result of the 1993 election was lower by only 0.15 percent but according to the electoral law it was insufficient for obtaining representation in the Seym. A better outcome was achieved in the election to the Senate, where "Solidarity" gained nine seats. The structure of its electorate had not changed. It remained relatively differentiated but, as in 1991, the largest percentage was composed of workers (approximately 30 percent) and old-age pensioners (26 percent).

THE CONTINUATION OF VOTING PREFERENCES

An analysis of transformations, which took place in voter preferences and were disclosed by particular groups examined on the basis of two exit pool surveys, demonstrates a considerable instability of individual preferences.[17] On a mass scale, the electorate changed its preferences in the course of the two years that passed between parliamentary elections. This instability is not reflected well in results aggregated nationwide. By way of example, in both elections the Democratic Union won an almost identical number of votes but its electorate had changed substantially. Only 44 percent of those who had cast their votes for the UD in 1991 chose the same party in 1993. In the case of other post-"Solidarity" parties, the degree of the preference stability of their supporters in the 1991 elections was even smaller and oscillated around 25 percent; the least "loyal" proved to be the "Solidarity" electorate—only 15 percent of those who had voted for it originally reaffirmed their support in 1993.

Preference instability did not affect all the competing parties. The preferences of the SLD and PSL electorate did not waver. Some 90 percent of the SLD supporters from 1991 (approximately 83 percent according to INFAS/OBOP) and 75 percent of the PSL electorate upheld their preferences. These parties won not solely, and not even primarily, due to the "loyalty" of their voters. They had made a successful bid for the support of "new" voters, namely those who failed to take part in the election of 1991; they had also attracted adherents of other parties. Apparently, the barriers between the supporters of the post-"Solidarity" parties and those contenders which originated in the old system were not as steadfast as those between the political elites. The Democratic Left Alliance captured 14 percent of the former "Solidarity" electorate (slightly less—no more than 10 percent—according to INFAS/OBOP), 12 percent of the electorate of the Democratic Union and 9 percent of the KPN supporters. The PSL, on the other hand, assured itself of almost half of the votes of the former followers of the People's Agreement, a peasant party of "Solidarity" origin, about 14 percent of the former "Solidarity" electorate, and a significant percentage of those who had cast a ballot for the Catholic Election Action and other parties of "Solidarity" origin. No records were made of notable shifts of voters from the rightist "Solidarity" parties of 1991 to the SLD.

These data show that the former division of the electorate into post-"Solidarity" and post-communist is losing its importance. Furthermore, they demonstrate the significance of the polarization of the electorate to the right and left of the political spectrum. On the other hand, the considerable changeability of voters' preferences during the period between the elections of 1991 and 1993 points to the incomplete formation of the Polish party system whose foundations appear to have been laid. The 1995 presidential elections also cast some light on the continuity of election preferences. Truly absolute loyalty was evident among voters of leftist leanings. In the first round, A. Kwaśniewski was supported by 86 percent of those who voted for W. Cimoszewicz in the 1990 presidential elections and 89 percent of the SLD voters in the 1993 parliamentary elections. However, let it be said that SLD voters from 1993 could constitute 40 percent at the most of Kwaśniewski's supporters in the first round of the 1995 elections, assuming that they all voted.

This "loyalty" was smaller in Wałęsa's case—53 percent of his voters in the 1990 first round supported him in the 1995 first round, as did about 60 percent of the ZChN, Solidarność, and BBWR supporters taking part in the 1993 elections. Party loyalty for other candidates was much lower, with only 39 percent of 1993 UD voters supporting Jacek Kuroń, one of that party's leaders. W. Pawlak fared even worse, winning the support of only 23 percent of those who voted for the PSL in 1993 (all data quoted here come from OBOP exit poll). Thus, what is lacking is a strong right-wing party which would concentrate the numerous but dispersed votes of its electorate.

The leftist camp in particular crystallized and consolidated, the central position being taken by the Democratic Left Alliance (SLD) and within that Alliance, the Socialdemocracy of the Polish Republic—the party that had emerged on the ruins of the PUWP.

NOTES

1. The electoral system (the possibility of divided votes, the undefined party affiliation of many of the candidates) prevents us from obtaining a precise calculation of the support

index for the PUWP coalition in the election of 1989. Scholars are rather unanimous, however, in estimating that in the election to the Senate "Solidarity" had won 64–66 percent of the votes. Greater discrepancies are found in the estimated number of votes received by the coalition: from 17 percent to 25 percent.

2. Foreign scholars also draw attention to the limitations of the classical sociological approach to the transition to democracy in Poland.

3. Cultural determinants proved to be more relevant. For more extensive comments on this theme see Jasiewicz, 1990.

4. A review of prime conceptions concerning the determinants of electoral abstention and its political aftermath may be found in Lipset, S. M. 1981, *Political Man. The Social Bases of Politics*. Nonvoting in Polish conditions is discussed broadly by Skarżyńska and Chmielewski, 1993.

5. A similarly low attendance in post-communist countries was noted only in Hungary.

6. I discuss the results of this research in more detail in Raciborski (1991) and Raciborski (1993).

7. For a confirmation of this thesis in Polish conditions see Skarżyńska and Chmielewski (1993), Markowski (1992), and CBOS (Raports BS/167/136/93). The preelection survey conducted by CBOS showed that 52 percent of the lowest-income respondents declared their participation in the election, while in the highest-income group this index reached 75 percent.

8. This thesis was additionally confirmed by the results of research conducted by K. Skarżyńska, 1992, "The programs of the parties were little known to society either because they were badly articulated by the politicians or because the voters did not regard what the parties proposed in their programs as most important."

9. The analysis conducted by S. Gebethner (1993) indicates that an introduction of a nationwide 5 percent proviso would have reduced the number of groups represented in the Seym to nine but it would not have eliminated the dispersal of the mandates.

10. Correlations between the index of the religiosity of the surveyed and the ballots cast for select parties are rather high and statistically relevant; nonetheless, owing to the fact that these votes are dispersed among numerous parties, such correlations offer a limited explanation of the preference pattern within the entire electorate. More extensive comments on this topic are in Raciborski (1994).

11. The social reception of de-communization and lustration is discussed in detail by Bartkowski, 1993.

12. In accordance with a systematically published opinion poll conducted by the weekly *Wprost* upon the basis of research performed by the Institute for Opinion and Market research "Pentor."

13. A description of the electorate of particular parties, made according to sociodemographic variables, was founded upon the results of exit pool surveys carried out by INFAS/OBOP.

14. A portrayal of the ideological profiles of the electorate of particular parties is based on two sources: the author's own research (Raciborski, 1992: 147–56) and Dohnalik (1993).

15. The ideological profiles of voters who supported particular parties in the 1993 election were presented upon the basis of CBOS research: "Raport: Wyborcy zwycięskich partii" ("Report: The Electorate of the Winning Parties"), and the less systematized observations made by the author.

16. The description of the electorate of particular parties in the 1993 election according to socioeconomic variables is founded upon research conducted by INFAS/OBOP and CBOS.

17. The two studies mentioned include a survey by INFAS/OBOP on election day with a random sample of 50,000 respondents (the results are discussed by Żukowski, 1994) and another exit pool survey by the Social Studies Workshop from Sopot (a sample of 12,000 respondents) [the results are discussed by Krzemiński, 1993]. In both cases, the respondents were asked i.a. about their preferences in the parliamentary election of 1991. This method of examining electorate shifts is, unfortunately, burdened with rather grave errors due to the fact that the respondents tend to forget their preferences and commit conscious and unconscious lies. Numerical estimates, therefore, should be treated as approximate.

REFERENCES

Banaszkiewicz, A. 1992. "Identyfikacje światopoglądowe i identyfikacje partyjne jako czynniki oddziaływujące na zachowania wyborcze (Attitudes and partisan identification as factors influencing voting behavior")." In S. Gebethner and J. Raciborski (eds.), *Wybory '91 a polska scena polityczna* (Elections '91 and the Polish Political Scene). Warszawa: Fundacja Inicjatyw Społecznych "Polska w Europie."

Bartkowski, J. 1993. "Public opinion and 'de-communization' in Poland." In J. Wiatr (ed.), *The Politics of Democratic Transformation: Poland after 1989.* Warszawa: Scholar Agency.

Białecki, J. and B. Heyns. 1990. "Poparcie dla 'Solidarności' a wyniki wyborów z 1989 roku (Support for 'Solidarity' and the election results of 1989)," in L. Kolarska-Bobińska, P. Łukasiewicz and Z. W. Rykowski, eds. *Wyniki badań—wyniki wyborów 4 czerwca 1989 (Election Results—the Outcome of the Elections of 4 June 1989).* Warszawa: Polskie Towarzystwo Socjologiczne, p. 237.

CBOS. 1993. Raport: "Wyborcy zwycięskich partii (Report: The Electorate of the Winning Parties)."

Colomer, J. M. and M. Pascual. 1994. "The Polish games of transition." In *Communist and Post-Communist Studies* 27 (3): 276.

Dohnalik, J. 1993. "Profile światopoglądowe elektoratów poszczególnych partii i osób nieuczestniczących w wyborach (World outlook profiles of the electorate of particular parties and nonvoters)." In S. Gebethner, *Polska scena polityczna a wybory (The Polish Political Scene and Elections).* Warszawa: Fundacja Inicjatyw Społecznych "Polska w Europie."

Gebethner, S. 1989. "Wybory do Sejmu i Senatu 1989 (The 1989 elections to the Seym and Senate)," in *Państwo i Prawo,* no. 8.

———. 1993. *Polska scena polityczna a wybory (The Polish Political Scene and Elections).* Warszawa: Fundacja Inicjatyw Społecznych "Polska w Europie," p. 173.

Jasiewicz, K. 1990. "Zachowania wyborcze w świetle badań z serii 'Polacy' (Electoral behavior in the light of research from the 'Poles' series)." In L. Kolarska-Bobińska, P. Łukasiewicz and Z. W. Rykowski, eds., *Wyniki badań—wyniki wyborów 4 czerwca 1989 (Election Results—the Outcome of the Elections of 4 June 1989).* Warszawa: Polskie Towarzystwo Socjologiczne, p. 276.

Krzeminski, I. 1993. "Skoki po wyborviej szachownicy (Jumps on the election chessboard)." Rzevrpospolita, October 30.

Lipset, S. M. 1981. *Political Man. The Social Bases of Politics*. Baltimore: The Johns Hopkins University Press, chapter 6.

Markowski, R. 1992. "Milcząca większość—o bierności politycznej społeczeństwa polskiego (The silent majority—on the political passivity of Polish society)." In S. Gebethner and J. Raciborski (eds.), *Wybory '91 a polska scena polityczna*. Warszawa: Fundacja Inicjatyw Społecznych "Polska w Europie."

Raciborski, J. 1991. "Zachowania wyborcze Polaków w warunkach zmiany systemu politycznego (The electoral behavior of Poles during a change of the political system)." In J. Raciborski (ed.), *Wybory i narodziny demokracji w krajach Europy Środkowej i Wschodniej (Elections and the Birth of Democracy in Central-Eastern Europe)*. Warszawa: Instytut Socjologii Uniwersytetu Warszawskiego.

———. 1992, 1993. "Determinanty procesu krystalizacji preferenyi wyborczych (Determinants of the Crystallization of Voter Preferences)." In S. Gebethner and J. Raciborski (eds.), *Polska scena polityczna a wybory*. Warszawa: Fundacja Inicjatyw Społecznych "Polska w Europie."

———. 1994. "Kościoł i wybory (The Church and elections)." In M. Chałubiński (ed.), *Polityka i aborcja (Politics and Abortion)*. Warszawa: Wydawnictwo Naukowe "Scholar."

Skarżyńska, K. 1992. "Potoczna percepcja celów partii politycznych a zachowania wyborcze (The average perception of the goals of political parties and electoral behavior)." In S. Gebethner and J. Raciborski (eds.), *Wybory '91 a polska scena polityczna*. Warszawa: Fundacja Inicjatyw Społecznych "Polska w Europie," p. 119.

Skarżyńska, K. and K. Chmielewski. 1993. "Dlaczego ludzie nie głosują (Why people do not vote)" In J. Reykowski (ed.), *Wartości i postawy społeczne a przemiany systemowe (Social Values and Stands in the Face of Changes in the Political System)*. Warszawa: Instytut Psychologii PAN.

Żukowski, T. 1993. "Polska scena polityczna w latach 1991–1992 w świetle wyników wyborów: ciągłość i zmiany (The Polish political scene in the years 1991–1992 in the light of election results: continuation and changes)." In S. Gebethner, *Polska scena polityczna a wybory (The Polish Political Scene and Elections)*. Warszawa: Fundacja Inicjatyw Społecznych "Polska w Europie." pp. 250–54.

———. 1994. "Wybory '93: kto na kogo głosował (The 1993 elections: who voted for whom.)" In *Przegląd Społeczny* 20.

17

Patterns of Voter Alignments in Present-Day Romania

Petre Datculescu

INTRODUCTION

It is a widely acknowledged assumption of political science that, to be viable in the long run, a party needs a definite social base. Although a party will obtain many votes from outside its constituency, the strength and long-run viability of a party is based on its ability to represent a distinct social group and to advance the interests of the group it represents.

From 1990 to 1996, Romania had three general elections. On the surface they looked like elections in which stable political parties represented the interests of distinctive social groups. But a closer look at the three elections and the 1990 to 1996 period as a whole reveals an almost trendless fluctuation of political allegiance and deep-running changes in the social bases of most Romanian political parties. Quite naturally parties were gaining support or losing support from one election to another. Elections are like that. It is, of course, interesting to identify the groups where political parties lose or acquire supporters. But the crucial question is: who are the voters Romanian parties can count on and why? A related question refers to the significance of the changes in party support for the emergence of steady lines dividing voters according to their interests and political allegiance.

This chapter attempts to answer some of these questions. To begin with I shall look at the electoral records between 1990 and 1996, paying special attention to the changing social base of political parties. Using election results and public opinion polls, I will uncover some general patterns of voter alignment and attempt to explain the social and political origins of electoral change.

My principal sources of material are the official returns of the general elections and the exit polls conducted by IRSOP (Romania) and INFAS (Germany) in the 1990 and 1992 elections, and by IRSOP and IFES (Germany) in the 1996 elections. I was able to supplement this material by analyzing a large number of political polls conducted by IRSOP Market Research Ltd. during 1990–1997. I have thus been able to investigate trends in electoral attitudes and behavior and to arrive at certain conclusions about their origins and prospects. I do not pretend to have clear answers to the questions about the future of voter alignments in Romania. By looking at the sources of change, however, we can better understand the future prospects of Romanian politics.

THE ELECTION RESULTS

Although few people are registered members of political parties, election turnout has been remarkably high in all three elections—76 percent in 1996, 75 percent in 1992, and 86 percent in 1990. The turnout in 1990 was consistent with the general pattern of high voter participation in post-dictatorial elections.[1] Most interesting, the demographic composition of the new Romanian electorate was very similar to the voter structure which can be found in modern European democracies. Young voters (18 to 34) represented 35 percent of the electorate. Half of all voters (50 percent) were between 35–65, while older voters (over 65) constituted 15 percent.

Election research shows that voter participation tends to increase in times of political and economic crisis and that members of social groups who are more affected by political decisions are more likely to vote than voters who are less affected by a certain political decision (Curtis, 1968: 113). Pervasive economic distress across all sections of Romanian voters was the reason for high electoral turnout in both the 1992 and the 1996 elections. Voters felt that their vote was contributing to a political decision about the magnitude and speed of economic change, and that the political decision was crucial to the issue of economic well-being.

Because of many changes in the political landscape it is not always easy to trace the electoral record of individual parties over time. The results of the 1990 elections need to be presented separately, while relative comparisons are possible only for the 1992 and 1996 elections.[2]

In 1990 the overwhelming majority of voters felt that the National Salvation Front (FSN) was representing their interests related to increased economic well-being, freedom, national peace, and moderate social change. As a result, the 1990 election produced a political party with an absolute majority which controlled the Parliament for two years.

After 1990 there were two significant developments in the Romanian political community. First, the popularity of the FSN decreased and it split up in March 1992. Second, an opposition alliance was established under the name of

**Table 17.1
Returns of the General Election of May 20, 1990, in Romania and Party Preferences One Year Later**

	Chamber of Deputies (in %)	*Senate (in %)*	*IRSOP Poll April 1991 (in %)*
FSN	66.3	67.0	31
UDMR	7.2	7.2	5
PNL	6.4	7.1	10
PNȚCD	2.6	2.5	6
MER	2.6	2.4	5
AUR	2.1	2.2	8
PDAR	1.8	1.6	3
PER	1.7	1.4	3
PSDR	1.0	1.1	1
Other	11.5	12.1	4
Uncertain	–	–	25

Source: National Commission for Statistics, Bucharest, 5, 1995, and IRSOP Archives.

Democratic Convention (CDR). When the FSN hesitantly started to introduce unpopular economic reform measures, such as price liberalization, the living standard declined, unemployment increased, and the prices for goods and services skyrocketed. The former FSN voters felt betrayed and disappointed. As a result they started to turn their back on the party they had supported wholeheartedly twelve months before. But most interestingly, as the poll results in Table 17.1 reveal, no other party was able to attract the support lost by the FSN after one year in Government.

After the split of the FSN, the conservative wing was renamed FDSN and later PDSR. The more liberal faction under Petre Roman kept the name of FSN in 1992, but changed it to PD (Democratic Party) and entered the 1996 election in an alliance with PSDR under the name of Social-Democratic Union (USD).

Even more dramatic changes occurred in the opposition camp. A number of parties which had competed independently in the 1990 elections decided to form an alliance under the name of The Democratic Convention of Romania (CDR).[3] The CDR had a good start in the local elections of 1992 when it managed to attract 24.3 percent of the votes. But soon afterward it underwent a series of internal crises, nearly disintegrated a couple of times and entered each of the following two elections from 1992 and 1996 with a different internal party composition.

Table 17.2 presents a comparative view of the election returns of September 1992 and November 1996.

As expected by many analysts, the massive 66 percent support for the FSN in 1990 broke down to less than half in 1992. The majority of the FSN voters (41 percent) remained loyal to the conservative FDSN/PDSR and a small fraction migrated to Petre Roman's more liberal FSN. Together, FDSN and FSN managed to retain 60 percent of their former voters. Only 14 percent made a radical

Table 17.2
Returns of the General Elections of September 27, 1992, and November 3, 1996, in Romania. Chamber of Deputies and Senate (in percent)

	1992		1996	
	Chamber of Deputies	**Senate**	**Chamber of Deputies**	**Senate**
FDSN/PDSR	27.7	28.3	21.5	23.0
CDR	20.0	20.2	30.1	30.7
FSN/USD*	10.2	10.4	12.9	13.1
PUNR	7.7	8.1	4.3	4.2
UDMR	7.5	7.6	6.6	6.8
PRM	3.9	3.8	4.4	4.5
PSM	3.0	3.2	**	**
PDAR	–	3.3	**	**
Other	20.0	15.1	19.9	17.4

*Including PD, former FSN, plus PSDR, one-time member of CDR.
**Under 3% not in Parliament.

switch toward the CDR, while 20 percent moved further "left" to more nationalistic and conservative parties.

A dramatic illustration of weak political allegiance was provided by the fates of the National Liberal Party (PNL) and the Agrarian Party (PDAR). According to IRSOP polls the PNL had an electoral support of 17 percent when it defected from the Democratic Convention after the local elections of February 1992. During the same year, in the general elections of September 1992, the PNL was unable to collect 3 percent of the votes to get into Parliament. Similarly, the Agrarians who had won 7.9 percent of the votes in the local elections succeeded in entering the Senate by a narrow margin of 3.3 percent but failed to enter the Chamber of Deputies by several hundred votes.

In 1996, a massive realignment of voters from all sections of the electorate decided to achieve a complete change of political power in Romania. Evincing a different voting pattern than that of Western democracies, in 1996 the Romanian electorate ended the supremacy of a party (PDSR) in the three most important institutions of the state—Presidency, Senate, and Chamber of Deputies—and conveyed the entire political responsibility exclusively to the alliance of the opposition composed of CDR and USD. The explanation of this massive political shift is not very hard to find. During 1992–1996 the great majority of the working population experienced a steady, sometimes dramatic, decline in their living standards, with real earnings unable to keep pace with inflation. People learned to fear that year by year their work would fail to bring improved returns. President Ion Iliescu and the PDSR government were perceived as weak, ineffective, either corrupt or tolerating corruption, and lacking compassion about the hardships of the population. This led to disenchantment with the PDSR regime and impatience to try other people. The CDR projected an image of compassion, honesty, and determination to carry out real improvements of the living standard in a very short time. In 1996, the CDR vote was largely a vote of dissatisfaction. It represented movement away from Ion Iliescu and the PDSR rather than an ideological movement toward the CDR and its presidential candidate Emil Constantinescu.

Compared to 1992, the CDR registered a 10 percent increase, but overall the electoral performances of the parties in 1996 do not differ dramatically from their records in the 1992 elections. Yet an in-depth analysis of voter movements reveals that the 1996 political pattern was in fact produced by a massive shift of allegiance which indicates the absence of stable structures underlying voting behavior in Romania. Only 49 percent of the CDR voters of 1996 had voted CDR in 1992. One in four new CDR voters (25 percent) had cast their vote in 1992 for the FDSN/PDSR, and 7 percent had voted for the FSN, now USD. One in ten CDR voters (10 percent) did not vote in 1992 while 9 percent had voted for other parties in the previous elections. The second victor, the USD, displays an even more dramatic picture of voter instability. Only 19 percent of its voters of 1996 were the same as in 1992. Nearly half of the 1996 USD voters (42 percent) had voted for the FDSN/PDSR in 1992, while 14 percent were previous supporters of the CDR. The remaining 25 percent of the new USD voters had either not participated in the 1992 elections or had voted for other parties.

Some of the smaller parties, PNL 93[4] and PAC, members of the Democratic Convention, thought they could count on a stable group of supporters. They were wrong. When they defected from the CDR shortly before the 1996 elections to form a separate alliance, ANL, their supporters abandoned them, leaving the two parties outside the Parliament.

Miscalculations of voter support were all too common. The Agrarians (PDAR) who felt vulnerable thought they could increase their strength if they entered an alliance with parties which had been established just prior to the 1996 elections. But their extravagant move could not reverse the decline of the PDAR which had already begun in 1992. Neither could the PDAR remain in Parliament with the help of the newly formed alliance UNC (National Union of the Centre) nor could the alliance rise to Parliament on the shoulders of the Agrarians.

Finally, when one of the most leftist parties, the PSM, broke into two before the 1996 elections, each of the two factions was convinced it could keep a sufficient number of supporters from the old base and attract enough new ones under the guise of party renewal in order to pass the 3 percent parliamentary mandate threshold.[5] Both parties proved to be wrong and neither made it into Parliament.

THE PATTERNS OF VOTING BEHAVIOR

In analyzing the patterns of voting behavior in Romania, I shall make use of two theories which are widely employed in electoral studies (Health, Jowell, Curtice, 1985: 8–10). One theory is based on a sociological explanation of electoral choice.

It holds that voting behavior is influenced essentially by the social characteristics of the voters. Such characteristics as class, housing, income, education, and union membership are seen as the bases of voting behavior provided that political parties are shaped to reflect the interests of certain social classes. Social stratification theory emphasizes differences in the social characteristics of voters. In turn, social characteristics are associated with particular interests. There may be two kinds of interests: some may have no dividing effects, others may generate real cleavages splitting voters into opposing groups.

This approach to voter motivation, based on social stratification, does not exclude the influence of psychological factors related to group membership. But party choice is basically interpreted as a result of party identification based on solidarity with one's social group. A number of general tendencies in Western European societies regarding traditional party allegiance of various social and demographic groups have contributed to the longevity of this explanatory approach. The "voter stratification" theory has been refined and made more flexible in recent years to include the circumstances when voters break away from their traditional allegiance and vote for a party that has not traditionally represented their distinctive social interests.

A second theory is derived from economic models of human behavior. It holds that voting is based on rational calculation unrelated to group identity or group interests. Voting is then interpreted as an individual action of utility maximization. In other words, the voter will choose a party perceived as being able to maximize his or her interests.[6] It is widely assumed that voters assess the utility of parties in terms of promised change in the personal welfare of the voter that the party might bring about between this and the next elections. There are, of course, other promises that parties make apart from pledging that they will improve personal well-being. But social research conducted in Romania after the 1996 elections revealed that promises related to personal welfare were the most important factors considered by voters in making their electoral choice.

I believe that the voting pattern in Romania can be explained by combining the social stratification approach with the utility maximization theory. If the act of voting involves both cleavages or social stratification and utility maximization elements, then it is important to analyze the balance between the two elements.

The pattern of voting behavior in present day Romania appears to exhibit three broad characteristics: ethnic electoral divisions; rural versus urban divisions; cross-class voting; and differences between younger and older voters.

Ethnic Divisions

In all three elections since 1990, the Hungarian party UDMR received all or almost all the votes of the Hungarian ethnics living in Romania (7 percent of the population). The social base of this party is the same as the ethnic base and is located in seven counties in the North-West and Center of Romania (Covasna,

Harghita, Mureş, Cluj, Satu Mare, Sălaj, and Bihor). The counterpart of the Hungarian party is the Romanian nationalist party PUNR which attracts most of its supporters from about the same counties where the Hungarian ethnics live.

Hostile interethnic actions and rhetoric were more frequent during the five years after 1990 but declined markedly after the treaty between Romania and Hungary was signed in 1996. This is reflected in the voting records of the two parties. During times of intense hostility both the UDMR and the PUNR were able to effectively mobilize their supporters. When interethnic tensions subsided, the PUNR dropped from 8.1 percent (Senate) in 1992 to 4.2 percent (Senate) in 1996, and the UDMR also lost one percent of its traditional voters.

Rural versus Urban Divisions

From 1990 to 1996, the Romanian rural area consistently revealed a different voting pattern than that in urban areas. Soon after the overthrow of Nicolae Ceauşescu, the National Salvation Front (FSN) promised to dissolve the state-controlled agricultural cooperatives and divide the land among rural inhabitants. As a result of this promise in the 1990 elections the support for Ion Iliescu and FSN was 20 to 25 percent higher in the rural area and among farmers than in the urban environment. The honeymoon lasted more than two years. Table 17.3 shows the electoral choice in the urban and rural environments in 1992 and 1996 for the major five parties and alliances.

By the time the elections were held, by virtue of the new Land Law, 80 percent of the arable land and 65 per cent of the farmland had become private property, although ownership titles were issued with great delay. The mood in the rural areas was mixed. On the one hand, there was the enthusiasm of owning land, and the producers' freedom to produce what they wanted and to sell at their own prices. The distribution of land to farmers and the economic autonomy

Table 17.3
Party Choice in Urban and Rural Areas in the 1992 and 1996 Elections (in percent) (Romania)

	1992*		1996**	
	Urban	*Rural*	*Urban*	*Rural*
FDSN/ PDSR	19	35	16	34
CDR	34	18	43	26
FSN/USD	11	11	11	11
PUNR	8	7	5	4
UDMR	4	7	6	8
Other	24	22	19	17

* *Source:* IRSOP/INFAS Exit Polls, IRSOP Archives.
** *Source:* IRSOP/IFES Exit Polls, IRSOP Archives.

determined an unprecedented growth in the material resources of the rural population during the last fifty years. On the other hand, the hardships were overwhelming. Of the total population employed in agriculture two-thirds were women, and again two-thirds were over the age of 55. The lack of credits, tools, seeds and fertilizers, the low prices at which the produce was acquired by the government, the fact that rural households were not properly endowed for efficient farming, the small plots, plus the drought of 1992—all these made up quite a disheartening picture of the Romanian village.

The rural population needed strong support from the government to take off economically. They hoped that if they voted for the FDSN, which they perceived as believing in state intervention, the government would take over part of their difficulties, helping them to prosper and to maintain their property.

In addition, they feared that if the CDR came to power they would revise the Land Law and redistribute rural property in favor of the former landowners. A second explanation of the rural vote is that until 1992 the CDR made very few efforts to penetrate the countryside and to communicate its message to the farmers. The late Peasant Party leader Corneliu Coposu, who was also the leader of CDR, explained one year after the 1992 defeat, "We must accept the fact that we have not managed so far to penetrate the rural area according to our program; the rural population is still unfamiliar with our ideology and lacks information about our objectives" (Coposu, 1993: 9).

The rural community was not able to gain much from the PDSR government. The average size of the Romanian farm is a scant 2.5 hectares (barely seven acres). Chronically lacking capital and machinery, most farmers were forced to restrict themselves to subsistence agriculture. They were promised preferential credits by the government. But few of these credits were used effectively in agriculture. Funds usually arrived after great delays if they arrived at all, thus ruining the crop harvest. Failure to recoup the amounts invested resulted in defaults which increased the budget deficit. Burdened by corruption and bureaucracy, governmental aid for agriculture was unable to deal with the overwhelming problems of the rural community.

Yet the PDSR registered only a slight drop of one percent among rural inhabitants in 1996 and the CDR was able to increase its rural base by only 8 percent. Social research conducted by IRSOP in the rural area showed that farmers were extremely disappointed by president Ion Iliescu and the PDSR government. Yet they still feared that the CDR represented the interests of former big landowners rather than the interests of the small farmers. Moreover, pro-PDSR attitudes among rural inhabitants were probably shaped to a great extent by the state-run TV Channel 1, the only TV station with effective penetration in the rural area. In brief, the rural people were not happy with the way in which the PDSR had represented their interests, but they continued to support that party because they were either ignorant or distrustful or both about the CDR.

The Many Faces of the Social Classes

In 1992 it began to look as if a clear political division would emerge between voters with higher and lower socioeconomic status. Indeed socioeconomic status, measured by education and occupation—both separately and in combination—proved to be strongly correlated with party preferences, at least for the major parties.

The better educated and the nonmanual workers, particularly in urban areas, were more likely to vote for the CDR, while persons with a lower socioeconomic status were more likely to vote for the PDSR. But apart from these very general tendencies, a clear pattern of cross-class voting was apparent. It is true that the PDSR was overwhelmingly strong among farmers, while the CDR had an absolute majority among educated professionals. But the PDSR fared only slightly better than the CDR among workers, and the CDR emerged only a fraction stronger than the PDSR among nonmanual office workers and medium-level employees.

Four years later, in the 1996 elections, the cross-class voting pattern was still in place but the sides had changed. The CDR succeeded in taking a strong lead over the PDSR among workers, middle-level employees, private entrepreneurs, and intellectuals. But the PDSR was able to hold up among farmers and even among manual workers where it dropped only four percentage points. Table 17.4 presents the correlation between socioeconomic status and party preference for the PDSR and CDR in 1992 and 1996.

As can be seen in Table 17.4, the same parties receive consistent support from several social classes or strata. Thus, social class as a whole is not a sufficient explanation for how people have voted in Romania so far. The considerable political consensus which cuts across different social strata indicates that voters have both interests that are related to their class position and interests that transcend the boundaries of socioeconomic status. Typical class interests are perhaps stronger among farmers and intellectuals. Farmers rely heavily on state support

Table 17.4
Socioeconomic Status and Party Preference in 1992 and 1996 General Elections (Romania)

Socioeconomic Status	1992*		1996**	
	PDSR	CDR	PDSR	CDR
Farmers	43	18	53	18
Manual workers	25	20	21	32
Middle-level employees	21	23	21	35
Intellectuals	15	36	5	4
Private entrepreneurs	–	–	11	48

* *Source:* IRSOP/INFAS Exit Polls, IRSOP Archives.
** *Source:* IRSOP/IFES Exit Polls, IRSOP Archives.

and fear the alleged property restoration plans of the CDR. Intellectuals are primarily dedicated to the values of liberalism and worried about a possible restoration of the totalitarian past. But during the last seven years a number of criss-crossing interests emerged which were responsible for the rather eclectic voting pattern. Criss-crossing issues in Romania are of two kinds: broad consensus issues and consensus issues of a more narrow scope which affect smaller groups of people of all or most social strata. Social research shows that broad consensus issues include: keeping prices from rising, improving the economy, raising salaries, keeping unemployment down, and fighting corruption. Equally important in shaping electoral choice are a number of consensus issues of narrower scope. A large number of tenants of all social groups live in nationalized apartments and fear that they will have to surrender their homes to the former owners. Many urban voters of all social strata have rural properties and distinctive interests in the rural area. Millions of former members of the communist party, well represented in every population segment, are still worrying that some day they might be held responsible for their past political alignment. Large sections of the retired and of those nearing retirement are apprehensive of too much social change, while even larger sections of the young, the better off and the better educated are exasperated by too little social change. The monarchy has both supporters and opponents in all sections of the society. Electoral studies show that for broad consensus policies, such as keeping prices from rising or fighting corruption, the voters' assessment of the parties tends to differ only in the degree of their perceived inability to solve the problem (Himmelweit, Humphreys, Jaeger, and Katz 1981: 117). But voters rarely consider one issue in deciding for which party to vote. The voting decision is probably based on an amalgam of many issues, including broad consensus issues and consensus issues of narrower scope. In combining these issues voters are considering both interests related to their social group as well as interests they share with people from other social groups.

The Political Division of Age Groups

The differentiation of political preferences according to age groups is a characteristic of all electorates.

Based on the 1992 and 1996 elections, two political generations can be identified in Romania. The younger voters are more likely to vote for the CDR, while the older voters clearly support the PDSR. In 1996, one-third of all young voters under 24 voted for the CDR (35 percent), while only 17 percent voted for the PDSR. Among people over 65, 42 percent voted for the PDSR and only 24 percent for the CDR.

Social survey findings also show that favorable attitudes toward social change such as commitment toward privatization, approval of free enterprise and the right of foreigners to buy Romanian companies are definitely stronger among younger people than among persons over 65. The elderly are significantly more reluctant to approve economic reform. They are unwilling to suffer the hardships of economic transition because they have no way of expanding their resources to beat inflation and declining purchasing power. They also feel they would not live long enough to gain from the benefits of a successful market economy. Younger people are at least potentially better equipped to face the difficulties of economic transition and they tend to believe that changes will increase their chances in the future.

These results indicate that not age in itself but other underlying factors are responsible for the differentiation of political preferences. The political gap between generations is a consequence of differences in terms of resources for human well-being rather than a result of different generational value orientations.

THE FUTURE OF ROMANIAN POLITICAL CULTURE

For the time being, political parties in Romania do not have a distinctive social base. They have not yet established themselves as the parties of professionals, industrial workers, farmers, or private entrepreneurs. They do not have "heartlands." Their main concern is to attract followers from all segments of the society rather than work on securing the long-term loyalties of specific social groups with distinctive social interests.

In attempting to address all segments of the society, Romanian parties manifest a marked originality in comparison with political parties from established Western democracies. To attract voters they focus on the broad consensus issues and present themselves as being more capable than their opponents to solve all sorts of problems. They try to be very careful about consensus issues of narrower scope, and they often avoid taking a clear stance on such issues. Basically they opt for popular programs and then, after winning the elections, they try to move to a more radical ideological stance or "disclose" the necessity of introducing unpopular measures for advancing economic reform. This is what the FSN did after winning the 1990 elections. The same strategy was used by its leftist follower FDSN/PDSR after the 1992 elections. And exactly the same strategy was used by the rightist CDR for winning the 1996 elections.

If parties have no social bases it is extremely difficult to make predictions about how they will fare in the future. There is no way in which predictions regarding changes of the social structure can be related to changes in the growth or decline of political loyalty. Most probably, voter fluctuations will continue. And the fluctuations will reflect changing voter confidence in various political parties based on how well the parties will be able to carry out their promises related to broad consensus issues. But if votes keep switching from one party to another party, identification will have no chance to develop.

Lack of party identification indicates a deeply disturbed relationship between parties and individuals. It is true that voters engage in heated political debates and that they want the parties to find solutions to their problems. But few Romanians are deeply committed to a party and even fewer are ready to engage in party-building activities or to perform a service to a political party, other than voting.

The political divisions related to the speed of economic reform, private property, and socioeconomic status differentiation may develop further and may have a decisive influence on party development.

In the near future Romania is likely to witness economic polarization between a large group of unemployed and people living below the poverty level on the one hand and a thin upper class on the other, with no middle class in between. This polarization may turn into a structural cleavage that could generate opposing views on issues such as the amount of governmental centralism or taxation, the level at which private business should be regulated, or the desirable amount of public property. When articulated conflicts on these issues emerge they may become sources of political division and may lead to a restoration of the left-right continuum as an expression of conflicts between distinctive interests of various social strata.

NOTES

1. Election turnout tends to be high in the first elections after the breakdown of a totalitarian regime. Voter participation reached 92 percent in 1975 in Portugal after the collapse of the Salazar regime, 77.7 percent in 1977 in Spain after the death of Franco, 93 percent in East Germany after the fall of the Berlin wall, and 78.5 percent in West Germany in 1949 during the first democratic general election after the Nazi era.

2. Throughout this chapter I use the Romanian acronyms for parties and alliances. I provide here a translation for the names of the parties and alliances which entered Parliament in the 1990, 1992 and 1996 elections:

FSN	National Salvation Front
FDSN	Democratic National Salvation Front
PDSR	Party for Social Democracy in Romania
CDR	Democratic Convention of Romania (alliance of parties)
PDAR	Agrarian Democratic Party of Romania
PNL	National Liberal Party
PNȚCD	National Christian-Democratic Peasant Party (a member of CDR)
PRM	Greater Romania Party
PSDR	Social Democratic Party of Romania
PSM	Socialist Labour Party
PER	Romanian Ecological Party (a member of CDR)
AUR	Alliance for the Unity of Romanians (changed its name to PUNR)
PUNR	Romanian National Unity Party
UDMR	Hungarian Democratic Alliance of Romania (a member of CDR)
MER	Romanian Ecological Movement.

3. When it entered the 1992 elections, the CDR included PNȚCD, PNL, PSDR, MER, PER, and other nonparliamentary parties and political associations. But four years later the

composition of the CDR had changed significantly due to new admissions or defections, and even individual parties within the CDR had changed due to internal divisions.

4. PNL 93—The National Liberal Party 93, a splinter of the first National Liberal Party established in 1990. PAC—The Civic Alliance Party, a liberal party originating from the Civic Alliance Movement and mainly addressing intellectual elites.

5. The PSM—Socialist Labour Party split as a result of the emergence within the party of a less conservative group advocating the need to move the party in the direction of modern social-democracy. The group left the PSM and established a new party called PS—The Socialist Party.

6. For a more detailed discussion of the economic model of party choice see Becker, Gary S. 1976.

REFERENCES

Becker, Gary S. 1976. *The Economic Approach to Human Behavior.* Chicago: The University of Chicago Press.

Coposu, Corneliu. 1993. "Calitatea de intelectual nu îndreptățește înființarea unui partid," an interview granted to Andrei Cornea, *Revista* 22 (20): 9.

Curtis, M. 1968. *Comparative Government and Politics: An Introductory Essay in Political Science.* New York: Harper and Row.

Heath, Anthony, Roger Jowell, John Curtice with the assistance of Julia Field and Clarissa Levine. 1985. *How Britain Votes.* Oxford: Pergamon Press.

Himmelweit, Hilde T., Patrick Humphreys, Marianne Jaeger and Michael Katz. 1981. *How Voters Decide: A Longitudinal Study of Political Attitudes and Voting Extending over Fifteen Years.* London: Academic Press.

Further Readings

Ágh, Attila. 1996. "The Development of East Central European Party Systems: From 'Movements' to 'Cartels.' In Máté Szabó, ed., *The Challenge of the Europeanization in the Region: East Central Europe*. Budapest: Hungarian Political Science Association.
———. 1990. *Transition to Democracy in Central Europe: a Comparative View*. Glasgow: Centre for the Study of Public Policy, University of Strathclyde.
Ágh, Attila, and Gabrielle Ilonszki, eds. 1996. *Parliaments and Organized Interests: The Second Steps*. Budapest: Hungarian Center for Democracy Studies.
Berglund, Sten, and Jan A. Dellenbrant, eds. 1994. *The New Democracies in Eastern Europe: Party Systems and Political Cleavages*. Aldershot: E. Elgar.
———. 1991. *The New Democracies in Eastern Europe: Party Systems and Political Cleavages*. Aldershot: E. Elgar.
Bull, Martin J., and Mike Ingham, eds. 1998. *Reform of the Socialist System in Central and Eastern Europe*. New York: St. Martin's Press.
Casmir, Fred L., ed. 1995. *Communication in Eastern Europe: the Role of History, Culture, and Media in Contemporary Conflicts*. Mahwah: Lawrence Erlbaum.
Cowen-Karp, Regina, ed. 1993. *Central and Eastern Europe: the Challenge of Transition*. Stockholm: Sipri.
Crawford, Keith. 1996. *East Central European Politics Today: from Chaos to Stability?* Manchester: Manchester University Press.
Dahrendorf, Ralf. 1997. *After 1989: Morals, Revolution, and Civil Society*. New York: St. Martin's Press.
Dawisha, Karen, and Bruce Parrot, eds. 1997. *The Consolidation of Democracy in East-Central Europe*. Cambridge: Cambridge University Press.
Dawisha, Karen, ed. 1997. *Democratic Changes and Authoritarian Reactions in Russia, Ukraine, Belarus and Moldova*. Cambridge: Cambridge University Press.
East, Roger, and Joylon Pontin. 1997. *Revolution and Change in Central and Eastern Europe*. London: Pinter.
Higley, John, Jan Pakulski, and Wlodzimierz Wesolowski, eds. 1998. *Postcommunist Elites and Democracy in Eastern Europe*. New York: St. Martin's Press.

Huntington, Samuel P. 1991. *The Third Wave: Democratization in the Late Twentieth Century.* Norman: University of Oklahoma Press.

Hupchick, Dennis P. 1995. *Conflict and Chaos in Eastern Europe.* New York: St. Martin's Press.

Karasimeonov, G. 1995. "The 1994 Parliamentary Elections and the Development of the Bulgarian Party System." In *Party Politics 1* (4), 579–87.

Kitschelt, Herbert. 1995a. *Party Systems in East Central Europe: Consolidation or Fluidity?* Glasgow: University of Strathclyde.

———. 1995b. "A Silent Revolution in Europe?" In J. Hayward, and E. Page, eds. *Governing the New Europe.* Cambridge: Polity Press, 123–65.

———. 1992. "The Formation of Party Systems in East Central Europe." *Politics and Society 20:* 7–50.

Kopecky, Petr. 1995. "Developing Party Organizations in East-Central Europe: What Kind of Party is Likely to Emerge?" *Party Politics 1* (4): 515–34.

Lawson, Kay, ed. 1994. *How Political Parties Work: Perspectives from Within.* Westport: Praeger.

Lawson, Kay and Peter Merkl, eds. 1988. *When Parties Fail: Emerging Alternative Organizations.* Princeton: Princeton University Press.

Lewis, Paul G., ed. 1996. *Party Structure and Organization in East-Central Europe.* Cheltenham: E. Elgar.

Mair, Peter. 1997. *Party System Change: Approaches and Interpretations.* Oxford: Clarendon Press.

———. 1996. *What is Different about Post-Communist Party Systems?* Glasgow: Centre for the Study of Public Policy, University of Strathclyde.

Markowski, Radoslaw, ed. 1997. "Political Parties and Ideological Spaces in East Central Europe." *Communist and Post-Communist Studies* 30: 221–54.

Merkel, Wolfgang. 1996. "Institutions and Democratic Consoldation in East Central Europe." *Working Paper of the Centro de Estudios Avanzados en Ciencias Sociales, Instituto Juan March de Estudios e Investigaciones,* Madrid.

Miller, William L., Stephen White, and Paul Heywood. 1998. *Values and Political Change in Postcommunist Europe.* New York: St. Martin's Press.

Offe, Claus. 1996. *Varieties of Transition: The East European and East German Experience.* Cambridge: Polity Press.

Olson, David M., and P. Norton, eds. 1996. *The New Parliaments of Central and Eastern Europe.* London: Cass.

Plasser, Fritz, and Andreas Pribersky, eds. 1996. *Political Culture in East Central Europe.* Aldershot: Avebury.

Pridham, Geoffrey, and Paul G. Lewis, eds. 1996. *Stabilizing Fragile Democracies: Comparing New Party Systems in Southern and Eastern Europe.* London: Routledge.

Pridham, Geoffrey, ed. 1995. *Transitions to Democracy: Comparative Perspectives from Southern Europe, Latin America and Eastern Europe.* Aldershot: Dartmouth.

Pridham, Geoffrey, Herring, Eric, and George Sanford, eds. 1997. *Building Democracy? The International Dimension of Democratization in Eastern Europe.* New York: Leicester University Press.

Pridham, Geoffrey, and Tatu Vanhanen, eds. 1994. *Democratization in Eastern Europe: Domestic and International Perspectives.* London: Routledge.

Römmele, Andrea. 1997. "Communicating with Their Voters: The Use of Direct Mailing by the SPD and the CDU." *German Politics* 6 (3): 120–32.

Ronen, Dov. 1997. *The Challenge of Ethnic Conflict, Democracy and Self-Determination in Central-Europe.* London: Cass.

Rose, Richard. 1995. "Mobilizing Demobilized Voters in Post Communist Societies." Working Paper of the Centro de Estudios Avanzados en Ciencias Sociales, Instituto Juan March de Estudios e Investigaciones, Madrid.

Roskin, Michael G. 1993. "The Emerging Party Systems of Central and Eastern Europe." *East European Quarterly* 27 (1).

Tóka, G. 1997. *Political Parties and Democratic Consolidation in East Central Europe.* Glasgow: University of Strathclyde.

von Beyme, Klaus. 1996. *Transition to Democracy in Eastern Europe.* New York: St. Martin's Press.

Weidenfeld, Werner, ed. 1995. *Central and Eastern Europe on the Way into the European Union: Problems and Prospects of Integration.* Gütersloh: Bertelsmann Foundation Publishers.

Wightman, Gordon, ed. 1995. *Party Formation in East-Central Europe: Post-Communist Politics in Czechoslovakia, Hungary, Poland and Bulgaria.* Aldershot: E. Elgar.

Index

Ágh, A., 146, 153, 228
Allardt, Erik, 4
Analysis of Political Cleavages, The, 6
Andersen, Gosta Esping, 130
Andeweg, R., 62
Antall, József, 26, 74, 142–45, 226
anticommunism, 72, 124
Antonescu, Marshall Ion, 99
Appadurai, Arjun, 20–21
April Constitution, 90

Bad Godesberg decision, 10
Balcerowicz, Leszek, 162
Balcerowicz Plan, 162, 245, 251–54
Banaszkiewicz, A., 253
Bartkowski, Jerzy, 165
Bartolini, Stefano, 4–6, 10–11
"Basic Treaty," 145
Bauman, Zygmunt, 109
Benes, Eduard, 136
Berlin Reichstag, 78
Bertényi, I., 68
Bethlen, Count István, 70, 74
Bielecki, Krzysztof, 245, 254
Bill of Fundamental Rights and Freedoms, 134–35
Bismarck, 50

Blahož, Josef, 20, 21, 24–25, 123–39
Bokros, Lajos, 150, 151
Brehznev, Leonid, 102
"Brest election," 82
British Labour Party, 8
British Liberals, 22
Brokl, Lubomír, 20, 21, 24–22, 47–60, 123–39, 203–13
Brucan, Silviu, 102
Bruszt, László, 218
Bulei, Ion, 94
Bulgaria, 22–24, 37–45, 107–21
  communism in, 43–44, 111–12, 117, 199–201
  composition of electorate, 188–95
  Constituent Assembly, 38–39
  Constitution, 38–39, 117
  Eastern Rumelia and, 39
  Macedonia and, 39, 42
  parliamentary election results, 188, 201
  party pluralism, 111–15
  political culture, 197–99
  Popov government, 114
  Russia and, 37–41
  voter response, 185–202
Bulgarian political parties,
  Agrarian "Nikola Petkov," 112

Agrarian Party, 172
Bulgarian Peasant Union, 78
Bulgarian Peoples Agrarian Union, 41–43
Bulgarian Socialist Party (BSP), 113–14, 118, 119, 185–87, 192–98, 200–1
Christian-Democratic Party, 112
Club for Glasnost and Democracy, 112
Communist, 23
Conservatives, 22, 38–40
Democratic Party, 112
Ecoglasnost, 112
Left Wing Socialists, 41
Liberals, 22, 38–40
Movement for Rights and Freedoms (MRF), 23, 114, 117, 192
Radical Democratic Party, 41
Republican Party, 112
Right Wing Socialists, 41
Socialdemocratic Party, 41, 42, 112
Trade Union Podkrepa, 112
Union of Democratic Forces (UDF), 112–15, 118, 120, 185–87, 192–95, 197–98, 200–1
Burda, Andrzeg, 80

Călinescu, Matei, 171
Carol I, 96
Carol II, 99
Ceauşescu, Elena, 100, 104
Ceauşescu, Nicolae, 30, 99–102, 104–5, 169, 176, 267
Chirot, Daniel, 100
Christian Democrats of Italy, 8
Cimoszewicz, Włodzimierz, 248, 256
"Cleavage Structures, Party Systems, and Voter Alignments: An Introduction," 3
cleavages
  actual, 110
  ascriptive, 6
  attitudinal, 6
  authoritarianism vs. democracy, 160–61
  behavioral, 6
  center vs. periphery, 4–5, 8, 24, 49, 51, 61, 62, 150–51, 155
  centralist vs. autonomist, 51
  commodification, 151
  conflictual, 4
  cosmopolitan vs. nationalist, 24, 137
  cultural, 118, 155
  decommunization, 160, 165–66, 242
  divisional, 4
  economic, 23, 160–61, 167, 219–21
  emergent, 110
  ethnic, 28, 85, 159
  evolution of, in Hungary, 63–66
  federalist vs. antifederalist, 62
  formation of, 3, 19
  free-market liberalism vs. economic populism, 32–33
  functional, 49, 73
  historical, 28, 110–11, 116, 165–67, 219, 223, 226
  Hungarian post-Socialist, 147–51
  ideological, 221
  international policy and orientation, 118
  Kádárian, 75, 147–49
  labor vs. capital, 207
  modernizers vs. traditionalists, 44
  monetarism vs. antimonetarism, 242
  national, 57
  national-ethnic, 117
  organizational, 4
  owners vs. workers, 8, 137–38
  political, 4, 7
  political elite vs. technocrats, 30
  political elite vs. working class, 30, 102–3
  populist-urbanizer, 73–75
  potential, 110
  religious, 4–5, 8, 24, 28, 49, 118, 138, 159–60, 163–65, 167, 219, 221, 242
  residual, 110, 116
  rural vs. urban, 8, 49, 52, 62, 111, 137
  serfs vs. barons, 49
  social, 4, 7, 216, 221
  social democratic, 150

socioeconomic, 24, 28, 32, 116–17, 136–37, 162–63
sociopolitical, 117
state intervention vs. monetarism, 162–63
state protectionism vs. free market, 160
state secularism, 160
structural, 4, 138, 150
technocracy, political elite, 103–4
territorial, 49, 51, 73, 155
traditionalism vs. Westernization, 73, 141–44
transitional, 110, 111–15
Westernization vs. nationalism, 156, 161
Codiţă, Cornel, 170, 173
Commonwealth of Three Nations, 82
communism, 4, 12, 28, 30, 43–44, 54, 56–58, 62, 66, 69, 71–72, 80, 84–89, 98–106, 111–12, 117, 123–24, 129, 133, 141, 142, 152, 160, 165–66, 172–79, 177–79, 199–201, 210, 249
Constantinescu, Emil, 175, 265
Coposu, Corneliu, 268
Counter-Reformation, 4, 8
Czech and Slovak political parties
  abbreviations of current party names, 211
  Agrarian Party (AP), 52, 53, 59, 137
  Agricultural Party, 137, 206
  Association of the Republic–Republican Party of Czechoslovakia (SPR-RÇS), 125
  Christian Democratic Party, 125, 172
  Christian Democratic Union–Czechoslovak People's Party (KDU-ÇSL), 125, 203, 206, 208
  Civic Democratic Alliance (ODA), 125, 128, 132–33, 135, 205–6, 208
  Civic Democratic Party (ODS), 124–25, 128, 129, 132–33, 134, 135, 138, 204–8
  Civic Forum (OF), 172, 203, 204, 205, 210

  Civic Movement (OH), 204, 205, 206, 209, 210
  Communist Party of Bohemia and Moravia (KSČM), 125, 206, 208, 136
  Communist Party of Czechoslovakia, 24, 55, 57, 123, 203
  Czech Moravian Union of the Center (ÇMUS), 134, 135
  Czech Social Democratic Party (ÇSSD), 54, 56, 57, 125, 133–36, 172, 207–10
  Czechoslovak Democratic Party, 54, 59
  Czechoslovak National Socialist Party, 55, 57
  Czechoslovak People's Party, 54, 57, 123
  Czechoslovak Social Democratic Party, 124
  Czechoslovak Socialist Party, 123, 206
  DEU, 209
  DŽJ, 209
  Free Democrats (SD, SD-LSNS), 125, 134, 209
  Green Party, 130–31, 134, 206
  KDU-ÇSL, 125, 132–33, 134, 137
  Left Bloc, 125, 206
  Liberal National Socialist Party, 125
  Liberal-Social Union (LSU), 206
  Movement for Moravian and Silesian Self-Government (HSD-SMS), 203, 204, 206
  National Free-Thinking Party, 51, 52
  National Front, 56, 57, 123
  National Party, 51
  National Social Party, 52
  ODS-KDS, 205
  Old Czechs-Staročeši, 51
  Party of Czechoslovak Communists, 125
  Party of the Democratic Left, 125
  Slovak Freedom Party, 57
  Slovak National Revival Party, 57
  Slovak People's Party, 54
  Union for the Republic–Czechoslovak Republican Party (SPR-RSČ), 136, 206

VPN, 205
Young Czechs-Mladočeši, 51–52
cultural politics, 62, 64
cultural socialization, 217–18
Curtice, John, 265
Curtis, M., 262
Czech Helsinki Committee, 135
Czech Republic, 24–25, 47–60, 123–39
   assurance of security, 132, 136
   Catholic Church, 138
   Catholics and Protestants, 49, 51, 54
   civic society and political system, 128–30
   communism and, 54, 56–58, 123–24, 129, 133, 210
   decentralization, 131, 133–34, 135
   ecology, 130–31, 134
   economic transformation, 128
   election results, 204–10
   Federal Assembly, 123–24
   5 percent threshold, 207, 209–10
   FPTP voting system, 207, 209, 210
   German Question, 131–32
   Germany and, 25, 49–51, 53–55, 57
   House of Nations, 204, 206
   human rights, 131, 134–35
   industrialization, 52–53
   PR voting system, 207, 209, 210
   results of parliamentary elections, 126–27
   social security, 130, 134
   totalitarianism and, 55–58
   voter response, 203–13
Czubiński, Antoni, 86

Dahrendorf, Ralph, 133
Dalton, Russell, 9, 10, 215
Datculescu, Petre, 20, 21, 30–31, 93–106, 169–84, 261–73
Deák, Ferenc, 67, 68
decommunization, 28, 32, 113–15, 149, 160, 165–67, 242, 247–48, 252–54
Dimitrov, Dimitar, 119
Dmowski, Roman, 79
Dohnalik, J., 253
Dual Monarchy, 66–67

Dubet, 160
Duverger, Maurice, 89, 131

"earthquake election," 9
East Roman Empire, 64–65
Eastern Question, 37
Elcock, Howard, 131
Enescu, Constantin, 97
Enlightenment, 37
Epstein, Leon, 10
Erdei, F., 65
Ersson, Svante, 6, 7
European Union (EU), 132, 136, 137, 144, 161, 173, 200, 229–30, 249
Evans, G., 219

Fascism, 71
"Fatherland and Progress," 63, 65
Ferdinand, 40, 41
Flora, P., 61
Földes, Gy., 68
Franklin, Mark N., 11
Freedom Fight, 66–67
freezing hypothesis, 4, 8–11, 31–32, 47, 107, 153, 155
French Revolution, 22, 37, 39, 96

Gagnon, V. P. Jr., 180
Gallagher, Michael, 4, 7, 9
Garka, István, 146
Gdańsk-Szczecin agreements, 85
Gehmacher, Ernst, 22
Gemeinschaft, 64
Georgescu, Vlad, 99, 104, 106
German Christian Democrats, 10
German Question, 131–32, 136
German Social Democrats, 10, 53
Geró, A., 67
Gerschenkron, 63
Gesellschaft, 64
Gheorghiu-Dej, Gheorghe, 99–100
Gibson, Hugh, 81
Giczy, György, 155
Gierek, Edward, 85
Gömbös, Gyula, 70, 74
"goulash communism," 147–48
Great Depression, 43

Green parties, 11
Gronkiewicz-Walz, Hanna, 249
Gyapai, G., 68

Habermas, Jürgen, 79
Hapsburg monarchy, 50, 65, 67, 80, 53, 63, 81, 82, 129
Harmel, Robert, 9
Harvey, D., 142
Havel, Václav, 57, 136
Heath, Anthony, 265
Herzmann, J., 208
Heyden, Jacqueline, 164
Himmelweit, Hilde T., 270
Hitchins, Keith, 94
Hitler, Adolf, 70, 146
Hollar-Bohemus, V, 59
Holocaust, 28, 85, 159
Horn, Gy, 154
Horn, Syula, 153
Horthy, Admiral Miklós, 70, 71, 146
Hubai, L., 68
Humphreys, Patrick, 270
Hungarian political parties
  Alliance of Free Democrats (SZDSZ or AFD), 74, 141, 142, 149, 151, 154, 155, 216–17, 223, 228
  Alliance of Young Democrats (FIDESZ or AYD), 74, 143, 147, 149, 153, 155, 216, 223, 228
  Anti-Semitic Party, 68
  Arrow Cross Party, 70–71
  Bourgeois Democrats, 71, 72
  Christian Democratic People's Party, 216
  Christian Democrats, 26, 75, 142, 143, 155
  Christian Smallholders' Agrarian and Bourgeois Party, 69
  "cosmopolitan Liberals," 69
  Deák Party, 67, 68
  Democratic Opposition, 74, 142
  Democratic Party, 68
  Democratic People's Party, 72
  Free Democrats, 141, 143, 148, 149, 154
  Hungarian Council Republic, 69
  Hungarian Democratic Forum (MDF or HDF), 26, 74, 141, 142, 143, 146–49, 216–22, 229
  Hungarian Democratic People's Party (MDNP), 155, 228
  Hungarian Front, 71
  Hungarian Socialist Party (MSZP or HSP), 141, 142, 146, 149, 151, 152, 154, 216–23, 227–30
  Hungarian Socialist Workers' Party (HSWP), 141, 219, 220, 223, 226, 235
  Hungarian Truth and Life Party, 146
  Hungarian Universal Labor Union, 78
  Independence Party, 68–69, 72
  Independent Hungarian Democratic Party, 72
  Independent Smallholders' Party (ISHP), 216, 219, 222, 228
  Liberal Party, 67–70
  Moderate Oppositional Party, 68
  National Christian Alliance, 72
  National Labour Party, 68
  Party of Hungarian Life, 70
  Party of Hungarian Truth and Life, 155
  Party of Hungarian Workers, 72
  Party of Nonvoters, 69
  Peasant Party, 71
  People's Party, 68
  Smallholders, 26, 68, 71, 72, 75, 142, 143, 146, 155, 172
  Social Democratic Party, 69–71, 72, 142
  Socialist Party, 69, 142, 143, 147–49, 152–55, 221–22
  UDMR, 266–67
  United List of Workers, 71
  United Oppositional Party, 68
  United Party, 69–70
Hungary, 26–27, 61–76, 141–58, 215–37
  anti-liberal traits, 68
  cleavage translation, 146
  Communism in, 66, 69, 71–72, 141, 142, 152
  Dualist Period, 66–69
  educational system, 145
  election results, 217

foreign policy, 145–46
market socialism and, 72–73
media, 145
National Working Schedule, 70
patronage and dealignment, 153
suffrage, 68
support for democracy, 227
support for European integration, 229–31
support for market economy, 227
Huntington, Samuel P., 172
Hus, John, 55

Iliescu, Ion, 171, 175, 176, 178, 180, 264–65
Industrial Revolution, 8, 48, 52
industrialization, 129
Inglehart, Ronald, 7, 9
International Covenant on Civil and Political Rights, 135
International Covenant on Economic, Social and Culture Rights, 135
Iron Guard, The, 98
IX Extraordinary PUWP Congress, 88

Jaeger, Marianne, 270
János, Simon, 215–37
Jasiewicz, Krzysztof, 160
Jehliçka, P., 131
Jelev, Jelju, 114
John Paul II, 164
Joseph II, 63, 65
Jowell, Roger, 265
Jowitt, Kenneth, 94–95

Kádár, János, 147–49, 154, 217, 220, 226, 234
Kádárian compromise, 72–73
Kádárism, 73
Kanev, Assen, 119
Karasimeonov, Georgi, 20–24, 37–45, 107–21
Károlyi, Count Mihály, 69
Katz, Richard, 10, 270
Kirchheimer, Otto, 10
Kis, János, 154, 155
Kitschelt, Herbert, 12, 119

Klaus, Vaclav, 129, 133, 135
Klingemann, Hans-Dieter, 13, 110, 112
Knutsen, Oddbjørn, 9–10, 11
Komensky-Comenius, J. A., 59
Koroknai, Maria, 180
Kósa, Ferenc, 152
Kostelecký, T., 131
Krejčí, O., 209
Kroupa, Aleš, 135
Kubiak, Hieronim, 20, 21, 27, 77–91
Kulcsár, K., 63
Kulin, Ferenc, 63, 151
Kulturkampf, 65, 144–51
Kuroń, Jacek, 249, 250, 256
Kwaśniewski, Aleksander, 248–51, 256

Labuda, Barbara, 164
Lackó, M., 74
Lager, 144
Lane, Jan-Eric, 6, 7
Lasswell, H. D., 88
Laver, Michael, 4
Lawson, Kay, 10, 11, 19–34
Lerner, D., 63
Lijphart, Arend, 7
Lipset, Seymour Martin, 3–5, 8, 10, 13, 48–49, 51, 61, 64, 66, 109–10, 141, 144, 178, 181, 215–16
Lomax, Bill, 110
Lukács, Georg, 26, 74, 142
lustration, 247–48, 254
Luxemburg, Rosa, 79

Maastricht convergence criteria, 151
Machonin, P., 57
Maeckie, Thomas T., 11
Maguire, Maria, 9
Mair, Peter, 4, 5, 6, 10, 11, 12, 156
Mansfeldová, Zdenka, 20, 21, 24–25, 123–39, 203–13
March Constitution, 80, 86, 90
Markowski, Radoslaw, 134, 136
Márkus, György, 20, 21, 26, 27, 61–76, 141–58
Marxism, 70, 142, 152
Masaryk, Tomáš Guarrigue, 52
Mazowiecki, Tadeusz, 245

media, 12
Merkl, Peter H., 7
Micewski, Andrzej, 164
Michael I of Hohenzollern, 179
Michnik, Adam, 89, 165
Mikołajczyk, S., 86
Miroiu, Mihaela, 170, 173
Moczulski, Leszek, 249
modernization, xi–xii, 26, 42, 63–66, 73, 111–13
monetarism, 242
Moravia, 203–204
Moscow Duma, 78
movementists, 143
Müller-Rommel, Ferdinand, 11
multipartism, 84, 88, 124, 142
Mussolini, Benito, 70

narodniks, 64
National Revolution, 8, 48
Nazi Party, 54, 65, 70–71, 132, 165
New Democracies Barometer (NDB), 13
North Atlantic Treaty Organization (NATO), 24, 26, 118, 132, 136, 137, 144, 145, 161, 173, 249
Novák, M., 209
Nowak, S., 78

October Revolution, 82
Offe, Claus, 11
Oleksy, Józef, 248, 249
Olszewski, Jan, 249
Ottoman Empire, 37–38, 40, 42, 61, 63

Palouš, Martin, 135
Pappi, Franz U., 6
Parsons, Talcott, 84
partitocrats, 143
party response, 3, 19
Party Systems and Voter Alignments, 3, 10
Pasti, Vladimir, 170, 173
Patočka, J., 56
Pawlak, Waldemar, 248, 250, 256
Pedersen, Mogens, 9
Piłsudski, Józef, 79–82, 84
Poguntke, Thomas, 11
Poland, 27–29, 77–91, 159–68

agriculture, 163
Catholicism and, 82, 159–60, 163–65, 245, 246, 252–53
clericalization of the state, 247, 251–52
communism in, 28, 80, 84–89, 160, 165–66, 249
elections, 1919–39, 83
ethnic composition, 81
multipartism, 77, 78, 80
1995 presidential election, 248–51
parliamentary election results, 243–45
Senate, 240, 244–46, 255
Seym (Sejm), 82–84, 87, 88, 161–62, 166, 239–40, 242–46, 255
social structure, 83
Soviet Union and, 28
voter response, 239–59
voter turnout, 240–42
Polish Committee for the Defense of Workers (KOR), 65
Polish political parties
Agreement Center (PC), 246, 247, 253–54
Alliance of the Democratic Left, (SLD), 161, 162, 164, 166, 245–48, 252, 255–56
Catholic Election Action, 245, 252–53
Christian National Alliance (ZChN), 245, 246, 249, 252–53, 256
Civic Agreement Center, 253
Coalition for the Republic, 247
Confederacy for Poland's Independence (KPN), 246, 249, 254, 256
Confederacy of Independent Poland, 161, 162, 163–66
Democratic Party (SD), 86–87, 88
Democratic Union (UD), 161, 245, 247–49, 251, 255–56
Freedom Union (UW), 249
Jewish Socialist Union Bund, 80
Labor Party (SP), 86
Liberal-Democratic Congress (KL-D), 161, 162, 246, 249, 254
"Motherland" Catholic Election Committee, 246–48, 253
Movement for the Republic, 249
National Democratic Party, 78–80

Non-Party Bloc for the Support of
    Reforms (BBWR), 161, 162,
    164–65, 246, 247, 249
Party "X," 247
Peasant Party (SL), 79, 86
People's Agreement, 246, 256
Polish Communist Party (KPP), 79
Polish Peasant Party (PSL), 29, 79, 86,
    161–64, 166, 245–48, 253, 255–56
Polish Socialist Party (PPS), 79, 80, 86
Polish United Workers Party (PZPR),
    86–88
Polish United Workers' Party (PUWP),
    239–40, 245, 247, 252, 256
Polish Workers' Party (PPR), 79, 86
PSL-PL, 247
Social Democracy of the Polish
    Republic (SdRP), 161, 245, 256
Social Democratic Party of the Polish
    Kingdom and Lithuania (SDKPiL),
    79
Union of Labour (UP), 161, 164, 166,
    167, 245–49
Union of Liberty, 161, 162, 164, 166
Union of Real Politics, 162, 248
United Peasant Party (ZSL), 86–87, 88,
    245
WAK, 253
Polish Provisional Government of National
    Unity, 85
postmaterialism, 7, 9
Potsdam Agreements, 56
Prague Spring, 57–58
privatization, 133, 146, 170, 182, 198, 200
Przeworski, Adam, 4–5, 162

Raciborski, Jacek, 20, 21, 29, 239–59
Rae, Douglas, 6
Realpolitik, 143, 146
Red Army, 56, 71, 79
Reformation, 4, 8, 48
Renaissance, 37
Rendlová, E., 209
restaurationists, 112
Révész, 144, 145
Robertson, John D., 9

Rokkan, Stein, 3–5, 8, 10, 13, 47–49, 51,
    55, 61, 62, 64, 109–10, 131, 136,
    153, 178, 215–16
Roman, Petre, 175, 263
Romania, 29–31, 93–106, 169–84
    censorship, 101–2
    Communism in, 30, 98–106, 172,
        177–79
    "Cosmopolitan Liberals," 30
    Democratic Convention, 174–75,
        178–79
    economic reform and living standards,
        180–82
    election results, 262–65
    fascism, 98–99
    industrialization, 100–2
    Land Law, 267–68
    monarchy, 177, 179
    "National Conservatives," 30
    national stability and interethnic rela-
        tions, 177, 179–80
    party imageries, 176–77
    Securitate, 178
    social structure, 94
    voter alignment, 261–73
Romanian voters, 261–73
    age divisions, 270–71
    ethnic divisions, 266–67
    rural-urban divisions, 267–68
    social stratification, 266–71
Römmele, Andrea, 3–18, 19, 22
Romanian political parties
    Agrarian Party (PDAR), 264–65
    ANL, 175–76
    Civic Alliance Party (PAC), 176, 265
    Communist Party, 176
    Conservative Party, 96
    "Cosmopolitan-Liberals," 174–83
    Democratic Convention of Romania
        (CDR), 174, 263–65, 268–72
    Democratic National Salvation Front
        (FDSN), 175, 178, 182
    Democratic Party (PD), 175, 263
    Ecological Party (PER), 174
    FDSN/PDSR, 263–65, 268, 270–71
    Greater Romania Party, (PRM), 176

Iliescu party, 175, 182
Liberal Party (PNL-CD), 94, 96, 98, 174
list of significant parties since 1990, 173
"National-Conservatives," 174–83
National Liberal Party (PNL), 174, 175, 264
National Liberal Party 93 (PNL 93), 265
National Party, 96
National Party of Transylvania, 96, 98
National Peasant Party (PNT-CD), 98, 99, 174–75, 172
National Salvation Front (FSN or NSF), 171, 176, 180, 262–65, 267, 271
National Union of the Centre (UNC), 265
Party of Social Democracy (PDSR), 176, 182, 183
Peasant Party, 98, 174–75, 268
Roman Party (FSN, PD), 175
Romanian National Unity Party (PUNR), 176, 267
Social-Democratic Party, 96
Social-Democratic Union (USD), 175, 263–64
Socialist Labour Party (PSM), 176, 265
Socialist Party, 96, 98
"Totul pentru Țara," 98–99
UDMR, 175, 176
Rose, Richard, 7, 9
Rosetti, Radu, 94
Round Table contract, 85, 88, 91, 112, 239, 244
Rudai, R., 68
Russian Empire, 64
Russian Revolution, 8, 48
Russo-Turkish War, 37–38

Saatchi and Saatchi, 246
Sachzwang, 150
Sakharov, 65
Sartori, Giovanni, 64, 77, 87, 143, 144, 147, 204
Second Serfdom, 49

Seiler, Daniel-Louis, 59, 136
Sejm. *See* Seym
Seovik, Arne, 135
Seym (Sejm), 82–84, 87, 88, 161–62, 166, 239–40, 242–46, 255
Shamir, Michael, 9
Shopov, Vladimir, 20, 21, 23, 24, 185–202
Simon, János, 20, 21, 27
Slovak political parties. *See* Czech and Slovak political parties
Social Democratic Workers' Party, 51, 52
Social Democrats of Scandinavia, 9
Solidarity, 85, 160, 164, 166–67, 239–40, 242, 244–48, 253, 255–56
Solidarność, 249, 256
Solzhenytsin, Alexander, 65
Sonderweg, 65
Splichal, Slavko, 12
Sprague, John, 4–5
St. Stephen, 144
St. Stephen's Thought, 70
Stalin, Joseph, 99
Stalinism, 85
Stambolov, Stefan, 40, 41
Stoyanov, Petar, 201
Stráský, Jan, 135
Strzelecki, 160
Styrársdóttir, Audur, 11
Suchocka, Hanna, 245, 247, 252
Summers, Gene F., 135
Szalai, E., 73
Széchenyi, Count István, 63
Szelényi, I., 149, 150
Szűcs, J., 62

Talmon, J. L., 55
Taylor, Charles Lewis, 13
Taylor, Michael, 6
thresholds, 5–6
Tismăneanu, Vladimir, 171
Tisza, István, 68
Tisza, Kálmán, 67
Tökés, Laszlo, 105
Torgyán, József, 155
Torgyánism, 155
totalitarianism, 55–58

Touraine, Alain, 62, 156, 160
Transylvania, 94–96, 98, 105
Traub, H., 50
"trauma of Trianon," 143
Treaty of Berlin, 38
"triad capitalism," 62
Turnovo Constitution, 40

Urwin, Derek, 7, 9, 131

Vacaroiu, Nicolae, 182
Valen, Henry, 11
van Gennep, Arnold, 109
Verdeţ, Ilie, 176
Verheijin, Tony, 112
Versailles Conference, 81
Versailles Treaty, 64, 80, 142, 146
Visegrad Three, 132
voter alignment, 3, 19

Wasilewski, Jacek, 166
Wałeşa, Lech, 162, 164, 246, 248–53, 256
Weber, Eugen, 93, 99

Wessels, Bernhardt, 110, 112
Westernization, 28, 64, 155, 221–23, 230, 235
Whitehead, S., 219
Wiatr, Jerzy J., 20, 21, 28–29, 87, 159–68, 242, 247
Wien Reichsrat, 78
Wieviorka, 160
Witos, Wincenty, 79
Wolinetz, 9
Women's Alliance, 11
Workgroup on Political Parties and Elections, 21
World War I, 22, 24, 42, 43, 66, 78, 81, 96, 216
World War II, 7, 28, 30, 43, 56, 62, 65, 71, 85, 93, 97, 159, 165, 172

Yalta Conference, 85

Zamoyski, Adam, 79, 80, 85
Zdrahal, F. V., 49
Zelea-Condreanu, 98
Zieliński, Tadeusz, 249, 250

About the Contributors

JOSEF BLAHOŽ is a scientific collaborator at the Institute of State and Law of the Academy of Sciences in Prague, and professor of comparative constitutional law at the faculty of Law, University of West Bohemia, Pilsen. His recent publications include "Human Rights: Their Guarantees and the Constitutional Judiciary," in *Austrian Journal of Public and International Law*, vol. 43, 1992; "Human Rights Law in Czechoslovakia, Hungary and Poland," in David P. Forsythe, ed., *Human Rights in the New Europe*, 1994, and *Comparative Constitutional Law*, 1997.

LUBOMÍR BROKL earned his degree and began his career as a professor at Charles University in Prague, was dismissed for political reasons, worked for twenty years in industrial sociology, and was appointed in 1990 to serve as head of the research team working on "Change in the Political System" at the reestablished Sociological Institute of the Czech Academy of Science. His publications include "Von der 'unpolitischen' zur 'professionellen' Politik, Aspekte der Politischen Kultur der CSSR in der Periode des Systemwechsels," (with Z. Mansfeldová), in Gerlich P., Plasser F., Ulram P.A, eds., *Regimewechsel, Demokratisierung und politische Kultur in Ost-Mitteleuropa*, 1992; "Zerfall der Tschechoslowakei–strukturelle Ursachen und Parteihandeln," (with Z. Mansfeldová), in Dieter Segert, Csilla Machos, eds., *Parteien in Osteuropa*, 1995.

PETRE DATCULESCU, Ph.D. in Psychology from the University of Bucharest, is Managing Director of IRSOP–The Romanian Institute for Public Opinion, a private marketing and social research organization established in 1990. He is a member of ESOMAR (European Society of Marketing Research) and WAPOR (World Association of Public Opinion Research). His publications include *Rebirth of a Democracy: The Romanian Elections of May 20, 1990*, IRSOP, 1991; "Social Change and Changing Public Opinion in Romania After the 1990 Election," in Daniel N. Nelson, ed., *Romania After Tyranny*, 1992; and

"How Romania Voted: An Analysis of the 1992 Elections," in *Revista de Cercetari Sociale 1*, 1994.

ERNST GEHMACHER'S publications include *Das Ende des Nationalismus* with Michael Ley, 1996; "Die Politik der Evolution–Die Evolution der Politik," in *Die Ursachen des Wachstums*, Rupert Riedl and Manuela Delpos, eds., 1996; and "Wie demokratisch sind wir geworden," in *Zukunft*, vol. 8, 1997.

GEORGI KARASIMEONOV is professor at the Department of Political Science, Sofia University; managing director of the Institute for Political and Legal Studies, Sofia; and visiting professor at Ohio State University, USA, and the University of Örebro, Sweden. His research interests are political parties, political institutions, political change in Eastern Europe, and democracy theory. His major publications include *Socialdemocratic parties—political role and influence*, 1981; *Political parties in the USA*, 1991; *Political parties—general theory*, 1993; *Political parties in post-communist Bulgaria*, 1995; and *Politics and political institutions*, 1997.

HIERONIM KUBIAK is professor of sociology at the Jagiellonian University, Kraków. Among his most recent publications are "Hopes, Illusions and Deceptions: Half a Century of Political Sociology in Poland," in *Current Sociology*, no. 3, 1996; *Democracy and the Individual Will*, 1997; and "Partie Polityczne w Wielkim Mieście" in *Political Parties in a Big City,* 1997.

KAY LAWSON is professor of political science at San Francisco State University and visiting professor at the University of Paris (Sorbonne). She is the author and editor of numerous articles and books on political parties, including *The Comparative Study of Political Parties*, 1976, and the edited volumes *Political Parties and Linkage*, 1980; *When Parties Fail* (co-edited with Peter Merkl), 1988; and *How Political Parties Work*, 1994. She leads the international Work Group on Parties and Elections and is president of its parent body, the Committee on Political Sociology.

ZDENKA MANSFELDOVÁ is a senior research fellow at the Institute of Sociology, Academy of Science of the Czech Republic, in the research group "Change in the Political System." She is the author and co-author of numerous papers and books including, most recently, "The Pluralistic System of Interest Representation in Czech Society," in *European Studies 2, 1996;* "Social Partnership and their Actors in the Czech and Slovak Republic" (with M. Čambáliková), in *Sociológia*, no. 6, 1996, and "Sociální partnerství v České republice," in Brokl Lubomír, ed., *Reprezentace zájmů v politickém systému ČR. Pluralitní demokracie nebo neokorporativismus?* SLON, 1997. Her areas of interest are political sociology, political parties, institutionalization and interest representation, and social partnership.

GYÖRGY G. MÁRKUS is senior research fellow at the Hungarian Academy of Sciences, Institute for Political Science. His research interests are theory of political parties, party systems and cleavages, comparative analysis of party formations, party competition and party systems in East Central and Western Europe, social democratic politics, and policies, and the euro-conformity of political parties in Hungary. His research project "Party Politics, Party Systems and Dynamics of Political Cleavages in Hungary" has been supported by a NATO Research Fellowship. Among his numerous publications are *A szociáldemokrácia két modernitás között* (Social Democracy between two Modernities, 1995); "Party System and Cleavage Translation in Hungary," in *Working Papers of Political Science*, vol. 3, 1996; and "The Typology of Political Cleavages in East Central Europe–A Blueprint for the West? The Case of Hungary," in *HAS Institute for Political Science*.

JACEK RACIBORSKI is an assistant professor at Warsaw University, Institute of Sociology. His research interest is political sociology. His recent publications are "Whether and How to Vote? Confused Voters," in J. Wiatr, ed., *The Politics of Democratic Transformation: Poland after 1989*, 1993; *Nation-power-society*, 1996 (co-editor with A. Jasińska-Kania); and *Polskie wybory: zachowania wyborcze społeczeństwa polskiego 1989–1995 (Elections in Poland: Polish Voting Behaviors 1989–1995)*, 1997.

ANDREA RÖMMELE is a research fellow at the Mannheim Centre for European Social Research and editor of the ISA/IPSA newsletter on parties and elections. She received her Ph.D. in 1994 from the University of Heidelberg. She is co-editor of *"The Victorious Incumbent: A Threat to Democracy,"* 1994, and has published a book on comparative campaign and party finance (1995) as well as articles on political parties. She has also worked on several international projects including "Campaigns and Surveys" (with Hans-Dieter Klingemann); "Stability in Eastern Europe" (with Rudolf Wildenmann) and, most recently, "Representation in Europe." Her research interests are in political sociology, political parties, political campaigns, and campaign communication.

VLADIMIR SHOPOV earned his B.A. in Political Science at the University of Sofia, St. Kliment Ohridski, in 1996 and a Master of Science in Comparative Politics at The London School of Economics and Political Science in 1997. His research interests are regime change, party systems, coalition theory, and politics and nationalism. He is currently a researcher at the Institute for Political and Legal Studies and a lecturer at the Political Academy for Eastern and Central Europe, both in Sofia, Bulgaria.

JÁNOS SIMON is research director of the Institute for Political Science of the Hungarian Academy of Sciences in Budapest and lecturer of the Political Science Department of Eötvös Lóránd University of Budapest, director of Hungarian Erasmus Foundation for Democracy. His research topics are political culture, transitions, democracy studies, voting behavior, parliamentary, and elite studies. His main publications are *Silenced Majority,* with L. Bruszt, 1990; *The Change in Citizens' Political Orientations in Hungary,* with L. Bruszt,

1992, *Transition to Democracy in Spain,* 1996; "Comparative Electoral Systems in Central Europe," 1997; and *The Postcommunist Citizen* co-edited with Samuel Bames, 1998.

JERZY J. WIATR is currently professor of political sociology, Warsaw University. He was president of the Polish Political Science Association and Vice President of the International Political Science Association. He served in the Polish Parliament (1991–1997) and was Poland's minister of education (February 1996–October 1997). His latest contributions include *Political Sociology and Democratic Transformation in Poland,* 1996 and *Education for and in the Twenty-First Century,* Abu Dhabi: Emirates Center for Strategic Studies and Research, 1997.

HARDCOVER BAR CODE